Y0-BDG-396

HPB $5

12/09

CLEARANCE
$ 200

PRAISE FOR THE PREVIOUS EDITION

"Condemned to Repetition is the first extensive insider's account of U.S. policy-making toward Nicaragua during the crucial four-year period that began in 1977 . . . "
Washington Post Book World

"(Pastor) is dispassionate and thorough, letting the chips fall where they will. . . (he) does an excellent job of demonstrating how and why the United States has been 'condemned to repetition' in its behavior toward Latin America. He raises issues that should be at the center of any foreign policy debate . . . "
Atlanta Journal-Constitution

"There is . . . much here that will interest anyone who has ever wondered how our foreign policy is really made."
Wall Street Journal

"a valuable account"
The Economist

"straightforward and honest"
Shirley Christian
The New Republic

"A meticulously documented story . . . (Pastor) shows how all of the actors, from Cuba and Nicaragua to the U.S. and its Latin allies, acted in ways that made their nightmares come true . . . his book contains enough solid insight and information . . . to help readers understand what worked, what failed, and why."
The Christian Science Monitor

"Out of this very interesting and honest book, I would single one highly ironic section. Fidel Castro repeatedly urged Sandinistas to avoid the mistakes he had made . . . How are we to learn from history when it is Castro saying 'no more Cubas'?"
Newsday

" . . . by far the best study to date on the early years of the Sandinista revolution . . . (Pastor) managed to break free from the sterile polemics which have characterized recent debates over Central American policies, and provides the reader with fascinating, informative and frequently provocative insights into the dilemmas of policy formulation and implementation . . . He combines this insider's view of developments with massive research into available published and documentary sources, and interviews with key actors on all sides of the conflict. For this, and much more, *Condemned to Repetition* qualifies as must reading for anyone seriously interested in U.S.-Latin American relations."

Richard Millett
Caribbean Review

"This book is essential reading on U.S. policy making toward Nicaragua in the Carter and Reagan years . . . Pastor sidesteps the pitfalls of memoirs; he admits mistakes, including his own, and presents a well reasoned, critical analysis useful to both generalists and specialists."

Kenneth E. Sharpe
Political Science Quarterly

"a clear, well-written, and fascinating account of the evolution of U.S. policy towards Nicaragua . . . required reading for anyone wishing to understand the motives and outcomes of U.S. policy."

Herald Muñoz
Hemisphere

"very good: detailed, dramatic, and well-written . . . Pastor has mined the sources . . . Diplomatic historians can use it well."

Robert Schulzinger
Diplomatic History

"Pastor has been successful in walking the tightrope between the political memoir of a national security council official and an academic analysis of the evolution of U.S.-Nicaraguan policy during the presidencies of Jimmy Carter and Ronald Reagan."

Stephen J. Randall
Hispanic American Historical Review

"Should be read universally. It is a significant contribution to our understanding of a complicated and essential phase of our foreign policy. It is well-written, and other authors writing on such intricate and complex issues could benefit from taking note of the organization, clarity, and flow of this book."

William J. Williams
*The Annals of the American Academy of
Political and Social Science*

Not Condemned
to Repetition

OTHER BOOKS BY ROBERT A. PASTOR

Toward a North American Community:
Lessons from the Old World for the New (2001)

Exiting the Whirlpool: U.S. Foreign Policy Toward Latin America and the
Caribbean (Second Edition, 2001)

A Century's Journey: How the Great Powers Shape the World, Editor,
1999 (Translated and published in Chinese in Taiwan and the People's
Republic of China)

The Controversial Pivot: The U.S. Congress and North America (Edited with
Rafael Fernandez De Castro, 1998) (*El Actor Controvertido:*
El Congreso de Estados Unidos y America del Norte, 2001)

Collective Responses to Regional Problems: The Case of Latin America and the
Caribbean (Co-edited with Carl Kaysen and Laura Reed, 1994)

Democracy in the Caribbean: Political, Economic, and Social Perspectives
(Co-edited with Jorge Dominguez and Delisle Worrel, 1993)

Integration with Mexico: Options for U.S. Policy (1993)

Whirlpool: U.S. Foreign Policy Toward Latin America and the Caribbean (1992)
(First edition published by Princeton University Press) (*El Remolino: Politica*
Exterior de Estados Unidos Hacia America Latina y El Caribe, 1995)

Democracy in the Americas: Stopping the Pendulum (Editor, 1989)

Condemned to Repetition: The United States and Nicaragua (1987; with new epilogue, 1988) (First edition published by Princeton University Press)

Limits to Friendship: The United States and Mexico (with Jorge G. Castañeda,
1988) (*Limites en la Amistad: Mexico y Estados Unidos*)

Latin America's Debt Crisis: Adjusting to the Past or Planning for the Future?
(Editor, 1987)

Migration and Development in the Caribbean: The Unexplored Connection
(Editor, 1985)

Congress and the Politics of U.S. Foreign Economic Policy (1980)

NOT CONDEMNED
TO REPETITION

The United States and Nicaragua

REVISED AND UPDATED

Robert A. Pastor

Copyright © 1987 by Robert A. Pastor

Preface to the Paperback Edition and Epilogue copyright © 1988 by Robert A. Pastor

Revised and updated copyright © 2002 by Robert A. Pastor

All rights reserved. Printed in the United States of America. No part of this publication may be reproduced or transmitted in any form or by any means, electronic or mechanical, including photocopy,
recording, or any information storage and retrieval system, without permission in writing from the pub-
lisher.

Westview Press books are available at special discounts for bulk purchases in the United States by corporations, institutions, and other organizations. For more information, please contact the Special Markets
Department at The Perseus Books Group, 11 Cambridge Center, Cambridge MA 02142, or call (617)
252-5298.

Published in 2002 in the United States of America by Westview Press, 5500 Central Avenue, Boulder,
Colorado 80301-2877, and in the United Kingdom by Westview Press, 12 Hid's Copse Road, Cumnor
Hill, Oxford OX2 9JJ

Find us on the World Wide Web at www.westviewpress.com

A Cataloging-in-Publication data record is available from the Library of Congress.

ISBN 0-8133-3973-1 (HC) ISBN 0-8133-3810-7 (Pbk.)

Set in 10-point Minion by Perseus Publishing Services

The paper used in this publication meets the requirements of the American National Standard for Per-
manence of Paper for Printed Library Materials Z39.48–1984.

10   9   8   7   6   5   4   3   2   1

*To Tiffin Margaret and Robert Kiplin,
indisputable improvements on the past*

CONTENTS

LIST OF ILLUSTRATIONS

Cartoon

PREFACE

My first contact with Nicaragua was on a December morning in 1968, when I disembarked from a banana boat at the Caribbean port of El Bluff next to a small town called Bluefields. Most of the Nicaraguans were black and spoke English with West Indian accents. For a moment, I thought that during the days I had spent cleaning snakes out of the boat's hold, the boat had taken a wrong turn. It had not. Bluefields, inhabited by blacks and Miskito Indians and ruled indirectly by the British for more than a century, was the western part of the Caribbean but also the eastern part of Nicaragua. Tired of snakes and eager to see the country, I jumped ship.

A decade later, I found myself once again trying to avoid snakes in Nicaragua. This time, I was working on the National Security Council, and the United States was trying to find its way through Nicaragua's worst political crisis. The snakes were harder to find but just as deadly. I was accused of being a dangerous leftist by Anastasio Somoza's press secretary and a "hawkish" cold warrior by the Cuban national press.

Despite tireless efforts by the U.S. government to secure a democratic transition, the Sandinista National Liberation Front (FSLN) defeated Somoza in a violent revolution and seized power on July 20, 1979. Nicaragua's hopes for peace and justice proved elusive as it soon became engulfed in a civil war with each side financed by a superpower.

A decade after that, in July 1989, on the tenth anniversary of the Sandinista revolution, I found myself once again at the center of Nicaraguan politics. This time, working for a nongovernmental organization (NGO) chaired by former President Jimmy Carter, my first task was to persuade President Daniel Ortega and his opponent, Violeta Chamorro, to invite the Carter Center to observe the election scheduled for February 25, 1990. Ortega accepted the idea, and Chamorro enthusiastically endorsed it. All three—Ortega, Chamorro, and Carter—embarked on the most unusual journey of all, toward the first free and fair election recognized by all parties and the international community in Nicaragua's history. More than that, it was the first peaceful transfer of power in world history from a revolutionary government to its opposition. After failing to escape real and political snakes, and believing that Nicaragua would never escape repeating a tragic past, I witnessed the country discover a path to democracy. The experience of mediating that election was the most rewarding in my entire professional career.

This book, however, is not about my journey. It is about the journey of Nicaragua and the United States through the treacherous jungle of domestic and international politics. It is a story of how two nations—one small and one very powerful—tried to avoid being repeatedly bitten by the same snake. They succeeded only when they trusted international mediators and an electoral process.

The book has its own story. Although I have written or edited fourteen books, this one proved the most painful and difficult to write. I started the first edition in 1983 as the U.S. government began its support for what would become the contra war: a violent struggle for the future of the country in which the United States organized and financed a large "contra" army to overthrow the Sandinistas. The book sought to explain how the United States and Nicaragua had come to such a tragic confrontation, why the war would harm both countries but not succeed in dislodging the Sandinistas, and how a negotiated alternative could permit an exit. Like most other writers on Nicaragua, I was critical of the contra war, but unlike most I believed that the source of the crisis was neither U.S. intervention nor Cuban or Soviet interference. Nor did I conclude that the crisis was a product of social injustice or economic exploitation. Rather, in the first edition of this book I concluded that Nicaragua was condemned to repeat its tragic history because it failed to find a formula for a free election. The consequence was that the opposition had no choice but to seek power by violent means and request help from the enemy of the government. Thus, an internal struggle for power was inevitably internationalized. In the final paragraphs of the first edition, I wrote:

> Until the opposition believes it can win power legally and peacefully, armed struggles will continue, and local parties will always seek help from outside. This pattern cannot be broken easily. Internal strife can only be insulated from international intervention when the local government earns the trust of its opposition, and the superpowers show respect for regional governments. When this occurs, Nicaragua's future and its relations with the United States will improve on its past, and it will be easier to make peace in Central America than to make war.

I applied the lesson that I learned from writing that book in a second attempt to mediate a democratic transition. In 1979, President Jimmy Carter and his administration, including me as his national security advisor for Latin America, had failed to help the parties in Nicaragua navigate a democratic transition. A decade later, representing an NGO, the Carter Center of Emory University, we succeeded. One should not conclude from this example that NGOs are more powerful than governments, but rather that in certain delicate areas, such as an electoral process, NGOs might be better suited than governments. Part of the reason is that an NGO can be unequivocal in its dedication to the democratic process, whereas the U.S. government has more interests at stake and is far more focused on the outcome—in this case securing a Sandinista defeat—than on the process.

Although we were absolutely impartial, when Mark Uhlig, the *New York Times* correspondent based in Managua, asked me in late July 1979 who I thought would win a free election, I first asked him to pledge not to reveal the information until after the election. He agreed and then, based on my reading of dozens of polls that seemed at first glance to be contradictory, I estimated that Chamorro would win with 55 percent of the vote, and Ortega would get a solid 40 percent.[1] Seven months later, Chamorro won the election with 54.7 percent of the vote to Ortega's 40.8 percent.

The first edition of this book explained why Nicaragua and the United States were "condemned to repeat" a history of dictatorship and intervention because Nicaragua lacked free elections and the United States feared that instability could permit a foreign rival to gain a foothold close to the Panama Canal. This new edition explains how the two governments learned from the past and found the formula to avoid repeating it. The first edition served as a guide to several of us in the Carter Center, in the UN Mission, and in Nicaragua. We were all aware of the history and wanted to find a way to transform a mutually destructive self-fulfilling prophecy into a self-denying one that could end a war and begin a new democratic chapter for Nicaragua.

Organization of the Book

After an introduction to the principal themes of the book in Chapter 1, Chapters 2 and 3 describe the history of U.S.–Nicaraguan relations, the social and economic background to the revolution, and the different perspectives of its major protagonists. The next three parts of the book develop each of the major challenges faced by the two countries.

Part 2 (Chapters 4–9) covers the succession crisis from 1977 to 1979. How did the Sandinistas come to power despite considerable efforts by the United States to stop them?

Part 3 (Chapters 10–13) describes the confrontation with the Sandinista revolutionary government and the origins and evolution of the contra war. On reflection, the question, who lost Nicaragua, was the wrong one. In the 1980s everyone lost; everyone's nightmare came true. How did that happen?

Part 4 (Chapters 14–17) discusses the democratic transition. How did the United States and Nicaragua break the destructive patterns of the past and give the people of that small country a chance to choose their own leaders?

I have made modest changes in the first three parts of the first edition of the book but have completely rewritten Part 4. In the first edition, I used the chapters in Part 4 to explain why all the key actors—the United States, the Sandinistas, and the regional governments—lost in Nicaragua, how different decisions might have produced a different outcome in Nicaragua and other succession crises and revolutionary governments, and how the Arias Plan might be made to succeed. I have replaced those chapters in this edition with a description of how the the democratic transition emerged from the wreck of the contra war. In the final chapter of this edition, I summarize and seek to explain the patterns in U.S. foreign policy in relation to the three challenges—succession, revolution, and democratic transition—and the lessons to be drawn from them.

In reconstructing the Nicaraguan case, I have two advantages. I was a witness to, and sometimes a participant in, the policy process, and I was granted access to important classified government documents from the White House and the foreign policy agencies currently kept at the Carter Presidential Library. As the director of Latin American and Caribbean affairs on the National Security Council from 1977 to 1981, I am aware of all key government decisions during this period and was involved in most of them. Because of the Iran-contra scandal, most of the classified documentation of the Reagan administration's policy is also available, and during the election mediation I had a front-row seat to most of the key decisions.

The advantage of having participated in making a policy, however, often carries with it the disadvantage—from a scholarly standpoint—of having a stake in defending that policy. Although this book describes and explains the policy, it also tries to avoid defending it. Too often in memoirs, an administration's successes tend to have occurred when the author's recommendations prevailed, and its mistakes have happened when the author's ideas were rejected. The hard choices that any administration confronts are concealed from the reader. I have sought to avoid that tendency by reconstructing as fairly as possible the options, debate, and choices made by the government and by taking a number of precautions to reduce the chance that this work would be a single or one-sided portrayal of the case. In particular, I have interviewed many of the key participants in the United States as well as in Nicaragua and elsewhere, and their perspectives are incorporated in what follows.

As one tries to reconstruct a specific event or an entire case, one encounters many truths or, rather, many partial truths. Statements made at the time may have been intended to serve a specific purpose other than to depict events or describe the speaker's real intention. For example, on September 1, 1978, Somoza and the Sandinistas held separate press conferences. The Sandinistas accused the United States of sending mercenaries and CIA agents to prevent their victory; Somoza accused the United States of trying to overthrow him.[2] Newspapers tended to report one and discount the other, depending on their point of view. The purpose of both statements, however, was the same: to vent fears rather than to provide facts. Both were hoping their words would prove to be self-denying prophecies. The job of the historian is to include both statements and to evaluate them and their significance. I have tried to do that.

Another problem in reconstructing events is that most meetings and conversations are interpreted differently by the participants. In interviews as in memoirs, people usually remember events selectively and with the distorting prism of hindsight, which tends to reduce their role in failures and enhance it in successes. It is difficult to reconstruct an event even if one tries hard, and it is evident to the casual reader of books on Nicaragua that many authors did not try. For this book, I found government documents, memoranda, and transcripts of conversations to be an essential foundation for the preparation of a chronology, which I then used both to jog the memory of participants and to ensure that they did not unintentionally revise events. Readers will note an obvious difference in perspective and level of detail between my treatment of policymaking during the Carter, Reagan, and Bush administrations. Each administration faced at least one of the three challenges: the succession crisis, the revolution, and the democratic transition. I have chosen deliberately to give more attention to the question of how to relate to a crisis of succession because I believe this has been the least understood of the three, and I had access to all the internal documents and discussions during the Carter administration that addressed that crisis. In comparison, significant archives of classified material were disclosed during congressional investigations on the Reagan policy toward Nicaragua, and thus my chapters are more interpretive and briefer on that subject.

With the passing of a decade, I have decided to disclose the conversations of former President Carter, Daniel Ortega, President George H. W. Bush, and other participants in the election mediation to better understand how the democratic transition occurred. In the description and analysis of the third challenge—the democratic transition—I was directly involved in virtually all phases and meetings and thus I play a larger role in that narrative than in the previous sections. I have often been asked how Jimmy Carter mediated the election. How did a free election occur when so many people predicted the opposite? Part 4 of this book provides the only complete answer to that question that is available.

Although this book is informed by the present, it seeks to avoid the illusion of inevitability, which only hindsight makes possible. From today's perspective, the overthrow of Somoza looks inevitable, and even in 1978, about a year before it occurred, the U.S. government thought it was probable. However, no one was certain when, or even whether, Somoza would fall. Four months before the triumph of the Sandinistas, as Venezuelan and Costa Rican support for them appeared to end, many observers predicted that Somoza had weathered the worst.[3] Reminiscent of Lenin's famous prediction in March 1917 that he would "probably not live to see the decisive battles of the revolution," Daniel Ortega has admitted that as late as July 1979, days before Somoza's departure, he doubted he would live to see the Sandinista victory.[4] Similarly, the Reagan and Bush administrations did not believe that the Sandinistas would ever permit a free election in Nicaragua that would endanger their hold on power. Those who suggested otherwise were accused of naivete or worse.

Yogi Berra offered the best caveat against the temptation of asserting inevitability after the fact: "It ain't over till it's over." This book tries to recapture the uncertainty of the moment, which is the distinguishing characteristic of policymaking.

ROBERT A. PASTOR
Atlanta, Georgia
November 6, 2001

Acknowledgments

The author of a book with such a long gestation naturally accumulates numerous debts of gratitude. I could not have written it without the help of the many people whose interviews permitted me to understand dimensions of the case I missed the first time. I am especially grateful to Jimmy Carter and Zbigniew Brzezinski, both of whom gave me the opportunity to see firsthand how and why policy is made, and who both, after leaving office, were so generous with their time and recollections. Working with Carter on the second mediation from 1989 to 1990 helped me to realize how a person with determination and skill could change the course of history. It is ironic, but as we shall see, not surprising, that he was more effective in Nicaragua after leaving office. During the crisis, I admired Viron "Pete" Vaky, then assistant secretary of state, as he drew from vast reserves of patience and experience, but my appreciation for him grew as he read through this entire manuscript twice to ensure that it would fairly and fully represent the policy challenges faced by the U.S. government.

I consider myself especially fortunate to have scholarly friends who displayed no inhibition about slicing up previous drafts with rapier criticisms. Although not all of them will agree with the final product, I hope they all derive some satisfaction from recognizing how much better it is because of their efforts. Those who read and gave superb comments on the draft of the entire manuscript were Richard Ullman, Richard Millett, William LeoGrande, W. Anthony Lake, and David Ziegler. In addition, many people commented on individual chapters and sections: Jorge G. Castañeda, Jorge Domínguez, Richard Feinberg, Paula Gordon, Shelley McConnell, Rodolfo Pastor, Joseph S. Nye Jr., Robert Lieber, Carlos Rico, Rob Paarlberg, Manuel García y Griego, Cheryl Eschbach, and Carolyn Rose-Avila. I have benefited from competent and industrious research assistants over the years at the University of Maryland, El Colegio de Mexico, and Emory University: Charles Becker, Carola Weil, Frank Baitman, José Madrazo, Francine Mizell, Aaron Siegler, and Charles Hankla. Leona Schecter's perseverance and the editorial skills of Sandy Thatcher and Elizabeth Gretz helped transform the manuscript into the first edition of this book, Karl Yambert, Barbara Greer, and Sharon DeJohn helped take the book to its new edition.

Donald Schewe, the director of the Archives of the Carter Presidential Library, and Martin Elsey, his assistant, helped me locate important White House papers on Nicaragua. Brenda Reger, director of the Office of Information Policy of the National Security Council, had the dubious honor of being the first to review the entire manuscript, and I am very grateful that she cleared it for you to read. I hope you will be as well.

I thank Austin Hoyt of Public Television in Boston (WGBH) for permitting me to read the transcripts of interviews that were done for the documentary he produced on Central America. Parts of the book also benefited from the State Department cables that have been declassified as a result of requests by Scott Armstrong and Peter Kornbluh of the National Security Archive.

My largest debt is to my wife Margy, whom I married in June 1979 as the Nicaraguan crisis was reaching a climax. It is hard for me to imagine writing this book without her encouragement, patience, and, most of all, her perceptive editorial judgment.

This book may be about the past, but it is for the future, and so I dedicate it with hope to my two children, Tiffin Margaret and Robert Kiplin.

R.A.P.

The history of America's relations with Nicaragua well illustrates the truth that governments, no more than individuals, are all good or all bad. . . . At times, the United States has been a noble and unselfish hero to Nicaragua; at times, it has been the villain who would let nothing thwart his purpose. And often, it has been both hero and villain at once, as in its high-handed, yet absolutely necessary, enforcement of American supervision of the last Nicaraguan election [in 1928]. . . . As is usual in life, the United States has been punished the most severely when it was acting the most altruistically.

Harold Norman Denny, **Dollars for Bullets,** *1929*

Those who cannot remember the past are condemned to repeat it.

George Santayana, **The Life of Reason, Vol I,** *1905–1906*

You have to believe in free will. You don't have any choice.

Isaac Beshevis Singer

PART ONE

Setting the Stage

You are doubtless aware that the conduct of our relations with Nicaragua is considered by the peoples of other countries as a test of our policies.

SECRETARY OF STATE CORDELL HULL,
letter to the secretary of the navy, August 1936[1]

---

[1] Hull was reprimanding the secretary of the navy for praising Anastasio Somoza Garcia. Hull called the praise "unfortunate in every respect." Cited in Paul Coe Clark Jr., *The United States and Somoza, 1933–56* (Westport, Conn.: Praeger, 1992), p. 43.

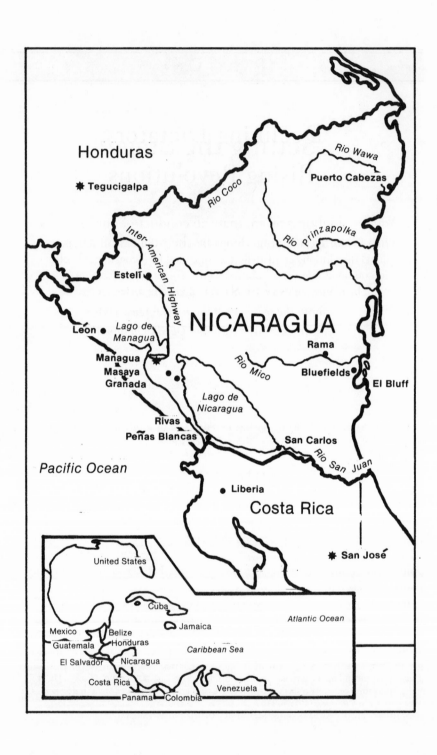

Declining Dictators, Rising Revolutions

"Revolution." In politics, an abrupt change in the form of misgovernment. Revolutions are usually accompanied by a considerable effusion of blood, but are accounted worth it—this appraisement being made by beneficiaries whose blood had not the mischance to be shed.

AMBROSE BIERCE, *The Devil's Dictionary*

"HE'S A SON OF A BITCH, but he's *our* son of a bitch." This comment about Anastasio Somoza by President Franklin Roosevelt has been widely known and used.[1] The Somoza family referred to it—to show they were tough, but their *partner*, the United States, was even tougher. Moderate critics of U.S. foreign policy cited the remark to show the myopia of a policy that supports right-wing dictators just because they are anti-Communist. Radical critics of the United States use the comment to show that U.S. assertions of idealism are hypocritical and mask a hegemonic or imperialistic purpose. Latin Americans referred to it to distinguish themselves from Somoza. The comment has been used by everyone to make so many points that no one has bothered to find out whether it was actually ever used by Franklin Roosevelt.

It probably wasn't. The first record of the statement is in a cover article on Somoza in *Time* magazine on November 15, 1948—three and a half years after Roosevelt died, and nine years after he was said to have made the comment. Donald Schewe, an archivist who worked at the FDR Library in Hyde Park for nine years, searched for the citation but never found it. However, after reading through thousands of pages of Roosevelt's correspondence, press conferences, and records, Schewe concluded "that was not the kind of language that Roosevelt used."[2] "Son of a bitch" was, however, the kind of language that Somoza *always* used.[3]

Some have suggested that the essence of U.S.-Nicaraguan relations can be found in the words attributed to Roosevelt. The real clue to the relationship, however, is in the way this apocryphal comment has been used. Although few believed the many outrageous statements of the Somoza family, many wanted to believe this statement because it was comfortable. It reinforced two myths—first, Somoza ruled only because of the support of the United States; and second, the United States *prefers* vassals and right-wing dictators. Somoza enjoyed the remark because he viewed the myth as a source of power. The United States, hardly a victim, did not mind the comment when it supported Somoza and could not dissociate itself from it when it did not.

Over time, as the Nicaraguan state developed, Somoza's myth backfired, antagonizing the nationalistic sensibilities of independent-minded people in Nicaragua and throughout Latin America. Indeed, the Sandinistas, who replaced Somoza, chose to use the mirror image of Somoza's myth—the United States as a hostile colossus—for the same purpose: to strengthen their regime. Instead of advertising U.S. friendship, the Sandinistas denounced U.S. imperialism in order to demonstrate their nationalist credentials and to attract youthful support.

"Nicaragua" and "the United States"—the ideas, not the nations—have often functioned as metaphors serving ulterior purposes. Among North Americans in the 1980s, "Nicaragua" became a metaphor for "Vietnam" or "Cuba," depending on one's political preferences, and to Nicaraguans, "the United States" was either savior or Satan. Both nations, of course, are more complicated than these metaphors, and their relationship—the subject of this book—is even more so.

The Ghost of Cuba Past

On July 17, 1979, Anastasio Somoza Debayle* resigned from the Presidency of Nicaragua, and three days later, a new government led by the Sandinista National Liberation Front (FSLN, or Frente) took power. The Carter administration had foreseen the possibility of a Sandinista victory about a year before it occurred. Viewing the key Sandinista military leaders as Marxist-Leninists who admired Cuba and despised the United States, the administration aimed to preclude a military victory by the Sandinistas but not to support Somoza, who was seen as indefensible. Over the course of the year, a subcommittee of the National Security Council met nearly twenty-five times to formulate policies to facilitate a peaceful democratic transition in Nicaragua and thus avoid a violent takeover by the Sandinistas.

---

*Spanish names have a second surname, which is the mother's family name. The patriarch of the Somozas was Anastasio Somoza García (1896–1956). García, his mother's name, will not be used, and sometimes he will be called Tacho I. He and his wife, Salvadora Debayle, had two sons, Luis Somoza Debayle (1923–1967) and Anastasio Somoza Debayle (1925–1980), who was also known as Anastasio Somoza, Jr., or Tacho II. His son is Anastasio Somoza Portacarrero (b. 1951) or Tacho III. In most cases, I will not use the maternal surname of Spanish names.

In the middle of the crisis, a group of young, well-groomed Americans arrived in Managua with a quiet determination to solve the conflict through transcendental meditation.[4] As it turned out, the U.S. government had about as much impact on the outcome of the Nicaraguan revolution as did this group.

How could that be? It was generally assumed by most Nicaraguans, ranging across the political spectrum from Somoza to the Sandinistas, that the United States was a crucial actor in Nicaraguan politics. While Nicaraguans were dying in Nicaragua, Somoza told reporters: "The battle is being fought in the U.S."[5] Most of those who have written about the Nicaraguan revolution assumed that the U.S. role was decisive. If that was the case, why did it not prevent a Sandinista victory?

Two major critiques of U.S. policy answer that question, though their authors contradict each other in their description, interpretation, and judgment. Jeane Kirkpatrick, who would become President Ronald Reagan's ambassador to the UN, wrote two provocative essays for *Commentary* in which she interpreted the Carter administration's policy as designed "to weaken the government of Anastasio Somoza and to strengthen his opponents." Her judgment is that Carter's policy "brought down the Somoza regime."[6]

An alternative view is offered by William LeoGrande, a professor at American University, in an article in *Foreign Affairs*. He criticizes the policy for always being several steps behind events, as it "labored mightily . . . to prevent the accession of a Sandinista government in Nicaragua." LeoGrande, Tom Farer, Shirley Christian, and others who have written about U.S. policy and the Nicaraguan revolution reach a conclusion the opposite of Kirkpatrick's—that the Carter policy failed precisely because it *did not* try to bring Somoza down.[7]

Ironically, both sides agree that the administration set an objective—in the first case, to bring down Somoza; in the second case, not to overthrow him—and achieved that objective, even though it was mistaken.

Analysts also differ on the causes of the policy failure. Whereas Kirkpatrick suggests that the Carter administration was insufficiently alert to the Communist involvement in the Nicaraguan opposition, Richard Fagen writes that the policy failed for the opposite reason—that the Administration's "twisted perceptions . . . [of a] Cuba-Sandinista connection" prevented it from taking the actions necessary to topple Somoza.[8] William LeoGrande also attributes the failure to misperception: "the fear of 'another Cuba,' and the questionable conviction that the radical opposition was intent on creating one."[9]

LeoGrande is correct that the Carter Administration feared "another Cuba," and that this concern influenced policy. Yet the Nicaraguan revolution evolved in ways that were strikingly reminiscent of the Cuban revolution twenty years before. Both revolutions were propelled by broad-based opposition to long-standing dictators who were despised by their own citizens and much of the international community. Rather than oppose the revolution, the middle class and the business community in both countries played leading roles, first in organizing general strikes, then in waiting for the United States to find a solution, and finally in ignoring U.S. advice and supporting the rebels. The United States deliberately withdrew support from the dictators and searched in vain for a middle, democratic option. Democratic leaders in Costa Rica and Venezuela passed arms covertly to rebel leaders in both cases.

In their memoirs, which were written for a North American, English-speaking audience, both dictators blamed the United States rather than themselves for their fall. A sense of *déjà vu* is perhaps most vividly conveyed, however, in the titles of those memoirs: *Cuba Betrayed* by Fulgencio Batista, and *Nicaragua Betrayed* by Anastasio Somoza, Jr.[10]

After the Sandinista triumph, many leaders—*even* Fidel Castro—expressed their hope that Nicaragua would *not* become another Cuba.[11] In Nicaragua and throughout the region, most hoped that the United States would support the revolution rather than confront it, and that is what the United States did at the beginning. But within eighteen months, the United States stopped supporting the Nicaraguan government and, one year after that, was financing a covert war to overthrow it. In the same period, the Sandinista government accelerated its revolution and became more dependent on Cuba and the Soviet bloc for military and economic aid.

The most fascinating and puzzling aspect of the Nicaraguan story was that all the key leaders in the United States, Nicaragua, and the neighboring countries were not simply aware of the Cuban events; they were preoccupied with the parallels. With the exception of Castro and the Sandinistas, they kept reminding each other during the revolution to avoid repeating the mistakes made in Cuba two decades before, but that's what they did. This was not only true of the United States, but of Venezuela, Costa Rica, the middle-class leadership in Nicaragua, and especially Anastasio Somoza.

The Cuban Drama in Seven Stages

What images of Cuba's history did decision-makers have in mind as they addressed the Nicaraguan crisis? The predominant image was of a long-standing dictator, Fulgencio Batista, who had been close to the United States, but whose repression sparked a general rebellion led by Fidel Castro, who professed democratic principles and overthrew Batista in 1959. The relationship between Castro and the United States deteriorated quickly. Castro sought support from the Soviet Union, and the confrontation with the United States almost led to a nuclear war. Those were the broad outlines of the Cuban revolution, but the details are even more fascinating because they are so similar to what occurred in Nicaragua two decades later.

Indeed, the relationship between the United States, Cuba, and Nicaragua was shaped by U.S. intervention in both countries at the turn of the century. Washington withdrew its troops from both countries, but sent them back whenever there was instability. However, by the mid-1930s, the U.S. finally replaced its periodic interventionism with a rigid non-interventionism.

Although Havana was beset by terrorism, President Franklin Roosevelt rejected two requests by his Ambassador Sumner Welles to intervene: "Certainly, we cannot be in a position of saying to [Cuban President] Machado, 'you have to get out.' That would be obvious interference in the internal affairs of another nation."[12] Welles continued to pressure Machado and conspire with the military, and on August 12, 1933, Machado left Cuba. The immediate effect was a period of instability and a political vacuum, which was filled by Sergeant Fulgencio Batista. As Chief of the Army, Batista ruled from behind the scenes until his election as President in 1940. By then, the United States was prepared to overlook the dictatorship because of the stability he brought to Cuba during a time of world war.

Batista relinquished power at the end of his term in 1944, but in 1952, he ran for President again. Behind in the polls, Batista staged a military coup in March of that year. On July 26, 1953, Fidel Castro led a group in a futile attempt to overthrow Batista. Castro was imprisoned, but Batista permitted him to leave the country.[13] By Christmas of 1956, however, he returned to Cuba and, with twenty followers, had launched his revolution in the mountains of the Sierra Maestra. U.S.-Cuban relations then passed through seven stages.

1. IDENTIFICATION. U.S. Ambassador Arthur Gardner (1953–57) was effusive in his praise of Batista, and in the first stop of a Latin American tour, Vice President Richard Nixon reinforced the impression that the United States stood firmly behind the dictator. The opposition to Batista therefore identified the United States with the dictator, although at the same time it tried to persuade the United States to change its position.

In order to be recognized among all the opposition groups, Castro had an interview arranged for him with Herbert Matthews of the *New York Times* in February 1957 in the mountains. Awed by Castro and by what he thought was a band of about 200 (although only 18 at the time), Matthews' articles made Castro an international figure. On July 12, 1957, Castro issued a manifesto calling for free elections, agrarian reform, a constitutional government, and an end to foreign intervention.

2. DISTANCE AND DISSOCIATION. The State Department was increasingly worried about the deterioration in Cuba and attributed it to Batista. The United States pressured him to hold free elections in 1958, hoping that they would provide an escape valve for the political pressures that were building. Earl Smith, an investment banker, arrived as the new U.S. Ambassador in mid-July, and he made a good impression in the country by criticizing "excessive police action."[14]

The Catholic Church also contributed to Batista's isolation. On March 1, 1958, Cuban bishops called for an investigation of the regime's brutality and asked Batista to step down in favor of a government of national unity. The statement influenced public opinion against Batista in the United States, forcing the U.S. government to reevaluate its military aid program. On April 8, 1958, Secretary of State John Foster Dulles announced an arms embargo against Batista, saying: "We don't like to have them [arms] go where the purpose is to conduct a civil war."[15] This was the clearest sign of U.S. dissociation from Batista. Hugh Thomas described the State Department's dilemma: "As democrats, they would have liked an alternative to Castro as a successor to Batista; but hostile to the idea of intervention, they shrank from any positive action to unseat Batista. The arms embargo seemed then the most positive form of negative action."[16]

3. THE LEFT LEGITIMIZED BY THE MIDDLE. Castro announced a general strike on April 9, 1958, and although it failed to unseat Batista, it added to his image as the center of the opposition. On July 20, 1958, representatives of all the opposition groups, including Castro's 26th of July, signed an agreement in Caracas—the "Caracas Pact"—which named an opposition government, with a moderate judge as president and Castro as commander-in-chief.

The Caracas statement represented a decisive shift in the balance of power within Cuba, as many in the middle class aligned with Castro. The Venezuelan site was as important as the message, because it connoted a new alignment of Latin American democratic forces behind Castro. Just six months before, Venezuelan dictator Marcos Pérez Jiménez had been overthrown, and the country was eager to demonstrate its solidarity with other democratic movements. Several democratic leaders from the region had already given covert support to Castro. José Figueres, Costa Rica's President, sent him a planeload of arms on March 30, 1958, and Carlos Andrés Pérez, who would become President of Venezuela during the Nicaraguan crisis, also sent arms to Castro on behalf of Acción Democrática.[17] Figueres later explained why Castro received so much help from democrats in the region:

> I helped Fidel Castro as much as I could because what was involved was the overthrow of a military dictatorship. . . . In the U.S., there's not enough knowledge of the fact that in Latin America for a long time, we have been trying to gather forces to establish a uniform political system based on the electoral system. . . . We were completely willing to help overthrow all military dictatorships. We didn't know, and I think nobody knows, what were Fidel Castro's ideas regarding Communism at the time.[18]

Batista recognized his international isolation and, using a psychological tactic familiar to the Somozas, he tried to change U.S. policy by blaming the United States for helping the rebels. Castro used the same tactic in reverse, he condemned the Eisenhower Administration for remaining too committed to Batista.[19]

4. THE SEARCH FOR A THIRD FORCE. The hope that Cuba's elections of November 1958 would offer an exit from the instability proved empty. Most of the opposition leaders refused to participate, and the results were manipulated by Batista. In late November 1958, senior officials in the Eisenhower Administration, realizing that time for finding an alternative to Castro was growing short, asked William Pawley, an American businessman with experience in Latin America, to undertake a secret mission. Pawley later recalled that his goal was to "get Batista to capitulate to a caretaker government, unfriendly to him but satisfactory to us, whom we would immediately recognize and give military assistance to in order that Fidel Castro should not come to power."[20] Pawley went to Havana and proposed that Batista transfer power to a provisional government involving Colonel Ramón Barquín, who was in prison for having led an unsuccessful coup against Batista in 1956. Batista refused, saying to an aide that he was inclined to "kick out this Pawley."[21]

In the last month before Batista fled, the Eisenhower Administration desperately sought to locate and support a "third force." Batista too realized his end was near, but tried to pretend that it was not, lest his own armed forces overthrow and kill him. The CIA wanted to get Barquín released and to link him with Justo Carrillo and other moderate civilians. Castro, wary of these plots, was concerned that the replacement of Batista by someone credible and independent like Barquín could bring a premature halt to his revolution. But Castro was saved by Batista. On New Year's Eve, 1958, Batista fled after handing power to one of his staff, General Eulogio Cantillo.

Cantillo decided it was futile to hold the Army together, and he handed power to Barquín, who had just been released from prison. Barquín then surprised everyone by telephoning Castro and surrendering the Army, giving up "what chance there was of a government of the center," according to Hugh Thomas.[22] The Cuban military disintegrated in a matter of days.

5. RELATING TO THE REVOLUTION. The United States recognized the revolution, but both Eisenhower and Castro had ample grounds for suspecting each other's motives. Castro knew that the United States had desperately tried to keep him from power, and the United States suspected that Castro's support for elections and the 1940 constitution concealed a more radical proclivity. Castro knew the power the United States had exercised in Cuba through nearly $2 billion of investments, and the United States could not doubt Castro's enormous popularity. Ambassador Smith was replaced with a liberal-minded professional, Philip Bonsal. The new Ambassador sought to meet with Castro to develop a good relationship, but Castro did not want to be like other Cuban leaders who took their orders from the U.S. Ambassador. He kept his distance from the Embassy.

Castro traveled to the United States in April 1959 at the invitation of the American Society of Newspaper Editors. Eisenhower decided to leave Washington, believing it would be more appropriate for Castro to meet with Vice President Nixon and Secretary of State Christian Herter. The United States was prepared to discuss aid to Cuba if Castro raised the issue, but he did not. Both sides tested the other, and both received poor grades.

Castro's revolution did not stop for breath. In March, he decreed a sweeping land reform law, lowered rents by 50 percent, denounced the United States, and nationalized the Cuban Telephone Company, which had been owned by Americans. By the fall, moderates within the government were replaced by radicals, and the independent revolutionary leader Hubert Matos was imprisoned. Castro's denunciations of the United States as Cuba's enemy increased in number and virulence.

6. DISTANCE AND NEGOTIATION. Bonsal continued to counsel caution, but another group in the Administration, led by Richard Nixon, urged a tougher approach so that other Latin Americans would not think the United States could be defied with impunity. Castro's own actions served to strengthen Nixon's arguments, and Nixon undoubtedly offered Castro a persuasive example that the United States was unwilling to accept the Cuban revolution. Nonetheless, in January 1960, Bonsal persuaded Presi-

dent Eisenhower to issue a statement that was both firm and conciliatory, urging Castro to begin talks with the United States and negotiate differences. Cuba accepted the offer in principle but continually delayed the talks. In the meantime, Castro hosted the visit of Soviet First Deputy Premier Anastas Mikoyan. And on March 4, 1960, Castro accused the United States of blowing up a French ship in the Havana harbor.

7. CONFRONTATION. The United States expressed shock at the charge, which it denied, but two weeks later, Eisenhower secretly authorized the Central Intelligence Agency to begin recruiting Cuban exiles for a possible attempt to overthrow Castro. Reports of CIA recruiting soon reached Castro, who responded by improving his nation's defenses, expanding the Army, and denouncing the United States.

Each action provoked a reaction by the other. In June 1960, after U.S. oil companies refused to refine Soviet oil, Cuba nationalized them. The United States then cut Cuba's sugar quota, and Cuba responded by increasing its sugar sales to the Soviet bloc and nationalizing most of the U.S. property in Cuba. Finally, on January 2, 1961, Cuba insisted that the United States reduce the size of its embassy, and Eisenhower, in one of the last acts of his Administration, responded by closing it. Three months later, the United States sponsored an unsuccessful invasion of more than 1,000 Cuban exiles at the Bay of Pigs. By the end of 1961, Castro had declared himself a Marxist-Leninist.

After the Cuban missile crisis in October 1962 brought the world to the brink of nuclear disaster, Cuba deepened its relationship with the Soviet Union and created a one-party Communist state. The United States continued to try to undermine the revolution, but with little effect. The worst fears and suspicions of both sides, however, continued to be confirmed, having achieved, in the words of one analyst, "a self-perpetuating momentum."[23]

All the participants in the Nicaraguan drama twenty years later continuously reminded each other of this history.[24] Needless to say, few of the key actors either knew or remembered the details, but the outline of what had happened was imprinted in their consciousness. And three men—Carlos Andrés Pérez, José Figueres, and Fidel Castro—did recall many details, since they were involved in both episodes.

Distinguishing Succession Crises from Revolutions

If U.S. policy appears repetitive, so too are the questions that writers ask of the government: Why can't the United States live with Latin American revolutions? How can events in such small countries affect U.S. national security?[25] These questions are not unique to Cuba and Nicaragua. The United States has wrestled with similar problems of declining dictators and rising revolutions in the Dominican Republic, Haiti, Vietnam, the Philippines, Iran, and Chile. Answers to these questions have proven unsatisfactory, perhaps because these are the wrong questions.

Part of the confusion stems from a misunderstanding of the word "revolution." Walter LaFeber described 'revolution" as "virtually the only method of transferring power" in Central America, and thus comparable to elections in the United States.[26] LaFeber's thesis is that the United States fears and resists all revolutions, but his definition would include every coup d'état in the region—most of which the United States accepted, and some of which it encouraged.

An alternative definition of revolution is a purposive, violent, and fundamental change in society in which power is transferred across social classes, or rather from one elite, representing the middle or upper class, to another, oriented toward a lower class.[27] Though LaFeber described revolutions as "inevitable," in fact they have been exceptional, occurring in only three countries in Latin America in the last sixty years. It is significant that all three great Latin American revolutions—in Mexico, Cuba, and Nicaragua—began as crises of political succession and only succeeded because virtually the entire nation agreed that the problem was the dictator. Moreover, the thesis that the United States and its "bourgeois lackeys" reflexively resist revolutions is not substantiated in these three cases, which succeeded in large part because the middle class supported and legitimized the revolt and the United States did not forcefully resist it.[28]

The distinction between succession crises and revolutions is significant because each poses a different challenge for U.S. policy-makers. The first—succession crises—is the result of an absence of clear, legitimate, and acceptable procedures for transferring power in a country, and, of course, this was the norm for most of Latin America in the 20th century. The United States tried to prevent Marxist or anti-American rebels from seizing power because once such a group takes power, it could legally invite a powerful, hostile government to defend it (or expand its influence). If such groups define the United States as their implacable enemy and the Soviet Union and Cuba as their friends, the probability is that they will seek a military relationship with the Soviet Union for defense against U.S. imperialism.[29] **The U.S. government long believed that its influence is greater, and the risks to world peace fewer, in preventing a hostile group from coming to power than in preventing a hostile government from asking the Soviet Union for help. Problems arise when the hostile group either disguises its intentions or has diverse or obscure goals. This was the case in all three "successful" revolutions.**

During a succession crisis, the main challenge and preoccupation of U.S. policy makers is not with the revolutionaries but with the incumbent dictator. The problem is not managing revolutionary change but, rather, trying to promote a negotiating process between parties that refuse to talk with one another.

If the revolutionaries come to power, as they have done in Cuba and Nicaragua, policymakers face a different challenge: how to promote U.S. interests to a regime that views the United States as opposed to its principal goals. But here again, in the cases of both Cuba and Nicaragua, the United States did not reflexively resist the new revolutionary government.[30] In Nicaragua, the United States was the major financial supporter of the revolution in its first stage. U.S. support did not end because of Nicaragua's internal policies but because of its support for international subversion.

The third stage—the democratic transition—was unprecedented in a revolutionary country, and the process that led to free elections was equally a surprise. But its importance cannot be overstated; it offered a formula for peaceful change.

The Thesis in Brief:
The Three Challenges of Nicaragua

This book aims to explain why the Nicaraguan revolution occurred, why it was radicalized, why the United States and other actors repeated much the same unsuccessful policies that each had pursued twenty years before in Cuba, and finally, why Nicaragua escaped the patterns of the past. Each question has its answer, but the thread that connects the answers is that mistrust between the United States and its friends—an attitude born of different histories, interests, and perceptions—undermined their common objectives until a new awareness permitted a change in approach.

One reason for the Sandinista victory in 1979 was that many thought the United States would prevent it, but no one acted on that assumption. All the key actors in the region thought the United States could control everyone else's behavior—except their own. The United States was perceived to be at the center of events, but that was an illusion—to which even the United States fell victim.

Although much of the literature on the Nicaraguan revolution views the United States as the actor and Nicaragua as the object, a much more complicated interaction occurred. The United States was at the center of the region's consciousness, but Nicaraguans always remained at the center of events. Though the United States is vastly more powerful than the nations of Central America, one should not assume that such power automatically translates into influence. Indeed, such power is sometimes reversible, with leaders or groups in the region using the United States to further their own political or economic ends, while ignoring U.S. attempts to influence them.

Some have found this role reversal difficult to interpret. For example, in summarizing U.S.-Nicaraguan relations over a forty-year period, LaFeber concluded: "As every President after Hoover knew, [the] Somozas did as they were told."[31] It is true that in order to strengthen their internal position, the Somozas cultivated the myth that they were working for the United States, but it was only a myth. The Somozas were no one's fools or servants. They cooperated with the United States only when it was in their interest to do so.

The roots of the revolution's radicalization were in the minds of the Sandinista and North American leaders. The different histories and deep suspicions each had of the other led each to perceive defensive actions as provocative ones. Both sides made policies that consistently evoked the worst in the other.

The repetitive policies of each of the actors also grew out of their national experience—each nation's history and political culture. This explains the continuity in each policy, but there were also some important changes over time, due in part to different leaders with markedly different perceptions of the nature and intensity of the threat to their national interests.

The clue for understanding both the mistakes of the past and the possibilities for the future lies at the *intersection* of U.S. and Latin American policies. The psychological baggage that both sides brought to the relationship distorted visions so much that it is a wonder there have not been more tragedies. The Nicaraguan case is a microcosm by which one can learn the pathologies of U.S.-Latin American relations in each of the three major challenges faced by the United States in the developing world—How to deal with succession crises so as to improve the prospects for peaceful change? How to relate to revolutionary governments so as to prevent a destructive confrontation? And how can the international community facilitate democratic transitions? These are the three questions that have perplexed American foreign policy-makers over the decades. We shall try to explain the reasons for the confusion and the possibilities for a long-term solution to each challenge.

A Fractured History

Peaceful changes between different factions of the ruling classes, which have been rather frequent in other Latin American countries, have not taken place in Nicaragua. This traditional experience predisposed the Nicaraguan people against electoral farces and in favor of armed struggle. There is no doubt, then, that the Nicaraguan people have a rich tradition of rebellion.[1]

CARLOS FONSECA AMADOR, 1969

The Subterranean Rhythm

ON A NARROW ISTHMUS between the world's two great oceans, Nicaragua and its Central American neighbors share a geopolitical burden worthy of Job. Not only does the Isthmus hold together two large and proud continents that sometimes appear to move in opposite directions, but it does this while being squeezed between two tectonic plates. The seismic pressures created as these two plates rub against each other turn rock into magma and ignite gases that search for weaknesses in the earth's crust. Not just life but also the earth itself is hard in the Isthmus, and there are few vents to permit the gradual release of the pressure. The result is volcanic eruptions or earthquakes of great severity. Nicaragua alone has been jolted in 1885, 1931, and 1972.

By some metaphysical law, Nicaraguan politics have conformed to nature's tantrums. Like its geology, its politics have been irregular, impulsive, and often explosive. Historical changes may be measured better on the Richter scale than by election results. Since the Spanish arrived in 1522, and perhaps long before, the indigenous people have suffered unbearable exploitation and cruelty. Of the nearly one million Indians estimated to be in the area now known as Nicaragua, Conquistador Gil González de Avila and his successors converted about 30,000 to Catholicism and sent nearly 500,000 to other parts of the empire as slaves. Diseases took their toll on those who survived the wars, poverty, and slavery.[2]

Nearly three hundred years later, as the region emerged from colonialism, the population of Nicaragua was approximately 200,000, still less than one-fifth the precolonial level. With the exception of a limited trade in indigo and cacao (chocolate), the economy, according to one scholar, was "static," the Spanish being uninterested in development.[3] There were hardly any schools and few roads. The little wealth created by the primitive economies was concentrated in the hands of a few families, and the region had no experience with democracy and little with self-government.

In 1821, Agustín Iturbide, the Mexican who declared himself Emperor, proclaimed independence for New Spain (Mexico and Central America) from old Spain. At the same time, on behalf of Central America, the Captain-General in Guatemala City declared independence from *both* old and new Spain. Only when colonialism became a chapter in the region's history did its single virtue become apparent: it had kept small, fragile political entities like those in Central America united. Independence in the early nineteenth century brought continual military struggles among families, cities, and the nations of Central America. Many of the conflicts were connected.

Within Nicaragua, two political parties emerged to represent the interests of a few families in two cities. Initially, the parties had distinguishable philosophies reflecting the different economic interests of the two towns: León, led by Liberals, was commercial and open-minded, and Granada, led by Conservatives, was more agricultural, clerical, and orthodox. (The labels remained in the twentieth century long after the philosophical differences had eroded.) Each town sought an international ally, with León looking to Mexico and Granada seeking help from Guatemala.

In 1823, before he could unite the region under Mexican hegemony, Emperor Agustín was overthrown. With Guatemalan leadership, Central America established a federation, but it was so loose that each state remained "sovereign," and the President of Central America was denied the power to enforce compliance with the government's statutes. The federation formally dissolved on May 30, 1838, but the "idea" of Central America persisted with an ironically perverse effect: it tempted powerful leaders in one nation to overthrow neighboring governments in the name of unity. The result was more fragmentation and instability.

Within Nicaragua between 1824 and 1842, Conservatives and Liberals fought seventeen major battles, and power changed hands eighteen times.[4] In 1845, Nicaragua's Conservatives, aided by Conservative leaders from El Salvador and Honduras and led by Fruto Chamorro, the great-grandfather of Pedro Joaquín Chamorro, defeated the Liberals, led by Bernabé Somoza, the great-uncle of Anastasio Somoza García. Somoza had received some help from Liberals in other Central American countries, and had requested aid from the United States, which denied it because he was considered "a notorious bandit."[5] In 1851, after sacking each other's capitals several times, the Conservatives and the Liberals finally compromised on a new capital, Managua, which was about half the distance between León and Granada.

U.S. interest in the region until then had been marginal and sporadic. With the end of the U.S.-Mexican war in 1848 and the discovery of gold in California the same year, however, there was a surge of interest in the Isthmus as a transit between the two oceans. The United States had previously acquiesced in the expansion of British influence on the eastern (Mosquito) coast of Central America, but in 1850, with the signing of the Clayton-Bulwer Treaty, the United States insisted on equal access to the Isthmus. Great Britain and the United States agreed that any future isthmian railway or canal would be jointly controlled and neutral and would charge the same tolls for ships from both countries. The treaty was symbolically important for two reasons: first, no Central American nation signed it or was even consulted; and second, the most powerful nation in the world at the time accepted parity in Central America with the United States.[6]

With the Isthmus secured, Cornelius Vanderbilt developed a transit route across Nicaragua in 1851, using a stagecoach and steamer. The U.S. government was too preoccupied with the sectional feud that would soon tear apart the Union to become involved in Nicaragua's internecine disputes, but this did not deter individual Americans.

One such adventurer, or "filibuster," to use the term of the times, was William Walker, a Tennessean who was small in stature but possessed a towering ambition. In 1855, the Liberals invited him to Nicaragua to help defeat the Conservatives. The U.S. government tried to discourage filibusters, and President Franklin Pierce issued a proclamation specifically aimed at Walker, which directed Americans not to join him.[7]

Walker and fifty-seven American soldiers of fortune ignored the warning. Together they quickly defeated the Conservatives and burned their capital in Granada. Walker allowed a Liberal leader to function as a nominal president for a short time while he kept control of the Army. Then, in July 1856, he named himself President of Nicaragua, legalized slavery, and made English the official language. To the surprise of many Nicaraguans and other Central Americans, who viewed Walker as a Trojan horse for U.S. imperialism, the State Department reprimanded the U.S. Minister to Managua, who had recognized Walker's government, and the United States officially withdrew recognition. When Walker sent a representative to Washington to seek recognition and support, Secretary of State William Marcy refused to see him.[8]

Yet Walker stirred deep and contradictory feelings in the United States on the divisive issues of slavery and manifest destiny. One year later, in a weak position politically, Pierce tried to gain Southern support for his renomination by recognizing the Walker government. After the Democratic convention passed him over, he again withdrew recognition.[9]

If Walker divided the United States, he succeeded in unifying both the Conservative and Liberal parties against him, a feat not duplicated in Nicaraguan history until the 1980s. Moreover, by seizing Vanderbilt's transit company, he made a formidable foreign enemy. With the support of the British, the combined armies of all the countries of Central America, and Vanderbilt's financial assistance, the Nicaraguans drove Walker out of the country in 1857. (When he returned in 1860, he was captured by the British, who delivered him to the Hondurans to be executed.)

The experience with Walker and the fear that Costa Rica might exploit Nicaragua's weakness to occupy the southern part of the country provided a stimulus for Nicaragua's two parties to declare a truce and jointly rule while drafting a new constitution. In August 1858 Nicaragua became a republic, with a president elected for a single, four-year term and a bicameral legislature. Because the Liberals were discredited for having invited Walker, the Conservative Tomás Martínez captured the Presidency.

The Conservatives were able to stay in power for thirty-five years because the party developed a system to rotate its leaders. When the Conservatives divided in 1893, however, the Liberals quickly seized the opportunity. José Santos Zelaya, a Liberal from León, took power. By rewriting the constitution, he was "reelected" twice and served sixteen years.

During these fifty years of Conservative and then Liberal rule, only the forms of democracy were maintained. The opposition was ignored or suppressed, and elections were rigged. Still, these were years of relative peace, and particularly under the Liberal Party rule of Zelaya, Nicaragua began to modernize and develop. A railroad was built connecting the major cities in the western part of the country; some agricultural diversification occurred; and the number of schools was increased and their quality improved. However, compared to the other countries of Central America, Nicaragua received little foreign investment and made little economic progress.[10]

Zelaya modernized the Army and established a military academy, staffed by a German captain, a Nicaraguan colonel, and several Chilean officers.[11] Shortly after taking power, Zelaya assisted a group of Honduran Liberals to take power there. Later, he tried to replicate his success in other Central American countries as well as in Colombia and Ecuador, but he failed.[12] Nevertheless, Zelaya transformed Nicaragua into the premier military power in Central America for the first time in its history.

U.S. Entry into the Caribbean

By the end of the nineteenth century, the U.S. had reached its continental frontier, and Americans, exuding the confidence and strength of a new, world-class power, sought new areas for expansion. A rebellion in Cuba provided the perfect opportunity both to defeat a European nation and assist a neighbor to achieve independence.

After the war with Spain, the United States turned its attention to building a Canal and excluding other powers from the Isthmus. U.S. and Nicaraguan interests coincided in expelling Great Britain from the Mosquito Coast. For this, Zelaya expressed his gratitude to the United States as the "natural protector of all the small Republics of the Americas."[13] Next, the United States negotiated the Hay-Pauncefote Treaty of 1902 with Great Britain, which granted the United States the unilateral right to construct and defend an isthmian canal. The Treaty was described by the eminent diplomatic historian Samuel Flagg Bemis as "the token of Great Britain's real decision to leave to the United States mastery of its own continental life-line."[14]

The U.S. decision to select Panama as the site for the Canal, however, led to the deterioration of its relationship with Nicaragua. It grew worse in 1907 when Zelaya invaded Honduras, replaced its President, and prepared to invade El Salvador.

Whereas internal instability and cross-border intervention in the region was hardly noticed by the United States in the nineteenth century, it generated profound disquiet and occasionally direct military action by the United States in the twentieth. The area had not changed; the reach and the investment of the United States had. The most important investment, of course, was the Panama Canal. The U.S. concern with stability in the Caribbean Basin was especially pronounced in Nicaragua, because it was chronically unstable, and it offered the only alternative canal route to that of Panama.

Nonetheless, Theodore Roosevelt, whose famous corollary to the Monroe Doctrine was designed to justify U.S. intervention in the Caribbean, preferred a different approach in Central America. He joined with the President of Mexico in inviting all five Central American governments to a peace conference in Washington, beginning on November 14, 1907, to negotiate treaties to resolve the region's disputes. All parties agreed to a ten-year Treaty of Peace and Amity and to seven conventions, including one establishing a Central American Court of Justice with compulsory jurisdiction and another denying recognition to any government that came to power by violent means. All parties also obligated themselves to prevent the use of their territory by rebels attacking their neighbors. By the middle of 1908, all the conventions were ratified. Implementing them was another matter.[15]

The Washington conference did not affect Zelaya's ambitions or behavior any more than it inhibited the United States. In addition to threatening his neighbors and forcing U.S. companies to renegotiate their concessions, Zelaya also contracted with a German company to build a railroad to the Atlantic and was reported to have opened separate negotiations with Japan and Great Britain for a new canal.[16] The United States was therefore pleased when the Conservatives launched a rebellion against him in October 1909 in Bluefields (on the Atlantic coast). The uprising, which was financed by U.S. companies and other Central American governments, recruited the governor of the province, General Juan Estrada, as its leader. The U.S. government did not take an official position on the rebellion, but it was privately sympathetic.

Zelaya quickly dispatched troops to the eastern coast, and the rebels, who were outnumbered, sought U.S. intervention. Under the guise of protecting American citizens in Bluefields, 400 Marines landed.[17] General Estrada was mistakenly encouraged by the arrival of the Americans, and he led his army to defeat against Zelaya's. Estrada then retreated to Bluefields and Marine protection, but not before two of his North American demolition experts were captured and executed by Zelaya's troops.

U.S. public opinion was outraged by the executions. The State Department condemned Zelaya's regime as "a blot upon the history of Nicaragua" and broke diplomatic relations. Zelaya succumbed to the pressure, and on December 16, 1909, he tendered his resignation to eliminate a "pretext" for U.S. intervention.[18] This was the first time the U.S. would help overthrow the Nicaraguan government, but it would not be the last. Twenty years later, a correspondent for the *New York Times* noted: "In 1909, the U.S. took a bear by the tail, and it has never been able to let it go. . . . Once in, [the United States] found that it could not get out. It tried to get out, and disaster struck Nicaragua, and dragged it in again."[19] The United States had become the arbiter of Nicaraguan politics.

The Nicaraguan Congress selected one of Zelaya's men, José Madriz, as President, but he was unsatisfactory to the United States, which withheld recognition until the rebels overthrew him. The new government of Juan Estrada was born with serious defects, not the least of which was that he enjoyed little, if any, popular support. The Liberals opposed the government, and so too did many Conservative generals, who considered themselves better qualified for the Presidency than either Estrada or his Vice President, Adolfo Díaz. As a result, the United States was pulled deeper into the details of constructing a stable and solvent government. This, in turn, caused the Nicaraguans, alternately to rely on the United States and to resent and resist it. Rebellions by Conservative and Liberal generals increased in number and scope, and in August 1912, Diaz, who had replaced Estrada as President, requested U.S. military support.[20]

Marines landed at Corinto on the Pacific side and at Bluefields on the Atlantic. With the exception of an eighteen-month period (August 1925–January 1927) when the Marines left Nicaragua, the intervention of 1912 lasted until January 1933. In the first phase, the United States used 2,700 troops and defeated the rebels by October 1912. The United States then withdrew all but 100 men, which was still a sufficient force to deter the Liberals from trying to overthrow the government. In defending the Conservatives from 1912 to 1925, however, the United States was accused of using them as surrogates, and they were accused of being puppets.

To build a more secure economic foundation, the United States organized the nation's finances, supervised the budget expenditures, and collected customs revenues.[21] U.S. banks managed the Nicaraguan railroad and national bank and nominated the collector general of the customs, subject to the State Department's approval.[22] An extended period of political stability permitted investment and some economic growth, and by 1920, the Nicaraguan government had paid off some of its international debt.

After the first World War, though the most powerful nation in the world, the United States turned inward, rejecting the League of Nations and withdrawing its military forces from most of the Caribbean area. The challenge for U.S. policy in Nicaragua, according to the State Department, was "to create a situation where the legation guard [the Marines] could be safely withdrawn" without provoking another rebellion.[23] This would require a government with broad support, and that only could be accomplished in a free Presidential election. The United States persuaded the Nicaraguan government to employ Harold Dodds of Princeton University to draft a new electoral law in 1924. Dodds did so, but he insisted that outside supervision by the United States was necessary to guarantee a free election. Nicaragua rejected that stipulation.

A coalition ticket with a Conservative, Carlos Solórzano, as President and a Liberal, Juan Sacasa, as Vice President won a fraudulent election, and the two were inaugurated on January 1, 1925. Solórzano asked the Marines to stay, but President Calvin Coolidge brought them home on August 1, 1925. In one month, the government began to unravel, and within a year, Nicaragua was engulfed in another civil war. Nicaragua's politicians continued to look to Washington for direction, but the United States decided in principle to limit its involvement. In practice, the United States was ambivalent because of a contradictory mission: the State Department wanted to limit its role, but U.S. diplomats in Managua were major actors in Nicaragua's politics, and their job was to prevent instability and avoid losing control of events.

The United States was also constrained by the results of a second meeting of Central American governments, which began in December 1922, to discuss ways to make the 1907 treaties effective. The conference agreed to another Treaty of Peace and the establishment of "tribunals of inquiry" or fact-finding missions. The United States proposed arms limitations, but the Central Americans were not interested. The conference also agreed on an elaborate formula to withhold recognition from revolutionary governments or leaders as a way to discourage revolutions.[24]

This conference did not bring peace to Central America any more than the previous one had. The Conservatives in Nicaragua took control of the government but could not defend themselves from attacks by the Liberals, who were then led by Juan Sacasa and José María Moncada. The Liberals were receiving arms from the Mexican government at a time when U.S.-Mexican relations were strained, and the Coolidge Administration suspected that the Mexicans were supporting Communist activities in Latin America. Therefore, when the Nicaraguan President urgently appealed for help and was seconded by the British, Italian, and U.S. embassies, President Coolidge dispatched 160 Marines on January 6, 1927. This was inadequate, and within a few months, U.S. forces expanded to include more than 5,000 Marines and eleven cruisers and destroyers.[25]

Coolidge defended the action, which was a departure from his policy of noninterference, by stressing the covert support that the rebels were receiving from Mexico and the "proprietary rights" of the Bryan-Chamorro Treaty, which in 1914 had granted the United States exclusive rights to build a canal in Nicaragua.[26] At the same time he wanted a solution that would bring the troops home, and on March 31, 1927, Coolidge dispatched former Secretary of War Henry L. Stimson to Nicaragua "to investigate [the problem] and report." "If I should find a chance to straighten the matter out," Stimson recalled as Coolidge's instructions, "he wished I would try."[27]

After arriving in Nicaragua, Stimson met with many Liberal and Conservative leaders. His conclusion, which he believed they shared, was that the cause of the problem was "that Nicaragua had never had a really free election; that the government habitually controlled the result and that the habit was so inveterate and ingrained that they could only hope to obtain a free, fair start through outside assistance in supervising the conduct of the polls."[28] Nicaragua was weakened by the war, and both sides had concluded that they could not win. It was also clear that both sides trusted the United States, but not each other, and believed that the United States alone could enforce a settlement.

With the exception of one Liberal general, Augusto César Sandino, the armies of both sides deposited their arms with the U.S. Marines. Sandino withdrew to the northeast of Nicaragua with 150 followers and continued the fight against his own government and U.S. forces. The U.S. government considered Sandino a "bandit," robbing and killing poor people and harassing small outposts,[29] but he was perceived as a nationalistic hero in much of Latin America.[30]

From the U.S. perspective, Sandino was irritating, but the larger problem was to establish a nonpartisan constabulary and ensure free elections. On November 4, 1928, the United States supervised the first "free" Presidential election in Nicaraguan history.[31] The Liberal José María Moncada won the election by a vote of 76,676 to 56,987. On January 1, 1929, power was transferred peacefully from a leader of one political party to another in an inauguration ceremony in which both leaders participated. After the election, the United States reduced the number of Marines in Nicaragua from 5,000 to 1,300, but Sandino pledged to continue fighting until all U.S. troops were withdrawn.

Henry Stimson became Herbert Hoover's Secretary of State, and he was determined that after supervising Nicaragua's elections in 1930 and 1932 as he had promised, the Marines would be withdrawn. Stimson's motives for advocating withdrawal were unambiguous. First, he believed that one of the U.S. objectives in Central America should be to secure the independence of the countries, and that meant using force only in exceptional and temporary circumstances. Second, he was sensitive to the mounting opposition to U.S. intervention in the United States and abroad. And third, he wanted to mobilize international opinion against Japanese aggression in Asia ("the Stimson Doctrine"), and the U.S. occupation of Nicaragua was obviously inconsistent with his own doctrine.

Liberal leader Juan Sacasa won the Presidential election in 1932, and on January 1, 1933, moments after the inauguration, General Calvin B. Matthews, the head of the Marine legation and the National Guard, "departed, leaving in such a rush that his Chief of Staff doubts that [Matthews] had time to finish packing."[32]

The First Somoza

Some in the State Department viewed the creation of a non-partisan National Guard as essential to ending Nicaragua's intermittent partisan wars. Others, including the U.S. Minister to Managua, predicted that the National Guard would become the army of the party in power as soon as the Marines left.[33] The two predictions were not incompatible, and indeed both came true. The United States helped create a modern military instrument that brought an end to partisan warfare, but when the United States departed, the party in power, the Liberals, quickly turned the Guard into their partisan army. President Sacasa consulted with his predecessor, Moncada, and with the U.S. Minister, and appointed Anastasio Somoza García, the ambitious and shrewd young husband of his niece, as the Director-General of the National Guard. Somoza, who had been Stimson's interpreter, used the Guard first to defend Sacasa, then to take power in 1936, and finally to keep power until he was assassinated in 1956.

Sandino ended his campaign after the Marines departed. He reached a peace agreement with Sacasa, and warned the President that the Guard was his greatest threat. Somoza worried that Sacasa might find the warning credible. On February 21, 1934, after dining with Sacasa, Sandino was arrested by a Guard patrol and executed.

Sacasa pledged an investigation of the murder, but Somoza, using his allies in the Nicaraguan Congress, effectively blocked any investigation. Evidently believing that if he could share the responsibility, he could lessen his culpability, Somoza claimed that the execution was approved by the United States, which also, he said, supported his political ambitions. Both statements were untrue, but that did not stop Somoza from repeating them. After several efforts, U.S. Minister Arthur Bliss Lane finally persuaded the Department of State to issue a public statement on June 25, 1934, rejecting both insinuations.[34] Somoza, however, was unfazed.

Somoza was the first Nicaraguan leader to recognize that the United States had really decided to withdraw from Nicaragua's politics. Sacasa did not understand this. Nicaraguans had become so accustomed to U.S. control that the psychology of their dependent relationship continued long after direct U.S. involvement ended. Somoza, having begun as an interpreter, proved most adept at manipulating the image of the relationship and made it appear that the United States condoned, approved, or even instructed him. For example, in the week before the murder of Sandino, Somoza made certain he was repeatedly seen talking with the U.S. Minister and even joining him at a baseball game.[35]

Somoza's attempt to identify himself and his cause with the United States infuriated his opponents and exasperated Washington, which was trying to remove itself from Nicaragua's internal affairs. When the U.S. Minister recommended that the United States block Somoza's attempts to take over the government, Secretary of State Cordell Hull, anticipating the debate that would divide the Carter Administration forty-five years later, endeavored to explain the basis of the new policy:

> It has for many years been said that the United States has sought to impose its own views upon the Central American states, and that to this end, it has not hesitated to interfere or intervene in their internal affairs. This criticism has been made particularly in regard to our relations with Nicaragua. We therefore desire not only to refrain in fact from any interference, but also from any measure which might seem to give the appearance of such interference.[36]

From 1934 to 1936, the United States agonized over defining and justifying its policy of noninterference, as Somoza gradually took control of the Liberal Party and solidified his hold on the Guard. Many people, both within and outside the Nicaraguan government, urged the United States to stop Somoza. President Sacasa personally argued that the United States had a "responsibility" to do so because it had created the Guard, but the State Department rejected that argument, saying that U.S. intervention ended in January 1933, and "in seeking advice . . . and requesting our opinion, Dr. Sacasa was in fact seeking to prolong or revive the intervention." Sacasa rebutted that "a word of advice or an opinion would not constitute intervention," but State insisted it could be interpreted as such. Sacasa pressed, saying "silence at this time might also be interpreted as a kind of intervention."[37] The Mexican chargé in Managua warned that if Somoza, the man "responsible for the death of Sandino, a hero in Latin America yet a mortal enemy of the United States" took power, it would appear as though the United States "had put him in power as a reward for having killed Sandino."[38]

The State Department would not respond, believing that Nicaragua could only learn self-government if the United States resisted efforts to be drawn into internal disputes. Although it was not the intention of the U.S. government, the effect of this policy was to permit Somoza to have a clear path to the Presidency. The United States had gone from one extreme—U.S. Marines—to another—silence. The Roosevelt Administration could have stated its public opposition to Somoza's takeover clearly and openly. Even if that failed to deter Somoza, it might have scotched subsequent allegations that the United States wanted him to be Nicaragua's President.

In June 1936, Somoza pushed his uncle out of office and the country. Somoza then quit his command of the National Guard in November, and with his opponent in exile, he ran for the Presidency. The opposition first asked the United States to stop the December 8 election. When the United States restated its policy of noninterference, the opposition decided not to participate. His landslide victory was no more surprising than the resumption of his post as Chief of the Guard two weeks later. At the end of his term, Somoza changed the constitution to permit him another "transitory" term until May 1947.

Like his predecessors, but much more so, Somoza used his office for profit as well as for power. Just as he had modernized the military, he also developed new sources of wealth. Most of his investments were in Nicaragua, and in almost every sector. By graduating his generals into his companies, he also used his investments as an additional means of securing his control of the Guard.

As World War II ended, dictators fell in Guatemala, El Salvador, and Venezuela, and Nicaraguans hoped theirs would be next. U.S. policy remained one of noninterference, but with the death of President Roosevelt, the State Department chose to interpret policy broadly. On August 1, 1945, the Assistant Secretary of State for Inter-American Affairs, Nelson Rockefeller, told the Nicaraguan Ambassador that "should Somoza run for re-election, it might create difficulties for him which would seriously affect relations between the two countries."[39] When he heard this, Somoza suggested the U.S. Ambassador join him in selecting a successor, but his offer was rejected.

Somoza nominated Leonardo Argüello, a previous opponent who was 70 years old, as the Liberal candidate. Argüello won an election that was reportedly stolen by the Guard.[40] However, on May 2, 1947, the day after his inauguration, Argüello reorganized the General Staff of the Guard and began replacing some of the officers, without consulting Somoza. Argüello informed the U.S. Embassy that he intended to assert control over the Guard. Somoza then called the Chargé to inform him of his views of Argüello: "Can you imagine what a stupid bastard? I took him out of León where he couldn't earn a dime, and he does something crazy like that."[41] On May 24, Argüello told the U.S. Chargé that he was asking for Somoza's resignation; two days later, he was deposed by Somoza.[42]

The United States deliberately withheld recognition from Somoza and demanded the return of all ammunition belonging to the military mission. The chief of the U.S. military mission and the American director of the Nicaraguan Military Academy were withdrawn. Internationally, the United States indicated to the Latin American governments that were then negotiating the Rio Pact that the "oppressive" Nicaraguan regime, which was "a puppet one and a creature of Somoza," should not be recognized, although the United States agreed to "follow the majority" of votes on the issue.[43]

By August 7, 1947, worried about economic sanctions, Somoza suggested to the United States a number of steps he could take—short of stepping down from the Guard—that could permit U.S. recognition. The United States did not respond, but in a meeting with Assistant Secretary of State Norman Armour on August 24, 1947, at the Rio conference, the Nicaraguan Ambassador to Washington "wondered . . . whether the departure of Somoza would not help in clearing up the situation and making recognition easier." Armour "entirely agreed," but only if the government was broadened after Somoza's departure to include "representatives of certain of the other groups."[44] Needless to say, Somoza did not agree. He felt the pressure from the United States but knew that his power ultimately derived from his control of the Guard. Thirty years later feeling similar pressures from the north, his son recalled this period and kept firm control over the military.

In April 1948, at the Bogotá conference, the foreign ministers of the American states adopted a resolution urging the continuity of diplomatic relations among members of the OAS (Organization of American States). As a result of that resolution, the United States extended recognition to the government of Víctor Manuel Róman y Reyes, Somoza's elderly uncle, who had been appointed President by a new constitutional convention.[45] He died on May 6, 1950, and a new constitution (Nicaragua's tenth) allowed Somoza to seek and win election as President. He was inaugurated on May 1, 1951. The constitution guaranteed the opposition party one-third of the seats in Congress.

Democrats vs. Dictators vs. Communists

After World War II, a new three-sided ideological struggle involving dictators, democrats, and Communists was grafted onto the traditional Central American landscape of mutual intervention. In October 1944, the democrats of Central America received a boost from a successful democratic coup in Guatemala. The new President, Juan José Arévalo, invited democrats from the region to Guatemala City on December 16, 1947, to sign a "Caribbean Pact" to help each other bring democracy to the region.[46]

In the Presidential elections in Costa Rica in February 1948, Rafael Angel Calderón ran against Otilio Ulate, a popular newspaper editor. Two of the three members of the Electoral Tribunal announced that Ulate had won the election, but Calderón's party, which controlled the Congress, annulled it. With help from the democratic "Caribbean Legion," José Figueres, a young follower of Ulate, launched a six-week guerrilla war and defeated Calderón. He then established an eighteen-month junta that inaugurated a second republic. In November 1949, as proof that he was a different breed than the traditional *caudillo*, Figueres passed the Presidency to Ulate. At the same time, Figueres honored an agreement he had made with Rosendo Argüello, Jr., a Nicaraguan leader, to help him overthrow Somoza after Argüello had helped Figueres overthrow Calderón.

Before Figueres and Argüello could attack Nicaragua, however, Calderón, who had received help from Somoza, led his small army from Nicaragua into Costa Rica in December 1949. The United States demanded Somoza stop supporting Calderón, and the Costa Ricans defeated the invasion.

Somoza had been trying desperately to obtain U.S. military aid, which he had received during the war in exchange for bases. With the emergence of a leftist government in Guatemala, Somoza saw an opportunity. He sent his Ambassador to the State Department on September 29, 1952, to seek "urgent" military aid and U.S. cooperation for a plan to overthrow the Guatemalan government. Somoza also expressed concern about two other "leftists" in the area, Figueres and Rómulo Betancourt. The Truman Administration was noncommittal about military aid, but precise in discouraging any conspiracies against Guatemala or Costa Rica.[47] In a memorandum to Truman, Secretary of State Dean Acheson acknowledged that Somoza was friendly to the United States but also described him as greedy ("his desire for personal gain is very great") and as "a one-man show."[48]

The U.S. view of Nicaragua and Guatemala changed with Administrations. The Eisenhower Administration viewed the existence of Communists in the government in Guatemala as a serious threat to the United States, and it gave less weight to the criticisms of Somoza as a dictator and more to his loyalty. In a telegram to the Department of State on March 6, 1953, Ambassador Thomas Whelan argued that the United States should sign a military aid agreement with Somoza, who, Whelan asserted, was "not a dictator in the true sense of the word." Whelan wrote that Somoza was prepared to be helpful against Guatemala and had promised not to "take any action" against Costa Rica, where Figueres had just been elected.[49] The Administration accepted the proposal and negotiated a military aid agreement with Nicaragua at the same time that the CIA began using Nicaraguan territory to train Guatemalan rebels.[50]

In August 1953, twenty years after a Republican President had withdrawn U.S. troops from Nicaragua, President Eisenhower decided to overthrow the

Guatemalan government. The United States was concerned about Communist participation in the Guatemalan government, but the U.S. action was interpreted in the region in more traditional ways. Somoza, in addition, saw his new alliance with the United States as permitting him to secure another term for the Presidency and overthrow Figueres, who continued to sponsor plots against him. As soon as the Guatemalan government was overthrown in June 1954, Somoza provided weapons and training to a group of 500 Costa Rican exiles, the Authentic Anti-Communist Revolutionary Army, under the leadership of Teodoro Picado, Jr., the son of a former Costa Rican President. Assistance also came from Dominican dictator Rafael Trujillo and Pérez Jiménez of Venezuela.

The United States tried to defuse tensions between Costa Rica and Nicaragua, but by August 12, 1954, it was clear that such efforts had failed. The Acting Secretary of State then decided to "let it be known to Somoza by appropriate means that he had impaired his position with the United States." This warning also failed to deter Somoza. On January 11, 1955, Picado's army invaded Costa Rica and was aided by air drops of war matériel by the Nicaraguan Air Force.[51]

The United States acted quickly to halt the war. It airlifted fifteen tons of light arms to San José and sold four P-51 fighter planes to the Costa Rican government for a dollar each. The OAS sent a team to the border to establish a buffer zone. The crisis was over, but Washington decided to reduce aid to Somoza, who, in turn, complained: "What advantage do we get from being friendly? You treat us like an old wife. We would rather be treated like a young mistress."[52]

In September 1956, after receiving his party's nomination to serve still another Presidential term, Anastasio Somoza García attended a Saturday night dance in León. There, Rigoberto López Pérez, a young Nicaraguan poet, shot him five times before being killed by Somoza's bodyguards. With U.S. help, Somoza was flown for emergency treatment to the Canal Zone, but within a week, he was dead.

Recurring Themes

Throughout its history, the vast majority of Nicaraguans have scraped a meager living from a rich earth while a few wealthy families controlled most of the economy and contested power. Force remained the currency of political change. Stability was imposed by either dictators or U.S. Marines, but every Nicaraguan faction sought help abroad.

The scars left by North American adventurer William Walker remain on the Nicaraguan body politic as the first mark of U.S. intervention. What is often forgotten is that Walker was invited by Nicaraguans and discouraged by the U.S. government. Zelaya also invited the United States to help him expel the British. When the United States turned against him, he looked for help from Britain and even Mexico, but to no avail. From 1912 to 1933, U.S. support was sought first by the Conservatives and then by the Liberals. Only Sandino fought the United States, but he too invited aid from Mexico and was the first to recruit international public opinion for his cause.

U.S. policy was shaped by its internal politics and its self-perception. U.S. policy toward Walker had much less to do with Nicaragua than with divisive American issues like slavery and manifest destiny. Its involvement in the Caribbean Basin and intervention in Nicaragua during the first three decades of the twentieth century were driven by strategic concerns regarding the Canal, but the character of U.S. involvement was shaped by ambivalent and contradictory ideas of its proper role. The United States did not want to control Nicaragua or the other nations in the region, but it also did not want to allow developments to get out of control. It wanted Nicaraguans to act independently, *except* when doing so would affect U.S. interests adversely. When it did intervene in Nicaragua's internal affairs, it did so thinking its involvement would be brief—but it was not.

The establishment of the National Guard and the supervision of "free" elections were the clearest examples of what happens when two such different nations interact. Both were done with the best of intentions—providing a framework for peaceful democratic change and facilitating the exit of the Marines—but with the worst of consequences—the beginning of the Somoza dynasty.

The complex psychology that accompanies a relationship between a powerful occupation force and a small nation was fully developed in Nicaragua. The United States became impatient with Nicaraguan greed and tyranny, and Nicaraguans became angry with U.S. arrogance. When the U.S. Marines left, Nicaraguans felt a combination of both pride and uncertainty about themselves, and admiration and resentment for the United States.

Only Anastasio Somoza García grasped the full implications of a United States that swung out of Nicaragua so fast it feared raising its voice about Nicaraguan politics lest the pendulum of intervention swing back. And so Somoza manipulated the absence of the United States as much as the U.S. presence had previously manipulated Nicaragua. Somoza's venality and his pretense of being a U.S. surrogate obscured a significant historic development: the expansion of the region's autonomy, its growing ability to control its own destiny. With minor exceptions or retreats, the governments in the region, whether friendly to the United States or not, had gradually but inexorably widened their area for decision making. In 1910, the United States could overthrow a government merely by withholding recognition; in 1947, the same tactic failed. In 1954, the United States could arm fewer that two hundred Guatemalans and topple the government; thirty years later, 30,000 contras could not shake the Sandinista government.

Anastasio Somoza had learned to dodge or ignore U.S. pressures, but in the end, he could not ignore Nicaragua's subterranean rhythm. He capped the pressures for political change for twenty years and met his end with a lethal blast, the volcanic fate of Nicaragua's geology and its politics.

Roads to Revolution

We are usually told that revolutions are set in motion to realize radical changes. Actually, it is drastic change which sets the stage for revolution. . . . Where things have not changed at all, there is the least likelihood of revolution.

ERIC HOFFER

The Brothers Somoza

THE DYNASTY began with the death of the old man. His two sons had been taught to view their country as their estate, and they moved rapidly and expertly to replace their father. Luis Somoza, 34, a graduate of Louisiana State University, was President of the Nicaraguan Congress at the time of the assassination, and he was chosen to complete his father's term and to receive the party's nomination for the Presidential election in February 1957. He was elected overwhelmingly.

Anastasio Somoza, Jr., 31, who was called "Tachito," had graduated from West Point and was Acting Director of the Guard and the Commander of the Nicaraguan Air Force. He was promoted by his brother, and his first decisions were to arrest hundreds of opposition leaders in Managua and to replace all officers of potential ambition or questionable loyalty.

The feud with Figueres was passed on to the next generation of Somozas, who suspected, incorrectly, that the Costa Rican leader had arranged the murder of their father. In May 1957, three gunmen were arrested in San José and charged with plotting to kill Figueres. A few months later, Figueres reported that he had uncovered a new Nicaraguan-supported plot to overthrow him. Two years later, in May 1959, Figueres equipped an expedition led by Pedro Joaquín Chamorro and Enrique Lacayo and airlifted them and two planeloads of rebels into Nicaragua to link up with another group that entered by land from Costa Rica. The Somozas defeated the expedition and imprisoned Chamorro and his followers.[1]

By 1961, the Somoza-Figueres feud was eclipsed by the geopolitical struggle between the United States and Cuba. The Somoza brothers became a target for a few

The Somoza dynasty: from left, Anastasio Somoza, Jr., his mother, Anastasio Somoza, Sr., and Luis Somoza in 1956. AP/Wide World Photos.

unsuccessful raids from Cuba by Nicaraguan rebels, and the United States, in turn, enlisted the Somozas in their effort to overthrow Castro. Luis Somoza eagerly volunteered facilities on Nicaragua's Caribbean coast to serve as a staging area for the Cuban exiles destined for the Bay of Pigs.

Nicaraguan guerrillas had long been trying to overthrow Somoza, but Castro's victory added a new purpose to their ambition. Prior to 1959, most "revolutions" were aimed at overthrowing dictators. Castro mixed Marxism, nationalism, and anti-Americanism in a new recipe that created problems for the United States and inspired leftists throughout Latin America. In Nicaragua, Carlos Fonseca Amador and Tomás Borge quit the pro-Moscow Nicaraguan Socialist Party because of its reluctance to pursue an armed struggle. They went to Havana, where they organized the Frente Liberación Nacional (National Liberation Front). The FLN then merged with several other groups, including the Frente Revolucionario Sandino led by Edén Pastora, who had been fighting Somoza since 1958. Together, in July 1961 in Honduras, these groups established the Frente Sandinista de Liberación Nacional (FSLN).[2] Fonseca, the leader of the new group, was clear on the source of inspiration of the FSLN: "With the victory of the Cuban Revolution, the Nicaraguan rebels' spirit recovered its radiance. The Marxism of Lenin, Fidel, Che, Ho Chi

Minh was acquired by the Sandinista National Liberation Front, which had undertaken again the hazardous and difficult guerrilla path."[3]

The Sandinistas, however, posed no threat to the Somozas in the 1960s. With increasing investment in Nicaragua as a result of the Alliance for Progress and the Central American Common Market, this was a period of unprecedented economic progress. Luis Somoza, an ostensibly more genial and accommodating politician than his father or brother, began to relax political restrictions and decided not to seek another term. Instead, in February 1963, he had René Schick, a lawyer who had served the elder Somoza as a private secretary, nominated as the Liberal candidate. However, when the Conservative candidate Fernando Agüerro did not receive guarantees of a free election and Luis Somoza refused to invite OAS observers because it would constitute "foreign interference" in Nicaragua's internal affairs, Agüerro withdrew. Schick won by a margin of more than ten to one. Luis Somoza, while retaining real power, allowed Schick more autonomy than his father ever considered. Schick was even allowed to implement several decisions against the wishes of the Guard, including trying one officer for murder and exiling rather than imprisoning or executing Carlos Fonseca Amador after his capture in July 1964.[4]

Brother Anastasio Somoza concentrated on securing the Guard's support before obtaining, on August 1, 1966, the nomination of the Liberal Party for the next Presidential election. The constitution required that he resign from the Guard, which he did, although he did not move out of his office. The opposition united behind the candidacy of Fernando Agüerro, and he mobilized a large demonstration in Managua in January 1967 to seek guarantees for a free election. The Guard put down the demonstrations ruthlessly, and Somoza won the election on February 5 with 70 percent of the vote. Like his father, Anastasio Jr. insisted on maintaining formal control of the Guard and the government simultaneously. In April 1967, Luis Somoza, who was said to have been a moderating influence on his younger brother, had a heart attack and died.

The election of Richard Nixon brought to the White House a man who saw the Communist threat in the hemisphere much as Anastasio Somoza did.[5] Nixon named as Ambassador Turner Shelton, who became a confidant of Somoza. Like Thomas Whelan, Shelton could not speak Spanish, and he made no effort to communicate with the opposition.

As his term was coming to an end in 1971, Somoza conspired to remain in power. He first reached an agreement with his former rival Fernando Agüerro to dissolve Congress, call a constituent assembly, and appoint a three-member ruling junta, composed of Agüerro and two of Somoza's representatives. The junta governed the nation from May 1972 until Presidential elections in December 1974. Other opposition leaders rejected the agreement, and for the first time the Church, led by Archbishop Miguel Obando y Bravo, issued a statement denying the pact had any Church sanction.

If the Archbishop's statement failed to shake Managua, nature succeeded. On December 23, 1972, the streets of Managua were lifted by a powerful earthquake, then dropped, and finally burned by a storm of fire. When the streets settled and cooled, the city was rubble, 8,000–10,000 people were dead, and hundreds of thousands of people were left homeless. For a moment, the regime also shook, as many members of the National Guard deserted either to help their families or to loot. With the moral support of Ambassador Shelton and the offers of aid from the United States and the international community, Somoza steadied himself and transformed a tragic national loss into a personal financial gain. He accomplished this by channeling aid through his companies and purchasing the parts of the city where he planned to undertake reconstruction. He also encouraged Guard leaders to profit from the foreign aid and the reconstruction opportunities in the city. The acts of the Guard further isolated them from the Nicaraguan population even while tying them closer to Somoza. The business community's deep-seated contempt for Somoza stemmed to a great extent from his exploitation of the earthquake. After this event, some of the children of the middle and upper classes began to leave school to join the Sandinistas.

Except for the Ambassador, most of the U.S. Embassy staff in Managua recognized the earthquake as a turning point politically; they recommended that the United States distance itself from Somoza. But Shelton continued to support Somoza as the latter maneuvered into position for another presidential term.[6] Once again, Somoza rewrote the constitution and feigned resignation from the Guard. Once again, the opposition, this time united by Pedro Joaquín Chamorro, refused to participate in the election and recommended abstention. Although 40 percent of the voters stayed away from the polls on September 1, 1974, 815,758 votes were counted, and Somoza won 748,985 of those. The bishops and the opposition refused to participate in his inauguration, on December 1, 1974, for a seven-year term. Years later, Somoza would confide to an aide: "My single biggest mistake was running for reelection in 1974."[7]

As a head of state, Anastasio Somoza was a most unusual hybrid, an American-Nicaraguan. Except for four years, all of his schooling had been in the United States. "I know the U.S. better than my country," Somoza once said.[8] A more accurate statement would have been that he knew some parts of the United States in the 1930s and 1940s better than he knew Nicaragua. "Next to Nicaragua, I loved the U.S. more than any place in the world," he wrote in his memoirs.[9] Several have suggested that he felt a greater affection and affinity with North Americans than he did for Nicaraguans, whom he treated either formally or with contempt.[10]

Although there was an obvious political motive in the title of his memoirs, *Nicaragua Betrayed,* the title also reflected a theme of the book and a personal obsession of its author.[11] He saw the world, as many conservative Americans did, as divided between Communists and non-Communists. When the United States deserted him, he viewed himself as a victim of an "international conspiracy" as vast as Joe McCarthy's, including not just Cuba but Venezuela and Costa Rica and people like Rómulo Betancourt ("a self-declared Communist"), Jimmy Carter, Edward Koch (then a liberal Congressman from New York), Edward Kennedy, and Jack Anderson.[12]

Somoza also saw himself as a shrewd politician and businessman; he viewed his political opponents as incompetent and other Nicaraguan businessmen as jealous of his success. He ruled with an iron hand and was not averse to having the Guard abuse and torture political prisoners. Still, he would suggest to Americans that his Liberal Party was comparable to FDR's Democratic Party, and that his political machine was no worse than Richard Daley's in Chicago. His grasp of the truth was tenuous, at best.[13]

Using American terms and counting on American disinterest in Nicaragua, Somoza believed he could persuade most Americans that Nicaraguan politics were not that much different from U.S. politics, except that Nicaragua was threatened by Castro and the Communists. When pressed to resign, Somoza would insist on the importance of respecting the constitution. He expected that Americans would be unaware of the numerous times the Somozas had changed the constitution to serve their purposes.

The United States: From Identification to Neutrality

Although Nicaragua's middle class generally dates the beginning of Somoza's downfall to the 1972 earthquake, the protagonists—Somoza and the Sandinistas—use different benchmarks. Characteristically, Somoza dates the beginning of his downfall to a change in U.S. administrations. However, it was not the arrival of Jimmy Carter that first troubled Somoza, but "Nixon's departure" and the subsequent replacement of Ambassador Shelton.[14]

Somoza was correct that U.S. policy changed after Nixon's resignation. The very next day, Secretary of State Henry Kissinger phoned William D. Rogers, a Washington attorney and formerly Deputy Coordinator of the Alliance for Progress in the Kennedy Administration, and asked him to become Assistant Secretary of State for Inter-American Affairs.[15] When Kissinger was appointed Secretary of State in 1973, he asked Rogers to take the same position, but Rogers declined to work under Nixon. This time Rogers accepted, subject to two conditions: first, the CIA would not do anything serious in Latin America, as had occurred in Chile, without his knowledge; and second, he wanted to make changes in policy and personnel, particularly with regard to several ambassadors.

Turner Shelton was one of those he had in mind. In appointing his replacement, however, Rogers had to defer to Vice President Nelson Rockefeller, who proposed James Theberge, a conservative Latin Americanist from Georgetown University.

To ensure a change in policy, Rogers drafted and cleared detailed instructions, and then he delivered the new policy directly to Somoza with Theberge present to underscore two points for both. First, "the U.S. was [henceforth] absolutely neutral both publicly and privately in all its actions" with regard to Somoza and the opposition, and the United States would begin a dialogue with the opposition. Second, the United States was going to be watching the accounts of the Agency for International Development (AID) much more closely to ensure that the money was not misspent.[16]

Somoza received the message, and later wrote that it:

came as a shock, and it was hard to take. . . . There were more surprises. Ambassador Theberge began to associate with Pedro Joaquín Chamorro, a known Sandinista. He was entertained by those people [Conservatives] in Granada and . . . was bent on establishing a close relation with the wrong side—an opposition coalition. It seemed to me that . . . my country and I were in for trouble.[17]

Actually, Rogers had replaced the collaborationist policy of Shelton with a variation on the policy of noninterference and neutrality as it had been developed during the Roosevelt-Truman years.

The Sandinistas

The Sandinistas celebrate the anniversary of their first spectacular raid at Christmas in 1974 as the first glimpse of light at the end of a tunnel leading to victory.[18] José María "Chema" Castillo Quant, a wealthy friend of Somoza and former minister of agriculture, hosted a farewell party for Ambassador Shelton. Tomás Borge, who had received two years of military training in Cuba, prepared a small group of Sandinistas to capture prominent officials at an Embassy reception, but when they heard about the Castillo party on the radio, they changed their plans. Shelton had departed by the time the Sandinistas arrived, but many guests were still there, including Nicaragua's Foreign Minister, Managua's Mayor, and Somoza's brother-in-law, Guillermo Sevilla-Sacasa, who was also Ambassador to the United States.

The Sandinistas killed Castillo, held the rest of his guests hostage, and demanded that Archbishop Obando act as mediator. On December 30, after tense negotiations, Somoza agreed to release fourteen imprisoned Sandinistas, including Daniel Ortega; provide $1 million in cash; and publish the FSLN's 12,000-word communiqué denouncing Somoza and U.S. imperialism and asking the people to rise up and join the Frente to overthrow Somoza. The Sandinistas then flew to Cuba. The raid, according to Borge, was a tremendous success: "It put the Sandinista movement in the spotlight world-wide, and our organization started to be recognized internationally."[19]

The raid helped to attract and recruit young people to the Sandinista movement, including the daughter of Chema Castillo and a young businessman, Alfredo César, who secretly began organizing a group of his colleagues to help the movement.[20] But these rewards were more than offset by the repression that Somoza unleashed to take revenge for the raid. At that time, the FSLN was estimated by Henry Ruiz, one of its leaders, to have about 150 cadre. In the next two years, the Guard arrested Tomás Borge and killed much of the Frente leadership, including Eduardo Contreras, Carlos Agüerro, and on November 6, 1976, its founder, Carlos Fonseca Amador.

There seemed hardly enough Sandinistas to make a revolution. Who were they? The Sandinistas' view of Nicaragua's history had much in common with Somoza's

Manichaean vision of the world, except that the saints and the sinners exchanged uniforms. Where Sandino is a bandit in Somoza's passion play, he is the Christ for the Sandinistas, and "the crime of February 21"—the date in 1934 when Sandino was murdered—is the date of his crucifixion. The United States is Pontius Pilate, who gave the instructions to Somoza to kill Sandino and then washed its hands of the crime. According to Carlos Fonseca Amador, Nicaragua had been "a victim of Yankee aggression for more than a century," and Nicaragua's history can be described most concisely as a list of U.S. interventions, beginning with William Walker. Every Nicaraguan who collaborated with the United States, like Adolfo Díaz, is a "traitor," and everyone who fought or defied the United States like José Santos Zelaya, is a patriot. Also central to the Sandinista outlook are the Marxist interpretation of history as a class struggle and the view of Nicaragua as a victim of U.S. transnational corporations and the Nicaraguan bourgeoisie.[21]

Given the centrality of the theme of the United States dictating to and exploiting Nicaragua, the origins of the modern Sandinista movement are as strangely ironic as Somoza's dual personality. The principal founders of the FSLN—Fonseca, Borge, and Silvio Mayorga—were members of the Nicaraguan Socialist Party, which was established in 1944, according to Fonseca, by a directive from Joseph Stalin sent through the leader of the American Communist Party, Earl Browder. Stalin had issued orders to all the Communist parties in the world to form a united front with all those who declared war against Hitler. That included Somoza, who had followed the lead of the United States and declared war against Germany. Therefore, the first act of the new Nicaraguan Socialist party was to proclaim its support for Somoza's government—on the instructions of an American, who was acting as a surrogate for Stalin.[22]

The Sandinista movement tried to marry a Marxist interpretation of history with a visceral hatred of Somoza, the National Guard, and the United States. Sandino— the great anti-Yankee Nicaraguan revolutionary—was a natural symbol for the movement, except that the Marxists had difficulty locating "class consciousness" in Sandino's actions and writings. Sandino welcomed "Internationalists," but he rejected all ideologies, calling his movement "essentially a nationalist thing."[23]

In 1973, after years of arguing with Borge and Ruiz, Pastora, who believed that Sandino was a nationalist and not a Marxist and that Marx was a democrat and not a Leninist, finally left the movement. He had recommended that the Sandinistas "discontinue implementing a Marxist-Leninist revolution and should implement a nationalist revolution of Sandinista character." His main argument for changing direction, however, was pragmatic: "A long time had gone by, and we had still not convinced the Nicaraguan people of a Cuban revolution, which they were trying to copy."[24] Pastora went to Costa Rica and started a shark-fishing business.

The formative experience of many of the leaders of the Sandinistas was a traumatic act inflicted on them or their families by Somoza's Guard. Both parents in the Ortega family were jailed by Somoza. "Family conversations and discussions," Daniel Ortega recalls, "always were anti-Somoza, and included criticisms of the U.S. for its permanent complicity with the Somoza government." All the Ortega brothers joined the FSLN, and one, Camilio, was killed. Daniel Ortega was imprisoned five separate times; the first in 1959 when he was 14, and the last from 1967 to 1974.[25]

Originating in Marxism, but driven by nationalism and hatred for the Somoza dynasty, the Sandinista philosophy naturally evolved as its membership changed. After the earthquake, a young group of idealistic Christian students from El Colegio de Centro America joined the movement, despite resistance by Henry Ruiz, who had been trained in Moscow. Radical priests like Ernesto Cardenal reinforced the Christian current in the movement.

The repression forced the movement to reconsider its strategy. In 1975, Humberto Ortega was completing his manuscript, *50 Años de Lucha Sandinista,* and he admitted that "we were in a precarious situation."[26] By its own account, the FSLN had failed in the 1960s, because of its inability to adapt to the jungle, and in most of the 1970s, because of the military power of the Guard.[27] After the decapitation of the Frente leadership, the next tier of leaders divided into three "tendencies" or groups. These reflected traditional Nicaraguan factionalism but also different strategies and constituencies. When interviewed in the fall of 1978, representatives of each faction called for unity but did not conceal their criticism of the other. Their main point of agreement was their fear that the bourgeoisie and the imperialists could overthrow Somoza before the revolution succeeded.[28] Fonseca, according to Henry Ruiz, had also given the group some precious advice. When someone proposed assassinating Somoza, he argued strongly against it, maintaining that "Somoza was an invaluable asset who personified all our country's contradictions."[29]

The original group, which included Borge and Ruiz, was called the "Prolonged Popular War" (GPP), and they remained wedded to the strategy of organizing the peasants from the mountains. After their Cuban "foco" strategy failed, they adopted the prolonged-war strategy of General Vo Nguyen Giap of Vietnam. They criticized the "Tercerista" faction for expecting a "great surge" to sweep away Somoza. They felt there was no alternative to working methodically with the peasants to build a guerrilla movement. Their weakness was that they could point to few peasants who had been converted.

A second group, "Proletarian Tendency" (TP), led by Jaime Wheelock Román, was younger, more intellectual, and concentrated its efforts on the workers in the urban areas. When asked about the difference between his movement and the other tendencies, Wheelock described the others as "currents of interest whose objectives, strategies, allies, and tactics are divergent and even contradictory." His group saw the road to revolution in organizing strikes.

The third group, "Terceristas" ("third force"), led by the Ortegas, was the least educated and the most pragmatic. They had absorbed the young, idealistic Christian recruits and had less patience for debates over Marxist purity. Asked to explain the differences between the tendencies, Daniel Ortega said: "Since 1973, we have forced ourselves to search for ideological-organizational ways to overcome within our ranks programmatic tendencies on the one side, and pseudo-theoretical tendencies on the other."[30]

In other words, the Terceristas were tired of talk, perhaps because they were not good at it. They wanted to overthrow Somoza and realized this could only be done by concealing their Marxist rhetoric and looking for allies everywhere. Their strategy was to undertake a few armed attacks and advertise them as major assaults on the dynasty. The Terceristas criticized the GPP for isolating themselves in the mountains and the TP for being "a small group of people of academic formation"; they saw themselves as "the front of the popular insurrection."[31]

In late 1976, Humberto Ortega persuaded Pastora and Carlos Coronel, a politically astute entrepreneur, to join the Terceristas. Had this new alliance and others that the Terceristas established not been formed, it is doubtful that the Sandinistas would have emerged from the wilderness. As a result of their strategy, however, the Terceristas did become the vanguard of the revolution, and the other two groups followed behind.

The Revolution before the Revolution

The Sandinista view of the Nicaraguan economy was that it was approaching crisis in the mid-1970s, the culmination of decades of neocolonial Yankee exploitation.[32] However, a closer look at the economic and social data of Nicaragua suggests that this revolution, like others, was the result not of poverty and backwardness but of economic growth. In the two decades preceding the Nicaraguan revolution, the social and economic progress was more profound than it had been for the previous two hundred years. The economic growth created new groups that placed pressure on an anachronistic political system.[33]

During the Alliance for Progress, from 1962 to 1970, Nicaragua received, on the average, about the same as each of its Central American neighbors: $92.5 million in economic aid (loans, grants, PL 480-II) and $11 million in military aid. During the next six years, owing to the earthquake, Nicaragua received nearly three times as much in economic aid, but less military aid.[34]

Loans from the World Bank and the Inter-American Development Bank also increased in number and value and, together with U.S. aid, provided the stimulus for an unprecedented surge in development. The average annual growth rate for Nicaragua from 1960 to 1970 was 7.2 percent, and from 1970 to 1978, 5.8 percent; this was almost double the rate for the United States during the same period, and among the fastest in the world.[35] Although agriculture in most developing countries declined sharply, Nicaragua's agricultural base remained strong and dynamic, particularly in exports, but food for local consumption was not neglected. Food imports as a percentage of total imports actually declined from 9 percent in 1960 to 8 percent in 1977.

Trade, which grew in the 1960s at about 10 percent annually, was a major engine of growth and diversification. Nicaragua is dependent on agricultural exports, but it is hardly a banana republic. It also exports beef, cotton, and coffee, and its overall dependence on these commodities declined from 95 percent of its exports in 1960 to 82 percent in 1977. Similarly, its dependence on the United States and the other industrialized countries as the source of all of its imports also declined during this period—from 91 percent of its trade in 1960 to 69 percent in 1978. The U.S. share of Nicaragua's exports fell from 43 percent in 1960 to 19 percent in 1974.[36]

The Central American Common Market, established in 1960, helped stimulate and diversify the economy. Trade among participating countries mushroomed from $32 million in 1960 to over $900 million in 1978, with manufactures accounting for 95 percent of the total.[37]

Population expansion, due to improved health conditions, was probably the major source of change. The population doubled in twenty years from 1.1 million in 1950. By 1975, over 50 percent of the population was under the age of 15.[38] The number of doctors as a percentage of the population increased. The infant mortality rate declined, and life expectancy increased from 47 years in 1960 to 55 years in 1980.

Education also improved and was extended to a wider segment of the population. The proportion of Nicaraguan children enrolled in primary schools as a percentage of all Nicaraguan children of that age group was 66 percent in 1960 and 92 percent in 1977; the figures for secondary schools were 7 percent and 29 percent.

In short, the growth in production and trade and the improvements in health and education were nothing short of revolutionary. Although per capita income was only $840 in 1978, this represented more than a four-fold increase for a population that more than doubled since 1950; it also reflected a doubling in income in the previous eight years. Put another way, if the total population had remained the same, per capita income would have increased nearly ten times between 1950 and 1978. New middle and working classes emerged, better educated, healthier, and more likely to live in the urban areas than their parents.

These changes and improvements, however, should not obscure the gross inequities that existed and that, in some cases, were exacerbated by the new growth. The most visible disparities were between the urban and rural areas and between the new wealthy and the new poor in the urban areas. But the most frustrating gap of all was the one that separated the Somoza family from the rest of the country. The Somozas not only controlled the nation's military and politics but had an expanding share in the nation's economy. They owned cattle, cotton, sugar, and rice farms, an airline, a shipping concern, a fishing fleet, a cement plant, a slaughterhouse, a construction company, and vast real estate holdings. There were no precise data on the Somoza family's wealth, but Anastasio Somoza reported his worth in July 1979 as $100 million. Other sources suggested it was closer to $900 million.[39]

The economy had grown and diversified; the population had grown and become better educated. People hoped that the time had also come to change the dynasty. But it did not change. New young, educated leadership pushed up against an immovable political system, like magma pushing up against a mountain peak. The pressures did not dissipate; they grew stronger, searching for vents to escape or a section of rock to detonate.

PART TWO

The Succession Crisis, 1977–1979

Our life is managed from behind the scenes; we are actors in dramas we cannot interpret. Of almost no decisive event can we say: this was of our choosing.

WALTER LIPPMANN, *Drift and Mastery*

4

Human Rights and
Nicaraguan Wrongs

Those who have been discriminating against dark-skinned people for years have nothing to tell me about human rights.

ANASTASIO SOMOZA, APRIL 23, 1977

AS JIMMY CARTER was taking the oath of office, Anastasio Somoza had more reason to be concerned with his weight than with the Sandinistas. At 267 pounds, Somoza was considerably heavier than his brother Luis was when he died of a heart attack in 1967. Moreover, as Somoza's girth was expanding, the Sandinista threat was shrinking. Since Somoza had decreed martial law in December 1974 after the Christmas party raid, the National Guard almost destroyed the FSLN. In June 1977, the Department of State estimated total Sandinista guerrilla strength at 50 fighting men.[1]

In the absence of any threat more serious than Somoza's weight problem, and with an ambitious domestic and international agenda, the Carter Administration had little time for Nicaragua at the beginning. The lack of high-level attention, however, did not mean that Nicaragua was neglected or that the United States did not have a policy. The U.S. approach was fashioned via a classical, deductive method: general policies, which were formulated at a high-level at the beginning of the Administration, were adapted by middle-level officials to the specific circumstances of Nicaragua.

Unlike most of his predecessors, Jimmy Carter had a deep personal interest in Latin America, and this was reflected in his choice of the first state visitor (from Mexico), his second foreign policy address (at the OAS), his highest priority in the first eighteen months (the Panama Canal treaties), and the six-country tour of Latin America and the Caribbean by his wife (May–June 1977).[2] In the overall policy that he developed toward the region, three specific themes had a special impact on Nicaragua.

41

First, his commitment to new Canal treaties with Panama communicated a willingness on the part of the United States to take the concerns of a small Central American country seriously. It also led Carter to develop close relationships with Panamanian leader Omar Torrijos and Venezuelan President Carlos Andrés Pérez, both of whom strongly opposed Somoza. Second, the advancement of human rights and democracy were central themes of his Administration. In a speech at Notre Dame in May 1977, Carter insisted that U.S. power should be used "for humane purposes." He also made a remark that had obvious if not specifically intended consequences for Somoza: "Being confident, we are now free of that inordinate fear of Communism, which once led us to embrace any dictator who joined us in that fear." Given the repressive, authoritarian rule of Anastasio Somoza, and the relative absence of a threat to the United States, human rights was the general policy that was initially judged to be most relevant to Nicaragua. Third, in his 1976 campaign, Carter had criticized the Nixon Administration for destabilizing the democratically elected government in Chile and then embracing the Pinochet dictatorship that overthrew it. He used his inaugural address to stress his opposition to overthrowing established governments: "We will not act abroad in ways that we would not tolerate at home." The first theme identified his allies; the second, his goal; and the third, limited the means that he would use to pursue his goal.

Human Rights Policy: Theory and Application

The Carter Administration's human rights policy was based on both a moral and a national security premise. By supporting a dictator, the United States would alienate his nation and especially its youth, which would identify the United States as part of its national problem. This, of course, is what had happened in Nicaragua. There were risks in withdrawing support from dictators, but the Administration believed that the prospect of violent revolutions would be greater in the long run if peaceful change were precluded.

Applying the theory to the Somoza regime, the Carter Administration viewed the dynasty's repression as the cause of the nation's instability. The Sandinistas were the symptoms of this problem, not the cause. Remote threats like the Sandinistas were less likely to become real if the political system were opened gradually than if the system remained closed. Therefore, the first question was how to promote human rights.

The way a government defines an issue determines the forum in which the issue will be debated. When Nicaragua was defined as a human rights issue, the central forum for debating U.S. policy to Nicaragua became the Interagency Group on Human Rights and Foreign Assistance, under the chairmanship of Deputy Secretary of State Warren Christopher. The policy became the sum of the committee's specific decisions on when and whether to increase or reduce foreign aid.

The Carter Administration's policy grew in part out of Congressional initiatives begun in 1973 to reduce foreign aid to countries violating human rights. Because the Nixon and Ford Administrations gave low priority to human rights, Congress passed laws requiring the President to give it higher priority in its aid programs.[3] The Carter Administration took office committed to Congress's priorities yet found translating the laws into effective policy difficult, partly due to inherent contradictions. For example, are human rights promoted by denying aid to poor people in countries ruled by dictators? Congress recognized the contradiction but walked around it, instructing the United States to reduce aid and vote against loans to countries that violated human rights "unless such assistance will directly benefit the needy people." One could argue either that aid should be approved because it would always benefit *some* needy people, or that aid should be denied because it would legitimize a repressive regime and prolong suffering. The Administration agreed that such questions could not be answered by any single formula; what was needed was a framework for case-by-case decision making that could also take into account other interests and review the kind of strategy that would be most effective toward each country.

The Christopher Committee was established by Presidential directive on April 1, 1977, to address these specific cases. Its mandate was to ensure that the aid program was used to promote human rights. The objectives were to discourage human rights violations, encourage improvements in human rights, and promote democratic institutions that could permanently guarantee human rights. If private diplomacy, the preferred method, failed to achieve its objective, the United States would raise the stakes by going public and demonstrate its seriousness by reducing aid.

The Committee debated specific human rights objectives and whether to provide aid to encourage good performance, deny aid to penalize bad performance, or use a combination of carrots and sticks. Participants included representatives from all aid-granting agencies as well as those with human rights or geographical responsibilities. Each agency generally had a vested interest in one of the options. By and large, aid-granting agencies and the regional bureaus, like the Bureau of Inter-American Affairs (ARA), would argue in favor of the carrot, insisting that only with good relations and the option to withdraw the carrot could one induce improvements in human rights performance. To deny aid would be counterproductive, they would argue. On the other side, the Bureau of Human Rights (HA) generally argued on behalf of the stick—denial of loans, reduction of aid—insisting that dictators would only take U.S. policy seriously if they had to pay a price. (HA did try to obtain additional aid to reward positive performance, but such efforts generally foundered because of budgetary constraints.) HA was led by political appointees, whose experience reflected both the domestic and the international origins of the Administration's concern for human rights. Assistant Secretary of State Patricia Derian had experience in the civil rights struggles in the South; her Deputy, Mark Schneider, had served as Senator Edward Kennedy's principal Latin American adviser and had drafted many of the human rights amendments. Derian was the articulate public voice of the policy, and Schneider, the adept bureaucratic operator.

The power of their small bureau derived from the personal skills of these two individuals and their colleagues, Carter's commitment, and most of all, from Warren Christopher, who transformed Carter's commitment into policy. Christopher judged that the best way to implement the policy was to combine both carrot and stick—denying aid for bad performance and supplying it for good performance, but because it was sometimes difficult to overrule the regional bureaus' argument that a particular strategy would be ineffective, he had to rely on the views of other regional specialists who worked in the State Department's Policy Planning Staff (PPC) and the National Security Council (NSC). These individuals were often political appointees, who shared the President's commitment to human rights but also had the regionalists' sense of the constraints of effecting change in a foreign country. After listening to the debate, Christopher would make a decision. The division that was built into the decision-making process was constructive, but when it spilled over—or rather leaked—into the public arena, it frequently left the impression of incoherence and inconsistency.

In brief, there was no specific policy toward Nicaragua early in the Carter presidency; there were only human rights policies that applied to Nicaragua. Outside of this framework, U.S. relations with Nicaragua received low priority. The new Ambassador, Mauricio Solaun, a Cuban-American professor of sociology from the University of Illinois, was not sent to Managua until August. Although among the more intelligent and informed of the Administration's ambassadors, Solaun was not particularly suited for the Nicaraguan post. He was a modest and unassuming individual who was well liked but not a good match for Somoza's gruff personality. Alfonso Robelo, a business leader and friend of Solaun's, recalled that the Ambassador "trembled when he went to see Somoza."[4]

There was a special poignancy in Solaun's service in Nicaragua. As a Cuban-American he, more than anyone, knew the cycle of events that had led to Castro's triumph and wanted to avoid a repetition. Yet Solaun could do little as he watched the worst-case scenario unfold before his eyes.

The Impact on Nicaragua

While some debated whether the human rights policy was having any effect, Somoza already felt it. In the words of one of his closest friends, U.S. Congressman John (Jack) Murphy, Somoza "knew that he was in deep trouble five days after the Carter Administration took office because it cancelled export licenses for the sale of ammunition for sporting arms. That was a message . . . [that Somoza] was out of favor with the United States. So early in 1977, he knew he would have difficulty with the Carter Administration."[5]

The press played a central role in publicizing human rights violations. Alan Riding, who had been covering Mexico and Central America for a decade for the *New York Times,* recalled that at the beginning of the Carter Administration he suspected that the purpose of the human rights policy was "just to needle the Russians." He sought a good test in Latin America, and in his mind, there was no better case than Nicaragua.[6] His articles on Guard repression therefore had a dual purpose—to criticize Somoza and to test the Administration.[7]

When the human rights reports were issued in Washington in April 1977, Somoza denounced the one on Nicaragua as "unacceptable," saying it "constituted interference in the internal affairs of Nicaragua." The report was brief and descriptive, citing the state of siege, the many reports of disappearances and torture, and summarizing the reports issued by human rights organizations.[8] Five Latin American military governments protested the reports by renouncing U.S. military aid, but that was not Somoza's style. He hired lobbyists and public relations firms in Washington to try to change the policy.[9]

Somoza's objective was to defeat an effort led by Rep. Edward Koch to eliminate the military aid program for Nicaragua. In this, he achieved some success, although the lobbyists were much less helpful than two influential Congressmen, Jack Murphy and Charles Wilson. Murphy and Somoza had been classmates at LaSalle Military Academy and West Point; their friendship had begun when they were 13 years old. From 1977 to 1980, according to Murphy, he spoke with Somoza "maybe two or three times a week. And I made many visits to Nicaragua."[10]

Charles Wilson, a flamboyant, conservative Democrat from Texas, became one of Somoza's most effective supporters even though he was not particularly fond of him. Wilson, like Murphy, thought the Carter Administration—particularly the State Department—was too liberal, too hostile to conservative regimes like that of Somoza, and blind to the Communist menace in the Third World. He also feared that Carter's foreign policy would make southern Democrats like himself vulnerable. Wilson therefore used his influence as a swing vote on the critical Foreign Operations Subcommittee of the House Appropriations Committee to change policy on Nicaragua.[11]

Although the Appropriations Committee narrowly supported Koch's amendment to delete military aid to Nicaragua, Murphy and Wilson succeeded in restoring the funds on the House floor. Their victory was short lived, however, because Carter undercut the vote by publicly assuring the House Appropriations Committee in June 1977, that it would not sign a military agreement without an improvement in human rights.

Somoza understood that over the long term he could not influence the United States unless the human rights situation improved, and in the spring of 1977, he instructed the National Guard to curb such abuses. The U.S. government learned of this directive, but many were skeptical of its significance until it was later confirmed by Amnesty International and the Catholic Church.[12]

On July 28, 1977, while visiting his mistress Dinorah Sampson, Somoza felt, in his words, "deep burning heat run across my chest." His doctors advised him to go to the Miami Heart Institute, which diagnosed the attack as angina.[13] Although he commanded an air force and owned Nicaragua's private airline, Somoza requested emergency evacuation by the U.S. Air Force. Aware of his condition but also of his family's long-standing tactic of trying to get the United States to identify with them at moments of vulnerability, the Administration said it would provide a plane, but he would have to pay. Somoza claimed to be "shocked and bitter," but he paid.[14]

His heart condition prevented him from his only opportunity to have a personal meeting with President Carter. In order to try to gain support for the Panama Canal treaties by showing the American people the treaties' importance to Latin America, Carter invited all the heads of state to the signing of the treaty on September 7, 1977. He met individually with each of the eighteen leaders who attended. Somoza's doctors insisted that he return to Nicaragua to rest and begin a strict diet and regimen of exercise.

Just as he and his brother had stepped in quickly to fill the vacuum created when his father was assassinated, his son, Anastasio Somoza Portocarrero ("Tacho III"), assumed a more visible role in the government when his father was incapacitated. Tacho III was born in 1951 in the United States and was educated at Harvard University. On returning to Nicaragua, he enlisted in the National Guard and, not surprisingly, rose rapidly. By 1977, he was commissioned a major and appointed Director of the Basic Infantry Training School, an elite group modeled on the U.S. Special Forces. As he shuttled between Managua and the Miami Heart Institute to pass messages to his father and return with instructions, Tacho III served as a visible reminder that the Somoza dynasty could extend another generation.

When Somoza returned to Nicaragua in September 1977, his colleagues urged him to step down. Luis Pallais, who was Somoza's cousin and president of the Nicaraguan Congress, argued that if Somoza transferred power to a unity government, he could undermine the opposition and preserve his interests. Pallais believes that he almost convinced Somoza, but as his health improved, so too did his interest in remaining in office. He finally put off Pallais by saying that he could "ride the waves" and remain in power, much as his father had done in 1947.[15]

Somoza was also visited by Costa Rican President Daniel Oduber, who suggested that the time was opportune for Somoza to step down from the Guard and the Presidency. Somoza rejected the idea. As the conversation shifted to Somoza's cool relationship with the United States, Somoza insisted that he still had friends there. Oduber, drawing on fragments of a brief conversation I had with him on May 30, said that the Carter Administration would not support him. Somoza said that this was not the first time that chilly winds had blown down on the Somozas from the north, and he would do as his father and brother had done, "crawl into his shell like an armadillo and wait for the wind to pass." He insisted he would remain President until the end of his term.[16]

Although unwilling to give up power, Somoza changed his Cabinet to make it more representative and then he responded to the most pressing U.S. objective at that time: on September 19, 1977, he ended censorship and lifted the state of siege that had been imposed since the Sandinista raid in December 1974. Immediately *La Prensa,* the only independent, antigovernment newspaper in Nicaragua, began publishing acerbic criticisms of the Somoza regime, and its editor, Pedro Joaquin Chamorro, the leader of a coalition of opposition parties called the Democratic Union of Liberation (UDEL), explored ways to democratize Nicaragua.

Somoza's decision to lift the state of siege put the human rights policy to a second test. Having withheld aid as an inducement to liberalize the political process, the United States should theoretically have released the aid after he took the step, and the Bureau of Inter-American Affairs argued that position. But the Human Rights Bureau argued that this was a small, insignificant step on the path toward a long and difficult dialogue. If the United States granted aid, the opposition would be demoralized and Somoza would have no incentive to pursue the dialogue. The classic division occurred, with ARA arguing to give the carrot and HA arguing to withhold it.

If the fiscal calendar had not forced a decision, the Administration would probably have avoided it, especially because the laws on economic and military aid were different, confusing, and easily misinterpreted. After listening to a heated debate, Christopher decided that since the Administration achieved its goal of getting Somoza to end the state of siege, it could not disapprove aid to Nicaragua. On the other hand, the Administration did not want to approve aid and lose important leverage to try to obtain free elections. Christopher chose to keep the options open: the United States would neither approve nor disapprove aid. The United States announced it would not provide any military aid *until* further progress was made in human rights. However, the law required the Administration to sign the 1977 military aid agreement before the end of the fiscal year, or the money would revert to the Treasury and future leverage would be lost. There were no similar constraints built into the economic aid laws, so the Administration merely postponed that decision.

In announcing the continued suspension of economic aid and military aid, the State Department said that the signing of the military aid agreement was required by law, but that it did not mean that the United States was sending military aid. Nevertheless, the *Washington Post* reported: "In a confusing turnaround, the Carter Administration has decided to withhold economic aid while approving military assistance."[17]

The Sandinistas were the last to recognize the significance of the human rights policy, but their view of it was the clearest. Humberto Ortega, a leader of the Terceristas and Minister of Defense when the Sandinistas later triumphed, recalled:

In mid-1977, there was great political activity among the bourgeois opposition resulting from the shift given to U.S. foreign policy by the Carter Administration. Imperialism and reaction were seeking ways of making changes in the regime without touching the basic strings of power: the tremendous economic and repressive power of the National Guard.[18]

The Sandinistas viewed the end of martial law and the U.S. effort to democratize Nicaragua as a threat, not an opportunity. The principal lesson that Latin American leftists had learned from the military coups against Guatemalan President Jacobo Arbenz in 1954 and Chilean President Salvador Allende in 1973 was that a revolution would fail unless the old military were replaced with a revolutionary army. The Sandinistas learned this lesson and, in Borge's words, remained "focused on the destruction of the National Guard and its replacement with a new armed force that would respond to a new program."[19] **Indeed, they alone in Nicaragua preferred Somoza to remain in power until the Guard could be defeated.**

Fearful that their revolution could be preempted, the Terceristas therefore accelerated a two-part strategy they had been developing since the Ortegas first contacted Edén Pastora in San José in 1976. Humberto Ortega said they "took note of the fact that the enemy had taken a step forward by lifting the state of siege and was considering an amnesty, and saw that if this happened, we would be in a difficult position. So we decided to speed up the offensive."[20]

On October 13, 1977, Pastora led a small group of Sandinistas in an attack on the Guard barracks in San Carlos, which was directly across the Costa Rican frontier. Simultaneously, other groups of Sandinistas attacked the police stations in Masaya (south of Managua) and at Ocotal in the northern part of Nicaragua.[21] The raids were "daring," in the words of Somoza, who also admitted surprise when he learned that the "sons of solid Conservative families participated in the battles."[22]

More significant was the Sandinistas' new public message: their goal was "not to install a Communist government but merely to overthrow the long-ruling Somoza regime and establish democracy" through free elections. The Sandinistas also insisted that they received "no money or weapons from the Castro regime and that no Nicaraguan guerrillas have been trained in Havana since" 1970.[23] They had learned the lesson Castro had learned from José Martí: "There are things, which must be hidden if they are to be obtained."[24]

On October 15, 1977, two days after the raids, a group of twelve prominent Nicaraguan businessmen, lawyers, priests, and educators issued a statement in San José and in Washington, D.C.: "There can be no permanent solution to the escalating armed conflict, which now threatens to envelop all of Nicaragua, without the participation of the Sandinista National Liberation Front."[25] The group, which became known as the Group of Twelve, seemed authentic and independent of the FSLN. Prior to this statement, the Sandinistas were generally viewed by the moderate opposition as a few Communist guerrillas. The three attacks demonstrated they were a viable threat, and the Group of Twelve offered them the legitimacy to be taken seriously by the country's opposition.

Only a few people then knew that the Group of Twelve was created by the Terceristas. In early 1977, Daniel and Humberto Ortega had asked Sergio Ramírez, a Nicaraguan novelist who had recently returned from studying and teaching in Europe, to organize "an alliance with the democratic sectors of the national bourgeoisie" to urge the recognition of the FSLN.[26]

In one case, Joaquín Cuadra Lacayo, who had been fighting with the Sandinistas since 1974, recruited his father, one of Nicaragua's wealthiest and most respected lawyers. Another person who joined the Twelve was Arturo Cruz, a Nicaraguan who was working at the Inter-American Development Bank. Cruz was brought to San José before the attack on San Carlos, and Ramírez told him "we would announce the installation of a provisional government on Nicaraguan territory headed by the Group of 12."[27] When the Sandinistas failed to hold any territory, the Twelve issued its statement in San José.

In repelling the attack against San Carlos, the Nicaraguan Air Force fired across the Costa Rican border at three boats on the San Juan River. On one of those boats was the Costa Rican Minister of Public Security, Mario Charpentier, who was nearly killed. The Costa Ricans protested to the OAS, and the sentiment in Costa Rica, always unfriendly to Somoza, became hostile and, for the first time, sympathetic to the Sandinistas. Prior to the raid at San Carlos, the Sandinistas had purchased their small supply of arms on the black market; afterward, they received support from Costa Rica. According to Pastora, José Figueres became the main source of arms and supplies: "He immediately gave us 300 M-1 rifles, rockets, bazookas, 50 machine guns, 30,000 bullets."[28] Figueres said that he opened his farm, "La Lucha Sin Fin" (The Endless Struggle), to the Sandinistas: "We did everything that was possible to do to help the Sandinistas."[29]

The moderate opposition reacted in different ways to the events of October. Pedro Joaquín Chamorro met secretly with a group of Sandinistas in an effort to get to know them better and perhaps develop a common strategy. Others tried to use the vitality injected in the anti-Somoza movement to begin a dialogue with Somoza on the question of a peaceful transition. A committee was established, composed of Archbishop Obando and Monsignor Pablo Vega from the Church, Alfonso Robelo and Felix Esteban Guardicki from the private sector, and Francisco Fiallos, a lawyer. With U.S. encouragement, Somoza agreed to meet with them in December 1977, but they found Somoza "completely stubborn" in his insistence that he finish out his term ending in 1981. They tried to persuade Somoza to begin a national dialogue on a transition before 1981, but he was unmoved.[30]

The Death of Chamorro

On January 9, 1978, in the Iranian city of Qom, the Shah's police opened fire on a demonstration, and the Iranian "revolution had begun."[31] The very next day, on the other side of the globe, the undisputed leader of the Nicaraguan opposition, Pedro Joaquín Chamorro, was assassinated, and another revolution began. More than any other individual in Nicaragua, Chamorro, the descendant of three Nicaraguan Presidents, represented the moderate opposition. His death energized the nation and had a profound effect on Nicaragua's neighbors.

His son, Pedro Joaquín Chamorro Barrios, was convinced that Somoza was not responsible for the assassination,[32] but practically no one in Nicaragua believed that at the time. Thousands marched in the funeral procession, and the businessmen decided that the time had come to split decisively with Somoza. Alfonso Robelo, the president of the major business association in Nicaragua (COSEP), directed and organized a general strike from January 23 until the second week in February. It was 90 percent successful. For the first time, businessmen, as an organized and cohesive political group, issued a public demand for Somoza's resignation. If the earthquake was a watershed in the private sector's view of the venality of the Somoza dynasty, the killing of Chamorro was the catalyst that moved the private sector toward political action.

Chamorro's death also had a profound effect on his close friend, Carlos Andrés Pérez, the President of Venezuela. After Pérez took office in 1975, Chamorro, who had been in exile in Costa Rica with Pérez in the 1950s, visited and told him excitedly: "Carlos Andrés, look, now you can do something for my country." Pérez responded much as the United States would have done: "Pedro Joaquín, you are the one who has to do it, and if you do it, I will support it." Pérez did give him moral and political support, but the death of Chamorro "made me compromise my previous position." He began to play a more direct and active role.[33]

Pérez's Presidency (1974–79) coincided with the sudden rise in the price of oil, which provided a windfall for Venezuela and gave Pérez the resources to assert leadership internationally. In December 1974, he launched a program to provide aid and oil at subsidized prices for most of the countries of Central America and the Caribbean. With aid came influence, and Pérez, the quintessential activist, used it. A strong advocate of human rights and arms control in Latin America, Pérez was delighted by the election of Carter, whom he viewed as dedicated to the same goals. For the first time since his mentor Rómulo Betancourt had established a relationship with John F. Kennedy, Venezuela's President seemed positioned to establish a new cooperative relationship with a U.S. President. And just as Betancourt was obsessed with eliminating Dominican dictator Rafael Trujillo, Pérez had a similar preoccupation with Somoza.

Venezuela, unlike Nicaragua, was relatively high on the Carter Administration's list of priorities, and Pérez was the first South American President invited for a state visit. In late June 1977, Carter met with Pérez for two days of meetings that covered almost every important international issue—human rights, arms control, North-South relations, energy and OPEC, the Middle East, Cuba, Zimbabwe, and the Caribbean. No other Latin American President discussed as extensive an agenda with Carter. By the time the two met again in September 1977 after the signing of the Panama Canal treaties, Carter would refer to Pérez as "one of my best personal friends and a great counselor and adviser to me on matters that concern the nations of the Caribbean and Central and South America."[34] Pérez and Carter agreed to coordinate strategies on a number of issues, but in neither June nor September did they talk about Nicaragua.

Their first exchange on the subject occurred when Pérez sent Carter a letter on January 31, 1978, three weeks after Chamorro's death. Pérez had just consulted with Omar Torrijos and Daniel Oduber on a strategy to overthrow Somoza, though he did not mention that in the letter. Instead, he described the situation in Nicaragua in dire terms and proposed joint action. Pérez gave the letter personally to the U.S. Ambassador, Viron Peter Vaky, in order to convey the importance he attached to receiving a quick response from Carter. In a classic case of diverging priorities, Carter was just then sending Pérez a letter on the Horn of Africa.

The First Policy Review

By January 1978, virtually all of the initiatives that Carter had begun a year before were beginning to create conflicts within the Administration and political friction with Congress. Carter was deeply worried that his first major initiative—the Canal treaties—could fail, and he devoted much of his time to persuading uncertain Senators. The centerpiece of his domestic policy—the energy bill—was stuck. Delicate negotiations on SALT and China were beginning to strain the relationship between Secretary of State Cyrus Vance and National Security Adviser Zbigniew Brzezinski.

Although many political analysts predicted a fight between Brzezinski and Vance from the beginning of Carter's term,[35] both entered the Administration in agreement on priorities and the basic outlines of the Administration's approach to foreign policy. In his book *Between Two Ages,* written at the end of the 1960s, Brzezinski had recommended that the United States abandon the Monroe Doctrine and the "special relationship" with Latin America, place relations with the region "on the same level as its relations with the rest of the world," and approach revolutionary change in "the developing countries with a great deal of patience."[36] Brzezinski had also thought about Central America: "American long-range interests would be harmed by continuing indifference to the mounting desire in Central America for greater social justice and national dignity, as our indifference will only make it easier for Castro's Cuba to exploit that desire. Much of Latin America could be antagonized by any resulting conflicts."[37] Vance's views on Latin America were strikingly similar.[38]

On the other hand, there was no denying their different temperaments and perspectives, and their positions at State and the National Security Council reinforced these differences. Vance, a corporate lawyer and skillful negotiator, had the patience and tolerance that made him well suited to be Secretary of State. As National Security Adviser and as a Polish-born professor of Soviet politics, Brzezinski was more conservative and apt to evaluate an event more in terms of its implications for the U.S.-Soviet strategic relationship than was Vance. Although some believed that Brzezinski's Polish background led him to see everything in anti-Soviet terms, it also made him more sensitive to recognizing that Latin America's view of the United States and its need for self-respect had much in common with Poland's view of Russia.

The first important issue that separated Carter's two senior foreign policy advisers was the question of how to respond to the Soviet-Cuban military intervention in the Horn of Africa. Vance argued that it would be counterproductive to approach the crisis as an East-West issue because this could embolden the Somalis and provoke the Soviets, and the United States would be in a weak position to respond. Brzezinski felt that the Cuban-Soviet involvement had injected an East-West dimension into a regional conflict. He insisted that the United States respond for strategic reasons, to raise the costs of intervention to the Soviets and Cubans lest they consider it again, and for political reasons, to counter criticism that Carter was soft on the Soviets.[39]

Much of this criticism stemmed from the nature of the agenda Carter was addressing—"giving away" the Canal treaties, arms control, normalization of relations with China, cancelling the B-1 bomber. But there was no question that conservatives in the Democratic as well as the Republican party were increasingly bothered by the direction of Carter's foreign policy. Indeed, the Murphy-Wilson defense of

Somoza was, in part, a reaction by conservative Democrats to the perception that Carter was tilting away from their world view. The disagreement between Brzezinski and Vance on the Horn was the first time this difference within the Democratic Party was aired within the Carter Administration.

In January 1978, Carter decided to consult with a number of world leaders about issues related to the Horn, and he sent a letter to Carlos Andrés Pérez. The letter requested Pérez's advice about the most appropriate response to Cuba's violation of the principle of nonintervention, a principle Latin America had championed. A week after Carter sent the letter, I tried to interest Brzezinski in the various issues raised by Pérez on Nicaragua, but he asked instead about Pérez's response to the letter on the Horn. I called Vaky in Caracas, and learned that Pérez would not receive our Ambassador or the letter until he had received a response on Nicaragua. When I relayed this to Brzezinski, he suddenly took an interest in Nicaragua and asked for a memo and a draft letter for the President, on an urgent basis.

The letter from Pérez, therefore, served its purpose: for the first time, the Carter Administration was forced to address the Nicaraguan situation as a political issue. Simultaneously, the moderate opposition in Nicaragua asked the U.S. Ambassador in Managua for a position, and he proposed a statement of support for democracy.

Warren Christopher, who had gradually assumed primary responsibility for Latin America and human rights on behalf of Vance, convened a small meeting to discuss what role the United States should play in Nicaragua and to review drafts of a statement and a letter for Carter. The Bureau of Inter-American Affairs suggested the United States directly mediate a dialogue between Somoza and the opposition. The representatives of Policy Planning and the Bureau of Human Rights and I, representing the NSC—all political appointees—argued that we should reaffirm our support for democracy, which the State Department did in a statement on February 6, 1978, but avoid becoming an intermediary. Christopher agreed.

Carter, in a letter signed on February 17, pledged to work closely with President Pérez on human rights issues and, as Pérez had suggested, would try to obtain Somoza's acceptance of a visit by the Inter-American Human Rights Commission (IAHRC). Second, with regard to Nicaraguan politics, Carter wrote: "We can and will voice our preference for increased democratization. . . . But we will not intervene or impose specific political solutions for individual countries." Ambassador Solaun was also instructed to encourage Somoza to accept a visit by the IAHRC.

Events in Nicaragua did not wait for the U.S. government to complete its abstract discussion on its proper role. The death of Chamorro unleashed a torrent of hatred against Somoza. Demonstrations were organized in most of the major towns and in several cases, as on the small island of Monimbó, a spontaneous, violent riot occurred.

The opposition united behind the business community during the general strike, and its organizer, Alfonso Robelo, soon found himself at the head of a middle-class movement to unseat Somoza. Robelo, born in 1940 and educated as a chemical engineer at Rensselaer Polytechnic Institute, owned 10 percent of an agrobusiness that processed cotton seed for cooking oil. His real interest, however, was politics. At the age of 32, he became president of the Chamber of Industry, and by 36, he was elected president of the Nicaraguan Development Institute (INDE) and the Higher Council of Private Enterprise (COSEP), the two major business associations in Nicaragua.

The personal experience of leading the general strike whetted his political appetite. On March 16, together with a group of about a hundred young professionals, he established the Nicaraguan Democratic Movement, which then immediately tried to bring other groups under a new umbrella organization, the Broad Opposition Front (FAO). In May 1978, most of the moderate opposition agreed to associate with the FAO, and in August 1978, the Group of Twelve also joined. The Twelve also arranged meetings between Robelo and the Tercerista leadership in San José, Costa Rica, in April 1978. This was the first time he had met the Ortegas, and they impressed him as pragmatic, leftist Social Democrats. He did not think they were associated with Cuba, but he did not ask because he was not concerned with this issue.[40] The Group of Twelve also met with officials and organizations throughout the United States, Latin America, and Europe. A human rights organization, for example, arranged for Miguel D'Escoto, a Maryknoll priest and member of the Twelve, who would later become Nicaragua's Foreign Minister, to meet with me on November 11, 1977. His message was simple: the Sandinistas enjoyed wide support. They were not Castroite Marxists, though they included some radical elements. Nicaraguans were tired of living on Somoza's "national farm" and would overthrow Somoza and his regime. He also said that he hoped the United States would take a neutral position.[41]

Somoza recognized the growing power of the opposition and although he was not reluctant to confront it, he was shrewd enough to try other approaches as well. In a press conference on February 26, 1978, he announced for the first time his intention to leave both the Presidency and the National Guard at the end of his term. He established a special commission to investigate the Chamorro assassination. He also promised that new political parties could register, and he offered a dialogue on whether to reform the television and radio code, expand rights of labor unions, and restructure the National Guard. A measure of the crisis within Nicaragua was that people were disheartened to hear Somoza say he would step down in 1981, because that meant he would remain until then. The reaction was expressed in continuing riots and gun battles in various parts of the country.

Washington was still focused on other issues, but Carter had an opportunity to review events during his trip to Venezuela and Brazil. On March 28, 1978, in Caracas, Carter and Pérez talked about Nicaragua for the first time, although it was neither the first nor the most important issue they discussed.

Pérez raised the issue and posed the problem: "Somoza's authority was diminished. . . . The danger is the increased strength of the Sandinistas. It is very similar to the fall of Batista." During the discussion, Pérez kept returning to the Cuban case, and Carter, who said he agreed with the analysis, tried to focus on what could be done. "As you have requested," Carter said, "we have encouraged Somoza to let in the Inter-American Commission on Human Rights, and we have frozen our aid program. But we have a difficult time proposing direct action by the U.S. to bring about Somoza's downfall." Carter reiterated his commitment to nonintervention and said that he did not believe the United States should engage in a policy of changing the governments of small nations.

Pérez could have disagreed; he could have explained that stating a principle and practicing it were different or he could have argued that Somoza was an exception, but he did not, even though his actions implied that was what he believed. Instead, he accepted Carter's point and urged multilateral pressure on Somoza using the OAS and other forums, though he could not stop repeating the Cuban case and said he was convinced Somoza would not last until 1981. Carter suggested that if Pérez could persuade Somoza, perhaps Somoza would step down.

Pérez was disappointed by the response and decided to press ahead independently without consulting or even informing Carter. In 1977, Pérez had established a National Security Council in the Venezuelan government. It was composed of a few military officers to coordinate and manage crises and to undertake special projects for the President. Their first task was a study of Nicaragua. As the study evolved, Pérez defined its objective as the overthrow of Somoza and decided to use Venezuelan funds and arms to increase his country's influence with the Sandinistas and to serve as an incentive to unite the Sandinista factions.[42] However, the principal recipient of the weapons and monthly financial allotments was Pastora.[43]

The United States unintentionally moved in the opposite direction. In May, after one year of delays, the Administration reluctantly approved two basic human needs loans to Nicaragua: $3 million for education and $7.5 million for nutrition. Congressman Charles Wilson forced a decision, and the Administration felt it could no longer delay.

Most members of Congress are unable to locate the point in the Executive Branch where effective leverage can force a deal, but Wilson found that point in the person of Henry Owen, who had become a virtual czar of U.S. foreign economic policy during the Carter Administration. Owen was sensitive both to the tenuousness of the aid program on Capitol Hill and to the pivotal nature of Wilson's vote. When Wilson told Owen that he would block the aid bill until the two Nicaraguan loans were signed, Owen judged that a credible threat.

In general, the Administration approved basic human needs loans, except in the most egregious cases of human rights violations. Although the response by the Guard to the riots represented a serious concern, Somoza did not reimpose martial law or censorship of the press. His subsequent concessions made it difficult to argue that the situation in Nicaragua at that moment was bad enough to justify a further aid postponement, particularly because the United States had made such loans to countries with worse human rights records. Somoza had taken many of the steps that the Administration had been demanding, and it was hard to argue against the loans without making it sound as if the Administration was pursuing a vendetta against him. Owen persuaded Christopher to go ahead.

In its announcement of the loans, the Administration sought to correct the impression of inconsistency conveyed by news reports of the September 1977 decisions. First, the Administration noted it had not given any military aid to Nicaragua since it came into office, and it did not even request fiscal year 1979 funding.[44] Second, to preclude Somoza's trying to use the loans to indicate U.S. support, the State Department issued the following statement on May 16 in Washington and in Managua: "The U.S. reiterates its policy of strict non-intervention in the internal political affairs of Nicaragua and our continuing desire for a steady non-violent transition to genuine democratic rule. Approval of A.I.D. projects for the needy is not intended as an expression of political support." The *Washington Post* paid no attention to the Administration's statement, preferring to report it as another "policy reversal."[45]

The Carter Letter

On June 19, Somoza held a press conference and promised to invite the Inter-American Human Rights Commission and allow the return of the Group of Twelve to Nicaragua. In addition, he said he would consider signing the American Convention on Human Rights and declaring an amnesty for political prisoners. This was the Carter Administration's agenda, and several of the points were also Venezuela's. Neither the *Washington Post* nor the *New York Times* covered that conference, but the Embassy routinely reported it. The key points were included by the White House Situation Room in its June 21 summary of events of the previous day. Carter read it and was impressed that Somoza had conceded most of the points the United States had been making. He instructed Brzezinski to prepare a letter for him to send to Somoza to express his support for the steps. Brzezinski asked me to do the draft. When I protested, he cut me off: "Write it. Put your concerns in the memo to the President and clear it with State."

Although I was uneasy about sending a letter to Somoza, I never guessed that it would turn out to be so controversial. The case is an interesting study of both the effect of the press on policy and the way in which the psychology of the U.S.-Nicaraguan relationship could transform something inherently insignificant into a major event.

Carter had sent similar letters to other heads of state in Latin America and elsewhere. His style was to encourage progress gently and to reinforce it when it occurred,[46] hardly a novel idea. Generals Pinochet of Chile and Videla of Argentina—leaders responsible for much worse repression than Somoza—had received such letters. Moreover, Carter had just returned from Panama, where he had met with five heads of state, and in the communiqué they jointly issued, no one had suggested singling out Nicaragua. In short, Carter had no reason to believe that Somoza should be an exception to his policy.

The letter I drafted noted each of Somoza's promises, as well as others he had previously made to reform the electoral system. The letter sought to encourage Somoza to fulfill his promises by explaining the importance Carter attached to each of them. For example, Carter expressed his "hope that your government can rapidly reach agreement with the [Human Rights] Commission on a date for their visit," and he underscored its importance by noting that "multilateral institutions can be a most appropriate and effective means of protecting human rights." The letter concluded: "I look forward to hearing of the implementation of your decisions."

I then sent the draft to the State Department. ARA joined HA in opposing any letter from Carter to Somoza, because they felt it could be misinterpreted to indicate that the United States was not serious about its human rights policy. Christopher asked about the origin of the letter, and I told him that the President had requested it. I did not offer my views about whether to send it because I did not feel strongly about the issue, and I had not yet made up my own mind. State then formally returned the letter to the National Security Council with marginal changes and a recommendation that it be delayed for a week, pending the negotiations between Nicaragua and the Inter-American Commission over a visit.

My job then was to prepare a cover memo for Brzezinski to send to the President, and I recommended against sending the letter for two reasons. First, Somoza did not have a good record of keeping his promises. Second, I feared Somoza would use the letter—"not necessarily the substance, just that you sent him a personal note—in a way which will lend support to him for partisan political purposes." Brzezinski, who at that time had more substantial disagreements with the State Department, decided to delete my argument against sending the letter and submit a simpler memo concurring with the department's recommendation. On June 26, Carter revised the letter to make the same points more gently and personally, expressing his "appreciation" for the steps. He also accepted the recommendation to delay sending the letter until June 30.

After the President signs a letter, the standard operating procedure is for the State Department to cable the text to the appropriate ambassador for delivery. This time, State procrastinated, finally cabling it on July 8. Ambassador Solaun presented it orally on July 11. On July 14, he informed the State Department that the Broad Opposition Front was planning a general strike on July 19, and fearful of the letter's possible impact, he asked permission not to deliver the physical letter when it arrived. Pete Vaky, the new Assistant Secretary of State for Inter-American Affairs, agreed with Solaun.

I was surprised to learn that Solaun had delayed implementing the President's decision for two weeks without informing the White House. I suggested that Vaky try to persuade Vance to ask the President's permission not to deliver the letter. Neither Vance nor Brzezinski thought it was worth the President's time or temper, but they accepted my recommendation that Solaun be told to stress the confidential aspect of the letter. If Somoza chose to use the letter and violate the confidence of President Carter, then that would tell us something about our ability to communicate sincerely with him. It did.

On July 21, Solaun delivered the letter, and after he left, Somoza was startled and confused. The letter arrived, Somoza later recalled, "at a time when I needed encouragement, and particularly from the U.S."[47] Somoza felt that he was finally "making headway," and for the first time, was communicating with "the middie" (midshipman), as he referred to Carter in his conversations with Representative Jack Murphy and Max Kelly, an aide and another fellow West Point graduate.[48]

Though Solaun had stressed the need for confidentiality, Somoza wrote in his memoirs of his first reaction: "The contents of that letter, if publicly known, could assist me greatly in warding off my other enemies. I was not interested in a collector's item, and without being able to use the letter, that's what it was."[49] He knew by then what the United States did not, that Pérez was the principal source of arms and funding to the Sandinistas, and he decided to use the letter on him first.

He immediately arranged a meeting with Pérez on a small island, La Orchila, off the coast of Venezuela. Both flew there for a tough and uncompromising four-hour confrontation in late July 1978.[50] Somoza surprised Pérez with the letter, and claimed he enjoyed the support of President Carter. Pérez was annoyed but not diverted: "I don't care what Carter says. Our position is firm. You have to go."[51] They talked about several possible solutions to the crisis, and Pérez offered to ease Somoza's exit by purchasing Somoza's property in Nicaragua and ensuring his security. But Somoza claims he insisted on the need to stay to forestall a Communist victory. At this, Pérez responded forcefully, as he recalled in a later interview:

Somoza, if you don't accept my advice to leave Nicaragua and give way to a democratic solution and to an agreement between the National Guard and the guerrillas for the rise of a government that would grant liberty in Nicaragua, you will be the greatest criminal in Latin America. Everyone is against you. You will not be saved from being overthrown.[52]

At the conclusion, they returned to where they started. "Regrettably," Pérez recalled, "he received all my advice with incredible cynicism, and we did not get any agreement." The letter had failed to serve Somoza's purpose.

A few days later, on August 1, the *Washington Post* published a front-page article, headlined "Carter Letter to Somoza Stirs Human Rights Row," by John Goshko. The lead paragraph read: "President Carter, overriding State Department objections, has sent a personal letter congratulating Nicaraguan President Anastasio Somoza for promises to improve the human rights situation in his country." Goshko wrote that the NSC had originated the letter "to give Somoza an encouraging pat on the back" and then forced the State Department to deliver it. The article indicated that "State Department officials are concerned that revelation of the letter . . . will raise questions about the credibility and sensitivity of the Administration's human rights policy." The article concluded that the human rights policy "seemed to veer back and forth, drawing charges that its policy toward Somoza is confusing, inconsistent, and ineffective."

In large part because of this article, Carter noted in his diary the next day: "The editorial policy of the *Washington Post* has been very good. The news policy abominable."[53] Carter was so angry with the distorted leak of the letter that he "came down on the State Department like a ton of bricks" and tried to get the leaker dismissed.[54] The source was not found, but Goshko later told me that it was a senior pro-human rights official in the Bureau of Inter-American Affairs. Goshko never saw the letter.

During the next two days, the White House provided a detailed briefing of the purpose and the contents of the letter. Rex Granum, the White House Deputy Press Secretary, emphasized that the letter's purpose was to encourage Somoza to implement his announcements, not to "congratulate" him on his progress. A brief clarification in the *Washington Post* the next day reported that Granum had said that both the State Department and the NSC had recommended the letter—which was technically correct—but the report still characterized the letter as "congratulating" Somoza, and that perception remained.[55]

The U.S. Chargé met with Somoza the day of the Goshko article, and Somoza promised that "no one has seen President Carter's letter." (Not aware of his meeting with Perez, the Chargé did not know he was lying. As Somoza read the letter more closely, his initial reaction of it as "a nice, friendly letter," gave way to a feeling that it was a devious trick and that Carter was "stepping up his attack" against him.[56] At the same time, because of the letter, Somoza acknowledged in his memoirs that he did permit the Group of Twelve to return and the Inter-American Commission to visit. The latter would seriously and adversely affect his position in the OAS.

The letter also represented a watershed for U.S. policy, although an ironic one in some ways. First, it impelled Brzezinski and Carter to focus on Nicaragua for the first time. Before the incident, my memos on Nicaragua were returned as too long; afterward, they were requested. On August 8, I offered a detailed analysis that Somoza's strategy was to play for time until 1981, but by then, the United States might have "to deal with a real possibility of a strong leftist revolutionary movement and an evaporating political middle." I recommended a formal Presidential Review Memorandum to develop a long-term strategy, but Brzezinski was not yet that interested, and Vaky, who wanted State to manage the process, also opposed the idea.

Second, the letter represented the last time Nicaragua would be defined solely in the bureaucratic context of the human rights policy. After the letter and the Sandinista takeover of the National Palace in August, the United States approached Nicaragua as a political-security crisis, and the Human Rights Bureau was excluded from the central deliberations, although it continued to play a role in defining the State Department position. In addition, as in many leaks directed at the White House from a department, the leak of this letter served to divide one from the other, heighten mutual suspicions, and shrink the number of people who would have access to policy-making.

The strongest argument against sending the letter was that Somoza might disclose it in a way that associated himself with Carter. Therefore, the most exquisite irony of the entire episode was that it was leaked not by Somoza, but by a State Department official who was reportedly committed to Carter's human rights policy, even though the letter was Carter's idea and the leak enraged him. Moreover, this official described the letter incorrectly as "congratulating" Somoza for improving human rights, rather than encouraging him to fulfill his promises. And that description of the letter—rather than the letter itself—confused or angered Carter's friends in Latin America and the moderate opposition in Nicaragua.

The letter accomplished Carter's purpose of encouraging Somoza to fulfill at least some of his promises. Somoza tried to use the letter on Pérez, but failed. The leak by a State Department official accomplished what the letter and Somoza failed to do: it associated Carter with Somoza in a way that the actual letter did not.

The Takeover of the National Palace

Nicaragua's political landscape was not changed by the letter, however, but by the bold act of Edén Pastora and a group of twenty-five Sandinistas on August 22, 1978. Pastora captured the National Palace and 1,500 people in it![57] For the next two days, Pastora negotiated with Somoza with the aid of Archbishop Obando. Somoza was under considerable pressure by some of his officers to storm the palace, but instead he accepted most of the Sandinistas' demands. He released 59 political prisoners, including Pastora's old rival, Tomás Borge; paid $500,000 in cash (Pastora had asked for $10 million); and permitted their long communiqué to be published in the newspapers and read (105 minutes) over the radio three times a day during the next two days. The communiqué called on the Guard to rebel and the people to join them in overthrowing Somoza. Although describing the conflict as a class struggle, the Sandinistas welcomed capitalists to participate in the "anti-Somoza fight," provided they understood that they could not "try to impose formulas in which their personal interests come before those of the populace."

Somoza guaranteed the Sandinistas safe exit, and their trip to the airport was described by reporters as a "victory parade" because of the crowds cheering for the FSLN.[58] The Carter Administration was aware of the nation's distaste for Somoza, but it was startled and unsettled at how easily that hatred was transformed into support for the Sandinistas. An additional sign of their increasing legitimacy was the plane's destination. After the raid in 1974, the Sandinistas flew to Cuba; in 1978, they flew to Panama and Venezuela on planes provided by those two governments.

Tad Szulc, a former reporter of the *New York Times,* interviewed Pastora in Panama and reported that the Carter letter had provoked the palace takeover. Pastora told him: "How could [Carter] praise Somoza while our people were being massacred by the dictatorship?"[59] In an interview five years later, Pastora acknowledged that the letter had not provoked the raid. Pastora, like most of the Sandinista leadership, was aware that Somoza had lost U.S. support from the beginning.[60] Pastora played the press like a violin, stroking the letter to put the Carter Administration on the defensive. Humberto Ortega later revealed the real reason for the palace takeover. The raid, he said, was taken "to foil the imperialist plot, which consisted of staging a coup in August to put a civilian-military regime in power, and thus put a damper on the revolutionary struggle."[61] The Sandinistas knew that Somoza was the key to their victory; if the Guard replaced him, the Sandinistas would lose much of their popular support. The purpose of the raid was to preempt and thus prevent a coup against Somoza.

The Sandinistas were correct about the coup plot, but they overestimated the role played by the United States. Washington had no information—and certainly no policy—about a Guard coup. On August 28, however, eighty-five members of the National Guard, including Lieutenant Colonel Bernardino Larios and a dozen officers, were arrested for plotting a coup.[62] On September 9, General José Ivan Alegrett and several others, who had conveyed to reporters their anger over Somoza's surrender of the National Palace, died in a plane crash. There was widespread speculation that Somoza had them killed to discourage further plots.[63]

The Sandinistas also were determined to stay in front of the anti-Somoza movement. In the two weeks before the raid, Archbishop Obando issued a declaration urging the establishment of "a national government of transition."[64] A few days later, the private sector led by Robelo's INDE issued a statement supporting the Church and urging Somoza to withdraw from the government.

The raid fulfilled the Sandinistas' most optimistic expectations. It placed them in the "vanguard" of an increasingly broad-based opposition and captured the excitement and support of Nicaragua's youth—"los muchachos." After the raid, on August 25, the FAO called for another general strike to seek Somoza's resignation. This sparked another uprising. Matagalpa was seized by "los muchachos," and they held it until the Nicaraguan Air Force began aerial bombing three days later.

The FSLN and some elements of the business community began, for the first time, to coordinate their plans for an insurrection in September. The United States was unaware of such cooperation, although Somoza was. Indeed, throughout much of this period, the three key sets of actors—the Sandinistas, the FAO, and Somoza's Guard—all assumed that the United States knew at least as much as they did about their adversaries' plans and may actually have been orchestrating events. Neither assumption was accurate.

Somoza and the Sandinistas knew more about each other than the United States knew about either. Somoza knew the Sandinistas were planning a takeover of the palace, and although he did not know when it would occur, he had readied a special force to resist the attack. When Pastora struck, the force was inexplicably not at the palace.[65] One of the reasons Pastora gained entry so easily was precisely because the Guard stationed at the palace thought Pastora's group was the special force. Similarly, as Humberto Ortega noted, the Sandinistas planned the takeover to preempt a coup against Somoza. The U.S. government was not only unaware of the coup plot beforehand, it did not consider its implications afterward.

In September 1978, fighting spread to five major cities in Nicaragua. The FSLN struggled to stay in front of the prairie fire, but as Humberto Ortega would later admit: "The mass movement went beyond the vanguard's capacity to take the lead. . . . It was a spontaneous reaction on the part of the masses which, in the end, the Sandinista Front began to direct through its activists and a number of military units."[66]

The pressure for U.S. involvement increased dramatically. Many in the moderate opposition feared more violence and pleaded with the United States to replace Somoza. Venezuela and Panama pressed the United States to the same end. On September 1, 1978, both Somoza and a leader of the Sandinistas held press conferences.

The FSLN accused the United States of intervening in Nicaragua to defend Somoza, and Somoza accused the United States of trying to overthrow him. Somoza said the Carter Administration was "in the hands of leftists and communists."[67] The State Department spokesperson was asked about Somoza's allegation: "Our policy remains one of non-intervention in the domestic politics of other countries. . . . We are not in the position of suggesting the overthrow or downfall of any government."

The Frontier

The inauguration of Carter, Somoza's heart attack, the murder of Chamorro, the establishment of the Group of Twelve, and the palace raid—these five events between January 1977 and September 1978 shook the foundation of the Somoza dynasty. The crisis in Nicaragua forced a distracted Carter Administration to confront some hard policy choices—not between human rights and security, as some have suggested, but whether, and if so how, the United States should influence the process of political change in a small Central American country.

The Carter policy succeeded in opening Nicaragua to genuine debate through the lifting of martial law, the end of censorship, the restraints on the National Guard, the invitation to the Inter-American Commission, and the return of political exiles. Somoza was constrained, and the opposition had more space. As one observer noted during the 1977 insurrection: "For fear of alienating Washington, General Somoza has been unable to respond to the new offensive against his regime by declaring a state of siege and unleashing a wave of repression against his opponents."[68]

Although effective in Nicaragua, the policy had become increasingly controversial in the United States, with liberals criticizing the Administration for being too easy on Somoza and conservatives condemning it for picking on old friends. There was some validity to both criticisms. U.S. policy was deliberately reformist and gradualist. It would neither accept Somoza nor aim to overthrow him. In choosing this line, the Carter Administration drew unconsciously from elements of a political culture that reflected a wariness of sharp breaks and a preference for gradual change.

The issue for Nicaraguans, who were responding to a very different, volcanic political culture, was not how to get Somoza to democratize, but how to get him out. Nicaraguans were impatient for a sharp break with the past. Though the United States had the potential power, the struggle was among Nicaraguans, and the United States was forced to adjust to a process of revolutionary change for which it was philosophically and temperamentally ill equipped.

By September 1978, the frontier of U.S. human rights policy had been reached. As the war worsened in Nicaragua, the human rights policy proved to be less of a constraint on Somoza's behavior and less useful as a tool for pursuing U.S. interests. The issue became, what role the United States should play as Nicaragua became engulfed in civil war. The people of Nicaragua, however, were in the lead; they forced the pace of events, and the United States reluctantly reexamined the premises of its policy and adapted.

5

To Mediate or Not to Mediate: The Policy Question

The crisis in Nicaragua can be described as a simple problem: a mentally deranged man [Anastasio Somoza] with an army of criminals is
attacking a defenseless population. . . . This is not a problem for the
OAS; what we need is a psychiatrist.

OMAR TORRIJOS, SEPTEMBER 22, 1978

THE CHEERS that greeted Edén Pastora on his way to the airport after the palace
raid were the political equivalent of the tremors that seismologists detect before
earthquakes. Scientists can now judge with a high degree of probability whether
there will be an earthquake. What they don't know is when and how severe it will
be. It could be one month, three years, or a decade.

The science of politics is even more inexact. In a then-secret hearing of the Senate Foreign Relations Committee on the prospects for survival by the Shah of Iran,
Senator Frank Church warned: "All I know about history says he is not long for this
world, nor his system. And when he goes down, boom, we go with him." The prog-
nosis was perfect, but the timing was off by eighteen years. The hearing was held in
1961. In that interim, four U.S. Presidents came and went.[1]

The Carter Administration knew that Nicaragua would soon be jolted by a political earthquake; it just didn't know when. Therefore, like the people who live in San
Francisco today, the Administration was uncertain how or how much to prepare for
the inevitable. Once again, however, Nicaraguans set the pace. With each tremor inside the country, everyone grew anxious and turned to the United States for help,
just as they had after Nicaragua's natural earthquake in 1972.

There are standard operating procedures for responding to natural disasters, but
none for political disasters. Partly because of that, the U.S. government devoted
considerable energy to the task. Between September 1978 and January 1979, a senior committee of the National Security Council met eleven times to debate policy

to Nicaragua. This chapter will focus on the evolution of U.S. policy from noninterference in September 1978 to multilateral mediation in November 1978.

Motive for Movement

On September 9, the Sandinistas launched coordinated attacks on National Guard detachments in Nicaragua's major cities. Fighting for his political life, Somoza overcame whatever inhibitions he had acquired in the previous year and fought with the brutality a nation usually reserves for its enemy, not for its own people (and certainly not for its youth). It still took nearly a month for the Guard to regain control of the towns.

As the demands increased for his resignation, Somoza became more intransigent. Using an old family tactic, he claimed that the only choice was between the Communists and himself.[2] The depth and breadth of the opposition in Nicaragua belied Somoza's description of the options. However, on August 29 Somoza began to take steps that the United States interpreted as trying to make his false description true. He revoked the charter of the largest business associations and instructed the Central Bank to recall loans previously made to business leaders who organized the strike. Within a week, Somoza arrested about 50 leaders of the moderate opposition, including Adolfo Calero, a leader of the Conservative Party and manager of the Coca-Cola bottling franchise. Eventually 600 to 800 people were imprisoned.

Somoza's decision to strike at the moderate opposition was one of the major factors that triggered the United States to review its previous policy of strict noninterference in Nicaragua's internal affairs. Until then, the senior officials in the Carter Administration—Carter, Vance, Brzezinski, and Christopher—had a clear vision of the role the United States should not play as well as the one it should. The United States should avoid, in their view, a posture of paternalism in which the United States, acting alone, would dictate political solutions.

Carter's preferred policy had two dimensions. First, the United States should encourage dialogue among competing groups within a country but should not mediate or arbitrate that dialogue. Decisions on the political future of Nicaragua should be made by Nicaraguans, not by the United States. The Carter Administration realized that the history of interventionism had left many in the region psychologically dependent on the United States to resolve their nations' problems, but the Administration, like Franklin Roosevelt's, wanted to avoid being drawn into those quarrels. The goal was to seek more balanced relationships. The United States would state its concerns, for example, on human rights, but it would not determine who should govern.

The second dimension stemmed from Carter's interest in forging a more modern and balanced partnership with Latin America. This meant that if the Nicaraguan crisis required international help, the United States should not act alone, but rather should consult and coordinate its response with friendly democratic governments in the region.

The vision of U.S. policy based on these two elements was impaired by Somoza's strategy to eliminate a reformist, middle option, and it was impugned by the pragmatism of the new Assistant Secretary of State for Inter-American Affairs, Pete Vaky.

A decision to replace the Administration's first Assistant Secretary, Terence Todman, was made in February 1978 after he delivered a speech that sounded more like a critic of the Administration than one of its spokesmen. Todman, like many competent foreign service officers, was a charming and effective Ambassador, but he was not comfortable nor effective in the job of making policy in Washington. Vance replaced him with Vaky.

Vaky was the Foreign Service's first choice because he was the diplomat's diplomat—he was aggressive, but he achieved his objectives in a smooth, gentle manner that almost appeared deferential. He combined long experience in Latin America with a number of policy-making assignments in Washington. Having served on the National Security Council during the first year of the Nixon Administration, he understood, as his predecessor did not, how the process worked under a strong President. Having served most recently as Ambassador to Costa Rica, Colombia, and then Venezuela, he understood how the Nicaraguan crisis was viewed by three of its democratic neighbors.

Like the political appointees of the Carter Administration, Vaky shared a distaste for the Somoza regime and a commitment to Carter's core principles—human rights, nonintervention, and regional cooperation. But the experience of working through hundreds of diplomatic problems under seven different Presidents had led him to be wary of the slogans, "principles," or ideology of any particular White House occupant. Vaky thought only the United States could solve the problem of Somoza, and that it should use whatever force necessary—barring assassination—to remove him.[3]

On August 29, 1978, Vaky called the first interagency meeting to address the political crisis in Nicaragua. He argued that the United States needed to get in front of events and assemble a coalition government. Otherwise, the situation would polarize even further, increasing the probability of a Marxist victory. Anthony Lake, who had directed Carter's foreign policy transition team and had been a close adviser to Vance, was the Director of Policy Planning in the State Department. He and I both agreed with Vaky's analysis, but not with his recommendation. We believed that the United States should not pursue a policy of overthrowing governments. Our current problems in the region stemmed in part from the history of U.S. interventionism, which, although almost always undertaken with good intentions, frequently had adverse effects on U.S. interests that outweighed any shorter-term benefits.

In frustration, and reminiscent of Pérez's conversation six months before with Carter, Vaky kept repeating that a failure to take control of events in Nicaragua would lead to a repetition of the Cuban crisis of 1957–58. I suggested two preliminary steps before addressing the issue at a higher level: first, State should draft a paper defining the options for U.S. policy; and second, our ambassadors should seek advice on what should be done from the Presidents of Venezuela, Costa Rica,

Panama, and Mexico. Vaky agreed and scheduled the next meeting on Labor Day, September 4, 1978.

By then, the situation in Nicaragua had deteriorated markedly, and Somoza had begun to arrest the leadership of the moderate opposition. Carter received messages from Pérez, Costa Rican President Rodrigo Carazo, and Mexican President José López Portillo. Brzezinski called me into his office on Labor Day at 9:00 A.M., and told me that Carter wanted a recommendation by the end of the day on how to respond to those messages. I told him that fortunately Vaky had scheduled a meeting that day at State; Brzezinski rescheduled it for the White House, to be chaired by his Deputy, David Aaron. Unhappy with the change in venue, Vaky did not object since the meeting's purpose had changed; now, it was to make a recommendation to the President. Henceforth, policy toward Nicaragua would be hammered out in the National Security Council.

The National Security Decision-Making Process

The National Security Act of 1947 established the National Security Council (NSC) to coordinate and advise the President on national security matters. The statutory members are the President, the Vice President, the Secretaries of State and Defense, but all Presidents have added others, depending on the issue and the individual.

Like any executive committee, the NSC has been adapted to serve the special needs of each President, but since President Kennedy, the NSC has consistently become known less as a Cabinet council and more as a part of the Presidential staff. The NSC staff expanded to more than fifty professionals under Nixon and Kissinger, and it acted as almost a surrogate State Department. President Carter reduced the staff to thirty-five professionals and made it less hierarchical, but he soon discovered that his ability to be the premier foreign policy maker required a strong NSC staff. Its responsibilities are to coordinate policy, do long-term planning or propose initiatives, ensure that the President's decisions are implemented, and most importantly, to provide staff assistance for the National Security Adviser and President. What the NSC uniquely offers the President is a staff that views his problems from his perspective. That is why all Presidents interested in directing foreign policy increasingly rely on their NSC staff more than on the personnel of the Cabinet departments, whose views often reflect their institution's interests more than those of the President.

Under Carter, the NSC was divided into two committees: a Policy Review Committee (PRC), charged with coordinating foreign, defense, and international economic policy, and chaired by the Secretary of a department responsible for the issue; and a Special Coordination Committee (SCC), chaired by the National Security Adviser and charged with coordinating intelligence policy, arms control, and crisis management. President Carter seldom chaired a formal NSC meeting, and he never chaired one on Latin American and Caribbean affairs.[4]

Instead, Carter made most of his decisions by reviewing a memorandum that summarized a PRC or SCC meeting, listed and analyzed the options, and described the recommendations of each of the departments. Carter generally would receive these memoranda the day of the meeting and return it to Brzezinski the next day. Other important modes of decision making were correspondence; meetings with other heads of state; and the Friday morning breakfasts, which were informal opportunities for Carter to meet with the Secretary of State, National Security Adviser, and others, such as the Vice President. Carter also invited new ideas and memoranda independent of the NSC meetings, but he required that all memoranda state clearly and fully the views of all related agencies. Carter organized the process to ensure that he made all the crucial policy decisions on Nicaragua and on most other issues as well.

As the crises proliferated in the second year of the Administration and the time available to Carter's senior advisers became scarce, the PRC and SCC meetings were increasingly chaired by deputies. David Aaron, who had left the Foreign Service in the early 1970s to work for Walter Mondale in the Senate, returned to the NSC on January 20, 1977, as Deputy Assistant to the President for National Security Affairs. He chaired the mini-SCC meeting on Nicaragua on September 4. These mini-SCC's were efficient ways to refine options for higher-level decision.

When the action shifts to the White House, the power of the NSC to shape the agenda, select the participants, and interpret the results for the President naturally increases. However, the power to implement decisions remains in the Cabinet departments. Since almost all U.S. decisions on Nicaragua were diplomatic rather than military, economic, or covert, the State Department retained the principal position in policy making. The institutional tension between NSC and State derives in part from the former's control of the agenda and the latter's control of implementation. State Department officials tend to be anxious about the NSC usurping policy, and the NSC tends to be concerned that State either might not implement the President's decisions or might do so ineffectually to demonstrate to the President that the NSC had been wrong.

Over time, U.S. policy toward Nicaragua became principally the product of the debate and dialogue between the NSC and the State Department. At the working level, Assistant Secretary Vaky and I would seek concurrence from our principals on decisions on which we agreed, and force decisions up to the NSC level when either we disagreed, or I thought the President would want to make the decision. The Assistant Secretary, as the head of a bureau and, in Vaky's case, as a senior diplomat, was more inclined to make decisions independently or without clearing them. As a staff person, I viewed my principal responsibility as ensuring that the President made all "key" decisions, which I defined to mean any decision that would either substantially alter his previous policy or narrow his future options. My second responsibility was to monitor implementation of his decisions, and my third was to offer advice and ideas.

A representative of the CIA attended all SCC meetings to describe the current situation and to offer judgments about the likely consequences if a particular option were adopted, but in my experience, the career officers never proposed a policy, even when they were asked. They were trained to believe that the preservation of their institution's integrity to gather and analyze intelligence required that they avoid policy making.

Representatives of the Defense Department and the Joint Chiefs of Staff also attended the SCC meetings. In 1975, the Bureau of International Security Affairs of the Department of Defense had combined the two Deputy Assistant Secretaries of Defense responsible for Asia and Latin America into a single position. Given the important U.S. military installations in the Pacific, the post was given to an Asian specialist, who lacked knowledge or interest in Latin America. The Defense Department therefore generally played a secondary role in policy toward Nicaragua during the Carter years.

As a rule, Vaky and I tried to reach some agreement before the meeting on minimal objectives. In the case of the mini-SCC meeting on September 4, we agreed to support a mediation effort led by Costa Rica and other nations in Central America.

Aaron called on Undersecretary of State David Newsom to offer his department's assessment. Newsom said that ultimately Somoza had to go. However, our ability to deal with the issue would become more difficult if that objective became clear initially. Therefore, State believed that we should stimulate Central American efforts to promote mediation as a first step. Vaky then developed his own position: no moderate solution will emerge by itself. Somoza has dug in. The Sandinistas are extremists with links to Cuba. We should avoid contact with them. Everyone is ready for a change in Nicaragua. Ultimately, Vaky said, the United States was the only actor capable of forcing the change. Tony Lake offered an alternative view, arguing that for reasons of principle, as well as politics, he would oppose going to a chief of state to ask him to step down. That was my position as well, and that was the main reason I had Lake invited to the meeting. Carazo had announced his willingness to mediate the conflict in Nicaragua, and the meeting concluded with a recommendation that President Carter send a letter to Carazo encouraging him to do that. Then, follow-up letters to the Presidents of Venezuela, Colombia, and Mexico would be sent by Carter encouraging them to support the Costa Rican effort. I drafted the letters with Vaky and Richard Feinberg, who was Lake's Latin American specialist, and summarized the meeting in a memorandum for the President.

Carter and his senior advisers had been as preoccupied by other matters as the "Latin Americanists" had been with Nicaragua. Impatient with the lack of progress on negotiations in the Middle East, Carter invited the Egyptian President and Israeli Prime Minister to Camp David on September 5. Carter had been warned of the risks of such an initiative, but he decided they were worth taking. Before the negotiations, he vacationed in the Grand Tetons with his family. There, on August 30, Carter was informed by Vice President Mondale that he would lose his natural gas bill, his highest domestic priority, if he did not return to Washington a few days early to lobby Congress.

Carter returned, and four days later, after instructing Brzezinski to obtain a recommendation on Nicaragua, flew to Camp David. From September 4 until his return to the White House at 10:00 P.M. on September 17, Carter, together with Vance, Brzezinski and his senior Middle East advisers, hardly slept as they struggled to construct a framework for peace in the Middle East. Israeli Prime Minister Menachem Begin later recounted: "President [Carter] worked. As far as my historic experience is concerned, I think that he worked harder than our forefathers did in Egypt building the pyramids."[5]

Behind the Mediation

On September 5, before he began his talks, Carter reviewed the memorandum on Nicaragua and the letters to be sent to the Costa Rican President and others; and he approved the strategy. The fast pace of events in Nicaragua and Vaky's influence had caused a shift in U.S. policy from a position of strict neutrality in Nicaraguan politics to the acceptance, in principle, of mediation. The change was gradual and facilitated in three ways. First, the United States did not decide to mediate, but rather decided to support an initiative that had been proposed by Costa Rica. Second, the mediation was multilateral and thus would contribute to the goal of building a regional framework. Third, the United States had not yet defined what it meant by mediation, nor had it addressed questions of strategy or objectives for the mediation. Despite the pressures of the upcoming Camp David negotiations, Carter recalls that he was "able to focus on the issue and did view the shift as important."[6]

The decision came none too soon, because Carazo was having second thoughts. The letter from Carter bolstered him to continue to pursue the mediation, but he requested U.S. help to gain acceptance from the other Central Americans. Vaky thought this was a waste of time, and that only the United States could organize the mediation and make it work. In my view, even if the United States pressed the other Central American governments—all dominated by the military—there was at best a 50–50 chance of success; if we did nothing, however, the multilateral initiative would definitely die. Vaky agreed to send cables to our ambassadors in the region asking them to help the Costa Ricans. At the same time, the State Department made a public announcement indicating its support for the Central American initiative.

Another mini-SCC meeting was called for September 12. The participants were of a higher level and better prepared to discuss the issues. The Nicaraguan National Guard then had a force of 6,000; the FSLN had expanded their forces in the previous months to about 1,200. Although the Sandinistas had received training and some guidance from Cuba in the past, the CIA thought they were getting very little outside support at that time. Vaky explained that the Central American mediation was going nowhere because Somoza had persuaded most of the military governments not to participate.

Christopher outlined four options for U.S. policy:

1. neutrality, which he described as the status quo;
2. dissociation from Somoza;
3. support for Somoza; or
4. mediation.

He dismissed the idea of supporting Somoza for practical and moral reasons, and CIA Director Stansfield Turner agreed that such a strategy could only accelerate the polarization within Nicaragua. Dissociation was viewed as opting out of the crisis, and was discarded. The status quo option was a nonstarter, because the problem was worsening as we stood still. That left mediation, and the question was what kind.

Christopher proposed two variations: (4a) keep Central America in front; or (4b) do it ourselves. Vaky and Newsom supported "4b," but Christopher defended "4a," saying we should try that first. He also opposed the idea of sending someone to speak with Somoza at this point, because that would be a shortcut to "4b." We might recommend that eventually, Christopher said, but we were not there yet, and the option had so many unattractive qualities that we didn't want to do it if we didn't have to. However, the group agreed to send William Jorden, former U.S. Ambassador to Panama, to travel to several countries in the area, though not to Nicaragua, to consult. Christopher also proposed that we suggest to the moderate opposition that they issue an appeal for international mediation; that would provide a Nicaraguan handle for someone outside to grab. Christopher's recommendation carried the meeting by consensus. (Christopher set the position for State; Vaky had a voice, but no vote.) In effect the meeting agreed to try the same approach a little harder, but it also provided an opportunity to explore some new questions. For example, Aaron asked Vaky whether he felt the loyalty of the Guard was transferable, and Vaky said he thought it was.

But Vaky was frustrated by the meeting. He found himself caught between an Administration that was moving, in his mind, too slowly, and Carlos Andrés Pérez, who kept calling him, urging faster action. For two days, Vaky delayed sending cables to strengthen the Central American initiative or to encourage the moderate opposition to issue an international appeal for a mediation. He had opposed the former because he thought it a diversion and the latter because he felt the opposition was too weak and fragmented to make such an appeal. But the day after the cables were sent, on September 15, the Broad Opposition Front (FAO) issued an international request for mediation. I then suggested we ask the FAO to direct the appeal to the Central Americans or another appropriate audience; Vaky wanted it directed to the United States, but agreed to leave it up to the FAO to whom they would direct the appeal. The next day, the FAO directed the appeal to Latin America, not the United States! Nonetheless, the State Department immediately issued a statement supporting the opposition's call.

The United States was in front, in back, and on the side, pressing everyone, except itself, to mediate—to little effect. The Central American initiative was dying, partly because Costa Rica had found little interest among its neighbors and also because Carazo himself lost interest. The United States thought that Carazo was getting cold feet; in fact, he withdrew his proposal because his feet were getting warm. Instead of mediation, Carazo was preparing to offer his goverment's support to the Sandinistas. On September 12, just hours after the mini-SCC meeting ended, "a very important incident occurred," in Carazo's words. The Costa Rican frontier was strafed and bombed by the Nicaraguan Air Force, and students, who were celebrating independence day there, were injured. "That was the reason," Carazo later explained, "why I backed away from the mediation initiative. We were no longer completely neutral."[7] Prior to the incident, Pastora and the other Sandinistas had used Costa Rica, but without the permission of the government, which from time to time had harassed them. From September 12 until December 1978, Carazo allowed Edén Pastora to use Costa Rica freely to transport medicines and food for his forces, to organize and train his soldiers, and finally to receive armaments.

As the Central American initiative expired, the conflict grew more intense and more international. Costa Rica protested the Nicaraguan attack to the OAS, which sent a team to investigate, and Carazo requested help from Venezuela and Panama. Pérez and Torrijos sent planes and helicopters to Costa Rica on September 14. After our Chargé in Caracas reported a disturbing conversation he had with Pérez suggesting possible intervention, Vaky called on September 18 and said that he hoped that Pérez would do nothing that would "inflame the situation or complicate it." In what Vaky recalls as a "volcanic" response, Pérez said: "I do not trust the U.S. now." Pérez decided to raise his concerns at the OAS, but he warned Vaky: "Do not defraud us."[8] Pérez also said that he thought the mediation would fail, but he would support it.

Venezuela had originally requested the convening of a Meeting of Foreign Ministers of the OAS on September 2, but it was postponed twice to permit the Central American initiative time and also to allow an OAS mission to investigate the border incidents. Finally, the day of Vaky's conversation, Venezuela called for an OAS meeting, and the vote was 23 in favor, with only Paraguay opposed. Nicaragua supported the vote in the surreal hope that the OAS would investigate Costa Rican support for the rebels.

In the afternoon of September 18, Aaron convened another meeting of the mini-SCC. The Costa Rican mediation was dead, The Sandinistas had much more support than anyone had suspected, and the Guard was weaker. Christopher recommended that the United States try to use the OAS Meeting of Foreign Ministers to get a resolution to support a mediation effort, and that the United States indicate its willingness to be directly involved in such an effort, and, if necessary, to lead it. The mini-SCC still preferred a multilateral effort and recommended that Jorden be instructed to see Somoza in order to gain his agreement to a mediation and to make clear to him that the United States viewed the crisis as the result of his remaining in power. Aaron also suggested looking into the idea of a peace-keeping force during a post-Somoza period to reassure the National Guard and to keep the situation from being dominated by the Sandinistas.

The representative of the Joint Chiefs of Staff for the first time expressed unease with the course of events and asked who was worse, Somoza or the Sandinistas. That question evoked silence; then Aaron and Christopher patiently explained the consensus of previous meetings: that the choice between Somoza and the Sandinistas was a false one; the longer Somoza stayed in power, the more likely it was that the Sandinistas would replace him.

That evening, President Carter addressed a joint session of Congress to describe the Middle East peace accords that he had just negotiated at Camp David. The next morning he reviewed the memoranda on the mini-SCC meeting and approved a more active strategy for the United States to participate in a mediation in Nicaragua. Again, the decision was facilitated by the multilateral character of the mediation, by the fact it remained undefined, and because the alternative had failed.

Bombing the Bunker

On September 19, 1978, the State Department issued an appeal for a truce, a human rights investigation, and mediation. That evening Somoza was interviewed on the McNeil-Lehrer television program, during which he insisted that he would not accept OAS mediation and would not step down before his term ended. Over the next two days preceding the OAS meeting, there were numerous reports of widespread atrocities in Nicaragua as the violence peaked.

The OAS meeting opened in Washington on September 21, and Christopher addressed the group. He called for a fact-finding mission to be sent to the Costa Rican border to reduce the potential of international conflict. To narrow the chasm separating Somoza from the Nicaragua opposition, Christopher announced: "We believe the good offices of concerned governments should be offered. The United States is prepared to participate in such an effort."9

After the session adjourned, I had dinner with the Panamanian Foreign Minister, an old friend. When we parted at about 1:00 A.M., we could not have guessed that within hours a bizarre chain of events would carry our two governments to the brink of war.

There had been warnings. Torrijos had met with Jorden on September 18 and had told him that he and Pérez wanted to take direct action to remove Somoza. Noting ominously that Venezuela's bombers were at the San José airport, Torrijos then flew to Caracas. When he returned, his aide informed Jorden that Torrijos and Pérez had discussed a military solution. That day, as noted above, Vaky spoke with Pérez in an effort to calm him down. On September 21, Jorden met with Pérez in Caracas, and Pérez argued for more forceful action: "A Sandinista victory will open the door to Castro. . . . This will end in Cuban hands. The shame is this could be avoided, but the United States has not been decisive enough." Nonetheless, Pérez agreed to move his bombers from San José to David (in northern Panama) and Tocuman (Panama City's airport).10

Torrijos felt that the United States had not been paying attention to the crisis, and he decided to use the presence of Venezuelan planes in Panama to force the pace of events. Late in the evening of September 21, Torrijos instructed Gabriel Lewis Galindo, former Panamanian Ambassador to the United States, to inform the United States that Torrijos and Pérez would dispatch their planes to Managua the next morning to bomb "the bunker," Somoza's headquarters. Lewis told Jorden, who had just returned to Panama, and they conveyed the message to Washington in the early morning hours. Carter recalls that he was awakened at about 5:00 A.M. by Brzezinski with:

> word from Panama that they were launching an attack within an hour or so against Managua with their Air Force. I told him to send a message to Torrijos, to Pérez, and to notify our Ambassador in Nicaragua, and to place a call to Gabriel Lewis and also to Torrijos.
>
> Later, I joined in a conference call with them [Brzezinski and Harold Brown] on this. We decided to let General McAuliffe [U.S. Commander-in-Chief in Panama] alert his top officers and show some minimal sign of activity around our air bases in Panama, and for McAuliffe to visit Torrijos . . . .[11]

Brzezinski called me after talking with Harold Brown and President Carter. He asked me to rush to the White House to assist the President in placing a call to Torrijos.

In the meantime, Vaky called Pérez, who denied any knowledge of Torrijos' threat. Torrijos was at his remote retreat in Coclecito, a small poor village in the highlands of central Panama. By the time Washington was geared to respond, he had made himself unavailable ("he took a long walk to think," his aide said). Carter therefore called Gabriel Lewis, who had become a trusted friend during the Canal Treaty negotiations, and Lewis promised to convey Carter's deep concern to Torrijos. At 10:00 A.M., Lewis called back to tell us that the air strike would not occur that day, and that Torrijos had asked him to fly to Washington immediately.

At 11:00 A.M., Brzezinski called an urgent meeting in his office with Harold Brown, Air Force Chief of Staff General Lewis Allen, Warren Christopher, Stansfield Turner, Vaky, Aaron, and me. The issue was whether the United States should send F-4 interceptors to Panama to prevent the air strike. Aaron, Vaky, and I argued strongly against doing this because the action would appear to Central America as if we were trying to rescue Somoza. The rather heated debate that ensued could have been avoided if anyone at the meeting had known that Panama did not have any fighters or bombers. Since Pérez had previously told Vaky that Venezuela's planes would not be used, the issue was moot. Nonetheless, under great tension, with little sleep and less information, the participants weighed several serious options, and Brzezinski decided to keep the interceptors on alert until the President reached Torrijos. Christopher would meet with the Costa Rican Foreign Minister and make sure that they were not going to encourage an attack against Nicaragua. The consensus was that the United States should contain the crisis in Nicaragua and not permit it to expand.

Both Brzezinski and Carter were scheduled to meet with a group of editors who were in Washington for a conference on Latin America. No one was aware that the Nicaraguan crisis was on the verge of becoming an international war, and Brzezinski therefore stunned the group when, at one point, he said that the President and he were up all night working on Nicaragua. The President then explained that: "We are trying through peaceful means to . . . put an end to the suffering. . . . We don't want to intervene in the affairs of a sovereign country. . . . [But] we are trying to work with our friends and well-meaning neighbors of Nicaragua to perhaps mediate the disputes . . . using . . . the OAS as a vehicle whenever possible."[12] Brzezinski further explained U.S. policy as neither a "hands-off policy" nor "engaging in interventionism." Rapid mediation was necessary to resolve the crisis and halt the polarization that could only lead to "extremism." But Brzezinski also vented his concern: "I would hope that there are forces in Nicaragua which are sufficiently committed to the democratic process and sufficiently strong in terms of their own vitality to make certain that any further changes in the nature of the Nicaraguan political system will not create a repetition of the Castro situation."[13]

At 3:00 P.M. Washington time, Torrijos came down from the mountain and returned Carter's call. The friendship and respect that had grown between Carter and Torrijos were unusual, given the extraordinary differences in personality and culture. Torrijos, a soldier and a populist, had a flair for pungent metaphors. The son of school teachers, he liked to confound his leftist friends by saying he believed in the classroom struggle, not the class struggle. And he confounded his conservative friends with his frequent use of leftist populist rhetoric.[14]

In that September 22 conversation, Carter and Torrijos tried to communicate in their own styles, leaving those who were also listening to the conversation bewildered. Torrijos first explained the problem in Nicaragua as he saw it: "[It is] a simple problem: a mentally deranged man with an army of criminals is attacking a defenseless population." Carter tried to pull Torrijos out of the world of García Márquez' metaphors into Carter's practical world of problems and solutions. Carter suggested that the way to address the problem was by mediation through the OAS, but Torrijos continued: "This is not a problem for the OAS; what we need is a psychiatrist." Carter persistently tried to obtain Torrijos' agreement to four points:

1. coordinated efforts among all peace-loving nations in the area, which meant no independent bomb attacks on Managua;
2. a strong mediation effort, in which Carter personally assured him the United States would participate;
3. helping the Red Cross to aid the victims of the violence; and
4. a commitment to nonintervention.

"Please confirm this," Carter said, calmly but firmly. He repeated the request a second time. Torrijos confirmed it in his way: "President Carter, you have a great deal of prestige on this continent; there is nothing you can't solve if you work on it." Within an hour, Panama's Foreign Minister called me to convey a more direct message from Torrijos to Carter: Torrijos agreed to follow the U.S. line of nonintervention because of his respect for the President. I asked the Foreign Minister why Torrijos had threatened to attack in the first place, and he said that Torrijos had been receiving reports of unspeakable atrocities in Nicaragua and was advised that only something very dramatic would stop them. I suspected that was half of Torrijos' motive; the other half was to move the United States to displace Somoza. Carlos Andrés Pérez later said that Torrijos had dreamed up the entire idea, believing that it would scare Somoza into leaving.[15]

Saturday, September 23, was a day full of Nicaragua. It began at 9:00 A.M. with a stiff conversation between Brzezinski and the Panamanian Foreign Minister. Christopher, Gabriel Lewis, and I listened as Brzezinski omitted the routine cordialities and bluntly told him that Torrijos' threat was not appreciated. His tone and message surprised and upset the Panamanians, illustrating the gulf in perspective between the two governments even more vividly than the Carter-Torrijos conversation of the previous day. Having made his point about Panamanian military action, Brzezinski responded to their concerns on Nicaragua by saying that the United States was serious about getting rid of Somoza, but only through mediation and in a way that ensured the result was not a victory by the extreme left. The Panamanians were concerned about the possibility of intervention on behalf of Somoza from Guatemala and El Salvador, and Brzezinski said that we were concerned about intervention on behalf of either side. When the Panamanians pressed for a specific date for Somoza's departure, Brzezinski resisted. Christopher said that he didn't think Somoza would remain until 1981, but the precise date should be determined by the mediation. As he enjoyed doing, Brzezinski concluded the meeting by setting the crisis in a broader context. The issue was whether the United States, or Panama for that matter, should determine the composition of other governments. The United States was reluctant to consider such a role for itself, but it was prepared to consider such actions under extreme circumstances if there were "a genuine collective endeavor." The Panamanians, who were offended by Brzezinski's bluntness initially, were pleased and relieved by the clarity of his statement of U.S. policy at the end.[16]

Christopher and Vaky had been meeting with the foreign ministers at the OAS, and both concluded that OAS mediation was neither practical nor desirable. The prevalence of Latin American military governments whose claims to legitimacy were as tenuous as Somoza's made the OAS an unlikely organization to endorse an attempt to change the government in Nicaragua. The United States therefore sought an OAS resolution that would expedite a visit by the Inter-American Human Rights Commission and endorse the idea of a mediation.

Because of the many hands involved in drafting the resolution and the formidable conceptual task of reconciling the "principle of non-intervention" with international mediation of an internal political crisis, the resolution was a bit convoluted. The formula for providing an OAS "umbrella" above a mediation was that Nicaragua would be willing "in principle, to accept the friendly cooperation and conciliatory efforts that several member states of the Organization may offer toward establishing the conditions necessary for a peaceful settlement . . . ." With that, all that was needed was for the Nicaraguan government and the opposition to request a mediation, and for several governments to "volunteer." Experience had already convinced us that neither would happen without the United States.[17]

The same day, September 23, William Jorden met with Somoza. He read from instructions that had been carefully drafted by the administration.[18] He had been instructed to say that Nicaragua's relations with the United States would be negatively affected if Somoza did not accept the mediation unconditionally. Jorden also told him that in the view of the Administration, Somoza was the cause of the polarization. The longer he stayed, the more likely it was that Nicaragua would go Communist. That was as close as the U.S. government would go at that time to suggest his resignation.

Prior to the meeting, Christopher had called William D. Rogers, then an attorney in Washington, to ask whether he would accept the role as U.S. mediator. Rogers said that he would accept, subject to four conditions:

1. he would travel to Managua only after a meeting with the President in order to show Somoza the President was committed to the effort;
2. the purpose of the mission was not to determine whether or even when Somoza would go, but how and under what terms;
3. Rogers would be authorized to negotiate with Somoza certain inducements—e.g., his exile and assets—to persuade him to leave; and
4. he would complete the mission before Christmas.

After a short time, Christopher called Rogers back to inform him that the conditions were acceptable.[19]

Somoza responded sarcastically to Jorden's comment that he did not want to be too specific about the parameters of the mediation since it was unique: "The only one in America." When Jorden suggested Rogers as the U.S. mediator, Somoza rejected it out of hand: "He has stated biased opinions about the Somoza family." Jorden told Somoza that his "departure from office before 1981 [was] one of the possibilities that [had] to be considered" during the mediation.[20]

Somoza accepted the mediation on Monday, September 25, but he immediately began negotiating the membership of the mediation and its terms of reference. One of his demands was that the mediators include Argentina, Brazil, Guatemala, and El Salvador—four military governments. Christopher asked Vaky and me to his office that evening, and we agreed Jorden should tell Somoza that the team would include Colombia, the Dominican Republic, the United States, Guatemala, and El Salvador.

The Colombian President then sent a letter to the President of the UN General Assembly condemning Somoza, who insisted in response that Colombia be excluded from the mediation. (U.S. officials were later told that the Colombian President sent the letter to avoid being involved in the mediation.) To retain balance between democracies and dictatorships, Jorden was instructed to tell Somoza that El Salvador would be excluded along with Colombia, leaving the mediation team to the United States, the Dominican Republic, and Guatemala. The Administration was mistaken in accepting Somoza's rejection of Rogers. Instead the Administration considered a number of people and, at Vaky's recommendation, decided on William Bowdler, who was Director of the Bureau of Intelligence and Research in the State Department.

Over 250 pounds and six and a half feet tall, Bowdler was physically imposing, but he spoke softly and with a gentle manner. He moved slowly and carefully in gait and speech, and the impression he left was one of directness, integrity, and solidity. Born in Buenos Aires, Bowdler had lived and served in Latin America longer than he had in the United States. He not only spoke Spanish like a native but possessed a sense of honor, respect, and "dignidad" that was more characteristic of Latin than North America. Like Vaky, he had served on the National Security Council (under President Johnson), and subsequently as Ambassador to El Salvador (1968–71) and Guatemala (1971–73). Like Solaun, Bowdler had a personal feeling for the Castro revolution in Cuba, having served in the U.S. Embassy in Havana from 1956 to its closing in 1961. Bowdler had the skill and strength of Rogers, but as a career official, he lacked the independence to go directly to the President rather than through the State Department. Bowdler was assisted by Malcolm Barnaby, a reliable veteran, and James Cheek, one of State's most capable middle-level officers. Cheek concealed beneath his slow, deep Southern drawl an imagination and political savvy that were invaluable during the negotiations. He also knew many of the political actors, having served in the U.S. Embassy in Managua.

On September 30, the OAS Secretary General announced the commencement of the International Commission of Friendly Cooperation and Conciliation. The three governments then formally accepted the request from Somoza and the FAO to mediate, and the group traveled to Guatemala to define the terms of reference. Alfredo Obiols, former Guatemalan Vice Foreign Minister, Bowdler, and Dominican Admiral Ramon Emilio Jiménez agreed on a three-part strategy: (1) identify the positions of both sides; (2) promote direct negotiations; and (3) assist the negotiations. The instructions Bowdler had from Washington were more detailed, and included the objective of preserving the National Guard and indicating that if Somoza requested to come to the United States, that would be considered.[21]

The general strike had collapsed on September 25, and the next day the Guard regained control of the country, but the damage was extensive. The Red Cross estimated that 1,500 to 3,000 people had been killed during a month of civil war; a half-dozen cities had been devastated; and the homes of 30,000 people had been destroyed. The devastation was compared to the 1972 earthquake.[22] On October 3, the Inter-American Human Rights Commission arrived in Nicaragua to investigate. As a gesture to it, Somoza lifted press censorship on their arrival. The result was that the commission came face to face with the seething hatred people felt for Somoza.

Divergent Perspectives of the Mediation

GETTING NICARAGUANS ON BOARD. The task of the three mediators was formidable. No one really wanted mediation. For Nicaraguans, as for the Carter Administration, "mediation" was the fallback option, chosen because they felt they had no alternative.

Somoza probably accepted the mediation because he thought that he had no choice and that he could turn the mediation to his advantage. While giving him time to reinforce and reequip the Guard, he would use the mediation to coopt, or if possible, divide the opposition and shift the terms of the debate from his resignation to the conditions for a free election in 1981. On October 4, he announced his plan to double the size of the National Guard to 15,000,[23] and he secretly began buying arms.

Somoza welcomed the mediators with a sleight of hand: "In my opinion, the only thing wrong on the Nicaragua scene is the longevity of the name Somoza."[24] He admitted that this conclusion had emerged from his conversations with U.S. officials, but he then tried to explain why it was wrong. He made the familiar arguments that he was the head of a strong political party, a prestigious Cabinet, and the National Guard. He told the mediation team that a three-man delegation representing the Liberal Party would negotiate on his behalf.

The moderate opposition did not see any point to the mediation, and only accepted it because they felt they had no other alternative. Organized under the umbrella of the Broad Opposition Front (FAO), they also selected three representatives to negotiate on their behalf: Alfonso Robelo, the president of COSEP; Sergio Ramírez from the Group of Twelve; and Rafael Córdova Rivas, a lawyer who was the president of UDEL, the coalition created by the late Pedro Joaquín Chamorro.

On August 27, when Somoza first told the U.S. Ambassador he would negotiate, he also said that the problem was that the opposition would not. To a certain extent, he was right. The FAO did not want to have any direct contact with Somoza; they feared that he would divide and coopt them as he and his family had done repeatedly in the past. Pastora later described their concerns most succinctly: "Somoza was a lost cause. Whoever dealt with him was diminished by the experience."[25] Moreover, the FAO did not understand why the United States was insisting on what it viewed as a charade. The solution to the crisis, in their view, was simple: Somoza should resign.[26]

Although Nicaraguans and most people in the region seemed fixated on Somoza's resignation, some in the U.S. government, notably Zbigniew Brzezinski, were more concerned about what would succeed Somoza. The political counselor of the U.S. Embassy in Managua provided a diagram of sixteen opposition groups that composed the FAO, and the heterogeneity and fragmentation of the opposition was not reassuring to those who agreed Somoza was the problem (see chart).

Clearly, part of the problem was also the endemic factionalism of Nicaragua's politics, which Somoza exploited and exacerbated, but which was indisputable. Chamorro, one opposition leader who might have been able to unite the groups, had been murdered a year before. Probably the only point on which all the representatives of the political groups associated with the FAO could agree was that Somoza had to go, but they disagreed on the mode of departure, with some insisting that he go in a box.

The Sandinistas initially were divided on the mediation. Like the National Guard, they had been battered in the fighting, and they welcomed the time afforded by the mediation to regroup, train new recruits, and obtain more arms and financing. Though Somoza may have thought that the Guard's repression intimidated the population, it had politicized the youth and dramatically expanded the FSLN base.

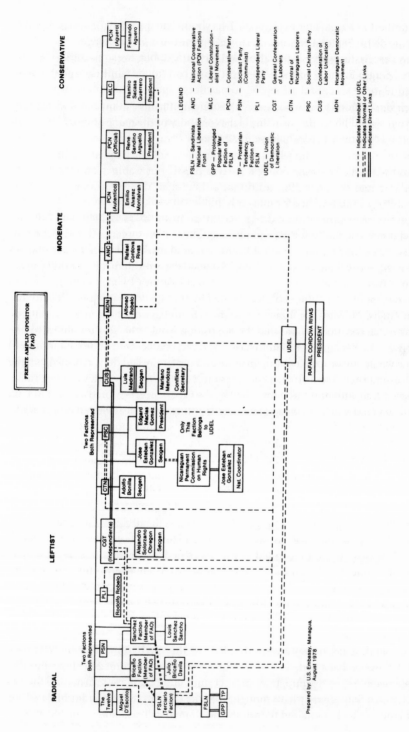

The Political Opposition to Somoza, August 1978

As Humberto Ortega later explained: "Everybody had a relative or friend killed in the struggle [in September], and there was a great thirst for revenge."[27]

The Terceristas were skeptical of the mediation, but ever practical, they appointed Sergio Ramírez to the FAO negotiating committee while they prepared for "a second more successful assault."[28] Tomás Borge spoke for the other two factions in their opposition to the mediation: "We opposed the mediation because we didn't believe it would affect the structural basis of the repression."[29] In other words, he was afraid that the Guard would be unaffected.

*   *   *

THE MEDIATORS. The Dominican Republic and Guatemala decided to participate in the mediation because the United States requested their help. The new Dominican government under President Antonio Guzmán owed Carter a debt for its very survival. Carter's timely and strong message to the Dominican military as they were about to steal the election in May 1978 made possible the first peaceful change in government in one hundred years of Dominican history. Guzmán may also have thought that participation with the United States in the mediation would help him domestically and with the military. Guatemala's motives were less clear, although it appears that President Lucas volunteered more as a favor to Somoza than with the expectation of receiving some reward from the United States. Fortunately, both Presidents appointed mediators whom Bowdler knew well, and Lucas did not pay much attention to the mediation until nearly the end, by which time it was difficult to alter the position of the Guatemalan mediator.

Although officially supporting the mediation as a gesture to Carter, both Pérez and Torrijos were pessimistic about what it would accomplish. This pessimism was shared by Vaky, who, like the opposition, was worried that a mediation might deflect the United States from the central issue: Somoza had to go.

Carter, Vance, and Christopher rejected two of Vaky's working assumptions: first, they did not want to be put in a position where they had to ask, let alone force, a head of state to resign; and second, they wanted to pursue a multilateral approach. These principles were not just moral abstractions but were grounded in a realistic calculation of the costs and benefits of intervention. To try to rearrange the politics of Nicaragua unilaterally would not only reinforce the protectorate mentality of Nicaraguans, it would saddle the United States with responsibility for ensuring that the outcome worked.

No one knew what would happen to the National Guard if Somoza left, or whether the opposition could cohere. If the Guard collapsed as a result of U.S. pressure, the United States would be responsible for eliminating the only barrier to a Sandinista military victory, or it would have to intervene militarily to prevent that. And this would occur at a time when most people believed that Nicaragua was reasonably stable by Latin American standards. The best approach seemed to be to work with other governments and to help Nicaraguans solve the problem themselves rather than try to solve it for them.

These were my views as well. In addition, I doubted that Somoza would step down just because the United States asked him. I suspected that he might be taping his official conversations (which he confirmed in his memoir), and that hours after our representative "talked turkey" to him, we would all be hearing it on the evening news. The President's Press Secretary would then be questioned the next day: "If President Carter is committed to the principle of nonintervention, why is he trying to overthrow Somoza?" If one juxtaposed the tape recording and the President's commitment to "never lie" to the American people, Carter would look foolish and impotent. Somoza would have a good laugh. In my mind, these were powerful reasons for not being too explicit in seeking Somoza's departure. Vaky believed that if we were clear and tough enough with Somoza, he would not try something like that, and would simply leave. It was never clear how tough the United States would have to be. Vaky also discounted the domestic political fallout, believing that could be managed.

The Administration returned to this issue several times, but the crucial point at this stage was that Vaky felt that Somoza had to be forced to resign as the key element of a negotiated transition. Bowdler shared Vaky's view, but the President and all his senior advisers disagreed. Both Vaky and Bowdler were dedicated professionals, who respected the President and would implement his decisions. Nonetheless, given all the pitfalls and roadblocks in the way of a successful mediation, the lack of enthusiasm on the part of the two key people implementing U.S. policy should have served as a warning signal, and would have, if the Administration had thought it had another alternative.

*   *   *

THE POLITICAL AMBIENCE IN THE UNITED STATES. Carter's policy may have been hitched to certain moral principles, but it was not made in a political vacuum. From the beginning, the Administration was subject to stinging criticism from Somoza's friends and enemies. While trying to heal the divisions of Nicaragua, the United States found itself contracting the same dreaded disease of political polarization. The debate increasingly divided between those who saw Somoza as either a defender against Communism or a brutal dictator; both sides attacked the Carter Administration for supporting the other, but their real purpose was to try to influence the Administration to support their position.

On September 22, 1978, President Carter received a letter from seventy-eight members of Congress, led by Murphy and Wilson, urging Carter "to come publicly to the support of the Government of Nicaragua during this period of crisis." The letter reflected Somoza's view that the Communists' "goal is to make Nicaragua the new Cuba of the western hemisphere." The letter was published in the *New York Times* and the *Washington Post* on a full page with a graphic illustration of a hammer and a sickle carving up the Central American isthmus.

No one captured the extent to which Nicaragua was a metaphor for other concerns better than Senator Carl Curtis, a conservative Republican from Nebraska, in a remark to his former colleague, Gale McGee, the U.S. Ambassador to the OAS.

Apparently confusing the Nicaraguan dictator with an Asian island, Curtis berated McGee: "Why are you guys [the Carter Administration] pushing around such a good friend of the U.S.? Why don't you leave Formosa alone?"[30]

Three weeks later, on October 13, eighty-six members of Congress sent a letter to Secretary of State Vance urging the Administration to "suspend all aid to the Nicaraguan government" on grounds that such aid sent "a misleading message of support" for Somoza. In fact, the Administration had suspended aid without ending the program in order to maintain a source of leverage to be used on Somoza if he rejected the mediation. Outside of Congress, some church groups and academics recommended that the United States support the Group of Twelve and the FSLN or incorporate them into a final settlement.[31]

What was the impact of Congressional and interest group pressure? Some thought that Wilson and Murphy had a hammerlock on the Administration that prevented it from taking the steps necessary to secure Somoza's resignation.[32] Wilson forced the Administration to make decisions on foreign aid that the Administration would have preferred to avoid, but the decisions themselves reflected the Administration's judgment of the merits of the case. Moreover, when the issue came to be viewed in a political-security context, Congress's influence diminished.

The conservatives had less influence on the Administration than the liberal bloc, but neither shaped the White House approach. Generally, when Congress divides on an issue, it permits decision-makers to follow their own instincts. This was the case with Nicaragua, where the public and Congressional debate reinforced the Administration's feeling that its defense of its two principles of nonintervention and multilateralism was the right course, and that either defending Somoza or trying to overthrow him was a mistake. Political pressure neither constrained nor changed the Administration's policy; it reinforced the approach the Administration had already selected.

Back in the Middle

The Carter Administration's preference was to avoid unilateral interference in the internal affairs of countries like Nicaragua, but the crisis in that country and the demands made by democratic friends in the region forced a modification of that policy. The Administration discarded it with reluctance and in small steps. First, it accepted the importance of outside mediation as a way to resolve the crisis. Next, it supported an international mediation of neighboring countries; then it tried to organize that mediation. When that failed, the United States finally offered to take the lead, although it continued to insist on its multilateral character. When the OAS authorized its member states to help mediate the conflict in Nicaragua, the country that took the lead was the United States.

These were all procedural issues; the tough questions of objectives and strategies to achieve those objectives remained to be answered. The United States once again found itself in the middle of Nicaraguan politics.

The (First) Mediation

To resign, which is what the opposition wants me to do, would be
to betray the aspirations of the people of Nicaragua to live in a free
society.

ANASTASIO SOMOZA, AUGUST 29, 1978

BETWEEN OCTober 1978 and February 1979, pushed and pulled by Somoza and
the opposition, the mediators tried to get both sides to agree to a process or a
plebiscite that would permit peaceful political change. Both sides preferred a simpler solution: Somoza said he would leave when his term ended in 1981, and the
opposition insisted that he leave the day before yesterday. The mediation came very
close to an agreement on a plebiscite, and that so frightened the Sandinistas that
they buried their internal differences and adopted a more effective strategy to take
power.

Building Bridges

It is hard to imagine a less propitious setting for negotiations to establish what the
OAS identified as its goal of an "enduring democratic solution." No one was interested in negotiations except the White House and the two senior officials in the
State Department. Fortunately for the United States, its mediator, William Bowdler,
was a dedicated professional with the patience of Job.

When the mediators arrived, Somoza told a press conference that he would be
prepared to discuss the 1981 election with them, but his resignation was out of the
question. The Broad Opposition Front (FAO) publicly stated that Somoza's resignation was the only solution. In their first meeting, the FAO told the mediation
team to obtain a date for Somoza's departure. Although sympathetic, the team encouraged the FAO to draft a realistic plan for a transitional government that could
be proposed to Somoza. The FAO had given no thought to a post-Somoza struc-

ture, and they first interpreted the advice to mean that the United States was not serious.

The FAO subsequently relented, drafted a plan, and submitted it to the team on October 25, 1978. The plan called for Somoza's immediate resignation along with that of his relatives in civil and military positions, the departure from the country of the Somoza family, a timetable for elections for a Constituent Assembly, the reorganization of the National Guard, and the installation of a new Government of National Unity composed of a Council of State and a three-man Junta. The Council itself would be composed of two representatives from each of the FAO's sixteen organizations and two from the Liberal Party. The Council would appoint the Junta that would implement the sixteen points of the FAO political program. The mediation team then presented the plan to Somoza's negotiating team and waited for a response.

The psychological relationship between the FAO and the mediators was delicate. Nervous about the outcome of the mediation, Alfonso Robelo sought some assurance that its purpose was to "get rid of Somoza in the most peaceful and efficient way." Robelo claimed that he received such an assurance from the Dominican mediator, Jiménez, and later from Bowdler.[1] The mediation team, on the other hand, tried to lower expectations and focus the FAO on constructing a "silver bridge"— "puente de plata"—that would induce Somoza to leave.

The FAO was fragile not just because of decades of Nicaraguan factionalism but because one of its members, Sergio Ramírez, was playing a double role, trying to lead the group and undermine it simultaneously. Though technically representing the Group of Twelve, Ramírez was actually representing the FSLN, and although designated by the Terceristas, he consulted regularly with leaders of the two other Sandinista factions.[2] The FSLN realized that if the mediation succeeded, they would fail. On the day the FAO presented its plan to the mediation team, the FSLN directed Ramírez "to make a dramatic gesture—to resign and seek asylum" in the Mexican Embassy in a manner that would shock and fragment the FAO. He did as he was told on October 25, denouncing any outcome that left the Guard in existence as "Somocismo sin [without] Somoza."[3] The Sandinistas then delivered an ultimatum to the mediators that said they would begin fighting if no agreement was reached by November 21.

With the FSLN denouncing the mediation, Carlos Andrés Pérez became worried about a new round of violence. He suggested a standby peace-keeping force of troops from the United States, Venezuela, Colombia, and Panama to be sent to Nicaragua if fighting resumed. The United States began thinking about the idea too.

The departure of Ramírez did not destroy the FAO, but it increased the pressure on it to quit the mediation if Somoza did not resign. Somoza consulted with his colleagues on a response and at the same time tried to influence the United States. He asked Manolo Reboso, the Cuban-American Vice Mayor of Miami, to see me on

October 30 in an effort to set up a secret meeting between Somoza and someone in the White House. I immediately informed both Brzezinski and Vaky. I thought such a conversation might be useful as a way of reinforcing Bowdler and purging Somoza of the idea of a possible back-channel deal, but the Administration was still so sensitive about avoiding even the most remote resemblance to anything Henry Kissinger had done that both the State Department and Brzezinski rejected the idea.

Vance and Brzezinski's differences on SALT, China, and Iran were beginning to spill over in unusual ways to other areas, like Latin America, where differences either did not exist or were insignificant. When Vaky decided that the mediation had gone far enough and new instructions were needed to push Somoza into accepting the FAO proposal, Vance insisted that there should be a PRC meeting to be chaired by State, rather than an SCC meeting chaired by NSC. Brzezinski was not averse to trading off the chairmanship of a meeting on Nicaragua provided he retained the chairmanship on other issues of greater interest to him. Brzezinski also knew that his views on Nicaragua policy at that time coincided with those of Vance and Christopher.

Christopher therefore chaired a PRC meeting on October 31. Vaky had called it because Bowdler and he were worried that Somoza would use his press conference on November 3 to reject the FAO proposal and that this would fracture the opposition. On October 24, Bowdler cabled a proposal to Vaky to apply pressure to Somoza to get him to face his departure seriously, and this proposal was put before the PRC.

In my view, the timing of the Bowdler/Vaky proposal was premature. There would be a time for sanctions, but not before Somoza had even responded to the proposal and not on the eve of U.S. Congressional elections. A second reason for waiting was that the Inter-American Human Rights Commission had recently returned from a visit to Nicaragua appalled by the atrocities of the Guard. The publication of their report would make such a step easier to take.

Brzezinski agreed with me, although for different reasons. He was more concerned about ensuring the solidity of the post-Somoza transition. He agreed that "Somoza had to go," but he threw Vaky's argument about the fragility of the moderate opposition back at him. If they were so fragmented and weak that they could not survive another round of negotiations or fighting, then what assurances did we have that they could take and hold power? He encouraged Vaky, as I had been doing, to work on post-Somoza leadership and on making contacts with the National Guard. Vaky's focus, like that of the FAO, Pérez, and Torrijos, was almost exclusively on Somoza's departure. Vaky recognized the importance of a post-Somoza plan, but, as he recalled, "it was very difficult to draw up plans and describe the scenario in the absence of Somoza's departure."[4]

General Smith of the Joint Chiefs of Staff shared Brzezinski's uneasiness about pushing out Somoza, but Brzezinski made it clear that he thought Somoza would have to go. Brzezinski wanted to press gradually so that the opposition would learn to organize itself and govern if the opportunity arose. Christopher agreed with

Brzezinski, and the two of them instructed Bowdler to speak with Somoza before the press conference to make two points. First, Somoza would be told that if he rejected the FAO proposal, that would signify that he had created a crisis to which the United States would have to respond appropriately. Second, to convey our seriousness, we would tell him that we were freezing aid and seeking a postponement of his government's request for a loan from the International Monetary Fund because approval at this time would be a political endorsement of his regime, which we would not make.[5] Christopher wanted the statement made by the entire team, if possible.

In addition, the PRC agreed to keep several democratic governments in the region fully briefed in order to be able to seek their support should the United States decide the time had come to pressure Somoza. In support of the objective of ensuring the continuity of the National Guard, the PRC decided that a U.S. official should communicate with a former General of the Guard, Julio Gutiérrez, who had distinguished himself as the commander of the battalion that had served in the Inter-American Peace Force in the Dominican Republic. Popular with his troops and known as so honest and incorruptible that even Pedro Joaquín Chamorro had singled him out for praise, Gutiérrez was exiled by Somoza—first as Defense Attaché in El Salvador and Guatemala, and subsequently as Ambassador to Japan.[6] The PRC decided to instruct U.S. Ambassador to Tokyo Mike Mansfield to meet with Gutiérrez.

Somoza sensed he had reached a crossroads. He wrote in his memoirs: "We went around and around in these negotiations, but were getting nowhere. However, one point was coming through loud and clear; the negotiating team had come to Nicaragua with instructions to get me out of office." He wrote that he then consulted with his Cabinet, the Liberal Party, and the General Staff of the Guard, and found that none of them could contemplate a future without him.[7]

On November 6, the Liberal Party—Somoza's mouthpiece—rejected the FAO proposal with a long and legalistic defense of the government and the constitution. The party insisted that Somoza could not resign for constitutional reasons, but it offered instead a plebiscite to measure the popularity of the opposition and the Liberal Party. If the opposition received a large share of the vote, Somoza would allot them a proportional share of the power in the Congress.

The next day, the mediation team met privately with Somoza. They noted the widespread sentiment in Nicaragua that peace would not be possible while he remained in power, and they asked whether he would resign to facilitate an arrangement between the Liberal Party and the FAO. This went beyond Bowdler's instructions but represented the consensus of the mediation team. Somoza rejected the idea, saying that he still enjoyed substantial support in the country, and that a plebiscite to measure party strength would be the fairest way to test his popularity.

Bowdler was feeling the pressure from the opposition and from the burden of his task. To hold the opposition and the mediation team together, he had to persuade them that the U.S. government would be prepared to deliver Somoza when the time came, but he was not at all certain his government would deliver, and he was uncertain whether U.S. leverage would work. In a private meeting with Somoza on November 10, Bowdler asked Somoza to reconsider, and felt Somoza might be wavering even though he said he would not resign.[8] Afterward he called Vaky, whose patience had already been exhausted. Vaky then informed me that the time had come to move to "step two"—full sanctions. We scheduled a PRC meeting on November 13, and Bowdler returned to Washington for it.

The Plebiscite

On Sunday evening, November 12, to review options for the PRC, Vaky asked me to meet in his office with Bowdler, Brandon Grove (one of Vaky's deputies), and Steven Oxman, Christopher's special assistant. Bowdler informed us that the essence of Somoza's counterproposal was a plebiscite; this was the first we had heard of it. Oxman and I asked some questions, but both Vaky and Bowdler abruptly dismissed the queries and the proposal. "It's a stalling tactic," Bowdler said. "He's throwing sand in our faces," Vaky added. They believed Somoza would use the plebiscite proposal to drag on negotiations, divide the FAO, and confuse the American people.

I agreed on Somoza's motive, but said that the purpose of the mediation was to negotiate a transitional government, and the United States could not dismiss an election as a method for accomplishing that. We needed to respond in some way, and I asked whether we could not turn the plebiscite proposal on its head: instead of voting on political parties, Nicaraguans would vote on Somoza. This would infuse the mission of the mediation—to have Somoza stand aside in favor of a new government—with legitimacy that would be impossible for Somoza to reject. The issue, I argued, was not whether to accept or dismiss a plebiscite, but whether negotiations could establish a free enough election to permit the Nicaraguan people to vote Somoza out. Negotiating those terms would be difficult, perhaps impossible, but we had to try. It would put us on a morally sound and defensible course, and if a plebiscite occurred, it would provide the FAO the opportunity to organize itself as a unified national party, which in turn would make it better prepared to govern. Whether or not negotiations succeeded, it seemed to me we had to call Somoza's bluff before he called ours. Both Vaky and Bowdler opposed the idea, but Oxman supported it.

The PRC meeting on November 13 started at 5:00 P.M. For nearly two hours, the Administration had its first high-level intense discussion on Nicaragua. Oxman and I suspected correctly that Vaky's two-page options paper would not mention the plebiscite, and we prepared another paper with the following three options for Vance, Christopher, and Brzezinski: (1) transform the plebiscite idea into a vote on Somoza's staying in power and negotiate terms that would ensure a free election; (2) dismiss the plebiscite and apply pressure (sanctions) on Somoza to negotiate his departure in accordance with the FAO plan; or (3) discontinue mediation and walk away from the problem.

The discussion of the three options reflected a sharp division. Vance, Christopher, and Brzezinski argued on behalf of option 1, Vaky and Bowdler for option 2.

General Smith from the Joint Chiefs of Staff was predictably cautious, arguing against pulling out the U.S. military group—one of the sanctions—on bureaucratic grounds: "why us?" There were no advocates for option 3.

Bowdler explained that the FAO had already rejected the plebiscite and felt exposed. He argued that they were capable of forming a government if Somoza stepped aside soon. Bowdler and Vaky argued that the plebiscite was diversionary; the opposition would never accept it and we would lose a crucial opportunity to resolve the crisis.

Brzezinski and Vance argued that we should tell the FAO that if they accepted the plebiscite idea, we would work to make it fair. If Somoza then rejected the plebiscite, we would back the FAO and impose sanctions against Somoza. If the FAO rejected it, however, Brzezinski said that the United States would be put in a bind. The meeting also emphasized the importance of implementing the previous decisions to meet with Julio Gutiérrez and consult with the Latin Americans—decisions that State had not pursued.

Brzezinski asked Bowdler whether Somoza would leave if we approved option 2 (sanctions). Bowdler said the odds were slightly better than 50–50. Following the logic of Bowdler's answer, Brzezinski hinted that if Somoza did not resign, the United States would be left without leverage, and the situation could become untenable very rapidly. International support for our position would be essential, but it did not exist at that time. That was Brzezinski's way of reminding State to consult with our Latin American friends, because it was believed that a strategy of isolating Somoza would be necessary and would elicit wide support. The PRC also emphasized again that the unity of the Guard was an important objective for U.S. policy. There was no disagreement on this latter point as everyone recognized that a post-Somoza government that lacked a firm military base could be overrun by the FSLN.

Vance said State would redo the memorandum for the President to reflect the three options. Vance permitted Vaky and Bowdler to make the strongest case for option 2 (sanctions) in the memorandum, and Christopher and his staff—with my help—made the case for option 1 (modified plebiscite). The next day Vance sent the memo to the NSC, which put a cover memorandum on top recommending option 1. Vance had deliberately chosen not to make a State Department recommendation, evidently because he did not want to undercut Vaky and Bowdler, his senior officers, even though he disagreed with them. Before making his decision, however, Carter called Vance, and he recommended option 1. Carter approved it.

The PRC debate showed that the major division within the U.S. government at that time was neither between bureaucracies—State versus NSC—nor between hawks and doves, but rather between the President's political appointees and career officials. The career officials—Vaky and Bowdler—were more attuned to the debate in Managua and more disposed to make the opposition's case for pushing Somoza out, whereas the President's appointees were more sensitive to developing a policy that was defensible in the United States and more inclined to advocate a North American approach to solving the problem—elections.[9] These alignments were neither unchanging nor predetermined, but the way the issue was then framed—

plebiscite or overthrow Somoza—increased the likelihood of such an alignment. For a foreign policy to be effective, of course, it needs to weave together these two strands and sensitivities, and that is the purpose of the NSC process.[10]

Before returning to Managua, on November 15, Bowdler met with Carter for a brief conversation and a photograph. The purpose was to show that the President had confidence in him. Carter recalled that Bowdler and he "agreed to push a strict plebiscite." If Somoza did not accept the terms, then, in Carter's words, Somoza's "incumbency will be difficult to sustain." Carter also asked Bowdler for his impressions of Somoza and several other political leaders.[11]

Despite this opportunity to communicate directly with the President, or perhaps because of it, Bowdler returned to Managua discouraged, but he did not flinch. He did his utmost to prove wrong his previous prediction that the FAO would never accept a plebiscite. First, he had to persuade his fellow mediators, a challenge made more difficult by the publication of an article in the *Washington Post* on November 14 that described the other two members of the team as being directed by the United States. Nonetheless, he succeeded, and together, the three approached the FAO. Robelo's first reaction was negative, but he and his colleagues eventually realized, as the United States had, that opposing a free election was like opposing motherhood. In the end, the remaining organizations in the FAO voted 9 to 3 in favor of supporting a plebiscite on Somoza. (Four groups, including the Twelve, had left the FAO by this time.)

Bowdler worked with the mediation team and the FAO to draft a specific plebiscite proposal in which Nicaraguans could decide whether Somoza should remain in office. The plebiscite would be organized, administered, and supervised by an international authority of perhaps as many as 2,000 officials. To ensure the credibility and impartiality of the election, the FAO demanded the lifting of the state of siege (reimposed in September) and several other steps. If Somoza lost, the FAO plan for a transitional government would come into effect: (1) Somoza would resign and leave the country; (2) the Nicaraguan Congress would elect an interim President, and then be reconstituted to reflect the predominance of the FAO; (3) Congress would elect a new President, who would serve until free elections in May 1981.

Essentially, the mediators used the plebiscite as a bridge between two ostensibly irreconcilable positions. If Somoza won the plebiscite, his Liberal Party proposal would be implemented and opposition leaders would join the government. If Somoza lost, the FAO's proposal would be implemented. On November 21, the team presented the integrated proposal to both sides, and for the next two weeks, the details were negotiated. During this time, the Inter-American Human Rights Commission issued a devastating condemnation of the Somoza regime's actions during the insurrection, and that added to the pressure on both sides to reach agreement. On November 29, the FAO agreed to the general plebiscite proposal, and the next day, Somoza agreed.

In response to the FAO demands, which the United States supported, Somoza lifted the state of siege, declared a general amnesty, and revoked the "Black Code" censoring radio and television. On December 4, 1978, four days after he accepted the plebiscite idea, Somoza sent Luis Pallais, his cousin and leader of the Liberal Party, on a secret mission to Washington. For the first time, Pallais believed Somoza would accept a genuine plebiscite and would resign if he lost.

In anticipation of one possible outcome, Pallais sought answers to three questions: (1) Could Somoza and his entourage get asylum in the United States? (2) Would the United States extradite him? and (3) Would his assets be secure from seizure? Vaky checked with Christopher, but not with the NSC, and responded that under the right circumstances, the United States would grant asylum. Explicit guarantees on extradition and protection of assets, however, would depend on international law and treaties. Pallais returned to Nicaragua to tell Somoza, who said the "answers were satisfactory."[12] It did not occur to Vaky to withhold answers to the three questions until Somoza's cooperation was assured.[13] This was a significant missed opportunity.

The clouds seemed to open for a moment. In a talk with newspaper editors on December 7, Carter explained how the United States "helped to shift the Nicaraguan circumstance from active and massive bloodshed and violence into a negotiation on the details of a democratic plebiscite. . . . We don't know that we will be successful, but I think that in itself is progress." The next day, for the first time during the mediation, both sides sat down across the table from one another to negotiate the specifics. Before this the mediators had been shuttling between both sides.

These events chilled the Sandinista leadership, who went to Havana to discuss strategy. On December 9, 1978, the leaders of the three factions of the FSLN issued a unity statement for reasons of fear and promises of help—the fear that the mediation might succeed combined with the personal influence of Castro and his promise of aid if they united. Their "communiqué," however, underscored their major concern:

> We have decided to unite our political and military forces in order to guarantee that the heroic struggle of our people not be stolen by the machinations of yankee imperialism and the treasonous sectors of the local bourgeoisie. . . . We reject the imperialist mediation. . . . A plebiscite . . . is no more than a trap that leads to compromise and to treason. The overthrow of the dictatorship through revolutionary means and the dissolution of the National Guard are the indispensable conditions for a true democracy.[14]

The leaders deliberately excluded Pastora from their meeting because they suspected his Social Democratic inclinations. However, Pastora was the crucial link to Carlos Andrés Pérez and Omar Torrijos, and they therefore appointed him Chief of the Army—actually of the southern front.[15]

On December 12, the *New York Times* published an editorial entitled "New Hope in Nicaragua," noting that "another round of civil war may now be averted in Nicaragua, thanks mainly to an inter-American team of mediators, led by the U.S." A *Washington Post* editorial on December 19 sang praises:

A month ago, Nicaragua seemed ready to resume a civil war that could only have ended with the ravaging of the country and the victory of an authoritarian regime either of the left or the right. Today, it is just possible to hope Nicaragua is on the way to becoming a democratic society. . . . American diplomacy has reached out to find and embolden and strengthen the democratic moderates of a war-torn country.

Bowdler had managed, through herculean efforts, to maintain the momentum of negotiations. On December 20, after more than eight rounds of negotiations and numerous drafts, the mediation team put forward a final detailed plebiscite proposal that reflected some of both positions but was closer to the position of the FAO. The major change from the November 21 proposal was that Somoza was permitted to stay in Nicaragua during the plebiscite campaign, although his son and brother would still have to leave. If he lost the plebiscite, Somoza would have to leave, but he could return if he so desired after a suitable period. The mediation proposal compromised on the outcome if Somoza won the election. Somoza insisted that the opposition join to help stabilize the government, but the FAO refused to associate with Somoza under any circumstances. The mediators proposed that the FAO become a "peaceful opposition" party in the new proposal and suggested that the vote occur on February 25, 1979.

Partly because the proposal was much closer to their own than it was to Somoza's, the FAO accepted it the next day. This was still a difficult decision for the FAO because of the relentless pressure on them from the FSLN and other groups to resign. Their acceptance reflected a greater degree of unity than anyone thought possible two months before. Since one of the purposes of the mediation was to encourage the unity of the moderate opposition, it was reassuring to know that this had occurred, even though the outcome was still in doubt.

Somoza's deviousness, however, tripped up the effort at its most promising point. His initial enthusiasm for a plebiscite had dissipated after it was turned back on him. Nevertheless, he sent Pallais to meet with Vaky again to discuss some of the details. Before leaving Managua, Pallais satisfied himself that Somoza was still serious about a plebiscite, and when Vaky asked him the same question, Pallais answered confidently that Somoza was serious. However, by the time Pallais returned, Somoza had changed his mind. Before he had an opportunity to explore the reasons for the change, Pallais was called by Somoza into a Cabinet meeting discussion of the plebiscite. During the discussion, Somoza did not say a word. The debate went against the mediators' proposal, and the Cabinet voted "no." Pallais was shocked. "All Somoza had to do was say, 'yes,' and the vote would have changed." Pallais later discovered that a number of people in the Cabinet, led by Foreign Minister Julio Quintana, "had persuaded Somoza that he would lose a free election, and he wanted to stay in power." This was the decisive moment.[16]

The Cabinet and the Liberal Party negotiators, however, decided that it would be better to quibble over the proposal's constitutionality than to reject it. The United States, unaware of either Somoza's uncertainty or his final decision, was losing its patience. General Dennis McAuliffe, head of the U.S. Southern Command in Panama, was authorized to accompany Bowdler on December 21. "The reason that I'm here," McAuliffe said, on behalf of the Pentagon, "is that we perceive that the co-operation you have given to the negotiating team is no longer evident."[17] McAuliffe continued: "We on the military side of the U.S. recognize . . . that peace will not come to Nicaragua until you have removed yourself from the presidency and the scene."

Somoza claimed his only objection was that the United States was demanding he permit an election "which would not be acceptable anywhere in the world. If the plebiscite is organized along traditional lines, which the people of Nicaragua understand," Somoza said, "there will be no problem." Of course, this was the problem. The Somozas had never permitted a fair election, and he knew that better than anyone.

Somoza was left with no doubt about the intentions and objectives of the U.S. government, and acknowledged as much: "What [General McAuliffe] has actually outlined to me is that if I turn right, I hit the wall; if I go forward, I hit the wall; if I turn left, I hit the wall."

Anti-Climax

It was the day after Christmas that Cyrus Vance convened a PRC meeting with Harold Brown, David Aaron, General Smith, Bowdler, Vaky, McAuliffe, U.S. Ambassador to Managua Solaun, and myself. Bowdler explained that the mediation team had presented its revised plebiscite proposal on December 20. The FAO had accepted it, despite their doubts about their ability to contest Somoza's machine and the lack of support from La Prensa and the Archbishop.

Somoza's party had raised several objections, which Bowdler and McAuliffe interpreted as signs of Somoza's unwillingness to permit a fair election. The PRC meeting did not explore the details of Somoza's objections, but rather searched for a strategy that offered the best chance for getting Somoza to accept the plebiscite. The only debate was between those who wanted to apply the pressure in a phased approach (option 1: withdraw the entire military mission and one-half of the AID mission, all Peace Corps volunteers, reduce Embassy) and those who wanted to apply it all at once (option 2: total withdrawal of the entire military and AID mission, all Peace Corps, all significant Embassy staff, and the Ambassador).

Aaron, representing Brzezinski, argued for option 1 in order to leave something as an incentive and as future leverage in case Somoza did not move. Bowdler thought it would have a greater impact on Somoza if all the sanctions were implemented at once, and Vance agreed, though for a different reason: he did not want to endanger those who would be left behind. He was already worried about hostages, and the Shah had not even left Iran.

On December 27, Carter reviewed the PRC's recommendation and approved a phased approach of sanctions as a first step to persuade Somoza to accept the plebiscite. But Carter also wrote on the memo that we should wait for Somoza's counterproposal before implementing the sanctions. As it turned out, the United States received the counterproposal the same day as the President's decision, and once again, Somoza managed a reprieve.

The principal arguments in Somoza's counterproposal were not new to Bowdler, but they were to the President, who saw the cable describing the counterproposal before it was reviewed by his staff. Somoza thought the plebiscite should be run by a national rather than an international authority, because the latter would constitute an infringement on Nicaragua's sovereignty. Carter noted that this objection did not seem unreasonable in the light of the importance Latin Americans attached to sovereignty. Sensitized by the Canal treaties, Carter accepted Somoza's argument that the international "organization, control, and supervision of the entire plebiscite" was "interventionistic" and "an excessive demand." Carter's hand-written note on the cable also included questions about several other items in the counterproposal.

Everyone had thought the mediation was over. The two other mediators had left Nicaragua with no intention of returning. Vaky and Bowdler insisted that we ignore Somoza's counterproposal; they were convinced that the FAO would never accept any revisions to the original proposal.

The PRC had failed to explore the details of the differences between the mediation team's plebiscite proposal and Somoza's objections for several reasons. First, almost everyone distrusted Somoza and respected Bowdler, and at this late stage in the negotiations, after Bowdler had worked so hard on a proposal that he did not even support, no one wanted to second-guess him. Second, in the course of trying to hold the FAO together and to gain their agreement to the plebiscite, Bowdler felt compelled to accept many of their conditions, though these appeared excessive to people unfamiliar with Nicaragua's history. After forty-five years of Somoza's rigged elections, the FAO wanted air-tight guarantees that the election would be fair. Finally, the PRC was exhausted with the issue of when and how to "talk turkey."

On January 2, I stayed late to draft a memorandum offering three options to respond to Somoza's counterproposal and Carter's comment. I gave the memo to Brzezinski the next morning and recommended that the President discuss it at a small meeting with Vance, Bowdler, Vaky, Brzezinski, and me. Brzezinski did not have the time to pursue this and decided instead to give the memo directly to Carter, who then called Vance. They agreed with my compromise proposal to accept Somoza's request for a national plebiscitary authority, but to insist it should work alongside an international authority that would fully monitor, mediate, and arbitrate problems. I also recommended that we draw a circle around this last set of issues, and set a deadline and phase-in sanctions if Somoza tried to stall or renegotiate. Finally, I suggested we go to the FAO first and tell them our plan. If the FAO accepted it and Somoza rejected it, we would impose the sanctions. My proposal was approved on January 5.

The next day, Bowdler met with Robelo in Washington, and he accepted all of the points. Bowdler then persuaded the other two mediators, and together, the mediation team returned to Managua. Vaky then asked me anxiously: "Are you people prepared to cross the Rubicon?" I checked with Brzezinski, and responded affirmatively.

For the second time, the story was interrupted before its climax. The three mediators delivered the final proposal on January 12, and Bowdler remained after the others had left to encounter an assertive, confident Somoza: "You [the Carter Administration] have been threatening me since January 1977." He had had enough. He argued that the FAO was weak and split, that he was strong, and that the United States should support him. Bowdler told him this was out of the question and insisted that Somoza accept the final plebiscite proposal. Bowdler now finally had authority to threaten sanctions, but for some reason, he did not use it. The State Department spokesman therefore said publicly that the mediators had presented the final proposal, and that Bowdler had stayed afterward to warn Somoza that if he rejected the proposal, the situation in Nicaragua would rapidly deteriorate and U.S. relations would be negatively affected.

On January 18, the negotiating committee of Somoza's Liberal Party accepted the proposal, but insisted on five changes: (1) they accepted the possibility of the OAS verifying the results of the plebiscite, but they opposed international arbitration of disputes; (2) they rejected absentee balloting and (3) the involuntary departure of Somoza's brother and son before the election; and (4) they insisted on prior registration and (5) a change in the plebiscite question. The change in the question was significant because it would have made it both confusing and subject to manipulation.[18] In retrospect, the other objections seem negotiable, but at the time, they just confirmed the Administration's suspicion that Somoza wanted to negotiate indefinitely. The Administration finally drew the line.

The next day, by coincidence, John Murphy and his wife had lunch with President Carter and the First Lady. Carter wanted to discuss a number of legislative issues, including legislation that would be reviewed by the House Merchant Marine and Fisheries Committee to implement the Panama Canal treaties. Murphy was the influential chairman of the committee.

Murphy tried to persuade Carter to support Somoza, but Carter refused outright, just as he refused to consider linking the Canal Treaty legislation with Nicaragua.[19] Instead, Carter convinced Murphy he was serious about Nicaragua, and as Carter recalled, he "made clear to [Murphy] that Somoza could not go on as he was." According to Carter, Murphy promised "to moderate Somoza's policies and bring Somoza to the realization that there could be some peaceful resolution of the problem." Afterward, Vance reported that Murphy was "shaken" by Carter's arguments, and Somoza himself concedes in his book that Murphy told him he thought that "Carter's mind was set against Nicaragua, and that he simply could not get through" to Carter.[20]

Carter and Murphy also talked about working together on a compromise bill on the Panama Canal Treaty legislation, which they did. (The bill that Murphy shepherded through the Congress was not the one that the Administration initially wanted, but it was satisfactory, and in the end, Carter lobbied for it.)

On the same day, January 19, the FAO issued a communiqué condemning "the brutal intransigence of the dictator" and declaring the mediation closed. *La Prensa* headlines read: "Somoza Buries Mediation." The opposition almost seemed to breathe a sigh of relief that it was over, and they had survived. Bowdler left Nicaragua, stopping to tell Somoza that he would return only if Somoza accepted the proposal.[21]

The day before a PRC meeting to decide how to respond to the failure of the mediation, Henry Owen called to tell me of a conversation he had just had with Charles Wilson. Wilson had told him that as a graduate of Annapolis, he had originally joined the House Appropriations Committee to work on the Military Affairs Subcommittee, but he had to accept a position on the Foreign Operations Subcommittee until there was an opening on Military Affairs. He had just been offered the position he coveted on Military Affairs, but rejected it so he could continue to oversee the Administration's policy on Nicaragua. Wilson told Owen that the aid bill would encounter serious problems if the Administration reduced aid to Nicaragua any further. "He can single-handedly eliminate Latin America from the aid program this year," Owen said. A few hours later, Owen's Deputy Rutherford Poats called me to say that Vice President Mondale had received a similar call from Wilson.

Christopher convened the PRC meeting on January 26. In attendance were Brzezinski, Aaron, Harold Brown, Assistant Secretary of Defense David McGiffert, Chairman of the Joint Chiefs David Jones, Stansfield Turner, Bowdler, Deputy Assistant Secretary of State John Bushnell, AID Administrator John Gilligan, Henry Owen, and myself. As in Nicaragua, the United States appeared relieved to have reached the decision point. Bowdler summarized the mediation and concluded that the impasse could not be broken without making concessions to Somoza that were unacceptable to the FAO and to the other two mediators. There was a generalized desire to get past this issue, and no further discussion of the specific points of disagreement.

The discussion shifted to the probable consequences of the mediation's end. Harold Brown summarized the consensus: the longer Somoza stayed in power, the higher the chances were of a radical takeover. The only question was when the Sandinistas would assume power. Turner said that Somoza had built up the Guard during the mediation and that the FSLN had lost support and were refocusing on a longer-term armed struggle. The moderate opposition was also weak. Therefore, Turner judged that the chances of Somoza remaining in power until 1981 were better than even.

Bowdler said that the Sandinistas had organized a Patriotic Front, an umbrella organization to induce further defections from the FAO. Unless the United States quickly gave the moderates an alternative, they would ally with the left, shortening the timing of a Sandinista victory. Thus he and Harold Brown argued that even though sanctions might not affect Somoza, they were needed to bolster the moderate opposition and keep them from turning to the left.

There was agreement to impose sanctions against Somoza; the only question was which steps would communicate disapproval most effectively without generating significant extraneous costs, such as those related to Wilson's threats against the aid program. Brzezinski put the issue in a strategic framework that permitted a quick consensus. He said that the principal actions the United States should take against Somoza were symbolic and should be military and political. We should withdraw the U.S. military advisory group, terminate all military aid, and seek to ostracize Somoza in the OAS. Cutting off all economic aid at this time was not necessary or appropriate; some room should be left for the next stage. Bowdler agreed that the steps that would have the most impact on Somoza and on Nicaraguans were political and military; steps to terminate economic aid would only cause an uproar in Washington without adding to our message in Managua. Bowdler suggested that two aid loans should remain suspended. The PRC also agreed that the United States would vote against all loans to Nicaragua in the international banks.

I returned to my office to write a summary of the meeting for the President and a decision memorandum. In addition, I wrote a memo for Brzezinski on a letter that John Murphy had sent the President after his luncheon. Murphy's letter read as if it were a legal brief for Somoza's counterproposal, making the case for each of Somoza's objections to the mediation team's proposal.[22] When I finished, I left the two items with Brzezinski's overnight secretary with instructions that part of the package was for the President and the other for Brzezinski.

This was an odd moment. Vaky and Bowdler had been advocating these actions for months, yet Bowdler acknowledged that the steps were unlikely to have an effect on Somoza. Although there was virtually no difference between the sanctions accepted on January 26 and those proposed earlier, Vaky and Bowdler feared that the sanctions might have less influence. And there was little discussion of what could be done after these steps. An unstated premise that hung over the discussion was that there was little more that could be done, even though all agreed that a serious crisis was looming.

It would have been logical to review the differences in the positions between the FAO and Somoza on the plebiscite more closely, because a plebiscite remained the only apparent method of moving Somoza out. But there was no discussion, partly because the U.S. government had no experience mediating elections, but also because of bureaucratic fatigue and the psychological need to reach agreement and move to the next issue. This was especially true for the principals, who had spent the previous month arguing over SALT, China, and particularly over how to deal with the collapse of the Shah.

The two revolutions in Iran and Nicaragua contained so many parallels that even the characters sometimes seemed interchangeable. During several discussions on the question of contacting General Gutiérrez as a possible head of a future National Guard, David Aaron and Harold Brown reminded each other that he was the Nicaraguan equivalent of General Fereidoun Jam, who had been considered a possible head of the Iranian armed forces, and therefore an alternative to both the Shah and the Ayatollah. Because the principals could not reach agreement on Iran, it was all the more refreshing for them to reach it on Nicaragua.

After the PRC meeting of January 26, attention shifted from Nicaragua so quickly that the decisions almost seemed to escape into a black hole and emerge in an altered state. On Saturday, January 27, I stopped by Brzezinski's office to see whether the decision memorandum had been sent to the President. I learned that Chinese Vice Premier Deng Xiaoping was coming soon for an official visit, and Brzezinski seemed more delightfully preoccupied than any time since he had worked on the President's schedule for his trip to Poland.

Proud of his role in what he considered the "historic" decision to normalize relations with China, Brzezinski was in the process of reviewing volumes of briefing books on China for the President. He suggested I speak to Aaron, who had the memorandum. Aaron had a penetrating intelligence, but organization was not his forte, and I feared the memorandum might be stuck. On Monday, I checked again, but by then the Chinese had arrived.

The memorandum finally went to the President on Wednesday, January 31, but by mistake, it included the extra section (on Murphy's letter) I had reserved only for Brzezinski. Carter, like Brzezinski, read voraciously, quickly, and generally, with high levels of comprehension. Memoranda were returned with comments the same day they were sent. Carter approved the recommendation of the PRC meeting to sanction Somoza.

But then Carter read through Murphy's point-by-point rebuttal of the mediation team proposal and jotted in his neat script those points, for example, on prior registration of voters, that struck Carter as sensible. Indeed, on many of the differences, Carter's notes suggest he found the Somoza/Murphy position better than the mediators' proposal. No better illustration of Somoza's effectiveness in transcribing Nicaraguan politics into the vocabulary of U.S. politics can be found than in the President's handwritten notes. Murphy/Somoza's objection to the degree of international supervision and the change of voting districts, for example, seemed reasonable if one were thinking in terms of a democratic nation. However, exceptional steps were necessary in Nicaragua to make an election credible. Carter had not grasped that point, nor did the memo make it because it was not supposed to be read by him.

I was rendered mute, and didn't know how to proceed. The implication of the President's notes was to reactivate negotiations. This would have required a heroic, probably futile effort in Washington, in the capitals of the other two mediators, and especially in Managua. I was certain that the best response we could obtain from Vaky and Bowdler was that the mission was impossible; at worst, they would resign.

Vance and Brzezinski were trying to cope with Iran and SALT. After obtaining his agreement to keep the information to himself until we figured out how to proceed, I informed Vaky over the phone of Carter's comments. I heard silence and then a thud, the sound of a forehead hitting a desk. If Carter's decision had leaked at that time, the embarrassment would have made us look back nostalgically to the leak of Carter's letter to Somoza. This was clearly the moment for the President to sit down with his principal advisers and infuse a new strategy with his own personal goals and commitment. But there was no time for that.

I therefore decided to break the logjam by drafting a brief "reporting item" for Brzezinski to include in his routine morning memorandum to the President. The item informed the President that the State Department would announce that the mediation had ended because of Somoza's intransigence, and the United States was responding with the sanctions he approved. I alerted Brzezinski to make sure that he understood the significance of the paragraph, and he sent it to the President on February 1. If the President wanted to change course, he would stop us. As it turned out, it was the same day that the Ayatollah flew to Teheran on a chartered 747, signaling the collapse of the Administration's Iran policy. The memorandum was returned the next day without comments. I told Vaky to go ahead.

Sanctions and Their Impact

Bowdler spoke to his counterparts from Guatemala and the Dominican Republic, and all agreed to sign a joint report announcing the end of the mediation. The United States then used the report as the basis for the State Department's announcement on February 8 that blamed the mediation's failure on "President Somoza's unwillingness to accept the essential elements of the mediators' most recent proposal. . . . Prospects for renewed violence and polarization, and the human rights situation . . . unavoidably affect the kind of relationship we can maintain with that government." The United States decided to take the following steps:

1. the U.S. military group would be withdrawn and the military assistance program, which had been suspended, would be terminated;
2. no new aid programs would be considered and the two loan projects would be held up, but those programs that were "well advanced" and aimed at "the basic human needs of the poor" would continue;
3. all Peace Corps volunteers would be withdrawn; and
4. Embassy staff would be reduced by more than half (from 82 to 37).

The statement urged other governments not to contribute to the violence and expressing the willingness of the United States to "resume the conciliation efforts should conditions and circumstances warrant."[23]

The next day, Carter received a letter from Senators Kennedy, Cranston, Javits, Sarbanes, and Hatfield supporting his decisions "to dissociate" the United States from Somoza. "They are a clear message that President Somoza can neither oppose democratic rule nor violate his citizens' human rights with impunity." They also urged him to take several additional steps if Somoza didn't reconsider his position, including enlisting other nations and the OAS; recalling our Ambassador; opposing all international loans; and reducing and possibly suspending meat and sugar import quotas.

La Prensa in Managua supported the Administration's decision, and the FAO breathed a sigh of relief that the United States had finally acted. The reaction in Latin America was generally favorable, but the State Department failed to coordinate sanctions with the other interested Latin American countries.

The mediation—from October 6, 1978 to February 8, 1979—had accomplished more than anyone thought possible at the beginning even though it failed in the end. The mediation team found both the FAO and Somoza unwilling to negotiate, but by cajoling, the team succeeded in eliciting both a plan for a transitional government from the FAO and a proposal for a plebiscite from Somoza. The opposition was fragile at the beginning of the mediation, but over time, despite surreptitious attempts by the Sandinistas to undermine it, the FAO became stronger until it could sit across the table from Somoza's negotiators in December. There is credible evidence that Somoza seriously toyed with the idea of a plebiscite, but in the end, he decided not to risk a vote. There was nothing inevitable in the failure of the mediation, and considerable progress made on the road.

The United States insisted that the mediation be multilateral, but assumed the unquestioning lead. It debated objectives—whether to do what was necessary to push Somoza out of office or whether to insist on an election through which the people of Nicaragua could make the determination. Carter chose the latter option, and then the mediation team tried to develop the kinds of guarantees that would permit an election in Somoza's Nicaragua to be genuinely free. This proved extremely difficult and eventually impossible, because Somoza did not want a free election, and the opposition was uncertain whether one was possible, or that they would win it. The Carter Administration also debated tactics—when to apply pressure and in what ways. Vaky and Bowdler thought that pressure would be more effective during negotiations; Carter decided to threaten during negotiations and impose sanctions only after negotiations failed.

In the end, the mediation failed. Instead of serving as a transition toward democracy, the mediation served as a resting place on the road to revolution. On that road, tragedy was wrapped in unintended irony: it was the very success of the mediation in almost achieving a plebiscite and a united moderate opposition that motivated the FSLN to bury their own differences and develop a winning strategy.

Marching to Different Drummers

Our ability to maintain broad alliances. . . . succeeded in isolating the Somoza regime, achieving nation-wide anti-Somoza unity, neutralizing the reactionary elements in favor of intervention. . . .

Our country is not an island like Cuba; we have to rely on neighboring countries. . . . We operated clandestinely in Costa Rica and Honduras. . . . The alliances . . . were of vital importance in our obtaining heavy weapons and sophisticated equipment. . . .

The progressives [the bourgeoisie] realized that ours was a revolutionary movement and that we weren't totally in accord with their ideology, but they also realized that we had a political program that was, to a certain extent, of interest to them, and that we had military power.

HUMBERTO ORTEGA[1]

FROM THE IMPOSITION of sanctions in February to the Sandinistas' "final offensive" in June 1979, the United States withdrew from the crisis. Others, "marching to different drummers," moved to center stage with the objective of overthrowing Somoza militarily.

Withdrawal Pains

On February 8, 1979, the Administration imposed most of the sanctions that had been proposed by those inside and outside the administration as a means of forcing Somoza's resignation. But Somoza did not budge.

The Administration considered additional steps. Instead of closing the Embassy, which would have precluded contact with the opposition as well as with Somoza should he decide to reconsider the plebiscite proposal, the Administration recalled Ambassador Solaun to Washington in late February for "consultations," and he never returned. He later resigned and returned to teaching. The Administration deliberately did not withdraw the mediation team's final plebiscite proposal in order to offer Somoza an exit if he should change his mind, though no one expected he would.

The threat of sanctions is more likely to influence behavior than its implementation, but if the threats fail, the imposition of sanctions is needed to maintain the Administration's credibility. Having used most of the sanctions, however, the Administration found its options limited. Vaky recalled that the mediation had left him exhausted, and after the sanctions, he simply "didn't know what to do."[2] He had been the motor behind the Administration's policy review; when his motor stalled, the Administration's policy did as well.

The United States and Somoza both experienced withdrawal pains, albeit for different reasons. Somoza thought he would remain in power because of the Guard; he was not sufficiently worried about the loss of U.S. support to consider resigning. With the passing of the atmosphere of crisis, and no new ideas or options, the Administration turned its attention to other areas that had been neglected.

As predicted, the collapse of the mediation accelerated the polarization within Nicaragua. In the fall, the FSLN had established a united front, the United People's Movement, to compete with the FAO and also to absorb the organizations that broke from the FAO because of frustration in dealing with Somoza. After the collapse of the mediation, the FAO merged with this organization to form a new National Patriotic Front. Bowdler had feared this might occur if the United States failed to impose sanctions; it happened anyway.

Like the Administration, the Nicaraguan moderates did not know what to do after the mediation, but they had an additional cause for disillusionment: they had thought that the United States would remove Somoza. When Somoza remained, the Latin Americans came to believe that either the United States was duplicitous or that it was weak. Nicaraguans could not believe the latter, so they accepted the former.

Alfonso Robelo traveled to San José in January 1979 to meet with his old friend and schoolmate, Edén Pastora. As one of the principal moderate leaders, Robelo was looking for alternatives, and he queried Pastora about the Frente. He was surprised when Pastora warned: "We should make a strong alliance because the Communists are getting together. And we, the true Social Democrats, will be left aside."[3] Soon after that, Robelo gave an interview that indicated that he understood Pastora's point: "I have come to the conclusion that if there is a military victory of the Frente, and I think that improbable, we would end up under a totalitarian regime of the Communist type."[4] Although aware of the danger, both Pastora and Robelo then acted as if it did not exist. Indeed, Pastora gave the Sandinistas their most effective military operation, and Robelo later provided them the crucial seal of middle-class legitimacy.

Somoza was bothered by the sanctions, though he pretended not to be. When asked by the *Voice of America* for his reaction, he said: "Yeah, how about those jerks?" But then he insisted that "things [will] go on as before."[5] His supporters in the United States continued to try to reverse the Carter Administration. Charles Wilson, in particular, kept the pressure on Owen, Christopher, and myself, insisting that he would "wreck the train" of foreign aid if the Administration did not leave Somoza alone. The Administration had in fact concluded that more sanctions would not move Somoza but would leave the United States with fewer options in the next crisis, and so Wilson's influence appeared larger than it actually was.

Somoza himself continued to try to influence the American public. On his Easter vacation, Somoza was interviewed on *Face the Nation* and bragged that he had stood up to the Carter Administration: "I even had your Ambassador come and tell me that . . . President Carter and Secretary Vance wanted me to get off the Presidency, and I said no. . . ." Somoza said he was fighting Communism on behalf of the free world, yet the Administration imposed an arms embargo: "Back in 1947, that was enough to overthrow a country." Then, displaying confidence and bravado, he said that he would "neutralize the Sandinistas," who, he predicted, would "wither away."

His optimism was not without some basis. The National Guard had increased in size (from 7,500 in September 1978 to 11,000 in March 1979), and had received new shipments of arms from Israel, Argentina, and Guatemala. In an article entitled "Nicaraguan Rebels Losing Key Support," Charles Krause of the *Washington Post* wrote that Venezuela, Costa Rica, and Panama were reducing their support for the rebels, and he cited one source, whom he considered well informed, who concluded this "will probably mean that Somoza will remain in power until 1981—at least."[6] Several correspondents who had been prepared to give the FSLN the benefit of the doubt in October were more skeptical about their boasts to overthrow the Guard in April.[7]

The FSLN may have been relatively quiet, but they were not passive. They were preparing. On March 7, the FSLN organized a single nine-man National Directorate composed of three leaders from each of the three factions to coordinate military-political strategy. They continued small attacks to provoke the Guard and gain recruits.

Robelo and his followers began organizing a general strike to overlap with an anticipated new round of fighting, but on April 30, Somoza jailed him and several of his colleagues. When he was released three weeks later, through repeated efforts by the U.S. Embassy, Robelo fled to Costa Rica to help the FSLN prepare a plan for a new government.[8] His imprisonment and subsequent departure was a first step in the transfer of legitimacy to the FSLN, although Washington failed to see that at the time.

Unfriendly Neighbors

Robelo found a sizable community of 60,000 Nicaraguan refugees in San José. One middle-class leader, Alfredo César, had left a comfortable job managing a sugar company to fight the Guard during the September insurrection. He had been captured and tortured, but he was not killed, in his view, because the jails were so crowded the Guard did not recognize him. When released due to the amnesty during the mediation, he fled to Costa Rica. Like César, some of those who fled

Nicaragua also joined the Sandinistas, who maintained their headquarters in San José. The FSLN recruited not just Nicaraguans but Costa Ricans, Panamanians, and other Latin Americans. The sons of José Figueres and Omar Torrijos were already fighting with Pastora.

Since 1824, when Nicaragua's most southern province, Guanacaste, seceded to join Costa Rica, relations between the two nations have almost always been difficult. Costa Ricans tend to be smug about their democratic institutions and condescending and not infrequently racist about the dictatorships that have ruled the mestizo population in Nicaragua. The postwar feud between Figueres and the Somoza family brought all the underlying prejudices between the two nations to the surface, and the presence of 60,000 victims of Somoza's tyranny transformed the Nicaraguan rebellion into a Costa Rican national *cause célèbre*.

Rodrigo Carazo Odío had been elected President of Costa Rica on February 5, 1978, and inaugurated on May 8. In a retrospective interview, Carazo identified three stages in Costa Rica's policy toward Nicaragua during his Administration: (1) neutrality; (2) acquiescence; and (3) support for the Sandinistas. Each stage corresponded to an act of Nicaraguan aggression and to his perception of the nature of the threat his nation faced.[9]

From May until September 1978, Carazo claimed there was no official Costa Rican support of the Sandinistas, although ex-president Figueres was helping them independently. During this first stage, Costa Rican authorities preserved their neutrality by occasionally intercepting and arresting Sandinistas. The second stage of Costa Rican policy was provoked by the Nicaraguan Air Force attack on the border on September 12, 1978. Carazo then permitted Pastora autonomy to transport medicines and food and to organize within Costa Rica. Gradually, Costa Rica became less neutral and more supportive of the Sandinistas. On November 21, 1978, another incident on the border occurred, and there were Costa Rican casualties. Costa Rica broke relations with Nicaragua and undertook a diplomatic offensive in the OAS and UN to denounce and isolate Nicaragua and obtain observer teams to investigate the border incidents.[10]

Carazo, Torrijos, and Pérez all supported the mediation and reduced the flow of arms to the Sandinistas during this second period. But after another border incident in late December and the subsequent collapse of the mediation, Carazo concluded that "Somoza was a national security threat to Costa Rica." In this third stage, Costa Rica became what Humberto Ortega would characterize as the "excellent rearguard network that made it possible to . . . end the war quickly."[11] Carazo at this point sought help from Venezuela, Panama, and Cuba. His strategy was to "support Pastora 100 percent. We saw him as the only alternative."[12]

Costa Rica became the key link in an elaborate logistic system that began in Venezuela and Cuba and passed through Panama. According to a report issued in 1981 by a special commission established by the Costa Rican Congress, "approximately one million pounds of arms and munitions entered" Costa Rica between December 1978 and July 1979. The munitions flights were deliberately undocumented, but the commission estimated there might have been as many as sixty flights. "The entire operation," the commission concluded, "was expressly authorized by the President [Carazo] and the Minister [of Public Security Juan José Echeverría]."[13]

The first arms that the commission could verify arrived on February 22, 1979, in a Venezuelan Air Force plane. Four hundred M-14 rifles and about one million bullets were unloaded. An earlier shipment of one hundred M-14s had arrived from an unknown destination. Panama also provided one planeload directly and then transshipped arms from Cuba. Cuban flights would land in David in northern Panama. The arms would be unloaded and transferred to planes that flew to San José. From there, the arms would either be flown to Liberia, a Costa Rican town near the border with Nicaragua, or be driven by Ministry of Public Security officials in trucks. This system became too risky, and so by April, Panamanian DC-3s flew directly from David to Liberia.

Costa Rica became the staging area for the war. But Costa Rica was unlikely to have played that role had it not been supported by Panama and initially by Venezuela. Torrijos viewed Pastora as he did himself, a romantic, independent military figure in a profession that rejected both adjectives. Pérez began supporting Pastora in early 1978, although when Ambassador Vaky left Caracas in July, he still "had no inkling that Pérez was involved in helping the Sandinistas."[14] After the mediation failed, Pérez invited Luis Pallais to Caracas, and Pérez made him a proposal: "It's real easy. You support Somoza; you are his relative; you are the president of the Congress. Try to convince your relative to leave Nicaragua. Ask Congress to name you President and then we can convene to negotiate with the guerrillas for a democratic solution."

Pallais responded: "I wish I could do that, but I don't know what Somoza would do if I mentioned this possibility."[15]

Perez sent Pallais to Panama to have Torrijos work on him, which he did. Torrijos put Pallais on a plane to Managua and then leaked a story to the press that Pallais would be the newly elected President of Nicaragua. When Pallais arrived in Managua, Somoza confronted him with the news report. Pallais apologized and explained, and Somoza told him to clear the public record with a press conference, which he dutifully did.[16]

That was the extent of the mediation efforts of Pérez and Torrijos. After this, both pursued the path of war. In March 1979, Vice President Walter Mondale attended the inauguration of the new Venezuelan President, Luis Herrera Campíns. The next day, Mondale had breakfast with outgoing President Pérez. When Pérez asked how the United States would get rid of Somoza, Mondale told him that we shared Pérez's distaste for the Somoza regime and his fear of the consequences if Somoza stayed in power, but the United States did not intend to overthrow Somoza. Pérez became upset, stood up, and said: "In that case, blood will flow."[17]

Though Pérez left the Presidency, his involvement in Nicaragua did not abate. He remained Vice President of the Socialist International (SI), the international organization of Social Democratic parties. At its regional meeting in San José on May 5, 1979, SI declared the Somoza dictatorship "the prime example of U.S. interventionism in the continent." It claimed Somoza was "still in power today thanks to U.S.

support," and said the only road was "the armed struggle." This was an unusually belligerent statement from a group of democratic parties.

Arístides Calvani, a close adviser to the new Venezuelan President, later estimated that Pérez might have spent as much as $100 million in support of the Sandinistas, but the new President decided not to investigate, in part because the war against Somoza was very popular in Venezuela.[18] Herrera was more cautious, conservative, and concerned about domestic issues than his predecessor, but he continued to send arms secretly to the Sandinistas, although at a much reduced level. He used the same people and the same operation in the Venezuelan National Security Council that Pérez had used.[19]

The change from Pérez to Herrera and the consequent decline in Venezuela's influence with the Sandinistas occurred as the FSLN was preparing its "final offensive." According to Pérez, who learned about it later, Carazo and Torrijos in late April "opened the door to Fidel Castro." Pérez said that both were frightened that Somoza might attack them, and they welcomed large shipments of arms from Cuba.[20]

In May, Pastora negotiated an arrangement with Cuban officials, Costa Rican Minister of Public Security Echeverría, and a commercial company called EXACO to fly arms directly to his troops in northern Costa Rica. At least 21 flights, each costing $8,000–10,000, went directly from Cuba to a small airstrip near the Nicaraguan border, Llano Grande. These flights began in late May and continued through the Sandinista triumph in mid-July and carried about 31,000 pounds of arms. Echeverría supervised the arms shipments and their transfer to the FSLN.[21]

There were also unconfirmed reports of flights of 707s from West Germany with 60,000 pounds of arms and from Portugal with 90,000 pounds. Several other flights from Colombia, carrying boots, uniforms, and medicines, were confirmed as well as many flights from Panama.[22] The Sandinistas also imported some arms through Honduras, obtaining the acquiescence of its military by bribery, but the quantity of arms received in Honduras was quite small compared to the arsenal assembled in Costa Rica.

The United States received some information about arms smuggling, but until late June it never suspected that the arms flow was very large or that both the Cuban and Costa Rican governments were directly involved. Intelligence was weak because State and CIA gave the region low priority and thus reductions in overall levels of U.S. personnel abroad were felt immediately in Central America. Whenever information was received, however, the U.S. Ambassador was instructed to meet with Carazo and Echeverría to express U.S. concern. Both denied any involvement and insisted that the government was doing what it could to curtail the illicit smuggling. When I asked Carazo years later why they had struck a deal with Cuba, he said: "It was more important for Somoza to fall than to keep out the Cubans."[23]

The Calm and the Storm

Unaware of the buildup of military equipment in northern Costa Rica and the plans for a major offensive in early May, the Carter Administration continued its cool approach to the Somoza government. The Administration faced another awkward decision—a standby loan for Nicaragua in the International Monetary Fund (IMF). Many confuse the IMF with the World Bank and the Inter-American Development Bank, although the latter two provide aid for development. The IMF does not give aid; it maintains the international monetary system by lending money to member countries that have chronic balance-of-payments problems or budget deficits. All members have a legal right to borrow on their own contribution if they accept an austerity economic plan.

The Executive Branch has always tried to prevent efforts by Congress to introduce any political criteria—whether human rights, expropriation of property, or anti-Communism—into the Fund's decision making. There was therefore some concern that the Administration itself had introduced such criteria in November when it persuaded the IMF to postpone a loan to Nicaragua.

Although the Administration had tried to use that decision privately to communicate its seriousness to Somoza, publicly, it had continued to insist that the decision was nonpolitical and the result of the failure by the Nicaraguan government to accept an economic plan. The principal reason the Administration had sought the delay, however, was that it feared that approval would be interpreted as a demonstration of political support for the Somoza government. By May 1979, however, the Nicaraguan government had not only negotiated an agreement to reduce its deficit by more than half in one year, it had already taken the most difficult step to implement it—a large devaluation. Because of the need to demonstrate consistency on its IMF position, the Treasury Department recommended voting in favor of the loan.

The issue represented a classic tradeoff between a global interest in maintaining "the rules of the game" for the international monetary system and a specific interest in avoiding any indication of support for a regime like Somoza's. The latter interest will prevail only when there is a compelling security crisis. In mid-May, there was a continuing security problem in Nicaragua, but it was difficult to argue that it was either compelling or a crisis at that time. The State Department decided to accept Treasury's position in exchange for a clarifying statement at the time of the vote: "The U.S. position on this request should not be interpreted as an act of political support for the Government of Nicaragua." That, of course, was exactly the way both the supporters and the opponents of the Somoza regime interpreted the vote. At best, the Administration's position was viewed as inconsistent.[24] It is worth noting that none of the Latin American democracies, including Venezuela and Costa Rica, voted against the loan.

From May 16–18, 1979, the senior Latin American policy makers from Washington—from State, Defense, NSC, Joint Chiefs of Staff, CIA, Treasury, and Commerce—met in San José, Costa Rica, with all the U.S. ambassadors to Central America and the key neighboring countries for a Chiefs of Mission (Ambassadors) Conference. Such meetings permit the ambassadors and policy makers from Washington to review events and narrow whatever perceptual gaps may have emerged. Vaky and I also used the opportunity to meet with President Carazo, who hinted that the Sandinistas might be preparing for a new round of violence but denied any specific knowledge of arms flows to the FSLN.

On May 2, 1979, in advance of the meeting, the CIA prepared a secret intelligence assessment that indicated that Cuba saw "the prospects for revolutionary upheaval in Central America over the next decade or so markedly improved" but had adopted a selective, sophisticated "low-key approach" aimed at a war of attrition and avoiding any actions that could provoke a U.S. response. Since the fall of 1978, the CIA estimated that the Cubans had supplied two or three shipments of arms to the Sandinistas through the Panamanian government and had increased their on-island training. The report also cited two Cuban diplomats in Panama who told officials "that Cuba no longer believed that the FSLN would be able to topple Somoza before his term expires in 1981."[25]

Both the State Department and the CIA agreed that Somoza's Guard was stronger, larger, and had better trained and equipped recruits. The FAO had splintered after the mediation. As for the Sandinistas, they were recruiting about 150 new soldiers per month, bringing their numbers up to 2,000, but they had experienced substantial losses in the fighting. The U.S. participants in the Chiefs of Mission Conference sensed the political tremors in the region, but they had no seismic device to predict when those tremors would reshape the political landscape. No one guessed how soon it would be.

On May 29, the Sandinistas launched an offensive, that they called "final." It was not until mid-June that the United States recognized that it truly was.

Like most nations, including the United States, Mexico tends to project its own internal structure and historical experience internationally. It supported revolution in Central America, believing every nation ought to have one like Mexico's. Starting in the fall of 1978, the ruling party (PRI) and the Ministers of the Interior (Gobernación) and Foreign Affairs gave money to the Sandinistas,[26] much as the Mexican government funds and coopts local leftist groups. The Foreign Ministry also offered its Embassy in Managua as a sanctuary for Sandinistas who needed to escape the combat.

But the payments were a reflex; the Mexican government did not focus on the Nicaraguan revolution until two months before the triumph, nor did it know much about Central America. Neither President José López Portillo nor the two men who served him as Foreign Minister, Santiago Roel and Jorge Castañeda, had ever visited Central America. These men were typical of the Mexican elite, which has historically looked to the United States and Europe, with almost no contact or interest in Central America, except Guatemala, since the 1930s.

Mexico's discovery of vast oil reserves in 1977 combined with oil price increases permitted López Portillo to pursue a more active foreign policy, and Nicaragua seemed an appropriate place to begin. Sandino was a hero in Mexico, where he had lived, and Somoza, a despicable North American client. In late May 1979, López Portillo met for two days with Fidel Castro. Castro's visit was his first to Mexico since he came to power and his first to Latin America since the fall of Allende in 1973. The meeting presented an opportunity not only to praise each other but to criticize the United States. Castro also denied reports that Cuba was intervening in

Nicaragua, suggesting that the United States was the guilty party through "the clearest product of U.S. intervention in Central America," Somoza.[27]

Two days later, Carazo arrived from Costa Rica with a message similar to Castro's. First, the Sandinistas were within a month of coming to power, but there was still time for Mexico to play an important role. And second, with Venezuela's role diminished under President Herrera, Mexico was needed to be the Latin American patron of the revolution. If the United States saw only Cuba as the major supporter of the revolution, it might intervene. López Portillo was convinced, and on May 20, he broke relations with Nicaragua.[28] He then sent two Foreign Ministry officials to Latin America to encourage others to break relations with Somoza, and he urged the United States to "modify its attitude" toward Nicaragua.

The Carter Administration was neither pleased nor surprised by the Mexican mode of consultation. Both Carter and Vance had previously sought advice from the Mexican government on Nicaragua, but they had not received much of a response. In September 1978, Vance had requested Mexican participation or support for the mediation. Santiago Roel later described his response: "I told Vance, you Americans created a monster, so you get rid of him. We don't want to be involved."[29] In February 1979, Carter explained U.S. policy toward Nicaragua in his visit with López Portillo and sought his advice. Once again, the Mexican leader rebuffed the request, responding with a discursive, conservative critique of Carter's human rights policy that implied that both Nicaragua's old and current troubles were wholly of U.S. manufacture.

The Mexican decision buoyed the hopes of the FSLN. One week later, on May 29, a Sandinista force of about three hundred crossed from Costa Rica into Nicaragua with the intention of reaching Rivas, about twenty miles from the border. The Nicaraguan government accused the Costa Ricans of harboring the FSLN, but the Costa Rican Deputy Public Security Minister, Enrique Montealegre, denied the guerrillas came from Costa Rica: "We do not understand what motivated the Nicaraguan government to come up with a such dangerous accusation."[30]

Sandinista radio announced the "hour for the overthrow" and urged Nicaraguans to participate in a general strike the next week. The attack received almost no press coverage in the United States, and the Administration viewed it in the context of the sporadic violence and repeated Sandinista threats of a major offensive that had been reported periodically since January.[31] Sniper fire was heard in León, Managua, and elsewhere, but the National Guard counterattacked and the offensive seemed to have been stopped.[32]

The CIA undertook a rapid assessment and concluded that the fighting could conceivably develop into a second insurrection on the level of the September crisis, but it would not be adequate to displace Somoza.

Secret Mission to Panama

At 1:00 A.M. on a Monday morning, June 4, I received a frantic phone call from Panama. Gabriel Lewis was calling at Torrijos' instructions. "General Torrijos,"

Lewis said, "is ready to move. He wants to speak to you right away." Ambler Moss, the U.S. Ambassador to Panama, was in Washington at the time, and at 11:00 A.M. that morning I was informed that President Carter wanted me to return with Moss to Panama on the noon flight. Moss reached the airplane first but had difficulty persuading the pilot that our mission was more important than his to leave on time. Fortunately, I arrived before the door closed.

During the flight, Moss and I discussed what we would like to be able to achieve, other than receive Torrijos' urgent appeal for Carter to rid the region of Somoza. We decided to try to calm Torrijos down in order to ensure passage of the Canal legislation, which was nearing a vote in the House of Representatives. Second, we would try to persuade Torrijos to stop sending arms to the Sandinistas. If at all feasible, we would try to obtain a pledge of noninterference in a letter from him to Carter. We thought there was little chance he would send such a letter, but we prepared one anyway. We cleared these objectives with Vaky and Brzezinski during our stopover in Miami.

We arrived at 7:30 P.M. in Panama, and a helicopter flew us directly to Contadora Island off the Pacific coast. Torrijos greeted us with abrazos and an uncharacteristic Wall Street metaphor: "It's too bad the United States is always so slow to recognize new realities, and that you didn't have the foresight to buy a share of Sandinista stock when I was first offering it." "General," I said, "we have not come to buy Sandinista stock, but to try to get you to sell yours."

Torrijos explained that the Sandinista offensive was the final one, and would triumph in a few days. We told him that we thought this would be a second, serious round of violence, but Somoza would survive it. However, this crisis could shock Somoza sufficiently that he might finally realize that he could not survive. We suggested this would be a good time to discuss a moderate transitional government.

More important for U.S.-Panamanian relations, however, was the legislation to implement the Panama Canal treaties, which would either pass or fail in the next few weeks. Panama's activities would be crucial in Congressional deliberations. Torrijos wasn't interested in the legislation: "I am out of the Canal Treaty business," he said. We tried to get him to reconsider, but his thoughts were filled with Nicaragua.

We differed on our interpretations of the FSLN, with Torrijos believing, as many Latin Americans did at the time, that the Carter Administration's concerns were symptomatic of the U.S. obsession with Communism. We questioned him about reports of Panama's involvement in transferring arms to the Sandinistas, and he denied the charges. Since the implementing legislation would be at risk unless he could offer assurances that he was not interfering in Nicaragua's affairs, we asked whether he could convey his assurance to Carter in a letter. After the third request, and after he received our assurance that we would be just as diligent in preventing intervention from El Salvador, Guatemala, and Honduras to bolster Somoza, he agreed to send a letter, but suggested one should also come from Panama's newly elected President, Arístides Royo. We agreed. Although Torrijos retained the real power as Commander of the Guard, the Carter Administration had been encouraging him to transfer his powers to the new President. We flew back to Panama to negotiate the text of the two letters with Royo.

Moss and I first returned to the Embassy, assembled the senior intelligence officers, and tried to determine whether Torrijos could conceivably have been telling the truth. Torrijos insisted that the flights from Cuba were not carrying arms but were for cultural or sports exchanges. We were very skeptical, but we had no evidence at that time to contradict his statements.

Early the next morning, without sleep, Moss and I negotiated the text of the letters with President Royo and his advisers. When the time approached for the departure of my plane, I told Royo I would have to go, and he pointed his finger to the Foreign Minister and said: "Ozores, hold the plane!" The Foreign Minister called the airport, and that was that. Moss and I looked at one another, thought about his heated exchange with the U.S. pilot back in Washington, and silently pondered the differences between a big, powerful country and a small, weak one.

We finished the letters, accepting most of their language in order to retain one key sentence in both: "I am not intervening and will not intervene in the internal affairs of any country."[33]

I then returned to Washington, almost exactly twenty-four hours after I had left. I wrote the memoranda for the President on the plane. He saw them the next day and was pleased with the assurances from Torrijos and Royo, although none of us was quite sure what they meant, and the reports were unclear. Subsequently, there was some evidence that Torrijos took our concerns to heart, and that Panama may have suspended transshipments for a time.[34]

Fate would have it that on my first full day back, June 6, two Nicaraguan officials, Max Kelly and Luis Pallais, testified before the House Subcommittee on the Panama Canal of John Murphy's Merchant Marine and Fisheries Committee. The subject was Panamanian involvement in the arms traffic between Cuba and Nicaragua. They exhibited weapons and tried to use the hearing to defeat the legislation implementing the Canal treaties.[35]

The same day Somoza declared a state of siege to permit him full powers to respond to the general strike and the widening guerrilla war. León, the second largest city, was now controlled by the FSLN, but the Guard was fighting back.

A New U.S. Plan

Begun in February 1979, the Presidential Review Memorandum (PRM) on Central America was completed in early June. The purpose of the PRM—the highest level interagency review—was to examine in a systematic way the emerging challenges throughout Central America, not just in Nicaragua, and to propose new policies. Christopher chaired a Policy Review Committee meeting on June 11 to review the PRM. The general assessment on Nicaragua was that the war was a standoff and the Guard would probably survive this round of violence, but that Somoza would not likely be able to serve out his term.

Brzezinski offered a three-point plan that followed from the discussion: (1) the United States should issue a clear statement calling for self-determination for Nicaragua and an end to the violence; (2) we should begin quietly exploring with other Latin American governments the idea of an inter-American peace force that would only act in conjunction with Somoza's departure; and (3) the United States should issue clear, forceful private and public warnings to cease the arms flow to both sides.

This would include a tough statement to the Israelis, who had been the source of some of Somoza's weapons. The Administration had agreed to do this several times before, but Vance was reluctant to put another demand on the table with Israel.

There was more discussion of the peace force idea, which had been first mentioned on September 18 and had been proposed by former Venezuelan President, Carlos Andrés Pérez. Vaky said he would not rule out the possibility of Latin American acceptance of such a force, provided that Somoza's departure was joined to it. Brzezinski acknowledged that he would be surprised if the Latin American governments accepted the idea at this time, but he thought that everyone ought to start thinking about it. Christopher asked the Pentagon to look into military contingencies, and Undersecretary of State Newsom made an implicit assumption explicit, that the United States would have to assume a major part of the responsibility for such a force, even though it would be a multilateral effort. "Yes," David Aaron quipped, "the peso stops here."

The proposal to link Somoza's resignation to a peace force seemed at that time to have some promise. Somoza might be persuaded to resign if he knew that the resulting vacuum would not be filled by the Sandinista military, and the Latin American democracies might support a peace force if that was required to obtain Somoza's departure and prevent a Sandinista victory. U.S. objectives were to gain support for a post-Somoza government, preserve the Guard, and negotiate free elections.

That evening, June 11, Carter, with Ambassador Moss, Secretary of the Army Clifford Alexander, and General McAuliffe of the Southern Command in Panama, met with a group of one hundred members of Congress. The principal purpose of the meeting was to persuade them to vote for the legislation to implement the Panama Canal treaties, but inevitably, they asked about the reports of Panamanian arms smuggling. In response to one such question, Carter said:

> First of all, I think the two issues [the implementing legislation and the Nicaraguan revolution] should be separated. . . . Panama has strong feelings that the Somoza government should not continue in power. This is a feeling shared by many other countries like Colombia, Venezuela, Mexico. I think most of the OAS. The negotiating efforts [the mediation] on our part . . . were unfruitful.
>
> I have inquired to the Panamanian leaders as to whether or not they were interfering in the internal affairs of Nicaragua. They replied that they are not. I cannot deny, however, that Panama and Venezuela and other countries that

I have already named might very well have given aid to the dissident groups opposing Somoza. . . . I think there is a general feeling down there among almost every nation that I know, and I have contacted almost all of them directly, that the Somoza government should be changed.

But I can't comment on whether or not Panama has given aid to the opposition forces in Nicaragua. My guess is that they have. It is a common procedure, apparently, by many other governments that disavow any desire to become involved in the internal affairs of Nicaragua.[36]

The next day Carter approved the recommendations of the PRC. Cables were then sent to U.S. ambassadors in Latin America, instructing them to meet with the Foreign Minister or President and seek support and advice on the idea of linking a peace force with Somoza's departure, and to stop the flow of arms. Ambassadors were told to discuss the possibility of reconvening the OAS to "pass a resolution calling for a ceasefire, a halt to the flow of arms to Nicaragua, and if possible, a high-level MFM [Foreign Ministers] mission to Somoza designed to urge and to help shape a peaceful transition to a representative government."[37] On June 14, the day after the U.S. Ambassador in Israel delivered the démarche,[38] an Israeli ship with arms destined for Nicaragua turned around and returned to Israel.[39]

On June 12, the CIA revised its estimate of the situation. The Guard was weaker and the Sandinistas stronger than they had thought. The Agency judged that Somoza might be able to hold on to power for a short time. The next day, as the violence increased, the U.S. Embassy began evacuating Americans.

In Different Directions

To understand U.S. policy toward Nicaragua in the month prior to Somoza's departure on July 17, it is essential to realize the extent to which President Carter and his senior advisers were absorbed with many other matters, which they viewed, with justification, as of far greater importance to the United States. During the final month of the Somoza dynasty, Carter, Vance, Harold Brown, and Brzezinski flew to Vienna (June 15–18) for a summit with Soviet President Leonid Brezhnev and for the signing of the SALT II Treaty. From June 23 to July 1, they traveled to Japan and South Korea for state visits and also for a summit meeting of the industrialized democracies. Carter returned to the United States to find his popularity at its lowest level and gas lines longer than the United States had seen since World War II.[40] By July 3, the President retreated to Camp David to review a speech on energy, but he remained nearly two weeks for an intensive and pivotal reassessment of the state of the nation and of his Presidency. When he returned to Washington on July 14, five Cabinet Secretaries were fired or resigned.

If the United States leadership was too distant from events in Nicaragua, Latin America may have been too close, concentrating on a gruesome, unforgiving war. The dominating questions were when and how Somoza would leave; few contemplated the implications of what would follow.

While Carter was flying to Vienna for a summit with the Soviets, the foreign ministers of the five countries of the Andean Pact—Venezuela, Colombia, Ecuador, Peru, and Bolivia—assembled to discuss Nicaragua. The Andean Pact had been originally established in 1969 an economic organization, but it had assisted Torrijos on the Canal treaties and facilitated the transition toward democracy in Ecuador, Peru, and Bolivia. By 1979, it began playing a political role. On May 28, 1979, on the eve of the "final offensive," the heads of state of the five countries met in Cartagena, Colombia, and issued a declaration that the situation in Nicaragua represented a threat to the peace of the Americas. After the meeting, the Venezuelan government sent a senior military adviser to Costa Rica, and the foreign ministers of Venezuela and Ecuador went to Managua to encourage Somoza to resign. Ambassador Bowdler met them before their journey, and asked what they expected would happen after Somoza left. They said they had not thought about it. They had no plan.

Somoza met with them, rejected the idea of a resignation, but expressed his interest in negotiating free elections in 1981. He had not grasped the new power of the Andean Pact or his own weakness. The Group of Twelve, representing the FSLN, did; they cultivated the Andean Pact countries, and when the foreign ministers met for a follow-up meeting on June 16, it was clear that the investment by the Twelve had paid off handsomely. The Andean countries declared the Sandinistas "legitimate combatants" in a "state of belligerency"; this implied that the FSLN and the Nicaraguan government were legally equivalent. The statement called on "all countries of the continent" to join in facilitating "the installation of a truly representative, democratic regime" in Nicaragua.

On the same date, from Costa Rica, Radio Sandino announced the names of a five-member Junta, which would serve as the head of the "Provisional Government." The members were Alfonso Robelo of the business community; Sergio Ramírez of the Group of Twelve; Violeta de Chamorro, the widow of Pedro Joaquín Chamorro; Moisés Hassán, a Sandinista leader of the National Patriotic Front with a Ph.D. in physics from North Carolina State; and Daniel Ortega Saavedra, one of the members of the FSLN Directorate. One week before the announcement, Robelo, Chamorro, and Ramírez met with the Ortega brothers and Borge in San José and discussed whether a member of the Directorate should be on the Junta. Robelo and Chamorro voted no, but the Directorate, which had designated them, also decided to put Daniel Ortega on the Junta. When Robelo and Chamorro insisted on the Junta's right to select the Cabinet, the Directorate accepted that point and told them: "We only want to set up a Sandinista Party, and we will organize the army." Robelo thought the moderates had won a victory.[41]

Also coinciding with the Andean statement and the announcement of the Junta was the invasion, led by Pastora, of a 400-man Sandinista force into Nicaragua to join with the 300-man force that had crossed on May 29. Pastora pledged to march to Rivas, twenty-five miles from the border, where he hoped to establish a Provisional Government. The next day, Ecuador broke relations with Nicaragua. It was rumored that the other Andean countries would soon follow, and that diplomatic relations would then be established with the new Junta.[42]

The United States had consulted with the Andean countries prior to their meeting and argued that such a decision would reduce the space for a moderate, democratic option, but U.S. views were dismissed. Many still thought that the United States was looking to save its longtime client, Anastasio Somoza, though the Administration had never considered this an option.

These three events—the Andean Pact's recognition of a "state of belligerency," the establishment of a Provisional Government in San José, and the invasion from Costa Rica—transformed the crisis. The United States had received some word beforehand about each of these events, but still—coming together—they stunned the Administration, which had not fully grasped, and was not yet prepared to accept, just how different the Latin American view of the Sandinistas was from its own.

8

The Reluctant Arbiter

The art of statesmanship is foreseeing the inevitable and expediting its occurrence.

TALLEYRAND

It ain't over till it's over.

YOGI BERRA

REVOLUTIONARIES, like politicians, predict victory to energize their supporters, but momentum occurs only when events convince skeptics that the predictions are credible. At that moment when minds are changed about the revolution's prospects, time is compressed: an endless revolution suddenly becomes imminent.

In the last month before Somoza's departure, the Sandinistas achieved momentum, and the Carter Administration's assessment of Somoza's tenure was squeezed from years into days. A combined CIA-State Department assessment in mid-May 1979 indicated that Somoza was likely to remain in power until 1981; on June 11, it was thought he would be forced to leave before 1981; on June 12, he was expected to last a short time; and on June 19, a week or more. The last assessment was repeated four times at approximately weekly intervals.

The Administration assumed that the Sandinistas would inherit Somoza's throne unless the United States could negotiate an alternative. A second judgment by the Administration was that a Sandinista military victory, as compared to a negotiated settlement, would significantly reduce the chances of democracy in Nicaragua and increase the probability that a pro-Cuban/Soviet, anti-American regime would emerge.

For these reasons, and without internal disagreement, the United States returned to its more traditional role as the arbiter of Nicaraguan politics. In August 1978, ten months before, the Administration had rejected a request to mediate because it feared it would directly involve itself in Nicaragua's internal affairs, violating its commitment to nonintervention. This commitment was eroded by the violence in Nicaragua, the fear that inaction could adversely affect U.S. interests, and the requests from friendly Nicaraguan and Latin American leaders. The United States therefore decided to mediate a plebiscite. By mid-June, the United States was prepared to arbitrate—to try to help choose Nicaragua's leaders. The atmosphere of crisis and the perception of an imminent threat were so vivid that few noticed the fundamental change in U.S. policy or raised a question to stop it.

The OAS Meeting

On Monday, June 18, 1979, the State Department proposed that the OAS reconvene the Meeting of Foreign Ministers to address the Nicaraguan crisis. The decision to use the OAS was a sign that the department had not fully grasped the implications of the Andean Pact statement issued two days before; the Andean countries were moving in the opposite direction from that of the United States. To invite an OAS meeting was to invite an embarrassment at best, a collision at worst.

The United States was not alone in failing to understand "the change in the correlation of international forces." The Sandinistas were very fearful that the United States would use an OAS meeting to obtain support for a peace-keeping force, as it had done in 1965.[1]

The President and his senior advisers returned to Washington on the evening of June 18, and Carter immediately went to Capitol Hill to address a joint session of Congress on the SALT II Treaty. In the course of that speech, Carter connected his discussions in Vienna with events in the region: "I made it clear to President Brezhnev that Cuban military activities in Africa, sponsored by or supported by the Soviet Union, and also the growing Cuban involvement in the problems of Central America and the Caribbean can only have a negative impact on U.S.-Soviet relations."[2]

The stage was set for a decisive SCC meeting on June 19. The Sandinista offensive had stalled south of Rivas, and the FSLN appeared to be having resupply problems. However, the Sandinistas had demonstrated considerable power in several towns, especially León. Somoza was expected to survive at least a week. The Guard, although showing signs of strain, was holding together. There were no signs of a coup.

Brzezinski chaired the meeting and began by connecting it with the Summit: "There is no interest in creating a crisis-like atmosphere after the summit, but events in Nicaragua would impact on U.S.-Soviet relations and on the President's domestic political standing, particularly in the South and the West." Then he crisply defined the objective for U.S. policy—to move Somoza out and create in his place a viable government of national reconciliation. The question was how to accomplish this goal.

Vance outlined a proposal that included (1) a cease-fire; (2) cessation of the flow of arms to both sides; (3) establishment of a government of national reconciliation; (4) humanitarian assistance; and (5) some basis for ensuring law and order during this period. Based on the initial consultations, Vance judged that the chances of gaining acceptance for a peace force were "slim." Brzezinski said that if the National Guard held together there would be no need for a peace force, but he feared a rapid process of disintegration after Somoza left, and steps should be taken to minimize that. He also pointed out that if Somoza were assured that the Guard could be preserved, he might resign.

Christopher and Vaky suggested that after Somoza's departure, a Government of National Reconciliation could invite help from the United States. Brzezinski questioned whether the government would hold together long enough. It was clear in the discussion that the major concern of the State Department was to ensure Somoza's departure while Brzezinski's was to ensure that the resulting government would be stable and capable of negotiating with the Sandinistas.

The SCC agreed to consult again with several Latin American governments on the five elements of a strategy, including the peace force idea. The peace force would not have to be an OAS force; like the OAS resolution the previous September, a regional blessing for a small ad hoc group would be sufficient. Vaky opposed Vance mentioning either Cuba or the peace force idea in his opening speech to the OAS meeting, because he feared it would be provocative. Everybody agreed to wait for feedback before making a decision. Stern messages would be sent to Torrijos and Carazo to get them to put a stop to the arms flow. Pezzullo would tell Somoza that the time had come to step down. Secretary of Defense Brown and Brzezinski proposed to inform the President that he may face two unattractive but possible alternatives: a Sandinista victory or U.S. intervention.

In the meantime, the fighting in Nicaragua grew worse. The destruction exceeded that of the earthquake; deaths were estimated in the tens of thousands. Since fighting had resumed in May, twenty thousand had fled the country, and many more were homeless. Virtually every city was under siege. Somoza warned the Guard that the Sandinistas would be savage if they came to power, and the Guard's fears made it merciless.

At the same time that reports of the brutality of the Guard were becoming almost commonplace, the Sandinistas were astutely reassuring the world about their democratic intentions. The announcement of the five Junta members was widely viewed as an important symbol of the moderation of the rebels. The Junta "stressed the need to maintain good relations with the United States, insisting that only two measures were not negotiable: expropriation of the Somoza family's business empire, and restructuring of the National Guard to eliminate officers directly responsible for repression."[3]

The FSLN receded from public view, letting Sergio Ramírez of the Junta be the main spokesman. He promised the new government "will take the route of representative democracy based on periodic elections, but with universal participation within a multi-party system, of course. We have had too much of a one-party system."[4] Regarding the Sandinistas' ties to Cuba, Ramírez said that the United States had to "talk about Cuba to justify military intervention in Nicaragua," but he insisted, "the United States knows this [Cuban support for the FSLN] is not true, and the CIA also knows it is not true. If Cuba had given help, we would have already won the war because Cuba would not intervene to give just a few old rifles."[5]

In fact, at the moment of Ramírez's denial, the CIA reported that the Sandinistas had received 8 to 11 planeloads of arms from Cuba during the previous month. This proved a conservative estimate. Carlos Andrés Pérez later learned that Cuban advisers had also arrived in Costa Rica, and that "Cubans actually participated in the last segment of the war."[6] U.S. Ambassador to Costa Rica Marvin Weissman met with President Carazo and delivered a chilling démarche about the impact of his collaboration on U.S.-Costa Rican relations. Carazo reacted emotionally and said he would put a halt to it, but he did not.

On June 18, one hundred members of Congress and five Senators signed a letter to the President, which was reprinted as a full-page advertisement in the *New York Times*. Under the ominous headline "Congress Asks: Please, Mr. President, Not Another Cuba!" the letter urged Carter to support Somoza as a traditional ally, warning that his departure would lead to a Communist government.

Then, on the eve of the OAS session, an event occurred that transformed the Nicaraguan issue from a concern of specialists to one that evoked the deepest and angriest emotions in the American body politic. ABC news correspondent Bill Stewart was stopped by a Guard patrol and then executed in cold blood. This was no wild rumor; the event was filmed and shown on the evening news. The response by the public was unlike anything I had seen since I had been in the White House. The phone rang incessantly and telegrams to the President, which passed my desk, poured in by the thousands. These were not the product of an orchestrated letter-writing campaign, as would occur after Vance's speech. The cables reflected the first installment on the national outrage that would reach its peak during the Iran hostage crisis. Here is a sample:

If there is no military retaliation for the reporters [sic] murdered in Nicaragua, it will convince us that the Carter Administration is as I have thought, gutless.

We feel it is about time the Presidency takes a firm stand against countries which commit such atrocities towards American citizens. Why is the United States being so docile? It's no wonder we suffer from a loss of national pride.

The United States should take some kind of stand. Send in the marines. Please protect us in foreign countries . . . . Punish Somoza and help the gorilla's [sic] bring him down.

The individual act of the Guardsman was obviously not authorized by Somoza, but by June 20, indiscriminate murder by the Guard was not unusual. One consequence of the tragedy was that it quieted the thunder from the right in the United States.

On June 21, the United States opened the OAS meeting. Given the complexity and controversial nature of the U.S. proposal, there was not sufficient time to consult about all its elements. The preliminary soundings, however, were not all bad, and the Andean countries suggested that they might even take the lead. On the evening before the OAS meeting, the Venezuelan government expressed interest in negotiating a horse trade: Somoza would leave and an OAS mission would arrive to help with a transition government that would invite a peace force, if necessary. Venezuela promised to raise this idea with the other Andean countries.

The State Department drafted Vance's speech. It followed the decisions of the previous SCC meeting, except it omitted any reference to either the peace force or Cuban involvement, despite the President's mention of Cuba three days before. Carter asked to see the speech and, after consulting with Brzezinski, he wrote both points into the text, which Brzezinski showed me before sending it to State. I told him that neither point would be well received by the OAS, but the single reference to Cuba was needed, given the President's statement in Congress and the facts. I was very uneasy about mentioning the peace force publicly at this time, even though I was in favor of the strategy of linking Somoza's departure to such a force. We had not consulted adequately, and although Brzezinski viewed the 1965 intervention in the Dominican Republic by the inter-American peace force positively, I tried to explain that this was not the way many Latin American leaders remembered it.

Though Vaky had accepted the strategy at the previous SCC meeting, he now opposed both the strategy and the public statement; he tried to persuade Vance to speak to the President about omitting any reference in the speech. Vance called Brzezinski to see whether the President had inserted the lines himself and, having learned that he had, decided not to pursue it. Although leaving the President's single insertion that the OAS "consider on an urgent basis the need for a peace-keeping force to restore order" and permit elections, Vaky redrafted parts of the speech to dilute the impact of the proposal by referring to an OAS "presence" or "appropriate elements" from OAS countries.[7]

Vance's speech tried to build on the Andean Pact's statement by proposing that the "solution [to the Nicaraguan crisis] must begin with the replacement of the present Government with a transition government of national reconciliation, which would be a clear break with the past." He called for a cessation of arms shipments, and in the single reference to Cuba, he noted that "there is mounting evidence of involvement by Cuba and others in the internal problems of Nicaragua." He also proposed a cease-fire and urged his colleagues to "immediately send a special delegation to Nicaragua to facilitate the formation by the Nicaraguans of a transitional government." He warned, however, that "we must not leave a vacuum," and therefore the new government" must have at its disposal appropriate elements from OAS countries, acting within the inter-American system, to assist it to establish its authority and preserve the peace."

Vance stressed, however, that such an "OAS peace-keeping presence" should only be sent after the departure of Somoza as a way "to assist the interim government" bring peace and reconcile the forces that were fighting. At that time, everyone, including the FSLN, assumed that the National Guard would survive the fighting. The OAS "presence" would oversee the cease-fire between the two forces while assisting both sides to negotiate a merger. Finally, Vance called for "a major international relief and reconstruction effort," and assured the group that the United States was prepared "to contribute generously to that effort."[8]

At the same time that Vance was speaking before the OAS, the House of Representatives was completing its debate on the legislation to implement the Canal treaties. The day before, June 20, several conservative Republican members called for the first closed session of the House since 1830 in order to examine the evidence of Panama's involvement in arms trafficking to the Sandinistas. The evidence of some Panamanian involvement—as it turned out, a small proportion of what was sent—was persuasive, but the proponents of the implementing legislation insisted that the two issues should be kept separate. Majority Leader Jim Wright admitted that it was no "secret that General Torrijos . . . sympathized with the Sandinistas and had a vendetta against President Somoza." Wright continued: "Yes, many of those countries [Venezuela, Mexico, others] sympathize with the Sandinistas. I wish they did not, but they do, and they will do more so if we give to them the impression that we are looking for a way to welch on our word, and they cannot trust us."[9]

The initial reaction in the U.S. press to Vance's speech was not negative. Bernard Gwertzman in the *New York Times* described the speech as "an anguished turning point." He noted that the Carter Administration "does not intend to be too far out in front of the Latin Americans. It did not act until eight other countries . . . had either broken relations or signaled their unhappiness with the Somoza government."[10]

The U.S. press highlighted the demand by Vance for Somoza's resignation while the Latin American press concentrated on the peace force, almost to the exclusion of Vance's call for Somoza's departure. The gentlest criticism came from *La Nacion,* the Costa Rican newspaper, which wrote that Vance had "an incomplete understanding of the true political situation in Nicaragua" where "the ferocity with which the National Guard has acted brought things to such an extreme that it is extremely difficult to speak of reconciliation."

In San José, the FSLN immediately rejected Vance's proposal. They urged a continuation of the war "until we win or die." The Cuban government denied its involvement and called the peace force a pretext for intervention. The reaction in the OAS followed similar lines. The Panamanian government waited until the U.S. House passed the implementing legislation. It then broke relations with Somoza, recognized the Provisional Government, and offered a seat on its OAS delegation to Miguel D'Escoto, who spoke to the meeting on the Provisional Government's behalf.

Mexican Foreign Minister Jorge Castañeda was in Europe when the OAS meeting was called and only returned because he was told to do so by his President, whose instructions were simple: block U.S. interventionism.[11] In his remarks, Castañeda praised the Sandinistas for exercising "the sacred right of rebellion against tyranny, just as the Mexican people had done seventy years before." He opposed any plan for the OAS to negotiate with Somoza or any compromise that could lead to "Somocismo sin Somoza." Mexico, Panama, and the Andean nations not only did not share U.S. anxiety and reservations about a Sandinista military victory; they had decided to run interference for the Sandinistas.

I returned from the OAS meeting to the White House to brief Brzezinski and found him in a very different world, contemplating military intervention. Since March 1979, Brzezinski had grown increasingly distressed with the "Soviets' creeping intervention in Afghanistan." He felt that Carter's credibility with Brezhnev required a similar willingness to use force.[12] I countered that if we intervened unilaterally, we would justify Soviet action and provoke a strong reaction in Latin America. The OAS needed to speak before the United States considered any action.

The news coverage in Washington followed the OAS debate, and quickly shifted from the demand for Somoza's exit to the question of U.S. intervention. Jody Powell, the White House spokesman, was asked at the noon briefing on June 22 whether the President ruled out the use of American forces in Nicaragua. He responded with a prepared answer: "That particular question is one on which we are currently consulting with our friends in the OAS. We will be guided by those consultations and by the needs of the situation."

The Decision Not to Intervene

Carter used his "Friday morning breakfast" as a vehicle to discuss foreign policy issues, much as Lyndon Johnson had used his "Tuesday lunches." Originally intended to offer Vance a weekly opportunity to cover his agenda, the meeting, over time, came to include others, and on June 22, Harold Brown, Hamilton Jordan, and Vice President Walter Mondale joined the President, Vance, and Brzezinski. This presented Brzezinski with the opportunity to make the case for intervention, and he recalls he did so forcefully. He spoke "about the major domestic and international implications of a Castroite take-over in Nicaragua. [The United States] would be considered as being incapable of dealing with problems in our own backyard and impotent in the face of Cuban intervention. This will have devastating domestic implications, including for SALT."[13]

After finishing his dark scenario, Brzezinski soon realized that his arguments were "not well received." According to Brzezinski, Vance reported that the OAS discussions were decidedly negative, particularly with regard to the peace force idea. Carter left no doubt that he had no intention of intervening unilaterally.

On Saturday morning, June 23, Brzezinski chaired an SCC meeting at 8:00 A.M. Harold Brown arrived in his jogging suit and greeted Vance, Christopher, General Lewis Allen, Stansfield Turner, Vaky, Bowdler, Pezzullo, Aaron, and me. The military situation in Nicaragua was viewed as a standoff. It appeared doubtful that Pastora could take or hold Rivas, and the fighting throughout the rest of the country reflected a rough balance.

Christopher briefed us on the discouraging debate at the OAS. Mexico, which had been the most antagonistic of the United States, was working with the Andean countries on a resolution that deleted the peace force and also omitted any reference to a cease-fire, a cessation of arms shipments, or any OAS involvement. Their objectives were to prevent any action by the United States and the OAS, force Somoza's resignation, and clear a way for the Sandinistas to take power. The Sandinistas had been successful in portraying the U.S. peace force proposal as a way to bolster Somoza, even though the first element of the proposal was his departure. Incredibly, this view took hold.

The U.S. proposal was dead; the issue for the SCC was whether to try to modify the Andean-Mexican proposal to permit the United States some authority to negotiate a transition in Nicaragua. The SCC agreed to pursue that route.

After the Friday breakfast, the talk of unilateral intervention had ended, except that both Brown and Vance put themselves clearly on record as opposing it. Both said that they would prefer to pursue multilateral mediation, but if necessary, the United States should pursue its own diplomatic-political strategy. The SCC discarded the peace force idea and accepted the State Department's "sequencing strategy"—after a new government was installed, the United States could help to support it while it opened negotiations with the Junta. Christopher and Vaky were authorized to explore this idea for a post-Somoza government with the Venezuelan Foreign Minister.

Brzezinski said that Jack Murphy had called the President the night before to tell him that Somoza was prepared to step down if he could receive assurances that the National Guard would be supported and the Liberal Party would be included in any post-Somoza government. The SCC discussed ways to keep the Guard from collapsing after Somoza left and agreed that a new Commander would have to be appointed and put in charge soon. When the subject was raised in the fall, the person who was recommended by many in and outside Nicaragua was Julio Gutiérrez, the former Guard General, who was now Nicaragua's Ambassador to Japan. U.S. Ambassador Mike Mansfield had spoken with him then. When he arrived in Tokyo for the Summit, Vance agreed to meet him and try to persuade him to return to the area, perhaps to Honduras or Venezuela.

The SCC also agreed that Somoza and Gutiérrez should be told that if Somoza stepped down, the United States would provide sufficient support to the National Guard to guarantee its stability during the transition period. (There was no discussion about either the magnitude or the kind of support that would be needed.) Bowdler would tell Somoza that. Finally, the SCC recommended that the President should again send messages demanding they stop their arms shipments to both Carazo, who appeared not fully in control, and to Torrijos, who appeared totally out of control. The President's decision to rule out a peace force had forced his advisers to focus on an alternative strategy, and the meeting was remarkable for the degree of consensus.

Christopher, Vaky, and I then went to the OAS to try to negotiate a satisfactory resolution. The Andean countries seemed initially eager to exclude the United States from the resolution, but they soon realized that their resolution was unlikely to pass without U.S. support. Christopher therefore worked with them and was able to insert several key passages in the resolution, including one that urged "member states to take steps that are within their reach to facilitate an enduring and peaceful solution of the Nicaraguan problem." The resolution did much else. It was unprecedented in calling for the "immediate and definitive replacement of the Somoza regime," which it declared "the fundamental cause" of the crisis. The resolution called for the "installation of a democratic government . . . [and] the holding of free elections as soon as possible."[14]

The resolution passed on June 23, 1979, by a vote of 17 for, 2 against (Paraguay and Nicaragua), and 5 abstentions. The resolution was far from what Vance had proposed, but considering the reaction by Mexico and the Andean countries, it at least did "permit constructive actions by the member countries." This was sufficient to permit the United States to negotiate a transition in Nicaragua legitimately.

After the OAS meeting ended and Carter had departed for the Far East, I completed a summary of the SCC meeting and the decision memorandum, and we cabled them to the President in Tokyo. On Sunday, June 24, we received a message that Carter approved all the recommendations of the meeting except that he was unwilling to offer support unconditionally to a post-Somoza National Guard. He decided that he would only offer such support if he determined that the transition government was legitimate, and he would judge that by whether it obtained support from other Latin American governments and from the Nicaraguan people. This June 24 decision by the President to make aid to a post-Somoza Guard conditional would be a crucial one.

The OAS resolution frightened Somoza. At 10:30 P.M. on the night of the passage of the resolution, several correspondents overheard Somoza on shortwave radio personally poll each of his military commanders in the field on their loyalty. Somoza condemned the OAS action as a "flagrant intervention into the internal affairs of Nicaragua," and asked his commanders if they were willing to fight with him to defeat the enemy. "I ask each of you to acknowledge," Somoza said, and then one at a time, each of the nineteen said: "Yes, sir, understood sir."[15] In a nationwide address that Sunday evening, he vowed to keep fighting, but in his memoirs, Somoza recalls his reaction differently. The defiance at the time was replaced in retrospect by sadness and the claim that he realized the OAS vote symbolized his end. He therefore wrote his resignation at that time and put it in his pocket for the appropriate moment.[16]

In Tokyo, Vance met with Gutiérrez and found him ready to return, but only after Somoza left and only if the Junta invited him to join. The report suggested that either Vance or Gutierrez did not understand the role he would need to play.

While Washington policy makers were preoccupied with the OAS, the Chargé of the U.S. Embassy in Managua had a pivotal meeting on June 24 with the leadership of the FAO—Rafael Córdova Rivas, Luis Sanchez Sancho, and Jaime Chamorro.

They expressed disappointment that the OAS resolution had given legitimacy to the FSLN. They had asked Alfonso Robelo to be the FAO's representative on the Junta, but as an organization, the FAO was still debating "whether to maintain its independent identity or to support the Provisional Government" in San José. Córdova and Sanchez were frank in their preference to maintain the FAO's independence, but they were seeking guidance and support from the United States. Although hinting that independence from the Provisional Government was preferable, the Chargé admitted that the United States did not have a position. This was an important opportunity that was lost because communications between the Embassy and Washington were poor, and the Embassy did not understand the debate in Washington well enough to know how to relate to it.[17]

Two Pillars

In order to hammer out a policy on Nicaragua, Brzezinski was asked by the President to remain in Washington for a few days after Carter departed. He convened an SCC meeting on Monday morning, June 25. Mondale attended along with Harold Brown and the usual cast. The Administration supported a strategy of trying to establish a second pillar of power that would be independent of Somoza and could then negotiate with the Sandinista Junta. Prior to the meeting, I briefed Brzezinski on my fears that State was slowly moving to a different strategy of accepting the Sandinista Junta as inevitable and trying to broaden and moderate it. To me, the question was not the breadth of the Junta but who controlled the military. If the Sandinistas were left with a monopoly on military power, the moderates in the Junta would be at the mercy of the Directorate.

The CIA updated us on the situation in Nicaragua, repeating their prediction of the previous week that Somoza had at least one more week. There was some discussion about whether there were Cuban advisers in Costa Rica, but the evidence was still uncertain. Brzezinski then posed the central question for the meeting: do we seek to widen and moderate the Junta, or create an alternative governing structure with an independent power base that would negotiate with the Junta? If the first option were chosen, the United States should encourage moderates to join the Junta; if the latter were chosen, we ought to try to discourage moderates from joining or endorsing the Junta and encourage governments to withhold recognition.

Christopher advocated pursuing both strategies simultaneously. We should begin talks with the Junta to moderate them and, at the same time, quietly try to negotiate the establishment of an Executive Committee, which could become an alternative source of power when Somoza left. This committee could ask General Gutiérrez to return and reform the National Guard. The United States could then call for a cease-fire, an arms embargo, and humanitarian assistance and urge both sides to negotiate with each other. If the United States could effectively work both strategies simultaneously, we would be well positioned to assist in the reconciliation process between the Sandinista Junta and the Executive Committee. Everyone agreed with this two-pronged strategy, even while accepting the chances for its success as about

50–50. David Aaron and I were concerned that the only way to encourage an Executive Committee at this time would be to offer some explicit assurances of help; otherwise, moderates would be vulnerable and fearful of joining. This issue was not addressed then.

Brzezinski summarized the consensus of the meeting to pursue both strategies—moderate the Junta while attempting to establish an Executive Committee—simultaneously. He would talk to Gutiérrez again when he reached Tokyo. Pezzullo would go to Managua to speak with Somoza and obtain his resignation, put together an Executive Committee, and work on ways to ensure the survival of the Guard. Bowdler would go to San José to talk to the Junta. At one point in the meeting, Mondale, who was attending his first SCC meeting on Nicaragua, asked where Somoza would go when he resigned. Brzezinski answered playfully: "We have a spot for him in Minnesota."

The main card the United States had to play was Somoza's resignation. Pallais and Murphy indicated that Somoza was prepared to resign under certain conditions, but the time had come to receive the answer directly. Pezzullo met with Somoza and John Murphy soon after his arrival at 4:30 P.M. on June 27. Somoza introduced himself as "a Latin from Manhattan," and Murphy as "a witness."[18] Pezzullo went straight to the point: "We don't see the beginning of a solution without your departure." Somoza said he was prepared to accommodate the United States, although he wanted guarantees that his country would not go Communist. Somoza said he had called the Nicaraguan Congress into session and was prepared to step down the next day, but Pezzullo asked him to put it off for a couple of days while he got "organized a little bit." Pezzullo assured him that one U.S. objective was to preserve the Guard in some form.

In my conversations that day with Vaky, I sensed a shift in his thinking toward a single strategy of trying to influence and broaden the Junta. I informed David Aaron, and he called a mini-SCC meeting the next day, June 28, at 8:00 A.M. Brzezinski had spoken with Julio Gutiérrez in Tokyo and had found his views unchanged since his conversation with Vance: he would only return to Nicaragua if invited by a new government. Those at the mini-SCC meeting understood the importance of someone of independent stature taking charge of the Guard soon. Therefore the group tried to think of how to encourage Gutiérrez to return before Somoza departed, without letting it appear that the United States was orchestrating his return. Somoza, who hated Gutiérrez, had learned of our interest in him and had already called him twice, letting him know that he could expose and undermine him if he wished.[19] One suggestion was to try to encourage Torrijos to invite Gutiérrez. Moss mentioned this to Torrijos, who said he liked the idea, but Moss does not know if Torrijos ever pursued it.[20] Another very serious problem was that as the war became more ferocious, the idea of permitting the survival of any part of the Guard became increasingly problematic.

A serious gap had opened between U.S. policy makers in Washington and policy implementers in Managua, though no one in Washington was aware of its breadth.

Pezzullo had a formidable task—obtaining Somoza's resignation, establishing an Executive Committee, preserving the Guard—but everyone had confidence in the new Ambassador. Larry Pezzullo was an unusual foreign service officer. The best officers, as a rule, are superb observers and reporters of politics in foreign countries; but few are political operators, and of these, fewer understand or appreciate the parameters of American politics as well as those of foreign governments. Pezzullo, who concealed his subtlety behind a blunt-sounding New York City accent, was one of those few. The Administration was so anxious for him to succeed and so confident in him that no one thought to ask whether he knew enough about the key factors in Nicaragua or whether the Embassy had enough capable staff to achieve these objectives.

The answers to these unasked questions were negative. When he arrived in Managua on June 27, he found an Embassy in "complete disarray." Since the sanctions had been imposed in February, the Embassy had been reduced to a very small size, and the officers were, with good reason, deeply concerned with the country's security as well as their own. The State Department had not informed them about the Administration's thinking or even its decisions. Their principal responsibility had been to organize evacuation flights for thousands of Americans and diplomats of other nations.[21] C-130s would fly to Montelimar, Somoza's small airfield on the Pacific coast, and the Embassy staff would organize convoys to drive the evacuees there.

Managua, to Pezzullo, was "like a war zone," with fighting in the streets. People were scared, tired, and uncertain of what would happen. Before his meeting with Somoza, Pezzullo decided to brief his staff quickly. They did not even know that Washington was focusing on Nicaragua. He assured them of Washington's attention but he was careful and selective in conveying information. A quick judge of people, Pezzullo sized up the principal members of the mission as either "nonsubstantive" or "unreliable." Many on the staff correctly perceived that Pezzullo did not trust them. Lt. Col. James McCoy, the Defense Attaché, recalls that many of the staff were uncertain or suspicious of Pezzullo.[22]

Until a new Deputy Chief of Mission arrived in two weeks, Pezzullo functioned as a one-man operator. Although he had had some brief contact with Nicaraguan affairs as Deputy Director of the Office of Central American Affairs from 1972 to 1974, he was unfamiliar with most of the leading political actors. There was obviously no time or opportunity to travel through the city or the country; indeed, the war made any travel perilous. He found himself negotiating more and more with Somoza in part because it was difficult and dangerous to arrange other meetings.

After meeting with Somoza on June 27, Pezzullo turned his attention to contacting people for the proposed Executive Committee. Had he arrived one or two days earlier, his prospects would have been better. Since their conversation with the Chargé on June 24, the FAO had been meeting regularly to decide whether to retain their independent status, which would have made them the ideal vehicle for the Executive Committee, or to offer their complete support and endorsement to the Provisional Government in San José. It was the same dilemma preoccupying the Carter Administration yet, tragically, there was little communication at this crucial moment because the embassy was weak and the State Department was concentrating on the OAS.

The FAO was bitter about the failure of the mediation and even more upset that the United States had hardly contacted them since the imposition of sanctions in February. On the day that Pezzullo met with Somoza, June 27, the FAO finally decided—after not hearing from the Embassy—to issue a communiqué: "The Junta, on which the FAO is represented, and which the FAO has supported and continues to support, constitutes the beginning of that democratic and pluralistic regime which must accede to power upon the fall of the Somocista government."[23] The Embassy staff had briefed Pezzullo on the moderates' mistrust, and the FAO statement implied that the space for a moderate alternative was closing rapidly. On June 28, after reading the FAO statement but before having had much opportunity to talk with moderates, Pezzullo cabled his quick assessment of the Executive Committee (ExCom) proposal: "After less than one day here, it is apparent that we have little if any chance of putting together an Executive Committee of any size." He recommended instead that Somoza turn power over to a member of Congress who would call for a cease-fire and form a Government of National Reconciliation.[24]

And yet this quick conclusion about the nonviability of the Executive Committee did not seem to be supported by the reports of his and others' conversations. On June 28, Pezzullo met with the Archbishop, who said that he would "convene his Presbyterian Council to come up with some names and ideas" for a transitional government. The Archbishop said that he doubted the FSLN would accept the idea, but according to Pezzullo, he "did not assert it would not work."[25]

The next day Pezzullo met with Ismael Reyes, the president of the Red Cross, who "appeared fascinated by the idea and viewed it [the Executive Committee] as a noble effort." Reyes said the proposal "would benefit from Andean or Central American sponsorship," but he would not commit himself to participating because there were "too many unknowns." Because he thought Somoza would leave before July 4, Pezzullo guessed that the committee could not be put together in time.[26]

The same day, the Director of Central American Affairs in the State Department met with Arturo Cruz, a member of the Group of Twelve, who had just arrived in Washington after a trip to San José. Cruz said that a broadened Junta was not the answer since the question was who had the guns? He supported the idea of a "neutral force [to] stand temporarily between the National Guard and the Sandinistas." Cruz said that the FSLN, with whom he had just met in Costa Rica, wanted to replace the National Guard with its popular militia, but he believed "that a compromise can possibly be found providing a role for the less-tainted elements of the present Guard."[27]

Although State was persuaded by Pezzullo's conclusion that an ExCom was not viable, the NSC gave more credence to the reports from his conversations as well as the one with Cruz that it was still possible, provided the United States offered clear assurances. Anxiety and urgency underlay both perceptions: State felt that the momentum was shifting toward the Junta in San José, and valuable time was being lost to influence it. NSC agreed that time was running short, and that this was all the more reason to do what was necessary to implement the ExCom idea. NSC feared that the lack of commitment by State to the ExCom idea would doom it, while State did not want to commit itself to a strategy that it judged would fail.

As in the fall, the issue was not seen this clearly at the time; indeed, it was perceived largely through interacting suspicions. Both sides felt the other was wasting valuable time pursuing a chimera. The issue that divided the government—really State from NSC—in the spring was whether to accept an FSLN victory as inevitable and adjust to that, or to believe that nothing is inevitable until it happens. When the inevitable is desirable, it is a pleasure to expedite its occurrence. When the inevitable—or rather the increasingly probable—is undesirable, then either one modifies objectives, as the State Department was doing, or one accelerates the search for alternatives, however unlikely, as the NSC was doing.

The mini-SCC meeting on June 28 decided not to decide; Pezzullo should continue to pursue the two tracks. Aaron and I agreed that the Administration had reached a crossroads; if we failed to make a clear decision, we would have to acquiesce to an inevitable Sandinista victory. We therefore wrote a memorandum describing the choice that the United States faced for Brzezinski to give to the President in Tokyo. We felt that the State Department's strategy of broadening the Junta missed the point. If Nicaraguan history contained any lessons, the key issue would be who had the guns. A strategy that offered the government to the Sandinistas would leave the democrats with no alternative source of power. The Executive Committee idea, though still a long shot, was the only viable option for preventing a total Sandinista victory. To induce moderate leaders to join such a committee and give it any hope for success, the United States would have to provide some assurances—physical, financial, and political. That was the choice.

State also sent a cable to Vance. Their main argument was that the momentum was shifting to the Junta, and the Executive Committee was not viable. State wanted to avoid any action that could antagonize the San José Junta, which knew of U.S. efforts to set up an alternative government and did not like it. If the United States demonstrated a sincere interest in working with the Junta, it would reap the benefits when the Junta came to power.

Brzezinski agreed with his staff, and Vance with his, and the two debated the issue in Tokyo. Aaron's cables and phone calls had made Brzezinski feel that the situation was "fast deteriorating." He met the President at the U.S. Embassy residence in Tokyo. Carter was preoccupied with "a very ugly confrontation [with] the Europeans." "This was not a time," Carter recalled, "when I wanted to forget about economic summit matters and spend a lot of time on Central America." Carter decided he wanted "to talk with Torrijos and see how the Central American leaders size up the situation," before making a decision. He recalled that he "wanted the Junta and/or Executive Committee to be representative of all democratic factions and friendly to the other democracies (Costa Rica, Venezuela, and Colombia) and Panama." He also thought Torrijos might be helpful in implementing any new decisions.[28]

In the afternoon of June 29, Aaron chaired a mini-SCC meeting to preserve as well as to develop some options for the President to consider in advance of his meeting with Torrijos. Aaron criticized a cable that State had circulated to U.S. embassies summarizing policy in a way that made it appear that the United States was pursuing a single track—to negotiate with the Junta—rather than the two tracks approved by the President. Pezzullo had been pursuing the Executive Committee strategy for only twenty-four hours, and had found some interest. It was too soon to abandon the strategy.

Vaky tried to turn the issue around and insisted that the question had become how to stop the fighting. This was the first time in a year of NSC meetings that anyone had suggested the central U.S. objective was something other than preventing a Sandinista victory. Christopher agreed with Vaky, and said we would be missing an important opportunity to moderate the FSLN if we didn't try to work with them now. His opinion was that economic aid after the revolution would be the main source of U.S. influence. Vaky said the Executive Committee idea was not viable; the time had come to choose which side of the street we wanted to work.

Aaron restated the Administration's initial objective, but sidestepped a debate by saying that the SCC had a responsibility not to reduce the President's options before his meeting with Torrijos. Christopher agreed to ask Pezzullo to continue looking for leadership in the Guard and for an Executive Committee or, if necessary, a single transition figure.

On June 30, Pezzullo responded to the questions the mini-SCC posed for him with two critical analyses. First, with regard to the military situation, he concluded that "the National Guard remains a strong fighting force, though somewhat enfeebled by shortages of essential material." He wrote that there was a "better than even chance" that "we can preserve a reorganized and reconstituted National Guard."[29] On the Executive Committee, he wrote that the key people would not join it "without greater assurances, one of the most important [of which] would be some tangible evidence that a reconstituted National Guard would stand firm and support them."[30]

At this time, the FSLN was working overtime to project an image of moderation. Alfonso Robelo and Alfredo César wrote the "Program of the Government of National Reconstruction," which, to their surprise and delight, the FSLN embraced.[31] The program described all the human rights that would be enjoyed by the people of the new Nicaragua. Two items omitted in the plan were who would control the military and who would guarantee respect for human rights. After forty-five years of the Somozas, the moderate leadership still had not discerned the sources of Somoza's power; the Sandinistas had.

The moderate members of the Junta never discussed who would lead the new army, or whether or how the Junta would command it. "We were totally blind to anything other than overthrowing Somoza," recalled Robelo. This was confirmed by César, who became Secretary of the Junta. They also ignored the United States when it proposed the Executive Committee or the appointment of a new Guard Commander. Robelo said he "never focused on military power." He admits that

Bowdler "tried to get me to do that, but I was too wary of being called a friend of the gringos, and so didn't do it."

On June 28, the *New York Times* disclosed the four parts of the U.S. plan: (1) the resignation of Somoza; (2) the appointment of a constitutional Junta (distinct from the FSLN Junta) by the Nicaraguan Congress; (3) the immediate appointment by that Junta of a broadly based provisional government made up of distinguished Nicaraguans (the Executive Committee); and (4) immediate contact between the provisional government and the FSLN Junta to form "the most widely based provisional regime possible." Public disclosure sabotaged this plan and strengthened the FSLN's defenses against a U.S.-sponsored government. The next day, the Junta, FAO, and COSEP all publicly rejected "the U.S. plan." They reiterated support for the FSLN Junta and said they would not participate in any competing administration.[32] From then on, the Junta, and of course the FSLN, insisted on eliminating the middle steps and transferring power from the Congress directly to itself.

Vaky called me several times on June 30 and tried to convince me to abandon the Executive Committee idea and move to a single track. There was no doubt that the *New York Times* story had hurt the prospects for an ExCom, perhaps fatally, but I questioned whether one could realistically expect to win over the military leaders of the Sandinistas in the last days of their revolution after they had been fighting U.S. imperialism for two decades. As long as there was any possibility of placing a buffer between them and exclusive power, should we not reach for it? Expanding the Junta seemed like an exercise in absurdity because the FSLN would decide what, if anything, the Junta would do. Moreover, that same day we received Pezzullo's cable that the Guard and the ExCom were viable if the United States provided assurances. Vaky argued that the Executive Committee was not feasible, and we were losing time.

After a conversation with Somoza on June 29, Pezzullo gave visas to his entire entourage. Murphy called Christopher to tell him that Somoza was ready to hear from the United States about when the plan should be set in motion. Unfortunately, there was not much of a plan left.

The Torrijos Conspiracy

When he was informed that President Carter had asked to see him secretly in Washington, Torrijos said he felt like a schoolboy being called to the principal's office for a scolding. And yet Carter, who had kept his word and paid a heavy political price for new and just Canal treaties, was one of the few people Torrijos trusted.[33] Torrijos had always wanted to work with Carter in Central America, but never knew how. This visit, he thought, might present such an opportunity.[34]

On the flight from Central America to Florida, Torrijos drank pink champagne as if it were water and he had been in the desert for weeks without liquid. As it turned out, he crashed minutes before the plane landed. Flat on his back and filling the small aisle in the jet, Torrijos' companions decided to create a diplomatic incident to keep the Customs and Immigration authorities from boarding the plane and seeing Panama's Maximum Leader in such a state. Gabriel Lewis bounded off the plane, and angrily insisted on calling the White House to protest the insulting behavior of the officials. He demanded an apology. Unaware of the specific circumstances, I apologized and asked local officials to expedite the trip.[35]

On July 2, the eve of Torrijos' trip, Bowdler, Pezzullo, and Moss returned from Central America for a long, sober SCC meeting followed by a meeting with the President to prepare for the discussions with Torrijos. The SCC, and the subsequent meeting with Carter, resolved the debate over the two tracks that had begun at the Deputy level. The State Department position prevailed, although not completely. The major thrust of U.S. policy would be to moderate the Junta rather than establish an Executive Committee.

At this SCC meeting, everyone was first brought up to date on events and the evolving views in the region. Turner explained that morale was beginning to slip in the National Guard as ammunition was running out. Bowdler said that both Torrijos and Carazo supported a cease-fire with both sides standing in place. Both wanted Somoza to leave but, according to Bowdler, neither wanted a Sandinista takeover. Their deeds impugned, if not belied, their words, but Moss confirmed that Torrijos believed anything was negotiable with the FSLN, even a possible fusion with the Guard.

Pezzullo said that Somoza was ready to go and was only waiting to hear of the date and the details. Although he thought the Executive Committee was viable two days before, at this meeting, Pezzullo called it impractical because there was only a handful of moderate leaders in Managua, and none of them had any confidence in the United States, nor did they want to be associated with a U.S. plan. Without clear support from the United States, all believed they would become victims. Pezzullo insisted there would not be a power vacuum after Somoza's departure, because the Guard would be turned over to a new individual. Some confidence-building measures would be necessary, however. Bowdler also tried to reassure the SCC and described the Sandinistas as an undisciplined fighting force. If the new Guard Commander had assurances of U.S. support, and if the foreign ministers of several Andean countries flew to Managua when Somoza departed in order to lend stability to the arrangement and give the Guard time to cohere, then a stable transition was possible.

Harold Brown, Brzezinski, and Aaron were skeptical that a transition could be managed or that the Sandinistas would hold to a bargain. As the discussion evolved, Vaky and Christopher advocated that the United States try to influence the Junta, and avoid becoming associated with the Guard for fear this would prolong the civil war. In response to a question from Brown about what would keep the new government from falling victim to the leftists, Vaky suggested that their desire for economic assistance was a great source of leverage.

Brzezinski, Brown, and Aaron feared that such a strategy might very well leave the Guard decapitated and demoralized. They thought that U.S. interests in a stable post-Somoza environment would be better served by focusing on ways to support the Guard. After more than two hours of debate, Brzezinski summarized the discussion in terms of four points of consensus: (1) the United States would actively seek a candidate for Guard Commander and gain Torrijos' acceptance as a first step toward gaining wider support for the new leader in the region; (2) the United States would seek to replace the Junta with a different one that included: Sergio Ramírez, Alfonso Robelo, Ismael Reyes, Mariano Fiallos (the Rector of the Leon branch of the National University), and the new Guard Commander; (3) the President would insist that Torrijos halt the arms flow or the United States would reserve the right to resupply the Guard; and (4) after Somoza's departure, the United States would provide humanitarian aid to help stabilize the new government.

These four points concealed the sharp division between the two strategies that were debated at the meeting. During the discussion, State appeared to be on the defensive, but the opposite was the case. Brzezinski suspected that their position was closer to that of the President's, and when he failed to persuade Christopher, he decided to concede the fundamental point—that we would aim to influence the Junta of the Provisional Government rather than try to establish a separate pole of power. However, Brzezinski conceded that point at the cost of proposing a plan that was unrealistic, and State did not object because they knew they had won their point.[36] The President was not well served by this compromise, and he was the first one to realize it.

In the afternoon, Harold Brown and the representatives from State and NSC met with the President to discuss the SCC's recommendations and propose a strategy for the meeting with Torrijos. Brzezinski was generally very effective in summarizing a complex meeting concisely and in a way that highlighted the critical issue even when it had not been obvious to its participants. This was not the case that afternoon, however. His summary of the SCC was abbreviated and unhelpful to the President, who began interrupting and questioning him.

Carter quickly grasped the unreality of the plan, and was impatient and sharp in his questions. How can you expect to negotiate with the Sandinistas a total revision of the Junta that virtually excluded them, he asked? State accepted his point, and suggested as an alternative adding the names to an expanded Junta, which would also include the Commander of the Guard. Brzezinski tried to focus the discussion on the connection between the Junta and the armed forces. Carter understood the importance of having a moderate on the Junta, which would have effective control over the army. "We don't want Ortega to be Minister of Defense," Carter said.

Brzezinski realized that he failed to persuade the President and so he retreated to his apocalyptic scenario, warning Carter that what was

> at stake is not just the formula for Nicaragua, but a more basic matter, namely whether in the wake of our own decision not to intervene in Latin American politics, there will not develop a vacuum, which would be filled by Castro and others. In other words, we have to demonstrate that we are still the decisive force in determining the political outcomes in Central America and that we will not permit others to intervene.[37]

Brzezinski's anxiety had caused him to abandon his forward-looking vision of the region in favor of a traditional "spheres of influence" approach. He knew the President was unsympathetic to his definition of the crisis or of the U.S. role and noted in his diary that "the State Department types were absolutely delighted by this exchange. One of them even grinned openly. My own judgment is that we are about to produce for ourselves another Iran but close to home."

Pezzullo was impressed by Carter. As he later recalled:

What struck me was the realism of the man. Carter seemed to sense just natively that the amount of things open to us was very limited. We didn't have a wide array of options. We couldn't demand anything; we couldn't really drive things in any direction. The most we could do was play a role and hopefully with deftness . . . of positive influence. That struck me because I think the tendency of policy planners in Washington is to assume that the United States can do more than it really can. . . . Carter instinctively realized that we had a marginal role to play, but we can play an intelligent one.[38]

Carter had both a different picture of the crisis and a different strategy than Brzezinski's. He wanted to preserve the Guard and secure a base for the moderates in the new government, but he believed the Guard would only survive if it were viewed as legitimate in Nicaragua and among a few of the democratic governments in the area. The President was the first person in his Administration to raise the issue of the legitimacy of the Guard as a key factor in its viability and in determining U.S. policy. Carter said that if Torrijos, Pérez, Carazo, or the Andean leaders were willing to accept Gutiérrez or Guerrero (two names of Guard Commanders that were being considered), then Carter would be willing to send help to the Guard. His purpose in bringing Torrijos to Washington was to try to capture international legitimacy for a reconstituted Guard. Turner suggested that the United States could support them indirectly through Israel, but Carter said that he would have no objection to doing it directly and overtly, provided it was legitimized by some of these countries.

Carter wanted to avoid a repetition of the defeat of the peace-keeping proposal at the OAS. As far as tactics, Carter said that he would try to make his plan appear as if it were just an endorsement of elements suggested by Pérez and Carazo. He understood that if the plan looked as if it had been made in the United States, that would be, in his words, "the kiss of death."

In effect, Carter adhered to his multilateral strategy—at this point, for practical reasons as much as for principle. If other countries chose to help the Provisional Government rather than try to preserve the Guard, then U.S. support for the Guard would guarantee a prolongation of the war, while allying the United States to an indefensible organization. Carter's motives were somewhat different from that of the State Department: he believed in a multilateral approach or at least one in which the United States would not confront the Latin Americans, whereas State wanted to try to influence the Junta. Nonetheless, Carter, as Brzezinski suspected, ended up closer to the recommendations of the State Department. He was unwilling to provide prior and unconditional assurances to the Guard or to an Executive Committee. Without such assurances, the ExCom was a dead letter. Carter preferred to try to influence the Provisional Government by expanding the Junta to include the leader of the Guard rather than to establish a separate political-military pole of power. He wanted to put the United States alongside its Latin American friends rather than in a position where it might confront them.

Overnight, several of us refined the specific plan, and at 9:00 A.M. on July 3, Carter presented it to Torrijos in the Oval Office. Carter was relaxed but firm with Torrijos. He explained that the reason for the invitation was because he knew Torrijos better than others in the region and the two of them had worked together well on another exceptionally difficult task—the Canal treaties. He then described a seven-part plan as if it were really developed by Pérez and Carazo, and just endorsed by Carter. (This was not entirely disingenuous, as the Administration had incorporated their views and those of others as it drafted the plan.) The seven parts were:

1. Agreement between Panama, United States, Costa Rica, and Venezuela on the specific names that should be suggested to expand the San José Junta.
2. Agreement on the Director of the Guard in Nicaragua during the transition. Two suggestions were Gutiérrez and Guerrero. The Commander should be on the Junta and perhaps serve as Minister of Defense.
3. The Junta would agree to a ceasefire, a standstill for the two military forces, no reprisal, and a merger of military forces when peace is restored.
4. No arms would be transferred to the FSLN or to the Nicaraguan government during this period.
5. The United States would ensure Somoza's departure and would organize a humanitarian aid program.
6. On Somoza's departure, the Nicaraguan Congress would name a President who would serve "for a brief time" (1–2 days; although Brzezinski later said "no more than 10 days"). The President would be someone independent like Fiallos or Reyes, and he would call for a cease-fire and would name the Commander of the Guard.
7. The new President would then resign and transfer power to the Junta, which in turn would organize elections.

After describing this plan, Carter tried to lighten the conversation for a moment by asking Torrijos whether it was satisfactory to him for Somoza to leave. Torrijos became animated, calling it the best thing that could happen to the world. He compared the plan, which he described as good, to taking a screw out of a DC-10 while the plane was flying. "The trick," he pointed out, "is to keep the plane flying." Torrijos insisted that it was very important that the plan not fail.

Both agreed that Torrijos would be the main exponent of the plan, and the United States would take a back seat, supporting and endorsing the proposals put forth by others at the appropriate time. However, though Carter agreed to a low public profile, he told Torrijos that the United States would remain involved in the

Omar Torrijos, head of Panama, told Carter: "Somoza is like the screw in a DC-10. The trick is to keep the plane flying after the screw comes out." Panamanian participants (left): Panama's Ambassador to the U.S. Gabriel Lewis (top): Torrijos (third from the top): and Manuel Antonio Noriega (bottom): On the U.S. side (right, from top): the author, Vice President Walter Mondale, Vance, Carter, Brzezinski, Todman, and U.S. Ambassador to Panama William Jorden.

transition. The United States, however, would try to influence events in Nicaragua, as it had many times since withdrawing troops in the 1930s, without using its hands.

Carter asked Torrijos if the Sandinistas would accept the plan. Torrijos said that he thought they would, but "I'll need a few hours to sell the list to them." He also gave Carter "a high percentage of assurance" of stopping the arms flow. Though Carter pressed him to confirm the details, Torrijos avoided them, saying that what mattered was the "attitude" and the flexibility of those who were negotiating. Carter stressed the importance of agreeing on a new Guard Commander, saying that he understood that Pérez and Carazo thought Gutiérrez would be the best. Torrijos was vaguely agreeable. Carter concluded the hour-long meeting by telling his staff to answer any additional questions Torrijos might have about the plan, and by asking Torrijos to offer advice on the content and timing of Carter's future public statements.

Torrijos was unfamiliar with either the names or the details involved in a possible transition. It appeared that he had not thought about anything beyond Somoza, and it was questionable whether he was doing this even after his conversation with Carter. As Torrijos thought out loud about the plan, his ideas coalesced around the emotions and the feelings of the Nicaraguan and Central American people. He became excited, calling the plan spectacular, indicating that it could transform the feelings of Nicaraguans overnight from hatred of the United States to love. He also spoke genuinely and with great warmth of his own relationship with Carter. It was clear that Torrijos wanted the Carter plan to succeed; what was less clear was whether he would remember the plan by the time he returned to Panama. He took no notes.

After his meeting with Carter, Torrijos spent the rest of the day with Brzezinski, Christopher, members of the State Department, and myself to work out the details of the proposal. But he continued to avoid details. Occasionally, one of his advisers, Marcel Salamín, a shrewd Panamanian leftist whose sympathies with the Sandinistas were more transparent than his motives, would mention that the Guard was totally discredited. It might be possible to integrate some Guard officers into a Sandinista army, but the idea of fusing the two armies was impractical. In discussing names of possible Guard leaders, Salamín mentioned the names of people who had defected from the Guard to join the Sandinistas. Torrijos did not comment on this point, but at other times his remarks suggested that he viewed the preservation of the Guard as of great importance.

Salamín's comments presaged the second crucial issue the Administration would address in Somoza's final month. The first issue—the Executive Committee or the Junta—was decided in favor of the latter. The second issue—whether to work for a fusion between two separate armies or a merger *under* the umbrella of the Sandinista Army—was never debated as openly or clearly as the first, but a similar dynamic—fed by the momentum of events in Nicaragua—led again to the latter option.

Torrijos returned to Central America exuberantly optimistic that he could sell the plan. Bowdler stopped in Guatemala to try to persuade Col. Inocente Mojíca, who was the Nicaraguan Defense Attaché there, to return to Managua to start to rebuild his contacts. Bowdler was unsuccessful. Vaky flew to Venezuela, Colombia, and the Dominican Republic. This was the beginning of the last attempt by the United States to piece together a more moderate Nicaraguan government.

Through June to early July, the position of the U.S. government toward Nicaragua was transformed and driven by events and fears as the possibility of a Sandinista takeover increased. The United States searched desperately for a "third force," an Executive Committee to serve as a buffer between the National Guard and the Sandinistas, but few moderates were left in Managua to consider it, and they would only do so if the United States provided the kind of unconditional assurances that Carter was unwilling to give in the absence of some international support. The moderates in Nicaragua finally abandoned hope of an alternative to the Sandinistas just when the United States was really prepared to develop one.

Though the United States thought it had stepped into the role of arbiter, it had not. Decisions on the future government of Nicaragua were being made in Washington, but they were not being implemented anywhere. Other decisions would matter more.

Denouement

Things which you do not hope,
Happen more frequently
Than things which you do hope.

TITUS MACCIUS PLAUTUS

DURING THE EARLY MORNING HOURS of July 4, after what seemed like only one hour of sleep, I was awakened by a telephone call from the White House Situation Room. The Duty Officer informed me that two letters had just arrived at the White House for President Carter from the Embassy of Nicaragua. I asked for an update on the fighting in Nicaragua, and was informed that the National Guard was being beaten badly. Another report indicated that Somoza would call the Nicaraguan Congress into session that day.

The Duty Officer told me that Brzezinski wanted an immediate analysis of the letters and a recommendation to bring to the President during his intelligence briefing that morning. Exhausted, but moving on spurts of adrenalin, my mind raced through hundreds of permutations of what the two letters might contain. I dressed and drove to the office. When I arrived, the Duty Officer handed me the letters as if they were heavy with the weight of history. I opened them anxiously and read them. They were two "July 4th Birthday Greetings," one from Anastasio Somoza and the other from the Nicaraguan Ambassador, Guillermo Sevilla-Sacasa. The Ambassador was famous for littering the White House with these cards. I wondered whether these reflected a machine that didn't turn off, a grotesque joke, or a metaphor heralding the last act of a Pirandellian play.

Translating the Plan into Panamanian

The first report that Torrijos sent us on his negotiations was upbeat. He indicated that he was moving on several fronts simultaneously, and that Carazo and Andrés Pérez liked the plan. This was the last such report we received from Torrijos, though his efforts continued. Needless to say, he did not complete his mission in a few hours.

The issue that became the biggest obstacle was in many ways the least important, the expansion of the Junta. The two moderates on the Junta—Violeta de Chamorro and Alfonso Robelo—were the most vigorous in their opposition to expanding it, for fear their own power would be diluted. Moreover, to compensate for their bourgeois background, they tried to sound more defiant and revolutionary than the Sandinistas.

The FSLN Directorate consulted with Castro, who indicated that he saw no problem with expanding the Junta.[1] (It is interesting that the FSLN felt the need to consult with Castro on this issue; it is more interesting that he had to tell them that the Junta did not matter.) The Sandinistas repeatedly showed their willingness to compromise on the issue of the Junta's composition, while the moderates were intransigent.

The public persona of the moderates and the Marxists therefore reversed. The Directorate tried to sound as moderate as it could, privately reassuring everyone while remaining in the background of a Provisional Government, which issued a "Plan of Government" and position papers as if it were a think tank or a Presidential commission. The combined impact of these two sounds—of militant moderates and moderate Marxists—was of a Nicaraguan government-in-exile, demonstrating its pluralistic character to the world.

By July 8, the United States had obtained ostensible support for the plan from the Latin American governments, but the Junta (by then called the Provisional Government) still blocked it. That evening the Junta spokesman Miguel D'Escoto called an aide to a member of Congress and asked that a letter be conveyed from the Provisional Government (PG) requesting a meeting with President Carter.

The *New York Times* reported the next day that the "fundamental obstacle to a negotiated settlement is still disagreement over the future role of the National Guard." In fact, despite herculean efforts by many, there seemed to be little progress on anything.

Brzezinski convened an SCC meeting at 5:00 P.M. on July 9 to review the negotiations. There was no progress on either the expansion of the Junta or the naming of a new Guard Commander. Gutiérrez had been ruled out since he would not return to the region. Panama continued to put forward names suggested by the FSLN, notably Bernardino Larios, the Guard officer who had been jailed after an abortive coup in August 1978. When he escaped, he joined the FSLN. The Defense Department thought he was a good man, but he lacked command experience and any real following in the Guard. It suggested several other names, including Col. Inocente Mojíca, whom Bowdler and Pezzullo had met briefly in Guatemala. Brzezinski urged State and Defense to agree on a new Commander, but resolution of that question was connected with the issue of what assurances, if any, the United States could give a post-Somoza Guard.

State opposed any aid to the Guard while the war continued, but it agreed to permit the Defense Attaché in Managua to inform possible candidates for Guard Commander that the United States envisaged a possible role for a purged Guard and would try to undertake rapid humanitarian assistance in a manner that it hoped would stabilize the situation. The SCC also discussed the letter from the Junta and agreed to hold out a possible meeting with the Secretary of State as an incentive for the Provisional Government to accept nominations for the Guard Commander and the expanded Junta.

The Directorate and the Junta rejected the conditions for the meeting with the Secretary of State; their tactics increasingly resembled those of Somoza's during the mediation. They appeared to be playing for time. Ramírez later confirmed this: "When the Yankees pushed for two more members on the Junta, I judged they realized that the Guard was defeated [and this] was the only way that remained for them to influence events."[2] The underlying reason for the Sandinistas' momentum and the systematic weakening of the U.S. negotiating position was the rather sudden shift in the balance of military power. The Embassy was aware of this shift. On July 7, Pezzullo sent a telegram to the State Department indicating that "the GN [Guard] supply lines have been severely restricted whereas the FSLN has an open supply line." He estimated that the Guard would run out of ammunition "within less than two weeks." Since their only effective instrument for fighting was air power, Pezzullo wrote that "it would be ill-advised to go to Somoza and ask for a bombing halt," as the FSLN was advocating, unless the FSLN agreed to a cease-fire, which, he assumed, they would not do.[3]

Since the United States could not stop the flow of arms to the FSLN and would not send arms to the Guard, U.S. negotiators were playing poker against a stacked deck. Their "ace in the hole," the resignation of Somoza, had become a liability. After nearly a week of negotiations, Torrijos, Carazo, and Peréz had failed to achieve agreement on anything, even a cease-fire. As the negotiations bogged down, Torrijos backed away, and as Bowdler filled the vacuum, Torrijos let it be known that the plan was "American," not Panamanian.[4]

The issue that the FSLN watched most carefully was the National Guard. They argued that the Guard was unsalvageable as an institution and sought to discredit and subvert any proposal that would leave it intact. Costa Rican President Carazo agreed,[5] but Torrijos disagreed. According to Gabriel Lewis and Ambler Moss, Torrijos believed right up until the end—July 19—"that the Guard would be saved."[6] But it is not clear what Torrijos did to preserve the Guard, and the person who often represented him in the region, Marcel Salamín, believed the Guard would have to be dismantled.

In their meeting with Bowdler on July 10, the members of the Junta indicated that they expected power to be transferred directly to them; to assuage United States concerns about the Guard, they expressed a willingness to incorporate some reformed elements in a Sandinista army. Brzezinski and Aaron recognized this as a turning point—perhaps the last before a Sandinista victory—and called an SCC meeting at 5:00 P.M. on the same day. Before the meeting, Vaky called to tell me that he thought the Guard would not hold together, and that we should discard the illusion that it would.

Brzezinski opened the SCC meeting on July 10 by asking sarcastically whether, in the light of Bowdler's conversation with the Junta, the United States should be a willing or an unwilling tool for dismantling the Guard. The war appeared to be wearing down the Carter Administration as much as the Nicaraguans.

The United States decided to force the pace of events for two reasons: first, the killing in Nicaragua was weighing on the Administration. As Somoza let it be known that he was only staying until the United States indicated the circumstances of his departure, the weight grew heavier.[7] Second, as the Guard's arsenal and petroleum stocks shrank and the Sandinistas' stockpile seemed inexhaustible, the Administration began to fear a complete collapse of the National Guard, which would leave the FSLN beholden to no one and restrained by no one.

The SCC meeting on July 10 therefore decided to bring the crisis to a head. First, the United States would seek the support of Torrijos, Carazo, and Peréz in asking the Junta one last time to expand its membership to be more representative of the Nicaraguan population and to call publicly for a cease-fire, standstill of military forces, and free elections. In the absence of such steps, the United States would consider alternative approaches to facilitate a transition. The Administration had no idea what alternatives were available, but threats made in desperation are not generally inhibited by the absence of rational alternatives. Second, the United States, hopefully with Torrijos, Carazo, and Pérez, would press for a new Guard Commander. The United States would also pledge to supply humanitarian assistance through him and a group of prominent civilians as well as through the FSLN. Third, the United States would inform Somoza that it saw no reason for him to postpone his departure.

Because the limits on the ability of the United States to influence the post-Somoza period were apparent, there was a discussion about whether the United States should walk away from Nicaragua. As he had in a previous meeting, David Aaron argued that the United States should not play the role of midwife to a Sandinista military regime; let the others sort it out. Like Mondale, his mentor, Aaron had an acute sense of the political dimension of foreign policy issues. His concern anticipated the criticism leveled against the Carter Administration by Richard Nixon. At a press conference in Mexico City, after visiting the Shah of Iran, Nixon said that Carter shouldn't "grease the skids for our friends." Nixon also repeated Somoza's refrain, which Somoza's actions had almost made true, that the alternative to Somoza was a "Castro-type government." The choice, Nixon said, was "not between Somoza and somebody better, but between Somoza and somebody much worse."[8] But except for Aaron, those at the SCC, including Brzezinski, felt that the United States was already in so deeply that it had a responsibility to see the project through and try, in the post-revolutionary period, to reduce the chances of vindictive violence, and increase the chances of democracy.

Bowdler presented the SCC ultimatum to the Junta on July 11 at 6:30 P.M. in Puntarenas, Costa Rica, where the Junta had been meeting with Carazo, Peréz, José Figueres, and a number of other leaders from the region. The Junta responded, though not in the way the United States had hoped. The Junta's "Plan to Achieve

Peace" would transfer power from Somoza through the Nicaraguan Congress directly to the Government of National Reconstruction, which would be led by the Junta and which would then dissolve the Congress and the National Guard. All those in the Guard who had not committed crimes and wanted to leave would be permitted to do so; others who wanted to be incorporated into the Sandinista Army would be considered. The Junta also announced a Cabinet, which included appointments of Bernardino Larios, the National Guard defector, as Defense Minister; Tomás Borge, as Minister of the Interior; Arturo Cruz, as head of the Central Bank; and Miguel D'Escoto as Foreign Minister.

At the same time, D'Escoto told the press that the Junta's new proposal "appears to move them closer to American notions of proper terms for settling the civil war." Although the Junta's proposal demanded power to be handed to them in a single step, Karen DeYoung, a *Washington Post* reporter, described it as "the most conciliatory [decision] made by the prospective junta government to date," and the State Department, viewing the outcome as inevitable, called it "positive."[9]

With regard to concerns about human rights, pluralism, and an end to the violence, Peréz suggested that the Junta should respond to the OAS resolution of June 23 to replace Somoza with a letter affirming its commitment to free elections and other human rights.[10] On July 12, the Junta sent a letter to the OAS Secretary General with a copy of the plan and a request that the Secretary General forward both to the foreign ministers of the governments of the OAS. In the letter, the Junta sought support from the OAS by referring to the "historic" OAS resolution of June 23. The letter pledged "full respect for human rights" and invited the Inter-American Human Rights Commission to visit Nicaragua as soon as the new government was installed. The Junta promised to ensure an orderly and peaceful transition and avoid a "bloodbath." It invited the foreign ministers of OAS countries to participate in the transfer of power to the new government as a way of lending stability to the process. Finally, it committed the new government to "the first free elections that our country will have in this century," although it omitted the resolution's recommendation that these be "as soon as possible."[11] The human rights pledges were important as a baseline from which democrats could measure the direction of a future government.

Bureaucratic defeats affect people differently. Vaky had been worn down in the early fall by bureaucratic losses, but until the failure of the mediation, his response had been to repeat the same recommendation—"talk turkey" and impose sanctions. Brzezinski responded differently to his repeated failure to persuade the President to his views in June and July. Rather than repeat the same option, Brzezinski chose instead to start and end almost every meeting with an impassioned statement that the United States was sitting passively as a historical change was occurring in Central America. He convened an SCC meeting on July 13 and spoke "of the baton being passed from the United States to Cuba. It fills me with unease," Brzezinski said. "We must lean harder on the Latin Americans to recognize that their security is involved."

Of course this was where the Administration, including Brzezinski, had begun, and it was fitting that was where it ended up. Brzezinski himself had written of the need for change in Central America, for social justice and greater national autonomy, but when the change came, it took a form and followed leaders that were hostile to the United States. It was especially discouraging to the Administration that many friendly Latin American governments appeared to view the United States as a more serious security problem than the Sandinistas. The gap in perceptions was symbolized by the decision of the Costa Rican Congress on July 11 to demand the withdrawal of U.S. aircraft sent to Costa Rica for purposes of evacuating U.S. citizens in case of emergency. Carazo had approved the request on July 8, but the Congress rescinded his decision three days later. At the time, it appeared that the Costa Rican Congress was trying to embarrass Carazo as much, if not more, than the United States. In retrospect, there were probably many in Costa Rica who feared that the U.S. personnel stationed in the region might learn the full extent of Costa Rican arms trafficking.

Brzezinski believed that the National Guard was going to collapse unless there was outside intervention, and he knew the United States would not intervene. The basic problem, he said, was that the President will not intervene alone, and the Latin Americans will not join. The United States would not support the Guard, because Latin Americans would be on the other side. There was no choice. The conclusion was that a left-of-center government would emerge; the question was whether it would be "Castro-ite." When Christopher asked for a definition, Brzezinski said that a Castro-ite government would be one that supported Cuban and Soviet foreign policy and insurgencies abroad—for example, in El Salvador. The SCC meeting on July 13 ended with a consensus that Somoza must go, but disquiet as to what would follow. Vaky, trying to facilitate a decision to bring the war to an end, reassured his colleagues that the Guard might not collapse, and even if it did, many democratic governments had a stake in helping Nicaraguan democrats.

By force of habit, the SCC usually made recommendations, and on July 13 it made five, which the President approved. First, Pezzullo was instructed to give a list of potential Guard Commanders to Somoza and to talk to him about it. Second, Vance would send a letter to various foreign ministers in Latin America urging them to play a more assertive role to ensure that Nicaragua would have a pluralistic future. Third, to counter a statement of the Junta that negotiations had broken down with the United States, we would reiterate our interest in talks and Bowdler would continue to press for assurances that the transition would be smooth and as bloodless as possible. Fourth, Pezzullo would ask Somoza to depart soon. And fifth, because Pastora was considered more independent than the Directorate, a meeting with him was authorized to explore future possibilities for cooperation. The Administration had already done considerable work on developing a humanitarian assistance strategy to help Nicaragua in a postwar period. These were the first decisions taken in preparation for a Sandinista Nicaragua.

For about eight months, Carazo and Torrijos had been trying to arrange a meeting between Pastora and U.S. government officials, and each time the Administration, after much soul-searching, rejected the idea. U.S. officials wanted to learn more about the Sandinistas, and especially about some of the leaders, but feared that if the meeting became known, as it suspected it would, this would unwittingly discourage the moderate opposition in Nicaragua and shower legitimacy on the Sandinistas. Because this was contrary to U.S. objectives, the U.S. government postponed the decision. By late June, however, it was clear that the Sandinistas would be a major—perhaps the only actor in a post-Somoza government, and U.S. officials finally met with several Sandinistas, beginning with Pastora, who proved to be as suspicious of the United States as the United States was of him. The initial discussions were unproductive.[12]

Preserving the Guard:
The Formaldehyde Solution

A central issue since the crisis began was the composition of the military in a post-Somoza Nicaragua. Given the history of the country, one would have expected all actors to have given this issue their highest priority, but the only group that defined and doggedly pursued a strategy on it was the FSLN. The U.S. government considered the problem, but its decisions were never formulated into a coherent strategy and almost no decisions were implemented.

Beginning on September 12, 1978, at one of the first mini-SCC meetings, Aaron had asked Vaky whether he thought the loyalty of the Guard was transferable, and Vaky responded that he did. The next week there was some discussion about what was needed to assist the Guard in an interregnum, but only at a PRC meeting on October 31, 1978, did the United States define the preservation of the Guard as a central objective. After that, at almost every meeting, there was some discussion about ways to achieve this.

The Administration recognized the moral problems and risks associated with helping a Guard that was corrupt and tied to Somoza. But so too did the FAO, and it included a restructured Guard as part of its proposal in October 1978 for a post-Somoza government. The Guard's atrocities during the insurrection were mostly committed by the "special forces" of Tacho III, Somoza's son, and one sign that the population did not identify all of the Guard with these excesses was that the Sandinista Army accepted some Guardsmen into their forces after the triumph.[13] The Carter Administration also understood that when the civil war ended, the side that controlled most of the arms would be the one that shaped the political future of the country. For that reason, the Administration looked for ways to build a military base under a moderate civilian leadership.

In June 1979, in the light of the "final offensive" of the Sandinistas, the SCC declared as one of its highest priorities that a post-Somoza government should not have to rely exclusively on the military power of the FSLN. Vance and Brzezinski both met with Julio Gutiérrez, and most in the NSC believed these contacts were just the tip of a much larger effort by the U.S. Embassy in Managua and by the Pentagon in Washington.

In my role of trying to report on the implementation of NSC decisions, I often asked people in State and the Pentagon about their contacts with the Guard. Instead of reports, I received comments like the following: "There is, after all, a war under way in Nicaragua." "No candidate for Guard Commander is willing to come forward." "Somoza doesn't like that particular candidate." The latter comment sent me into a paroxysm of anger as no one on the NSC would have thought Somoza's views should be the determining criterion for selecting his successor. The State Department accepted the importance of this objective, and as late as July 13, Vaky assured the SCC that the "objective was not unattainable," yet it evidently attached low priority to it. The Defense Department was distraught about the direction of events but, inexplicably, did not pursue it. Most of those who attended the SCC meetings, including myself, were never informed and therefore unaware of the Embassy's personnel problems and assumed that a wide range of contacts were maintained with Guard officers at all levels, and that plans were well advanced to ensure the continuity of the Guard after Somoza.

The assumptions were totally false. Ever since Anastasio Somoza García had first secured control of the Guard in 1933, the Somoza family had sought advice, assistance, and identification with the U.S. military, but they made sure that U.S. advisers worked through them—or through designated officers—and not directly with the Guard. Somoza instructed all Guard officers to report any and all contacts with U.S. officials to him immediately. Much of the information that the United States obtained on the Guard was therefore provided by Somoza! After the sharp reduction in U.S. Embassy staff in February 1979, information on the Guard and much else declined even further.

State Department political officers infrequently surveyed the Guard because they were careful not to tread on the bureaucratic turf of the Defense Attaché. The principal mission of the Attaché was to obtain information on military capabilities and requirements—"order of battle" information. They had a "trained incapacity," in Robert Merton's phrase, to think about, let alone pursue, questions related to the Latin American military as a political institution.[14]

By and large, the U.S. government knew less about the Guard than Somoza knew about the U.S. government. Indeed, as U.S. Ambassador to Managua Pezzullo suspected, Somoza used his longstanding contacts with the Pentagon to keep track of what the Embassy and the U.S. government was doing.[15] Pezzullo was therefore selective in what he permitted the Defense Attaché, James McCoy, to know about U.S. policy. He was so selective that McCoy never learned of the crucial June 24 decision by President Carter to support the Guard after Somoza's departure *only if* it could demonstrate some domestic or international legitimacy.

From at least 1976 to July 1979, U.S. government officials had no independent, unauthorized contacts with Guard officers. McCoy said he would never arrange a meeting on his own. The Embassy would have to make a recommendation as a "country team" to Washington, and that was unlikely in his view, while Mauricio Solaun was Ambassador. After Solaun left, there were no initiatives from the Embassy whatsoever. Moreover, McCoy opposed such contacts because in his view, "it would have looked like we were trying to replace Somoza. This would have upset Somoza." Besides, Tacho III had already warned McCoy that he might have an "accident" if he contacted a Guard officer without clearing it with him first. McCoy's statement illustrates the chasm that separated the Embassy from Washington. Washington policy makers would never have been concerned about importuning Somoza, but would have been outraged had they learned that Somoza's son threatened an Embassy official.[16]

After numerous decisions by the SCC to expand contacts with Guard officers, McCoy finally received instructions. He arranged a meeting on July 10 with four or five lieutenant colonels and asked them what they thought a post-Somoza Guard would look like. The officers were dumbfounded at such a question; none had contemplated such a future. After the meeting, the officers immediately informed Tacho III, who called his father. Somoza, who was meeting with Congressman John Murphy at the time, placed a direct call to General Edward Meyer, Army Chief of Staff, and denounced McCoy in the strongest terms. Meyer then cabled the Embassy to inquire what McCoy was doing. The cable arrived even before McCoy had returned to the Embassy from his meeting.[17]

At the same time, Somoza called Pezzullo and asked him to meet immediately in the back room of a small restaurant. This was the first time that Pezzullo had met with Somoza alone, and Pezzullo was struck by how nervous and angry he was.[18]

"He let me have it as soon as he came into the restaurant," Pezzullo later recalled. "You're going to get me killed," Somoza barked at him.

"What are you talking about?" Pezzullo asked.

"McCoy was going around talking to people in the Guard about what it would be like after I'm gone," said Somoza.

Pezzullo recalled that Somoza's "point was that if the Guard knew he was leaving, they would kill him." Pezzullo failed to grasp the significance of Somoza's indiscretion, or the leverage Somoza had provided him. Instead, Pezzullo responded in kind, saying that Somoza could only blame himself for his interview with the *Washington Post*, in which he suggested he was about to leave.[19]

Somoza admitted he had been drunk and that the interview was a mistake, but Pezzullo then conceded: "O.K., I take your point. We shouldn't get too far out in front until we get everything decided." He then returned to the Embassy to tell McCoy not to talk to any people in the Guard without his prior authorization. Pezzullo did this because he didn't trust McCoy, who he thought was trying to figure out a way to resupply the Guard, and because he thought Somoza and his son were the keys to preserving the Guard. McCoy felt betrayed by this single encounter with the Guard, and reciprocated Pezzullo's distrust. In McCoy's view, Pezzullo's "objective was to put the Sandinistas in power," and McCoy could not understand that.[20] This failure to bridge the divide between U.S. diplomats and military officers made it virtually impossible to achieve the Administration's objective of maintaining a modified Guard for a post-Somoza regime.

Both Somoza and Tacho III agreed with Pezzullo that the Guard's senior officers—the "Somocistas"—would depart with them. The son was helpful in describing traits of the junior officers. Both suggested candidates for Guard Commander, and Pezzullo forwarded these to Washington or directly to Bowdler in San José to clear with the Junta. Because Washington was unfamiliar with most of the officers, Pezzullo and Bowdler were left to swing back and forth between the outgoing Somoza government that sought through this appointment to maintain its influence in Nicaragua and the incoming revolutionary government that wanted a figurehead to preside over the collapse of the Guard.

Because Pezzullo did not use the Defense Attaché and had no one else to rely on, the U.S. government had no independent channel to the Guard in the final month. This problem was not addressed because Pezzullo, by his own admission, did not consider the maintenance of the Guard a high priority, and he thought Somoza would handle it. Pezzullo, instead, focused on making sure that "the countdown for the plan" would work.[21] He also thought that the "plan" was the most effective way to ensure the preservation of the Guard. Once a cease-fire and a stand-down occurred, the Guard would win the time and space to redress its wounds. Pezzullo thought that after Somoza left, the FSLN forces, which were mostly brave young people with no training or military experience, were likely to disintegrate more quickly than the Guard.

The first irony was that the strategy relied on Somoza when his interests were clearly at odds with those of the United States. Second, the strategy depended on Somoza's judgment of people and Nicaragua's future—two subjects in which his previous track record was something less than stellar. Somoza had personally conveyed to Pezzullo his fears about what his officers would do if they knew he was leaving, but Pezzullo did not see this for what it was—an admission that Somoza's most important interest was to keep the Guard completely uninformed and unprepared for his departure. It is true that Somoza's long-term interests would have benefited from a Guard that remained strong after his departure, but Somoza's own political demise was the result, in part, of his chronic myopia. To the last minute, Somoza kept the Guard completely dependent on him, and under these circumstances, the Guard could not have been expected to cohere. In retrospect, Pezzullo believed: "If Somoza had told [the Guard] to tough it out, they could have, but he lied to them because he feared he would be killed."[22] To have relied on Somoza was a colossal mistake.

Even if the United States had developed and implemented a sound strategy to preserve some portion of the Guard, it is by no means certain that it would have succeeded. Not only had the corruption and atrocities of the Guard transformed some of the nation's youth into Sandinistas, it had embittered many Nicaraguans. Moreover, the incestuousness of the Guard and the Somoza family led to the question whether one could survive in Nicaragua without the other. For these reasons, a good strategy might not have succeeded; a non-strategy, however, was guaranteed to fail.

The Last Days

At 6:15 P.M. on July 13, Anastasio Somoza placed a telephone call to Jimmy Carter. Jim Wright, the House Majority Leader and a friend of John Murphy, had spoken with Vance, who assured him that the President would talk with Somoza. But after consulting with the President, Christopher, Somoza's nemesis, and I received the call. Somoza said that he wanted to come to Washington to explain to the President how he could contribute to the national security of the United States. He informed us that the Andean Pact was intervening in Nicaragua's internal affairs. Christopher promised to convey the message to the President, but at the same time he urged Somoza to meet with Ambassador Pezzullo.

Wright called Christopher the next day to complain that Vance had broken his word in not permitting Somoza to speak to the President. At Christopher's suggestion, Brzezinski spoke with Wright and explained the situation in Nicaragua and U.S. policy. When informed that the United States had asked Somoza to resign, Wright protested that asking a head of state to step down was extreme. Brzezinski explained that the circumstances were extreme, and the longer Somoza stayed in power the more ominous the outcome. He said that even staunch anti-Communist governments like Brazil had broken relations with Somoza. Like Brzezinski, Wright was uneasy about the change that was coming, but he agreed that the American people would not support intervention to preclude it. Wright was essentially playing back to the Administration the arguments for not overthrowing Somoza that it had found persuasive in the fall. Circumstances had indeed changed since then.

In San José, Bowdler and U.S. Ambassador to Costa Rica Marvin Weissman were preoccupied with the possibility of a "paredon"—lining people up against the wall for executions as Bowdler had seen in Cuba after Castro came to power. They encouraged the Junta to be explicit about how they would implement guarantees of safe haven for those who wanted to leave the country, and they succeeded in reaching an agreement that involved the Church and the Red Cross. This may have been the one most important and tangible achievement of the United States in the final month of negotiations.

Suspicious of U.S. intentions, the Junta turned to an old Somoza trick of trying to make it appear that the United States supported them. Their purpose was to reassure the international community and advertise their legitimacy. After a meeting with Bowdler, Sergio Ramírez told the New York Times that "there is no point of disagreement between us." Miguel D'Escoto said that Bowdler had told them: "You are the government of Nicaragua."[23] Neither statement was accurate, but at this late stage there was no incentive for the United States to deny them. This was not the only tactic that D'Escoto and Ramírez had learned from Somoza.

Somoza was still worried about the Guard. He had assured his officers that military aid would arrive after he left, despite repeated statements to the contrary by Pezzullo.[24] The night of July 13, he decided to make one last effort to marshal support for the Guard, and flew to Guatemala. President Romeo Lucas García had been an important source of his arms, via transshipment, but that had stopped. Somoza asked Lucas to bring together the other military leaders of Central America for two purposes: to discuss the possibility of intervention to help the Guard at the last moment; or to obtain a pledge of a planeload of supplies for the Guard to arrive after Somoza left. At a minimum, he hoped to obtain a statement of political solidarity that could reassure the Guard.[25] In the middle of the night, the U.S. government learned of Somoza's trip and of the possibility of Central American intervention under CONDECA (the Central American Defense Organization). The governments were not inclined to intervene on behalf of Somoza, but the United States was asked its view. Brzezinski phoned me at 1 am to ask my view. We were both distraught that the Sandinistas seemed poised to take power, but agreed that Central American intervention would be a mistake. The United States indicated that it would oppose such intervention.[26]

In frequent conversations with Somoza, Pezzullo had developed a plan that he thought would work for the transition. Bowdler negotiated the same points with the Junta. The script went as follows. Somoza would resign from the Presidency and the Guard. He and his entourage—family, all the generals, and most of the colonels—would then fly to the United States. A new Chief of Staff, whose name would be approved by the Junta, would be appointed. The Nicaraguan Congress would accept Somoza's resignation and appoint a new President, who would meet at 8:00 A.M. at the Camino Real Hotel at the airport with a delegation of representatives from the Junta, the Directorate, Ambassador Bowdler, and Archbishop Obando y Bravo. The delegation would have arrived by plane from Costa Rica. The President would announce an immediate cease-fire and a standing-in-place of the two armies.

The Archbishop would then deliver a speech, declaring an end to the war. He would also seek to reassure Nicaraguans that both sides had pledged not to undertake any reprisals and to respect sanctuary in the churches and in Red Cross facilities. The Junta would discuss the political issues and the formal transfer of power with the President, and the new Commander of the National Guard would discuss the details of the cease-fire and a fusion of forces with the Directorate. Within 72 hours, power would be transferred formally from the new President to the Junta.

On July 12, Somoza decided that Francisco Urcuyo Maliaños, the speaker of the lower house of the Nicaraguan Congress, would be the next President. Urcuyo was a physician in his mid-60s, and, according to Pallais, was chosen because of his loyalty. Pezzullo, in his words, "didn't know Urcuyo from a hole in the wall." On July 14 and 15, Pezzullo discussed the scenario step by step with Somoza and Urcuyo. After the second meeting, Pezzullo asked his new Deputy Chief of Mission, Thomas O'Donnell, to meet again with Urcuyo to make sure that he understood the plan. Urcuyo was silent in these meetings. When asked whether he accepted the plan, he was evasive, saying that he could not commit himself since he was not yet President.[27]

Urcuyo recalls his meetings with Pezzullo and Somoza, but says that the plan called for him to stay in power for "a reasonable amount of time, six or seven months." Then he would hand power to a democratic junta, which would call elections. He did not consider the Junta in San José "democratic." After his second meeting with O'Donnell at the Hotel Intercontinental on July 15 at 6:00 P.M., Urcuyo was called across the street to "the Bunker," Somoza's office in the military compound. Somoza asked Urcuyo about his Cabinet, and Urcuyo said that it included representatives of the Conservative, Liberal, and Social Christian parties, "and even a Sandinista."[28]

On July 15, Bowdler told Pezzullo that the Junta was sending two representatives to Managua to discuss the transition with Urcuyo. Pezzullo met with them when they arrived, and learned that they wanted to compress the transition to about five minutes—an immediate transfer from the Congress to the President to the Junta, as they had told Bowdler on July 10. Pezzullo told the delegation that he thought the revised plan was "unrealistic," but he also said that he didn't want to get in the middle of their talks. He gave them Urcuyo's number and told him that they would be calling.[29]

One of the Sandinista representatives, Noel Rivas, a former leader of the Nicaraguan Chamber of Commerce, called Urcuyo to congratulate him and tell him the plan called for an immediate transfer of power to the Junta. Urcuyo was very upset and told Rivas "it couldn't be." Urcuyo then called Somoza, who after speaking with Pezzullo, informed Urcuyo that Rivas had fabricated the story.[30] Urcuyo therefore ignored the statement.

Although the SCC meeting on July 13 instructed Pezzullo to identify immediately a Guard Commander, two days later, Pezzullo gave Somoza a list of six names from which to select one. The list had been developed by McCoy and others in the Embassy. Somoza rejected Col. Mojíca and chose Col. Federico Mejía, a National Guard engineer in his mid-40s. "You know your onions," Somoza said, approving of the list, which had mainly been developed by himself.[31]

Pezzullo recalls sending a flash cable about the new Guard Commander to Washington and San José on July 15, and Bowdler indicated that the Junta approved of the choice. The plan, according to Pezzullo, was that Mejía would be Chief of Staff rather than Commander, and Humberto Ortega would also be Chief of Staff of the FSLN. The third member of the triumvirate responsible for negotiating a cease-fire and fusion of forces would be Bernardino Larios. Pallais insists that the final arrangement involved Mejía being promoted to General and designated National Guard Director and Army Chief of Staff.

A decision was then made that Somoza would leave early in the morning of July 17. The night before, Somoza phoned Pezzullo and warned him about allowing the Sandinista military to arrive at the airport the next day. "After all, we're in the middle of a war, and somebody [could] get trigger happy." "That sounded reasonable to me," Pezzullo recalls thinking. "I hadn't thought of it; I don't think anybody had."[32] Pezzullo then called Bowdler, who spoke with the Sandinista leadership, and all agreed that the United States would provide an Army plane for the new Guard Chief of Staff, Col. Federico Mejía, to fly with McCoy to Costa Rica to meet with the new Sandinista leadership to discuss the terms of a cease-fire. The purpose of sending McCoy was to assure Mejía that he wouldn't be taken hostage. Pezzullo tried to reach Somoza and Urcuyo to confirm this, but could not.

Pezzullo then called Mejía directly at 10:00 P.M., July 16. It was the first time that he or anyone from the U.S. Embassy had ever spoken with the new Guard leader, and Mejía knew nothing of this plan. Pezzullo, assuming Mejía did know, did not bother describing it; he just told Mejía that McCoy would meet him at the airport at 7:00 A.M. the next morning. A U.S. Army plane would fly them to Costa Rica for the meeting. Mejía listened quietly, and Pezzullo became uneasy. At 1 A.M., he sent McCoy to the bunker to make sure that Mejía was going to the airport in the morning. This was also McCoy's first meeting with the new Guard leader. After a brief conversation, McCoy called Pezzullo and told him that Mejía could not go because the President had ordered him to stay to discuss the military situation at a meeting at 10:00 A.M. Pezzullo shouted: "Which President?" McCoy wasn't sure. Pezzullo then called Mejía repeatedly, but Mejía refused to receive the phone call. The next morning, he did not go to the airport.[33]

Washington was even more bewildered about what was happening. Brzezinski chaired an SCC meeting on July 16. Most of the SCC members did not know that Somoza was leaving the next day, that Mejía had been selected as Chief of Staff, or the complex arrangement that had been worked out with Larios and Ortega. The meeting actually discussed for the fourth consecutive time Col. Mojíca, the Nicaraguan Attaché in Guatemala, as a possible head of the Guard. In the last week, events were moving rapidly in Central America as well as in Washington. There were so few people doing so many things that there was hardly enough time to read cables let alone write them. Communications broke down.

The major issue for the SCC was how to distribute food and medicines after Somoza left. The SCC decided to distribute aid in two ways that would strengthen moderates—through the Red Cross and the Provisional Government. Aid in Managua would be dispensed mostly through the Red Cross, but the United States would ask the president of the Red Cross, Ismael Reyes, to broaden the leadership of the organization and to consider using the National Guard. At the same time, the special AID representative, David Lazar, who had been sent to San José, would tell the Junta that the United States was prepared to be helpful if they broadened their capability to provide aid. The SCC also recommended a large airlift to Managua to begin immediately after Somoza departed, and the new government requested it.

The Andean Pact ministers were considering flying to Managua to lend their support to the new regime, and the United States encouraged them. Torrijos noted that he wanted to train the Nicaraguan military, lest the Sandinistas become a "hippy military force." The SCC decided to encourage Panama and the Andean countries to take the lead in dealing with the Sandinista government, and the United States would support them.

Exit

At 1:00 A.M., July 17, the Nicaraguan Congress convened in the Hotel Intercontinental and quickly accepted Somoza's resignation. Somoza then traveled in a convoy to the airport and left at about 4:00 A.M. The Congress elected Urcuyo President. In a nation-wide address, Urcuyo declared that Somoza's departure marked "an era which is definitively canceled." He urged his fellow Nicaraguans "to forget the past in the name of the present, with our eyes on the future." Instead of calling for a cease-fire, however, he asked "all of the irregular forces [to] lay down their weapons." Instead of transferring power to the Provisional Government in San José, he invited the Inter-American Human Rights Commission to visit and called "fervently for dialogue" with "all the democratic groups of the nation."[34] Though he did not actually say that he would complete Somoza's term, as the press and Ambassador Pezzullo reported, he did not sound like a man who would be leaving in 48 or 72 hours.

Urcuyo then walked to the bunker—his new office—and Pezzullo phoned him there at 4:00 A.M. The Ambassador reminded Urcuyo of the plan, which required Mejía's departure at 7:00 A.M. for Costa Rica and Urcuyo's welcome to the Archbishop and the Junta at 9:00 A.M. (It had been postponed one hour.) Urcuyo rejected both requests, insisting that Mejía was needed in Managua for a meeting at 10:00 A.M. with the Guard commanders "to discuss military strategy."

Tired and strung out, Pezzullo called Vaky and told him "the whole thing is coming apart." Vaky suggested he try again. Bowdler told the Junta to wait. Pezzullo and McCoy then went to the Presidential House and woke up Urcuyo. Urcuyo later wrote that he told Pezzullo that he would turn over power in a constitutional process to a democratic junta, but not a Communist one. He claimed he did not know anything about Pezzullo's plan. The two traded insults, and then Pezzullo returned to the Embassy and called Washington. Vaky told him to try yet again. In the meantime, there was an SCC meeting scheduled that afternoon to decide what the United States should do.[35]

Beginning at 3:30 P.M., the SCC met for one hour. Because of the rapid flow of events, few outside of the State Department knew the details of the elaborate plan that had been negotiated during the previous week. State—Vaky and Christopher—thought the plan was workable, but feared that Urcuyo rejected it. Their comments reflected the anger of Pezzullo, who judged that Somoza was responsible for Urcuyo's decision to stay; and they also were sensitive to the Junta's suspicions, which were being conveyed in colorful language to Bowdler in San José. The Junta was convinced that the latest turn of events was part of a U.S. plot. State therefore decided to force out Urcuyo.

Brzezinski and David Jones suggested that the Latin Americans should be encouraged to play a larger role, and that the United States should issue a statement that Urcuyo was acting on his own. Although the SCC was uncertain of Urcuyo's intentions, there was a certain irony in his scheme, which was essentially the Executive Committee idea that State had declared a nonstarter three weeks before. Urcuyo did not want to hand over power to the FSLN in one step; he claimed he would transfer power to a broadly based group of democratic opposition leaders, some of whom he wanted for his Cabinet. But the situation was much more fragile than Urcuyo realized.

Bushnell said that several C-141s filled with food were prepared to fly to Managua, and Gen. John Pustay noted that Torrijos proposed that our "silhouette loom large" with such planes. But the Sandinistas were worried that these planes might be carrying something other than food, and asked us to wait. State agreed. Pezzullo was instructed to try to get the plan back on track, and Bowdler to reassure the Junta. Pezzullo called Mejia, and explained the entire plan to him for the first time.

Pezzullo warned him that Urcuyo was "going to destroy the National Guard." Meijia did not agree.[36]

Early in the morning of July 17, after hearing of Somoza's resignation but before hearing Urcuyo's speech, Carlos Nuñez, a Sandinista leader, recalled that "the Frente made a rapid evaluation of the state of their forces and ordered a mass advance on Managua, calculating that they would need three days to take the capital and wipe out the last of the Guard." During the day and into the night, some of the "heaviest" fighting occurred.[37] Humberto Ortega later told Pezzullo that the FSLN never intended to negotiate with the Guard or accept a cease-fire or standstill. They intended to march into Managua and destroy the Guard.[38]

Urcuyo met with the new High Command of the Guard and told them of Pezzullo's proposal—that Mejía meet with the Sandinista commanders to plan a cease-fire and unification of forces. Mejía then phoned Humberto Ortega, who demanded unconditional surrender, attributing this change to the fact that Urcuyo violated the first understanding.[39]

The senior officers of the Guard met in the evening of July 17 to assess their military supply problems. They were aware that the Sandinistas had redoubled their efforts and controlled León, Granada, Chinandega, Estelí, and Puerto Somoza. Some units of the Guard had deserted during the day. After the meeting, about 8:00 P.M., Nicaraguan Lt. Col. Alberto Smith called McCoy and then Pezzullo to ask whether U.S. military aid would be coming. Pezzullo encouraged Smith to keep the Guard united, but said they could not expect aid from the United States. Smith then accused Pezzullo of destroying the National Guard. "Weapons were promised," Smith said. "Somoza told us he had an understanding with the United States that they would rush in and help us." Pezzullo asked about the morale in the Guard, and Smith told him the Air Force had already fled and that Tacho III's elite force was breaking up. Pezzullo encouraged Smith to preserve what he could of the Guard and call for a cease-fire.[40]

McCoy was called again by the Guard commanders at 2:30 A.M. "They said that the National Guard commanders had decided it was all over without U.S. support, and they were getting on planes to Honduras and so forth." McCoy had an assistant check, and by 6:00 A.M., July 18, he concluded that the Guard no longer existed and informed Washington.

To dissociate the United States from Urcuyo's actions, the State Department announced that Pezzullo was leaving with most of his Embassy staff on July 18. Pezzullo described the airport as pure pandemonium. Guard officers and enlisted men tried desperately to get out. Based on Pezzullo's judgment that Urcuyo was responding to Somoza's instructions, Christopher called Somoza in Miami and demanded that Urcuyo keep his agreement. Somoza turned on the amplifier on the telephone for everyone to hear. Murphy, who was present, recalled that Christopher began the conversation: "You're not welcome here because you haven't lived up to our arrangement.' Somoza said: 'What's the matter?' He [Christopher] said, Urcuyo refuses to leave. Somoza says: 'Tell him to leave. You told me to leave, and I left.'"[41]

But Somoza called Urcuyo anyway and, according to Pallais, said: "Look, Chico, you are in a very difficult situation because they just told me that all the promises of safe haven in this country will be taken away from me and my family. . . . You must do something." Somoza suggested that he resign and transfer power to the military, and Urcuyo agreed.[42] Somoza, fearful the United States might carry out its threat and extradite him, decided to move that same day to the Bahamas.

In the afternoon, Urcuyo asked the Guatemalan President, Lucas, to send a plane to evacuate him and his government. Prior to his departure, Urcuyo tried to transfer power to Mejía, as Somoza had suggested. Two hours later Mejía called back and said: "Mr. President, leave with your presidency because we are not going to share power with these Communists. We are also leaving."[43] Forty-three hours after assuming the Presidency, Urcuyo left.

When the plans for the transition ceremony in Managua fell apart, Costa Rican President Carazo asked the Mexican government to provide a plane to fly several Junta members into León in the early morning of July 18. Having waited so long for the denouement, Robelo, a member of the Junta, and Alfredo César, the Secretary to the Junta, were startled by the rapidity of events. Both had expected that the Guard would survive through the stand-in-place formula, even though the Directorate had told them the Guard would collapse. Neither had thought about how military power would be organized after Somoza's exit. Bowdler had tried to get them to focus on the need for a "counterweight," but in Robelo's words, "I didn't see it then."[44]

Costa Rica immediately recognized the Junta as the Government of Nicaragua. The next day, the Junta and all the Sandinista leaders arrived in Managua amid much cheering and rejoicing. The Archbishop, Bowdler, and numerous foreign diplomats witnessed their swearing in. At the suggestion of the United States, Costa Rica, Mexico, and the Andean Pact all pledged an active role in Nicaragua, to prevent it from becoming "another Cuba."[45]

At dawn on July 19, soon after Urcuyo's departure, Mejía also left, leaving Lt. Col. Fulgencio Largaespada, the head of the traffic police, to be the last Director of the National Guard and negotiate the surrender with the Sandinistas. In Nicaragua—a nation, but also a metaphor—the man who presided over the final collision between the Guard and the Sandinistas was, appropriately, a traffic cop.

The cynicism of the Somoza family permeated nearly a half century of Nicaraguan politics and provoked the cataclysm that brought it to an end. Anastasio Somoza Garcia, the patriarch, had once told reporters: "It took 20,000 lives for the Liberals to get into power. It will take 40,000 to get us out of here." He was right.[46]

From the U.S. government's perspective, the Somoza dynasty ended in much the same way it had begun. In 1934–36, the United States was displeased by the gradual accretion of power by Anastasio Somoza Garcia, but it decided that stopping Somoza would be costly. President Roosevelt was so determined to avoid re-involvement in Nicaragua's internal politics that the United States did not even raise its voice in protest.

In 1978–79, the United States raised its voice and reduced its aid to demonstrate its displeasure with the Somozas, but that was insufficient. To most Nicaraguans and Latin Americans, Anastasio Somoza Debayle was anathema, and if the United States would not overthrow him, then the Sandinistas—with wide support—would, and did. In the fall of 1978, the United States deepened its role in the conflict in order to keep the Sandinistas from taking power, but by June 1979, after the Sandinistas had won broad support from the middle in Nicaragua, the Andean countries, and the OAS, the United States judged that the moderate "third force" alternative had evaporated. Both times—in October 1978 and June 1979—President Carter chose to support the Latin American democracies and not intervene.

In 1934–36 and 1978–79, Nicaraguans were certain the United States was controlling its politics, but in both periods, that was an illusion. A Nicaraguan—Anastasio Somoza García—took power in 1936 and his son was replaced as a result of a violent revolution in 1979. On both occasions, the United States was a witness to events it did not like.

PART THREE

Relating to the Revolution

In that new world which is the old . . .

ALFRED, LORD TENNYSON, *The Departure*

Carter:
Mutual Respect and Suspicion

If you don't hold me responsible for everything that occurred under my predecessors, I will not hold you responsible for everything that occurred under your predecessors.

JIMMY CARTER'S ADVICE TO THE FSLN[1]

Avoid the early mistakes we made in Cuba, the political rejection by the West, premature frontal attacks on the bourgeoisie, economic isolation.

FIDEL CASTRO'S ADVICE TO THE FSLN[2]

AFTER THE SANDINISTA TRIUMPH in July 1979, United States policy toward Nicaragua changed from open and ample support for the revolution to indirect war. In the beginning, the United States government deliberately suspended its suspicions about the Sandinistas; three years later, the United States wanted to believe and publicize the worst charges against the Sandinistas. In contrast, the Sandinistas always believed the worst about the United States, and within three years, their worst fears were confirmed.

Despite mutual suspicions, or rather because of them, both governments initially sought to construct a non-hostile relationship. Such a relationship was motivated more by fear than respect, but it represented a genuine and reciprocal effort nonetheless.

U.S. policy was not so neatly divided between the Carter and the Reagan Administrations as partisans maintained. There was some continuity, and indeed some irony. Both Administrations sought to moderate and contain the revolution. Neither was successful. Ironically, the Carter Administration was on the verge of terminating its aid program to Nicaragua when it left office, while its successor entered with a mandate to end aid but delayed for nearly ten weeks.

Despite a few connecting threads, the differences between the Carter and Reagan Administrations in the perception of the revolution and the strategy to relate to it dwarfed the similarities. The next four chapters describe how and why the two U.S. Presidents tried to relate to the Nicaraguan revolution and how and why their best efforts were stymied.

The Carter Administration's Lessons

The ghost of Cuba past, which had haunted U.S. policy makers as Somoza was falling, continued to taunt them after the Sandinistas marched into Managua. The question was what lesson should be drawn from the U.S. relationship with revolutionary Cuba that would be useful as the United States approached revolutionary Nicaragua. Some writers concluded from the earlier experience that the United States pushed revolutions to the left and to the Soviet Union by a self-fulfilling prophecy. By calling Castro a Communist and acting as if he were one, according to this argument, the United States helped make him a Communist and his revolution, anti-American.[3] Others suggested that Castro deliberately provoked the United States to gain nationalistic support, consolidate and centralize his control, implement a thorough revolution, and justify a closer relationship with the Soviet Union.[4]

The principal lesson that the Carter Administration drew from the previous experience was that Castro's slide toward Communism and the Soviet Union was partly the result of confrontation with the United States in 1959 and 1960. The United States had not "pushed" Castro to the left, but the tough response to Castro's decisions to gain control of Cuba's politics and economy had accelerated its revolution and hardened its anti-Yankee posture.[5] With each U.S. reaction to each Cuban provocation, the relationship worsened and the United States moved further from its interests in a moderate, non-Communist regime. Cole Blasier described the essence of the action-reaction cycle that led to the destruction of the U.S.-Cuban relationship: "Almost from the beginning, Castro and the United States expected the worst from each other, and neither was disappointed." Philip Bonsal, who was U.S. Ambassador to Cuba during this period, reflected on U.S. mistakes and concluded that a less hostile response by the United States to Cuban nationalizations might have deprived Castro's revolution of its nationalistic fervor and offered more space for internal criticism.[6]

Different members of the Carter Administration drew different conclusions, but overall, the Administration's policy was premised on this last lesson. The Administration believed that hostile policies by the United States had been counterproductive, giving revolutionary regimes the excuse or the reason for radicalization. Having failed to prevent the Sandinistas from coming to power, the Administration wanted to avoid repeating the rest of the Cuban experience in Nicaragua.

The Benefit of the Doubt

On the first full day of the new Nicaraguan government, July 20, the United States government convened a meeting of the SCC to define its policy. Nicaragua, however, was not the only subject of debate. Attention had shifted to the rest of Central America. Having failed to manage political change in Nicaragua, the issue before the SCC was whether to try a different approach toward the other countries. The question was fundamental, and therefore hardly debated by the Administration.

The choice was whether to bolster the military governments in the region or to try to pressure them to open up to the new social and political groups demanding reforms. Henry Kissinger would argue that the "moderate, democratic alternative" that the Carter Administration sought did not exist. Many at the other end of the political spectrum made the same argument, only with the opposite prescription: instead of defending the status quo, the left argued that the United States should ally itself with the forces of the future.[7] The Carter Administration had, of course, made its choice: it was both philosophically and temperamentally incapable of supporting either military dictators or leftist guerrillas. Carter himself sketched the outlines of the policy at a Friday morning breakfast before the SCC meeting.

Brzezinski opened the meeting on July 20 by elaborating on Carter's outline. He said that a historic change had occurred in Central America. The United States could not and did not want to support a mindless bolstering of the status quo. The Carter Administration would continue to support moderate change as the only alternative to violent revolution. No one disagreed, and the discussion shifted to Nicaragua.

Once the Sandinistas entered Managua, the Administration unified in its prescription for U.S. policy. No one argued for either dissociation or hostility toward the new regime. People had questions and doubts, but few had illusions about the Sandinista Directorate's preferences for Cuba and Marxism, and its visceral hatred of the United States. Still, the governing coalition was broad, and even within the Directorate, there were likely to be some important differences, say, between a Tomás Borge, who had been a member of the Communist Party, and the rest of the leadership, which was young, much less educated, and unlikely to have his doctrinal convictions. Some Sandinistas might be social democrats; others might only be superficial leftists or Marxists without being Leninists. The question was who would prevail, and whether ideology could be moderated by a tolerant U.S. policy.

These issues were not debated at any length because no one saw a viable option other than to seek a good relationship with the new government. Having decided against intervention before the Sandinistas marched into Managua, the Carter Administration naturally viewed intervention afterward as out of the question, particularly given the warmth with which the revolution was greeted by its democratic neighbors.

Some thought that perhaps the United States could turn the self-fulfilling prophecy to its advantage. Whether the Sandinistas were Communists or not, perhaps it would be better to treat them like democrats, and maybe the Sandinistas—or rather some of the key leaders—might even begin to behave like democrats. As they dealt with the hard realities of governing and trying to meet the needs of their people, the new Nicaraguan leadership might come to realize that the United States and the Nicaraguan private sector had more to offer than Cuba or ideology. This thesis was first proposed by a Venezuelan leader, who suggested that instead of trying to lift the "mask of democracy" from the faces of the Sandinistas to show they were really Communists, it would be better to try to take the mask seriously, and by doing so, try to sew the mask to their faces.

Because of the consensus on goals and tactics, the SCC discussion of Nicaragua concluded rapidly and with no important disagreements. U.S. objectives were:

1. *internal:* to assist the revolution to fulfill its stated promises of political pluralism, elections, and a vigorous private sector, and conversely, to reduce the chances that the revolution would become Communist;
2. *strategic:* to deny the Sandinistas an enemy and thus a reason for relying on Cuban and Soviet military assistance; and
3. *regional:* to make clear that a good relationship with the United States was contingent on Nicaraguan non-interference in its neighbors' internal affairs.

To achieve these objectives, the United States would: (1) rapidly seek to establish good relations with the regime; (2) provide emergency food and relief supplies and develop a long-term aid program; (3) work with friendly democratic governments in the area and Europe to encourage them to be helpful as well; and (4) find ways to help the moderates in and outside the government, who were more likely to favor a democratic Nicaragua. The political premise underlying this strategy was that the majority of the national coalition that was taking power in Nicaragua was interested in democracy and was not hostile to the United States. Therefore, a strategy of patience, assistance, and restraint was more likely to produce a friendly, non-Communist regime than one that ignored, threatened, or attacked the new government. In fact, the converse more nearly reflected U.S. policy: the Administration believed that a Communist regime was more likely to emerge if the United States adopted a confrontational approach.

The United States decided to play for the long term. To implement the policy, Carter, like Eisenhower twenty years before with Castro's new government, sent as his representatives people who were liberal, active, and potentially sympathetic. Lawrence Pezzullo, who had deliberately not presented his credentials to Somoza, became the Ambassador to the new government, and Lawrence Harrison, who had more than twenty years experience in Latin America and the Caribbean, was made the AID mission director. The new government passed the United States a note on July 23, 1979, indicating that it wished to uphold its international agreements and continue good relations with the United States. The United States confirmed the request and affirmed its interest in good relations.

"Ah, yes, Senorita Sandinista, how beautiful you are when you're angry, yes, indeed! Him? Oh, a small libation or two, together. Hardly know the scoundrel . . . Ah, may I come in . . . ?

As the Junta paraded through Managua, it felt the euphoria of a people, who were relieved to have removed the Somoza dynasty and excited with the prospect of creating a "new Nicaragua." The Junta would need all the nation's exuberance and unity to cope with the formidable task of reconstruction. Managua had not recovered from the earthquake of 1972 when it was wracked by insurrection in 1978 and 1979.

Two studies by the United Nations and the Inter-American Human Rights Commission estimated that during the war against Somoza as many as 45,000 people had been killed (80 percent civilians), up to 160,000 were wounded, and 40,000 orphaned. About one million Nicaraguans were in dire need of food, and 250,000 of shelter. To pay for the war, Somoza had increased his country's debt to $1.5 billion—most of it in short-term loans and at high interest rates—and had looted the Central Bank. Economic losses due to the war were estimated at $2 billion.[8]

President Carter approved a generous relief package. In less than two weeks, the United States sent 732 metric tons of food by air and another 1,000 tons by ship. It purchased 9,600 pounds of medical supplies and funded other international relief efforts as well. Carter sought a symbol to demonstrate his sincerity and considered sending his son Chip on a special flight. Instead, on July 28, Ambassador Pezzullo returned to Managua with a message that the "President is sending this special plane [Air Force One] as an expression of his personal good will to the people of Nicaragua and to the new government."[9]

Though the Administration was united in its approach to Nicaragua, there was no consensus in the country. During a press conference on July 25, Carter therefore welcomed the chance to respond to the conservative critique that Nicaragua was a victory for Cuba and a loss for the United States:

> It's a mistake for Americans to assume or to claim that every time an evolutionary change takes place or even an abrupt change takes place in this hemisphere, that somehow it's a result of secret, massive Cuban intervention. The fact in Nicaragua is that the incumbent Government, the Somoza regime, lost the confidence of the Nicaraguan people. There was a broad range of forces assembled to replace Somoza and his regime. . . . We worked as closely as we could without intervening in the internal affairs of Nicaragua with the neighboring countries and the so-called Andean Group. . . .
>
> We have a good relationship with the new government. We hope to improve it. I do not attribute all the change in Nicaragua to Cuba. I think the people of Nicaragua have got enough judgment to make their own decisions, and we will use our efforts in a proper fashion without interventionism to let the Nicaraguans let their voice be heard in shaping their own affairs.[10]

Because of the Administration's confidence in its new Ambassador and his AID mission director, the details of Nicaragua policy were left to them. The Embassy was encouraged to continue doing what it had been instructed to do during the Somoza regime—seek out moderate and independent elements and encourage and assist them to play an active role in defining the structures and policies of the new regime.

One of those independent leaders was Edén Pastora. U.S. officials had met with Pastora as the insurrection was reaching a climax in late June and again after Somoza left. They listened to him and informed him that the United States was prepared to support social democracy in Nicaragua, if that was his objective. He listened, but nothing in his previous experience led him to trust or even believe the United States. Panamanian and Venezuelan officials also approached Pastora and urged him to keep his supporters together with the arms they had used or captured. He was "euphoric" at the time, and in his words, "didn't pay attention" to such advice. Later, he would acknowledge that "it was a mistake."[11] Pastora was excluded from the Directorate, but he remained the most well known and attractive of the Sandinista leaders. Moreover, he also led the bulk of the Sandinista Army—over 2,000 soldiers on the date of the Junta's arrival in Managua out of a total of about 5,000 Sandinista soldiers.[12]

The Distribution and Purposes of Power

On July 20, 1979, a coalition representing the complete spectrum of non-Somocista political and economic groups took power in Nicaragua. There were many predictions about who or which group would prevail, but these predictions were founded less on analysis than on fears or hopes. American conservatives saw the Sandinistas as committed Marxist-Leninists who served the Soviet Union. But several well-known Marxists visited Nicaragua in the months after the revolution and returned distressed that the more pragmatic elements of the Sandinistas seemed to mortgage the future of the revolution to cope with the immediate needs of the people.[13]

At the time, no one knew how deep the divisions were between the three factions of the Sandinistas. Their unification appeared "tactical," much like their alliance with the bourgeoisie. Nor was it clear who would control the military, because Pastora had the most cadre. Of the five-member Junta heading the Government of National Reconstruction, two were moderates; two, Sandinistas; and the alignment of the fifth, Sergio Ramirez, was unclear. A poet who had lived and worked in Costa Rica and Europe, Ramírez had been the Group of Twelve's representative on the mediation, before resigning on October 25. Many viewed him as a moderate social democrat. According to the "Plan of Government" of June 18, 1979, that Robelo had written, the Junta would function as the executive branch of the new government and would share legislative functions with the Council of State, which would be created later with representatives of 33 organizations. The FSLN would only control 12 of 33 seats.[14] The 18-member Cabinet included Bernardino Larios, the former Guardsman, now Minister of Defense, and a number of other moderates, particularly in the economic ministries.

Like most everyone in Nicaragua, the members of the Junta celebrated, and paid little attention to how power was being divided. According to Alfonso Robelo, it took several months before he realized that "someone in olive green," a representative of the 9-member Directorate (the Comandantes), was present at every Junta meeting. Before any important decision, the Junta heard from the Comandantes, and their views always seemed to prevail.[15]

On July 20, the day the U.S. National Security Council met to decide on a new approach to Nicaragua, the Directorate met in the bunker that Somoza had used as his war room. The Directorate had fought with guns so long that it was quite natural that they—alone of all the Nicaraguans—considered first how to organize military power in Nicaragua to ensure that they could make the last, if not the first decisions. The Guard had disintegrated, and one issue they discussed was the manner in which Guardsmen should be arrested and treated. The views of the United States and friendly governments in the region reinforced those who wanted to be fair with those members of the Guard who would not pose a threat to the revolution.

The main issue, however, was how the Directorate could take power from Edén Pastora. Some argued for an open fight; others, opposed that, insisting that unity was imperative. At that moment, Pastora burst through the door. Part of him noticed that the noise in the room he had heard outside a moment before had ceased as he entered. It was the kind of incriminating, embarrassing silence that suggested he was the subject of the discussion. Another part of Pastora, spontaneous and flushed with the joy of victory, prevailed, and he greeted the others with abrazos. Then, without knowing the question the Directorate had been debating, Pastora turned to Humberto Ortega, the Commander of the Sandinista Army, and answered it, probably to their disbelief, most assuredly to their satisfaction. He told them that he had brought his entire 2,000-man army to the outskirts of the city of Managua and left them there because he did not know where to put them. "What do I do with these people? Whom do I turn them over to? Where do I take them? Do I disarm them? What do I do?"[16]

Pastora was told that the Directorate would be sending people to take command of his force, and they asked him to be the Vice Minister of Interior. He accepted, even while recognizing that he would be junior to his old rival, Tomás Borge. With Cuban advisers, the Directorate focused its efforts at organizing the army, establishing the police and internal security, and organizing "popular," mass organizations, including the Sandinista Defense Committees, which were based on the Cuban block Committees for the Defense of the Revolution. The Directorate postponed the establishment of the Council of State until the new mass organizations were established and could be represented.

In the beginning, of course, there was considerable chaos in Managua. The "muchachos," the boys who did most of the fighting and dying during the insurrection, still had guns and felt powerful; but they were young and unemployed. The FSLN had important positions, but as Borge put it, they "didn't even have offices."[17] On July 28, the members of the Directorate held a press conference at their newly established military barracks in Managua. Their purpose was, as the first speaker put it, "to make one thing clear . . . The only official spokesman for the Sandinista Front are the members of the National Directorate." Then, Borge introduced himself as "organizing the national police force [and] . . . the state security organizations," and Humberto Ortega said that he was "organizing our Popular Sandinista Army."[18] Larios, the moderate Defense Minister, was not present.

The moderates in the Nicaraguan government had learned from Somoza the need for an apolitical armed force; the FSLN had learned the opposite lesson. In Borge's view, there was no such thing as neutral education or an apolitical army; education and the armed forces either served the revolution (government) or they undermined it.

By September 21, 1979, the Directorate had consolidated its power and organized a three-day conference with the cadre of the Sandinista Party to review how they took power, how they would keep it, and what they would do with it. At the end of their meetings, the Directorate wrote a summary of conclusions—the 72-Hour Document—and then circulated it widely in order to permit all "militants, both within the country and abroad" to understand the "political guidelines" of the revolution.[19] It confirmed the main interpretations of the Carter Administration.

The Directorate identified four enemies of the revolution: the "traitorous bourgeoisie, vestiges of Somocismo, the ultra-left sectors, and American imperialism, the rabid enemy of all peoples who are struggling to achieve their definitive liberation." The Directorate had designed the government as "a special class alliance . . . to neutralize Yankee intervention." The Marxist jargon is thick, but if one focuses on substance, the document reveals a realistic leadership that understood that its success stemmed from "political pragmatism." "We should avoid unnecessary theoretical arguments," the Directorate warned, because the "most serious internal danger" is factionalism. Unity is key. Their principal objective: "develop bold social plans in the fields of education, health, and housing in order to bring the revolution to the masses. Give priority to the peasant population, particularly on the northern border and the Atlantic coast." This represented a joining of their idealism (social programs), their constituency (peasants), and the two strategic regions where they expected U.S. intervention to occur.

Because of the power of U.S. imperialism, they recommended "an instinctively defensive posture." Their revolution should spread by example rather than by being exported. They should be "conservative" domestically and internationally.

From the beginning, there was a debate among the moderates and within the FSLN about whether the latter's commitment to political pluralism, a mixed economy, and nonalignment was genuine or merely "tactical"—whether the Sandinistas would implement these objectives or postpone them indefinitely.[20] Although some Sandinistas wanted a "socialist revolution" immediately, the 72-Hour Document accepted that the country was not ready for it, and a more cautious strategy prevailed. As the moderate groups deepened their understanding of the Sandinistas, they began to accept the Carter strategy—that the most likely way to transform "tactical" decisions into permanent ones was to prove to the FSLN that friendship with the local middle class and foreign democracies was beneficial, and it would be costly to sever such ties.

The ideological rhetoric was disconcerting, but the policies that emerged from the government reflected a commitment to the revolution's three objectives—pluralism, a mixed economy, and nonalignment—albeit with reservations. There was ample space in the Nicaraguan political scene for groups and organizations that were independent of the Frente. The new government issued a comprehensive bill of rights, ended the death penalty, lifted press and broadcast censorship, and took great care that the National Guardsmen arrested after the victory would be treated with due process.[21]

Somoza's National Guard had burned the offices of *La Prensa* as an act of vengeance in the closing days of the revolution. Soon after the triumph, the newspaper's owners quickly reestablished its voice, and it did not suffer serious censorship until after the declaration of the state of emergency in March 1982. COSEP, the business association, played an important role articulating the private sector's interests and concerns. The Sandinista leadership repeatedly approached COSEP to negotiate a wide range of issues. Finally, the independent labor unions that had struggled with the Somoza dynasty found room to organize and grow in the aftermath of the revolution even though they would soon face stiff and unfair competition from Sandinista-sponsored unions.

In time, the FSLN would try to bring each independent group under its umbrella, much as the Mexican ruling party had done. If a group resisted, the Frente would test its mettle with a combination of inducements and harassment, but if the group—including the Church—still resisted, the FSLN often retreated.

In terms of foreign policy, the new government immediately joined the non-aligned movement and established close relations with Cuba. Relations with the Soviet Union were established later, and a Soviet Ambassador only arrived in early 1980. On the UN vote to condemn the Soviet invasion of Afghanistan, Nicaragua abstained, while Cuba and Grenada supported the Soviet Union. Nicaragua also cultivated relations with its Latin American neighbors and with Western European governments.

Economically and socially, the government brought Nicaragua into the modern era, albeit by Central American standards. It initiated a number of health and welfare services for the poor and announced a national literacy program. Like its neighbor Costa Rica, Nicaragua nationalized the banking industry, trade in agricultural products, and mineral companies. As promised in its program, the revolutionary government also nationalized all of Somoza's properties. As a result, the public share of Nicaragua's gross domestic product increased from 15 percent in 1978 to 41 percent in 1980.[22]

Although some of the government's early decisions aimed to reassure the middle class in Nicaragua and democratic governments abroad, their rhetoric often inflamed suspicions. In October 1980, Borge explained the essence of the problem, without appearing to be aware of why he was a part of it. Regretting that "we have a backward capitalist class" in Nicaragua, he proceeded to divide the country into the masses, who were insecure before the revolution but were now secure, and the "social groups that ruled the country":

> Those who before caused insecurity to the big majority of the population now feel insecure themselves—even though this revolution has been extremely flexible and has given everyone an opportunity. They feel insecure even though we have seriously proposed—and this is not just a tactical or short-term thing—that we maintain a mixed economy and political pluralism. We mean it when we talk about political pluralism and a mixed economy.
>
> But what happens is that a thief thinks everyone else is like him. And these people think we are tricking them, when in fact we are going to great pains to show them that we are not lying, that in fact they are the ones who historically have been the liars. . . Obviously, this is a vicious circle, because this insecurity causes them to decapitalize their businesses. But when they do that . . . the revolutionary government becomes concerned."[23]

Borge was incapable of understanding how people on the other end of his class rhetoric—the "liars" and "thieves"—would interpret his remarks. Some were prepared to discount it and try to solve problems one at a time. Others believed that a relationship with Marxists was not possible.

Relating to the United States

Deciding on a policy toward the United States could not have been easy. The Sandinistas, including Pastora, had felt that they had been fighting the United States for as long as they had been fighting Somoza. They knew, and expected, the Carter Administration to try to prevent them from coming to power, and indeed, were surprised that they succeeded. Their ideology was publicly anti-imperialist when it wasn't more candidly anti-American. Tomás Borge asked a composer to write an FSLN anthem to be sung with the Nicaraguan national anthem. Borge told me that he asked that a phrase, "Yankees—enemy of humanity," be included to remind Nicaragua's youth of the danger from the north.[24]

The Sandinistas reciprocated the suspicions that U.S. policy makers had of them, but their mistrust was related to the asymmetry in power: the Sandinistas had to be much more suspicious because the capacity of the United States to undermine their revolution was infinitely greater than their capacity to affect U.S. interests. Moreover, a chasm of differences in personal experiences separated the two sets of leaders. North Americans engaged in the bureaucratic intrigue of leaking memoranda; Sandinista intrigues were literally matters of life and death. With a median age in the mid-50s and a global perspective in which Nicaragua was of marginal importance, U.S. decision makers could rationally step back and decide not to call the Sandinistas "Communists" for fear they could become them, if they weren't already.

One could not expect a comparable detachment from the Directorate, whose median age was about 30 and whose principal experience was fighting the National Guard. To survive in such a world, one had to develop an acute sense of paranoia and trust only a very few people or none at all. In a democratic system, the people who rise to the top generally have the most friends; the Sandinistas, who lived to govern, rose because they treated the world as their enemies. Compromise, essential to a democratic system, was alien to the guerrilla. Given their temperament and experience and the emotions of the moment, it is hardly surprising that few of the Sandinistas could restrain themselves from repeated references to the United States as an imperialistic enemy of humanity. Just as Borge was unaware how his description of businessmen as "thieves" might affect their views of him, the Sandinistas appeared unaware that their charges of U.S. imperialism confirmed suspicions in the United States.

Without knowing the specifics of the Directorate's debate, one can imagine that there might have been three views on what to do about the United States. The practical view argued that U.S. aid and friendship were essential to Nicaragua's development. The more cynical, or perhaps realistic, view would be that the United States would use its aid to strengthen the bourgeoisie and try to divide the left; it would be safer to insist on an arm's length approach and not accept aid. A third view would insist that the FSLN have no illusions about U.S. imperialism, but that the Sandinistas were intelligent enough to use the aid to serve their purposes rather than the Americans'. It would appear that the third view prevailed, but not without a snigger. The Junta, for example, complained that U.S. aid was inadequate, even though it then exceeded all other countries'.

High officials from both the United States and Nicaragua met on August 10, 1979—the occasion being the inauguration of the new Ecuadorean President, Jaime Roldos. Attending the meeting were Rosalynn Carter, Secretary of State Cyrus

Vance, Pete Vaky, and I on the U.S. side, with Edén Pastora, Violeta de Chamorro, and Miguel D'Escoto representing Nicaragua. Pastora warned that Nicaragua would turn to the "Socialist bloc" for weapons if the United States did not provide them. When asked why Nicaragua needed more arms if it had enough for two armies, Pastora admitted: "We have enough arms to equip the Sandinista Army from the Israeli Ghalils and American M-16s captured from the National Guard, but these weapons represent the suppression of the Nicaraguan people, and we would like to exchange them for other arms." I then queried why he thought another shipment of M-16s would be different from those. The discussion drifted inconclusively. To ensure colleagues knew of his resolute defense of Nicaragua, D'Escoto, in a condescending style that mimicked the way he felt the United States had treated Nicraragua, informed the *New York Times* what "he" had told Vance:

> The Nicaraguans are fully aware of the role the United States has played in Nicaragua and that the resentment against the American government is very deep. I [D'Escoto] told him [Vance] the United States should keep a low profile when making suggestions to us, and he said he understood. At no point did he try to contradict me, and he was very correct.[25]

Some photographers had learned of the meeting, and as the group assembled for a picture, Pastora whispered impishly to Vance: "I wonder who will be hurt more because of this picture?" Vance laughed, and judged that he would.

He was wrong. The next day in Managua, Borge held a press conference to criticize his subordinate for speaking out of turn. Borge said that Nicaragua would not buy arms from Communist nations because it did not want to leave the impression that it was aligning with Communism.[26] Borge enjoyed confounding the public perception of him as the "hard-line Communist" and Pastora as the independent. At the same time, he could not resist the opportunity to embarrass Pastora.

Whether wittingly or not, Borge's contradiction of Pastora did the Carter Administration a favor. A request by Nicaragua for military aid raised questions that the Administration preferred to avoid. One does not want to arm a potentially unfriendly nation, nor does one want to offer an excuse to request aid from the Soviet Union or Cuba. Nonetheless, the issue did not go away, and the United States resolved the dilemma by offering "nonlethal" military equipment—trucks, medical supplies, communications equipment—and military training.

When Torrijos informed the U.S. Ambassador to Panama that he was sending his officers to advise the Sandinistas on the organization of a police force, the United States encouraged him, particularly because the United States was prohibited by law from helping foreign police forces. Torrijos said he wanted to "try to beat Fidel at his own game of conspiracy" and give the Sandinistas an alternative to Cuba. He told one senior U.S. military officer: "The coloration of the new government will be neither Castro nor Iran. It would change colors depending on who's looking." But he also said that he thought it would be "moderate," a word he had learned had great significance to North Americans.[27] By the time the Panamanian officers arrived in Managua, hundreds of Cubans were already advising the Nicaraguans. Torrijos began to suspect that he was more interested in alternatives than the Sandinistas were. Instead of training the police, the Panamanians were assigned the demeaning task of training Nicaragua's traffic police.[28] Just as he seemed to buy stock in the Sandinistas before others in the region, Torrijos appeared to be among the earliest to become "disillusioned" with them.[29]

The United States decided to offer military advice and aid to the Sandinistas for much the same reasons as Torrijos: to offer an alternative, to begin to build military relationships with the Sandinistas, and to learn more about their officers and their organization. Three U.S. military officers stationed in Panama were sent to Nicaragua to discuss military training with the Sandinistas. This, in turn, posed a difficult question for the Sandinistas, and the slowness and the ambiguity of their reply suggests that Borge's comment in August may have had an additional purpose other than to embarrass Pastora. Borge did not want a military relationship with the United States for all the reasons that the United States wanted one. In the end, the Directorate never formally requested or formally rejected military aid and training from the United States, which for similar reasons was neither generous nor negative. However, the FSLN restricted access by the U.S. Defense Attaché in much the same ways that Somoza had.[30]

On August 1, 1979, before Pastora's conversation with Vance, Venezuela privately put the Sandinistas to the test. Foreign Minister José Alberto Zambrano and General José Antonio Olavarría, Deputy Director of his country's National Security Council, visited Managua and met first with the Minister of Defense, Bernardino Larios. The Venezuelans offered military aid and advice, and Larios accepted it enthusiastically. However, Larios suggested they also speak with Humberto Ortega, the Chief of Staff of the Armed Forces. Ortega was just as clear as Larios, except that he rejected the aid, saying that they had already received enough arms from Cuba. The Venezuelans were stunned, but chose not to publicize the response or to inform the United States.[31]

The Sandinistas preferred the United States to help rebuild the economy. To discuss this issue as well as the overall relationship, three members of the Junta and the Foreign Minister requested a meeting with President Carter in advance of a speech that Daniel Ortega would be delivering to the United Nations. The Administration recognized the political delicacy of such a meeting, and also its parallel with the visit of Fidel Castro in April 1959, when President Eisenhower did not meet with him. Commentators asked later whether such a meeting could have prevented the subsequent confrontation between the United States and Cuba.

On September 24, 1979, Daniel Ortega, Sergio Ramírez, and Alfonso Robelo from the Junta and Foreign Minister Miguel D'Escoto were escorted into the Cabinet Room of the White House, where they met with Carter, Mondale, Christopher, Vaky, Pezzullo, Henry Owen, and me. Carter welcomed them and reiterated his desire for friendship. Then Carter emphasized the importance he attached to three U.S. concerns: nonintervention by Nicaragua in the affairs of its neighbors, a truly nonaligned status, and human rights and democracy. The United States planned to

President Jimmy Carter's meeting with three members of the Nicaraguan Junta in the White House on September 24, 1979. On the U.S. side, from the top (left): Vaky, Pezzullo, Henry Owen of the NSC, Brzezinski, Carter, Mondale, and the author. On the Nicaraguan side, from the top (right): Embassy staff member, Foreign Minister Miguel D'Escoto; Sergio Ramirez, Daniel Ortega, and Alfonso Robelo of the Junta; and Rafael Solis, Nicaragua's Ambassador to the United States.

give aid, but Carter wanted to make sure that Nicaragua understood that these items "do concern us."

Ortega was equally direct, though considerably less diplomatic: "We are interested in obtaining frank and unconditional support from the United States. We know you can provide a lot." Responding to Carter's principal concern about Central America, Ortega insisted that Nicaragua's principal task was reconstruction. "Nicaragua is not a factor in the radicalization of El Salvador—now, in the past, and it will not be in the future. Nor in Guatemala." Although clearly an overstatement, Ortega's comment reflected the Sandinistas' decision at that time not to aid their Salvadoran and Guatemalan comrades.

Carter concluded by referring to the anti-American statements that Ortega and other leaders had made, and said that good relations are difficult to establish in the light of such statements. With his tongue in cheek, Carter said: "If you don't hold me responsible for everything that occurred under my predecessors, I will not hold you responsible for everything that occurred under your predecessors." There were smiles around the table, and Ortega mentioned to Carter as he was leaving that "we will not link you with the past."

Carter then excused himself but asked the other U.S. participants to remain and discuss in greater detail with the Nicaraguans their economic needs and U.S. concerns. Christopher explained, to Ortega's apparent surprise, Carter's goal to reduce the budget deficit and its implications for aid to Nicaragua. Nonetheless, through reprogramming, the United States had already provided $8 million of disaster aid and had approved another $39 million for projects. The Nicaraguans said that their priority was to reschedule their debt, and asked the United States to pressure the banks. Owen responded that the best first step toward obtaining bank compliance was to reach agreement with the International Monetary Fund. Significantly, there was no discussion of military aid.

Christopher explained that the concern the Administration felt about human rights in Nicaragua under Somoza would remain as important under the new government. Ramírez said that a similar motive propelled the revolution, and the new government was determined to make human rights a reality in Nicaragua. Ortega complained of former Somocistas, who were organizing with "agents of the CIA" to attack the country. He mentioned "Comandante Bravo," Somoza's most famous colonel, who had fought Pastora to a standstill in the south. Christopher assured him that the United States opposed any such efforts and that the CIA was not involved.

Four days after his meeting with Carter, on September 28, 1979, Daniel Ortega addressed the UN General Assembly and asked the international community to assume the Nicaraguan debt. (He later withdrew this proposal.) He then announced that Nicaragua was still "a target for imperialist policy. The most aggressive circles of the United States and of Central America dream of restoring Somozaism to our country. A macabre alliance . . . is trying to develop the idea that Sandinoism is a threat to the government of El Salvador." The speech sounded as if the meeting with Carter had little if any impact on Ortega, but *Barricada*, the Sandinista newspaper, reported the next day that Ortega had denounced CIA maneuvers in Central America, though he had not. Possibly, that deletion was a concession to the meeting.

The American People Debate Nicaragua

When the Sandinistas requested aid from the United States, they were probably unaware of George Washington's warning that "it is folly in one nation to look for disinterested favors from another; . . . it must pay with a portion of its independence for whatever it may accept." The price paid to the Soviet bloc for aid was large, but privately contracted; the United States generally demands less and gives more, but its demands are public and thus more embarrassing to a recipient, particularly those that are acutely sensitive to infringements on its sense of dignity.

The need to obtain Congressional approval for new aid to Nicaragua opened a national debate in the United States. Though the aid might have brought the two governments together, the debate inevitably separated them. For their blasts at U.S. imperialism, the Sandinistas received from Congress the American equivalent of rhetorical retaliation.

On September 11, 1979, after a month of interagency reviews on Central America, Assistant Secretary of State Vaky and Ambassador Pezzullo presented the Administration's policy on Nicaragua and Central America before the House Subcommittee on Inter-American Affairs. Vaky stressed the importance of the economic dimension in shaping the future course of the Nicaraguan revolution:

> While it is true that Marxist elements are well-positioned to exert power, they do not yet dominate the situation. Moderate democratic elements capable of exerting influence and power of their own also exist in key places in the Government and in society. . . . Nicaragua's future internal policies and relationships with the outside world will, in fact, be determined by those Nicaraguans who best define and meet the country's needs during the reconstruction period. . . . The course of the Nicaraguan revolution can thus be affected in no small way by how the United States perceives it and relates to it.[32]

He and Pezzullo encountered some stiff questions from friends as well as foes of the Administration. Democratic Chairman Gus Yatron asked whether the Sandinistas were "Marxist ideologues." Pezzullo responded that there were many "who have been weaned on Marxist philosophy," but "the practicality of running a government with economic difficulties of monumental proportions forces them to be pragmatic." Rep. Dante Fascell sought explanations for the Sandinistas' anti-American statements, their treatment of the press, and the arms they received from the Soviet Union. Fascell, however, conceded that the only sensible policy was to compete with the Soviets by providing aid.[33]

As soon as AID's program was ready in November, President Carter sent it to Congress, requesting $80 million as a supplemental in Economic Support Funds for Central America and the Caribbean. The message announced that the region was in a "crisis" and U.S. national interests required a quick response. Almost all of the money was requested for one country—Nicaragua—and of that, $70 million would be a loan (60 percent of that to the private sector) and $5 million a grant for private organizations working in the country.[34]

The debate on aid to Nicaragua tested the tolerance of an American people who had grown impatient. The issue was whether the United States should help a group of young revolutionaries who, at best, disliked the United States, and were very fond of Cuba. The Administration, of course, did not frame the issue that way, nor did the Sandinistas see the issue in those terms. The Administration's basic argument was summarized by Clement Zablocki, then Chairman of the House Foreign Affairs Committee: "I cannot give my colleagues any assurances that if we approve this assistance that Nicaragua will not fall within the Marxist orbit. But . . . if we do not, we will be abandoning the field to Castro and his Soviet bosses—with adverse consequences for our own national security."[35]

That argument and Administration muscle ultimately carried the bill through an extremely grueling debate. Conservative Republican Rep. Robert Bauman insisted that Nicaragua was already lost, and the United States was foolish to give money to Communists. Rep. Edward J. Derwinski, who would join the Reagan Administration as Counselor to the State Department, opposed the bill because of the "major presence of Cubans and to a lesser degree, East Germans in Nicaragua."[36]

Rep. Lee Hamilton, a supporter of the aid, was aware of the Sandinistas' "hyperbolic, bombastic condemnation of 'Yankee intervention,' [and found it] very disturbing. It has not been explained to my satisfaction. Moreover, if it is taken seriously, then it must be seen as inconsistent with the claim that Nicaragua desires cordial relations with the United States." Still, Hamilton noted a recent article in *La Prensa* headlined "U.S. Had Helped More Than During the Earthquake." He argued that as long as *La Prensa* was free to publish such articles, the United States would be making a serious mistake to abandon the revolution.[37]

On February 25, 1980, the House held its third secret session in history in order to examine classified data on Soviet-bloc involvement in Nicaragua. At its close, Rep. Jim Wright concluded that the information did not convince him Nicaragua was Communist-controlled. Congress then passed the aid, but only after adding numerous amendments, requiring the President to take into account the Sandinistas' commitment to human rights, labor union rights, free press, and much else. Most important, before disbursing the aid, the President would have to submit a certification to Congress that Nicaragua was not supporting insurgents abroad.

Though the Senate passed the bill in January and the House in February, a delaying maneuver impeded final passage of the authorization act until May 19, 1980. Several private groups, including the Council of the Americas, which represented 80 percent of U.S. businesses with investments in Latin America, lobbied hard for the aid. On May 9, 1980, the Council sent a telegram to all members of Congress, acknowledging that the aid had some risk, but: "We believe . . . that the risk is worth taking." The economic aid survived the battle, but Robert Bauman succeeded in defeating the military aid portion, arguing: "We have given them more than $60 million in the last fifteen months. All we have gotten back, in every international forum . . . was vile, consummate attacks on the people who have paid the bill."[38]

The President signed the bill into law on May 31, but the appropriations process provided the opponents another opportunity to delay its passage until July 2, 1980, and a last-minute amendment prevented the President from disbursing the funds until October 1, 1980. By that time, Ronald Reagan was the nominee of the Republican Party, whose platform deplored "the Marxist Sandinista takeover of Nicaragua" and recommended the end of the aid program.[39] The Republican Convention was only one of many harbingers that the mood of the country had changed. The nation and the world would have to wait until November 1980 to learn just how definitive was the transformation.

Symptomatic of this change was the number of articles by conservative columnists during the summer of 1980 about Nicaraguan collaboration with Cuba and support for leftist guerrillas. In fact, as we shall see, the Sandinistas were still trying to deflect or divert internal and external pressures to help the Salvadoran rebels. To compensate for their lack of real solidarity, the Sandinistas sought other means to prove their radical credentials. In March 1980, Daniel Ortega attacked the United States for "trying to drown Jamaica and Grenada, and threatening to intervene in El Salvador."[40] Hugo Torres, the Deputy Minister for State Security, accused the CIA of "trying to promote unrest . . . [and] divide the Nicaraguans . . . "[41] The charges were untrue, but each accusation made it more difficult for U.S. supporters of the aid to defend it.

The Sandinistas became much more open in their Cuban and Soviet relationships and less tolerant of the moderate elements in their coalition. Robelo found himself engaged in a losing struggle with the FSLN to implement the Council of State as originally envisaged. On April 16, 1980, the Junta met to consider the Frente's proposal to expand the Council of State to 47 members in order to include the new mass organizations created by the FSLN; this would give the FSLN an absolute and fixed majority. Robelo and Violeta de Chamorro voted against the proposal, and Ramírez and Moisés Hassán voted in favor. Daniel Ortega was out of the country at the time. Three days later, Chamorro resigned in protest, though she concealed her real concerns by citing health reasons. On April 21, the proposal was published as a decree with all five names at the bottom.[42]

The next day, Alfonso Robelo resigned from the Junta and held a press conference to criticize the FSLN for imposing changes on the Plan of Government without obtaining a consensus. The Council of State was only one issue for Robelo; he had also been pressing for an electoral timetable and greater access to the news media by political parties. He said that he resigned to force the FSLN to "reflect on what it is doing. We hope they will reconsider." The Directorate responded by calling Robelo a wealthy capitalist who could not identify with the people or their revolution.[43]

Events within both countries were becoming linked and entangled. The resignations in Managua impeded the Congressional effort to approve the aid to Nicaragua, which in turn exacerbated divisions within Nicaragua. Ambassador Pezzullo decided that both the U.S.-Nicaraguan relationship and the future of pluralism in Nicaragua depended on whether the moderates and the FSLN could refashion a compromise. He encouraged COSEP, the business association that had become the center of the political opposition, to accept the Council of State, participate in its inauguration, and support two new moderates for the Junta, Arturo Cruz, the president of the Central Bank, and Rafael Cordova Rivas. In exchange, the FSLN agreed to announce a timetable for elections by July 19, 1980, the first anniversary of the revolution. [44]

Robelo decided to test the limits of the new political bargain. In a speech on May 10, 1980, to gain support for his party, the Nicaraguan Democratic Movement, he openly criticized the Sandinista ideology for the first time: "We are openly against the reign of terror which Communism implants in the nations which it oppresses. . . . We reject class hatred. . . . We must not forget that only work produces wealth and that without production, we can only divide poverty."[45]

The resignations of the moderates in Managua and the changing mood in the United States affected Congressional perceptions of Nicaragua. Many North Americans were beginning to feel as if radicals were taking advantage of U.S. patience and generosity. The Sandinistas did not understand this any better than North Americans could understand or accept the anti-American rhetoric of the Sandinistas.

Carter: Mutual Temptations

The only way to get rid of a temptation is to yield to it.

OSCAR WILDE

THE FIRST ANNIVERSARY of the Nicaraguan revolution—July 19, 1980—occurred, appropriately, between the Republican and Democratic Party conventions. Both nations were sitting on the proverbial fence trying to decide how to view the other. The American people were about to choose between two profoundly different perspectives, one that saw the Sandinistas as a direct threat to U.S. interests and another that saw them as a difficult problem. The first, Republican vision pledged to end aid and stop the Marxist-Leninists, and the second, Democratic vision counseled patience and perseverance.

The Nicaraguan government was also uncertain about the United States. One faction demanded confrontation with the United States and support for revolutions throughout Central America; the other counseled caution.

These two visions competed to define each nation's policy, but the competition did not occur in a political vacuum. On the contrary, changes within Nicaragua and in its international relationships as well as increasing tension in the global struggle between the Soviet Union and the United States strengthened the credibility of the narrower, more bellicose vision in both countries. From mid-1980 to the inauguration of Ronald Reagan in January 1981, both governments communicated their fundamental concerns to the other and both were tested by high-risk, but also potentially high-yield, temptations to resolve the ambiguity in the relationship with a lightning change. Ultimately, it was the decision by Nicaragua to succumb to its temptation that defined the future relationship.

Changing Internal and International Relationships

By July 1980, the revolution had not mellowed, but neither had it hardened. International observers could still draw on diverse phenomena to confirm their fears or their hopes. Alan Riding described the ambiguity, albeit with a positive spin:

Rather than adopting a Cuban or other revolutionary model, the Sandinistas have been feeling their way along a narrow path between their dreams and their capabilities, with realism generally winning. Their rhetoric, above all in foreign policy, remains leftist, but their policies are pragmatic and, at times, even conservative.[1]

The regime still wanted to maintain relationships with Nicaraguan moderates and international democrats and was willing to compromise to do that. At the same time, the FSLN was ready to take some risks to declare its revolutionary credentials. For the first anniversary celebration, Fidel Castro was invited to be the principal foreign speaker, even though that cost Nicaragua the attendance of both Omar Torrijos and Rodrigo Carazo.

But revolutionary Nicaragua still wanted good relations with democracies in Latin America and Europe and "normal" relations with the United States. Recognizing the regime's need to be recognized, the Carter Administration sent to the anniversary ceremony a senior delegation led by U.S. Ambassador to the UN Donald McHenry and William Bowdler, who had become Assistant Secretary of State for Inter-American Affairs when Vaky resigned in December 1979. The delegation included a banker, a Senator, and the National Commander of the Veterans of Foreign Wars.

Castro had been told by me directly in a secret meeting in January 1980 that the Carter Administration would interpret any criticism of Reagan or praise of Carter as unfriendly and unhelpful. Nevertheless, in a forty-minute speech in Managua, he blasted Reagan and the Republican Party platform and complimented Carter for adopting "a more intelligent and constructive policy" toward Nicaragua than previous Administrations had adopted toward Cuba. And he couldn't resist a chance to poke the United States: "We welcome the aid that the United States has given, but our only sincere regret is that it is so little, so little for the richest country in the world that spends $160 billion on defense."[2]

Daniel Ortega delivered the main speech for the Nicaraguan government and devoted most of it to criticizing past U.S. interventions. His only allusion to elections was to say that they would be held "appropriate to the spirit of democracy."

The Sandinistas tried to placate Carazo, who had declined to come, by inviting him to speak at the closing ceremony of the Literacy Crusade on August 23, 1980. The Nicaraguans were justifiably proud of the success of their first major project, which involved one-fifth of the population over a five-month period and reduced adult illiteracy from 50 percent to 12 percent. With considerable Cuban assistance, the regime viewed the crusade as an opportunity to reduce illiteracy, show the poor that the new government was pursuing their interests, and indoctrinate the people to the revolution. Costa Rica had also offered its teachers, but the FSLN preferred Cubans.[3] As a result, 1,200 teachers from Cuba participated, along with 40 from Costa Rica, 70 from Spain, and 39 from the Dominican Republic. The FSLN would not accept Peace Corps Volunteers, because they viewed them incorrectly as CIA agents.

Carazo's visit in August 1980 served as an important marker, both for pluralism in Nicaragua and for Nicaragua's relationships with those democratic countries that had been crucial for the Sandinista victory. The visit also had an interesting parallel with an event twenty-one years earlier. Carazo made a plea for elections. A similar plea had been made by José Figueres in Havana on March 22, 1959, on a platform shared with Fidel Castro. When Figueres, who had sent arms to Castro during the revolution, completed his speech, Castro openly insulted him for having "been influenced by the campaigns in the international press attacking the Cuban revolution."[4] Humberto Ortega did the same to Carazo, calling the demand for elections part of an international counterrevolutionary conspiracy. Ortega then read an FSLN communiqué that defined "democracy" as "participation [that] does not begin and end with elections." He said the electoral process would begin in 1984, leading to elections the next year. Their purpose would be to "improve the power of the revolution, not a raffle to see who has power, because the people have the power through their vanguard, the FSLN and its National Directorate."[5]

Humberto Ortega's speech infuriated COSEP, which felt that the Frente had betrayed its promise of May 4 to announce a timetable for elections. Of course, Ortega did announce a timetable, but it was considerably different and more distant than what COSEP wanted. The speech also embarrassed Carazo, who was already in serious political trouble because a Costa Rican legislative commission was investigating charges of arms trafficking by his Administration. Carazo therefore decided to cool relations with Nicaragua, and by 1981 and 1982, the relationship had chilled.[6]

The Costa Rican trajectory symbolized the changing character of Nicaragua's international relations in the year since the revolution. After the Sandinistas triumphed, Venezuela decided to help the moderates play a role in assisting the revolution to fulfill its pledges. On February 27, 1980, Venezuela pledged to guarantee Nicaragua's oil supply, and in July, Mexico agreed to sell Nicaragua one-half of its oil needs. Although Venezuela and Mexico used the same instrument to help and influence Nicaragua, the two governments pursued different ends. Venezuela, especially under Herrera Campíns, was vigorously anti-Marxist and determined to help Nicaraguan moderates build a democracy, like Venezuela's. Mexico saw its interests served by helping a Marxist, anti-American government in Central America as it built a hegemonic political party like the PRI of Mexico.[7]

Compañeros and Contras

Although Nicaragua wanted aid from the United States, and the United States wanted democracy for Nicaragua, these issues were secondary to their security interests: the FSLN wanted to prevent the United States from helping the counterrevolution, and the United States wanted to prevent Nicaragua from supporting revolutions in other countries.

Shortly after the Sandinistas marched into Managua, former National Guardsmen began to plot their return. In September 1979, when Ortega complained that

Comandante Bravo was conspiring with "agents of the CIA" to overthrow the Sandinista government, he was half-right. Bravo had begun to conspire, but not with the U.S. government, which was not even aware of it. However, one month before, on August 1, 1979, Enrique Bermúdez, who was the Defense Attaché in the Nicaraguan Embassy during the revolution, "Bravo," and several other former Guard officers had met with Rep. John Murphy in Washington and had then held a press conference in which they tried to warn of the threat of Communism. They received almost no press attention. They met afterward to talk about plans to overthrow the Sandinistas. Two months later, Bravo went to Honduras to meet with some of his men. The Sandinistas were waiting for him. On October 10, 1979, he was tortured and murdered.[8]

Guardsmen in Honduras sought help from other governments, though not from the United States. They distrusted the Carter Administration almost as much as they hated the Sandinistas. Later reports hinted that the contra war in Nicaragua was actually begun by the Carter Administration, but these reports are false, and Carter himself later denied them.[9] The Carter Administration did not believe there were any significant efforts by ex-Guardsmen to attack the Nicaraguan government, and interpreted Nicaraguan charges as an excuse for militarization or as evidence of the regime's paranoia. Testimony to the World Court later confirmed that the Nicaraguan government also did not take seriously the reports of conspiracies by ex-Guardsmen. Luis Carrión Cruz, Vice Minister of Interior, told the Court that "organized military and para-military activities" began in December 1981. Prior to that date, Carrión said, there were "a few small bands very poorly armed, scattered along the northern border. . . . They did not have any military effectiveness."[10]

The United States, however, took seriously reports about possible Nicaraguan support for leftist guerrillas in Central America, and the Sandinista government was sensitive to these concerns. In their first press conference on July 28, 1979, the Directorate specifically denied

> that we are organizing internationalist brigades in Nicaragua to fight in Guatemala and El Salvador. Nothing could be more false and absurd than this. At this time, and ever since we started our struggle, the Sandinista Front's primary concern has been the fate of the Nicaraguan people. Today, our task is reconstruction. . . . We are not going looking for conflicts elsewhere.[11]

The 72-Hour Document confirmed that the Directorate was saying this privately as well as publicly. According to Pastora, however, the debate within the Directorate about whether to help their Salvadoran and Guatemalan compañeros began almost immediately after the triumph; it was not resolved for more than a year.[12] The U.S. Congress remained skeptical about the Sandinistas, and that is why they amended the aid bill for Nicaragua to prevent disbursement until the President's certification.

Given the deluge of intelligence reported in the newspapers on Sandinista support for the Salvadoran rebels, few expected Carter would certify. In mid-September 1980, *Time* magazine predicted that Carter would "put off signing the bill until after the November elections. To sign it now might give the Republicans a campaign issue that the President scarcely needs."[13] The politics of the issue did not deter Carter. He signed the certification, which read: "On the basis of an evaluation of the available evidence, the Government of Nicaragua 'has not cooperated with or harbors any international terrorist organization or is abiding, abetting, or supporting acts of violence or terrorism in other countries.'"[14]

Conservatives were upset by Carter's decision, particularly because Anastasio Somoza was murdered in Paraguay five days later. Though many suspected the Sandinistas were ultimately responsible, the only evidence pointed to South American terrorists.[15] Rep. Robert Bauman called for a Congressional hearing. Its results were inconclusive, like the evidence.[16]

The certification was a short statement at the end of a long review. The Administration had received reports of arms smuggling through Nicaragua to the Salvadoran rebels, and there were analysts—particularly in the Defense Intelligence Agency but also some in the CIA—who judged that the reports were probably accurate. However, the State Department interpreted the law as setting two minimal criteria for judging the reports. First, was the Nicaraguan government involved in the arms trafficking? Reports suggesting that some Nicaraguans might be aiding the Salvadoran insurgency would not meet this test, unless there was proof of government involvement. Second, was the proof conclusive? This required a judgment by the intelligence community on the reliability of the reports.

In September 1980, Carter's senior advisers—Secretary of State Edmund Muskie, Brown, Brzezinski, and Turner—found cause for concern that the Nicaraguans *might* be involved, but the evidence was not conclusive. However, before recommending that the President sign a certification, they instructed Ambassador Pezzullo to meet with Nicaraguan officials. The Nicaraguans denied any "governmental" involvement, but asserted that the government of Nicaragua could not be held responsible for the activities of individual Nicaraguans. Pezzullo warned them that U.S. concerns extended to all activities within their borders.[17]

After examining the evidence, the Secretaries of State and Defense, the Director of the Central Intelligence Agency, and the National Security Adviser all agreed that the proof was not conclusive that the Nicaraguan government was directing the arms smuggling. Carter signed the determination, but the Administration decided to send Deputy Assistant Secretary of State James Cheek to Managua. He told Daniel Ortega and other members of the Junta that if the United States found that Nicaragua was cooperating with or aiding rebels in other countries, it would terminate the aid program. The argument that the Sandinistas could not control all activities in Nicaragua was not acceptable. The Nicaraguan leadership said that they understood the message, and they promised that all steps would be taken to ensure that such activities not occur.[18]

According to documents captured later from the Salvadoran guerrillas, Cheek's démarche achieved its purpose. On September 27, the Nicaraguans told the Salvadorans that the United States had sensitive information, and therefore the Nicaraguans would not permit any arms shipments. The Salvadoran in charge of organizing the arms shipments wrote: "It seems very strange to us that a gringo official would come to them [the FSLN] to practically warn [them]. . . . If they have detected something concrete, it is logical that they would hit us and they would arm the great propaganda machine and not that they would warn us."[19]

U.S. information was not "concrete," but the Sandinistas told the Salvadorans it was in order to justify a halt to the arms shipments. That left the guerrillas bewildered, and the Sandinistas with more time. Since the Sandinista victory, the Salvadoran guerrillas, who had provided money (through kidnappings) and cadre to the Sandinistas during their revolution, had sought FSLN help.[20] The FSLN felt a camaraderie and supported the Salvadoran revolution morally, but it was reluctant to translate that abstract support into arms or training, which could endanger the Nicaraguan revolution.

During the first anniversary celebration, a senior delegation of Salvadorans arrived in Managua and, by their own account, "were told to keep ourselves locked up and not to go out" for nearly two weeks. Their report on the trip is revealing: "The Frente undervalued them and ignored them. . . . There was not a relationship of mutual respect but rather one of imposition. The Frente was very conservative, and it had a tendency to look down on the situation [in El Salvador] and to protect the Nicaraguan revolution."[21]

The FSLN promised their support, but continued to attach conditions that infuriated the Salvadorans. First, Nicaragua insisted on Salvadoran unity, on the grounds that aid could not be used effectively until that occurred. In 1979 and 1980, with Cuban help, the Salvadoran guerrilla groups united to form the military Farabundo Martí National Liberation Front (FMLN). At that point, the Sandinistas offered the Salvadorans the names of arms smugglers from Costa Rica and Panama who had helped ferry arms during the Nicaraguan revolution. However, that was halted in June 1980 when a small Panamanian plane crashed in El Salvador with arms that had been stockpiled in Costa Rica during the Nicaraguan revolution.[22] In July 1980, the FSLN criticized the Salvadorans for inflating the number of their forces, having bad propaganda, and lacking concrete plans. Nicaragua postponed its assistance again by suggesting the Salvadoran guerrillas develop direct relations with Cuba and other Communist governments. Jorge Shafik Handal, the leader of the Salvadoran Communist Party, and others traveled throughout the Communist bloc. Vietnam, with the largest stock of surplus U.S. arms, was the most forthcoming. Several other governments promised to provide token support, and Cuba promised to transship the weapons to the guerrillas.

The FSLN therefore successfully diverted the Salvadorans for fifteen months. However, by September 1980, the Sandinistas could no longer avoid the Salvadorans' supplications. About 120 tons of weapons from Vietnam had been stockpiled in Nicaragua. On September 26, the Salvadorans complained that they had received less than four tons; the next day, they were told of Cheek's démarche and of the suspension of all shipments.[23]

The Sandinistas continued to stall through October. The FSLN decided not to host a meeting of Communist parties of Central America in mid-October because they wanted to keep their distance from the Salvadoran conflict. Cuba hosted the meeting instead. However, to compensate, the Sandinistas agreed to permit the Salvadoran guerrillas to operate a clandestine radio station in Nicaragua.[24] It appears that the goal of avoiding a hostile relationship with the United States continued to inhibit, though not completely to preclude, the FSLN's revolutionary inclinations.

On October 10, 1980, Tomás Borge was probably partly truthful when he said:

> We have promised in all seriousness not to send arms or troops to help the Salvadorans, and we have kept our promise. Mr. Carter can rest assured that we are keeping our promise. . . . There is not the slightest danger that someday it will be revealed that we sent arms because we haven't.[25]

Beginning in the fall of 1980 and lasting until April 1981, the United States and Nicaraguan governments passed through exceptionally awkward transitions—within each country and between the two. The Iranian revolution had asserted its national purpose by taking the United States "hostage," and this provoked a nationalistic surge in the United States, which contributed to Ronald Reagan's landslide victory on November 4, 1980. Governing during the "lame duck" period was especially difficult with regard to an area like Central America, where the views of the incumbent and the incoming President appeared most different. The Carter Administration continued its policies, but the region began to respond to a different President who had not yet taken office.

The Nicaraguan government also was under stress. The Directorate saw the beginning of a militant internal and external opposition, and it feared that the Reagan Administration might exploit any division within Nicaragua to undermine the revolution. Some believed that the new Administration would undertake the "imperialistic intervention" that they had long expected but nevertheless hoped would not occur. The challenge for the Sandinistas was how to defend themselves and their revolution.

During this uncertain period, both governments were tested by temptation—the possibility of attaining the "perfect" solution. In this case, as in many others, the "perfect was the enemy of the good." For the Sandinistas, the temptation was disguised as a successful revolution in El Salvador. For the United States, the temptation was a coup that would eliminate the Marxists from the Nicaraguan government. Biting this tempting apple poisoned the relationship each had been trying to nurture.

Salazar and the Counterrevolutionary Temptation

Humberto Ortega's speech in August 1980 postponing elections and distorting their purpose provided the spark that ignited Jorge Salazar, the young and dynamic president of the Union of Nicaraguan Agricultural Producers. Salazar had a reputation of integrity, and many viewed him as a natural leader of the opposition. In October 1980, the U.S. Embassy was told that a group of moderate civilians, led by Salazar, and non-Marxist Sandinistas in the Nicaraguan military were conspiring to overthrow the Directorate. The Ambassador was informed; he was not asked for help.[26] Less than one month before the U.S. Presidential elections, Pezzullo passed this time bomb to the NSC. If an attempted coup in Nicaragua occurred, it would undoubtedly affect the campaign, but the precise nature of its effect was difficult to assess because so much depended on how it would occur and whether it would succeed.

The conspiracy posed the same difficult question for the Nicaraguan moderates who were contacted by Salazar as it did for the United States. Most moderates within and outside Nicaragua hoped for a change in government or at least a change in leadership that would be less attached to the Soviet Union and Cuba and more interested in democracy. Some were coming to believe that would only occur by force. Some Americans shared this view. Both sets of actors felt the moment had arrived when Salazar, a popular and charismatic leader, informed them that there existed such a group in the military and they had already contacted him.

The question for the United States was what, if anything, it should do. If the moderates tried to overthrow the Directorate and then were eliminated by the Sandinistas, that would extinguish any hope for moderation. If the U.S. remained passive, it would appear once again to have been several steps behind events, or worse, irrelevant (at a moment when the President needed desperately to look assertive).

If the plot were genuine and stood some chance of success, should the United State help? Some in the Administration were prepared to pay the price of again being labeled "interventionistic" if the coup succeeded, but if it failed, the Administration would be blamed for ineptness, and its strategy of trying to moderate the Sandinistas would be finished. On the other hand, if this conspiracy was actually just a sophisticated entrapment, then the United States should discourage the moderates, or keep its distance.

The conspiracy, in short, was a high-risk temptation. It could be the last chance to depose the Communists in the Nicaraguan government. Or it could erase the non-Marxists from the Nicaraguan government in a single stroke. Some of the suspicions that the Carter Administration had about the Directorate had been confirmed in the past year. Those who were most pessimistic and suspicious of the Sandinistas tended to favor supporting a coup; and those who were less pessimistic both about what had happened in Nicaragua and what could be expected in the future were more inclined to resist the temptation.

Pezzullo, in the latter camp, believed the conspiracy was an entrapment. Another senior official with considerable experience with Cuba explained that Castro started entrapping his enemies in Cuba shortly after taking power. Using agent provocateurs, Castro would raise the hopes of his enemies, and when a critical number of the opposition had committed, he would arrest them all. Castro and his government had improved this skill since then. The kind of conspiracy that Pezzullo described looked to this individual as if it had been made in Havana. There was a second tough question that the Administration would need to address: if it were genuine, how should the United States anticipate or respond to any effort by Cuban military forces to defend the Sandinistas?

All of the agony of trying to forge answers to these tough questions as the Presidential election approached was preempted by Pezzullo's growing conviction that the conspiracy was an entrapment. He warned Salazar. Edén Pastora, who learned that the Directorate knew of the plot and had condemned Salazar to death, also warned his friend, but to no avail. Salazar restricted his contacts. The election passed in the United States. On November 16, the security police confronted Salazar in a gas station and shot him. It was not known whether the conspiracy was a government entrapment from the beginning, or whether the Sandinistas only learned about it later and then turned it to their own ends. It was also not known whether there was any support within the military for a more moderate approach to domestic and international problems.

El Salvador and the Revolutionary Temptation

Just as the Carter Administration was grappling with what to do about the Sandinistas, the Directorate was probably addressing the mirror question: How should Nicaragua respond to the election of Ronald Reagan? No doubt there were some who said that Reagan's election confirmed the Sandinistas' expectations about U.S. imperialism; the Directorate should accelerate the building of its defenses. Others may have argued that a new Administration should be given the benefit of the doubt and time to adjust its preconceptions to international realities.

The two arguments were not necessarily incompatible. The FSLN strengthened its armed forces and stepped up its harassment of internal moderate groups. The police arrested Robelo on November 9, 1980, and censored press coverage of his political party's upcoming rally at Nandaime. Salazar was killed one week later, and the government began to harass and restrict the access to the radio by the Church and especially Archbishop Obando y Bravo.[27]

Central Americans followed the U.S. election as if their future depended on it, and in a sense, it did.[28] With Reagan's victory, right-wing leaders danced in the streets of Guatemala City. In El Salvador, the right unleashed a wave of repression, killing six opposition leaders, four American nuns and religious workers, and two American labor organizers.

The Salvadoran left, believing Reagan would intervene in El Salvador, decided to try to complete the revolution before he could stop them. The guerrillas therefore posed for the Sandinistas almost the same question that Salazar posed to the United States: should Nicaragua support the Salvadoran guerrillas' "final offensive" to seize power? The probability of success was low, but the outcome was optimal. On the other hand, if the Sandinistas did not help the Salvadoran guerrillas and they were defeated, that might set back irrevocably the chances of revolution in El Salvador. If the FSLN failed to help in the hour of need, what effect would that have on its image among leftists in the world? If the Sandinistas provided strong support to the Salvadorans to achieve victory, the United States would almost certainly discover it, and that could permanently affect relations with the United States, particularly with the new Administration.

There were two major differences between the two questions the two governments faced. First, the Salvadoran guerrillas (and the Cubans) posed the question of aid directly to the FSLN. Salazar had not asked for help from the United States. Second, the Salvadorans were determined to launch the "offensive" on a specific date, so the Sandinistas may have believed that they would not have a second chance: either support the Salvadorans and hope they can win, or passively watch their compañeros' revolution die.

Through the questions were similar, the differences might partly explain why the two governments answered differently. The United States was not really asked for aid, and available evidence seemed to suggest that the coup was not genuine. The United States therefore did not have to make a decision, and it did not. The FSLN was asked, and there was no doubt that the bus was leaving; as Ken Kesey wrote in another context: you either had to get on the bus, or get off. The Directorate chose to get on, but the available evidence suggests it was not an easy decision.

Several years later, after exploring this issue with a number of Sandinista leaders, Pezzullo concluded: "They were torn. They were pressured by their so-called friends in Salvador, and yet there was a desire to have a relationship with the United States, even though they found us to be a little difficult to comprehend or to trust."[29] Humberto Ortega later admitted they had made a critical error and "paid a heavy price for our internationalist romanticism."[30]

On November 1, 1980, the Salvadoran logistics coordinator in Managua informed the guerrilla general staff in El Salvador that the Frente had finally approved their plans and had scheduled the first shipment of arms to begin on November 4. But the Salvadoran said the FSLN were nervous—"it is such a hot potato for them"—and they wanted to expedite the shipment of 109 tons of arms in November. Apparently, they were feeling pressure from Cuba, which expected to send 400 tons to Nicaraguan warehouses ready for transshipment. The Nicaraguans had "taken a firm step," and suddenly, the Salvadorans had more equipment than they could handle.[31]

A senior Nicaraguan government official told me that the Directorate thought the rebels would win the El Salvador. Like the Mexicans coming to the support of the Sandinistas two weeks before the final offensive, the Nicaraguans thought they could gain influence with the Salvadorans if they helped at this critical juncture. (They apparently failed to remember how limited and illusory the Mexican influence on them proved to be after the victory.) Whatever the reasons for the Directorate's decision to help the Salvadoran guerrillas, the long-term consequences were grave for both.

On January 2, 1981, CIA aerial photography revealed a C-47 on a small airstrip at Papalonal, 25 miles northwest of Managua and just a short hop across the Gulf of Fonseca to El Salvador. The CIA had been watching the field change from a small dirt airstrip of 800 meters used for agricultural purposes in July 1980 to a 1,200-meter graded strip with turnarounds, hard dispersal areas, and storage buildings by late December. The pattern and speed of construction convinced the experts of its military function. The CIA analyzed the pictures from the aerial photography together with a vast quantity of new intelligence from many different sources that had been collected during the previous month and sent a report to the White House on January 6, 1981.

That report for the first time, in my opinion, provided conclusive proof that the Nicaraguan government was providing significant amounts of aid to the insurgency in El Salvador. Such an airstrip could not have been built or operated without a decision by the Nicaraguan Directorate or its Military Commission.[32] The law on Nicaraguan aid did not allow any option but to terminate aid. I called Assistant Secretary of State William Bowdler and then David Aaron, who scheduled a mini-SCC meeting the next day to review the intelligence and develop options for U.S. policy toward El Salvador and Nicaragua. Carter, Brzezinski, Christopher, and numerous others were working full-time to obtain the release of the American hostages in Iran, and it was decided to seek the President's decision only after the options were fully developed.

The intelligence community had developed four separate sources that confirmed Sandinista arms shipments by boat, land (through Honduras), and most recently, by air. In November, a Costa Rican arms trafficker had sold several planes to a Honduran aviation company that was a Sandinista front. The company took possession of the planes and sent them to Papalonal for flights to Lempa and Santa Teresa airstrips in El Salvador. On November 25, one of the planes crashed at Santa Teresa, and because of that, the FSLN suspended flights. They began again on January 2, and plans called for four flights per week until the offensive when daily flights would begin. Cuban and Nicaraguan officials were directing the operation.[33]

Those at the January 7 meeting decided to instruct Ambassador Pezzullo to deliver a stiff démarche to Sandinista officials. There was much discussion about how to use the evidence at international forums to both condemn the Nicaraguan intervention and forge an international response. The intelligence community was asked to develop options on how to capture planes or encourage people to defect and testify on the actions. A debate, which continued and deepened during the Reagan Administration, ensued between the political appointees and the officials of the intelligence community. The political appointees argued that the intelligence should be declassified and offered as proof in international forums; the intelligence community was naturally more sensitive to protecting its sources and methods. It was also decided to send a foreign service officer, Jon Glassman, to El Salvador to help that government prepare a case for the OAS against Nicaraguan intervention based on the reports captured from the guerrillas.

Pezzullo received the instructions, and on January 9, he "reminded Borge of the government's promises not to become involved in the Salvadoran conflict, warning that the first casualty of any such action would be U.S.-Nicaraguan relations." He was assured that Nicaragua's policy had not changed. Borge "acknowledged the possibility that some arms might have passed through Nicaragua and some people connected with the government might have assisted in some way, but insisted that Nicaragua was acting responsibly and had even recently intercepted a truckload of arms passing from Costa Rica to El Salvador." Borge was slow to realize that this cover story had been blown away. Pezzullo alluded to some of the specific reports and demanded that the Frente stop using the Papalonal airstrip and close down Radio Liberación, the Salvadoran guerrilla radio station.[34]

The timing of the démarche was perfect, but the Sandinistas evidently decided that they could not hold back the momentum of the revolution. The next day, January 10, 1981, Radio Liberación broadcast to guerrillas in El Salvador that "the decisive hour has come to initiate the . . . battles for the seizure of power." Shortly after, Radio Managua, the FSLN station, reported: "A few hours after the FMLN General Command ordered a final offensive to defeat the [Salvadoran] regime, . . . the first victories in the combat waged by our [sic] forces began being reported."[35]

The "final offensive" was a fiasco. The guerrillas expected a popular insurrection and the assassination of Napoleón Duarte and other leaders. They struck at about forty locations throughout El Salvador and destroyed a major army arsenal, but the army remained united and the population was unresponsive to the rebels' rhetoric. The guerrillas proved they were much weaker than they had thought. By Monday, January 12, the final offensive apparently peaked.

On January 14, a mini-SCC meeting was held to review the situation. Because the Salvadoran military had taken most of the steps that Duarte and the United States had demanded[36] and because of the urgent need to replace the arsenal, the group recommended sending $5.9 million of arms and ammunition to the Salvadoran government. The President approved the proposal, and the decision to send lethal military aid was announced on Monday, January 19, after members of Congress were briefed. On Friday afternoon, January 16, Aaron chaired a mini-SCC to develop a ten-day strategy that would give the new Administration time to decide what it would do. Carter approved instructions to Pezzullo to inform the Nicaraguans that aid was suspended and that their continued support of the Salvadoran rebels could lead to a rupture in relations. In response, the Sandinistas promised to close Radio Liberación, which they did on January 20, and to take "strong measures" to prevent the "funny business" at the airfields and other "unofficial activities."[37]

Carter later had an opportunity to explain to the Sandinista leadership in person his decision to suspend aid:

> I had no alternative but to cut off aid to the Sandinistas before I left office, because there was evidence that was clear to me that the Sandinistas were giving assistance to the revolutionaries in El Salvador, and the law required me to stop the aid. I was very eager to give the people of Nicaragua economic aid after the revolution, but it was not possible under those circumstances.[38]

On Monday night, January 19, 1981, the General Services Administration shipped the last files—the historical record of the Carter Administration—to Atlanta. As I was cleaning out my desk, I received a draft memo from the State Department for Carter to give to Reagan the next day on whether to terminate aid to Nicaragua. The next day was the inauguration. Both Carter and Reagan had other things on their minds.

The State of Relations

As Carter left office, the relationship between the United States and the revolutionary government of Nicaragua had been tested over an eighteen-month period. Neither side scored very well, but both sides passed.

Neither the internal situation in Nicaragua nor its relationship to the United States had met the hopes of the optimists or the fears of the pessimists. By the standards of most revolutions, Nicaragua's was reasonably moderate. There were no executions or "blood-baths," as occurred in Cuba and Iran. In fact, Nicaragua outlawed the death penalty, and there were few reports of human rights violations in the first two years.

There were signs of moderation and signs of Marxism-Leninism. There was space for political parties and groups, but the FSLN began to build powerful internal security and armed forces. The government negotiated to reschedule rather than repudiate its international debt, and there were few expropriations beyond Somoza's estates. Eighteen months after Castro took power, he shut down or seized all the independent press and media and limited the role of the Church, but in Nicaragua, *La Prensa* remained a vigorous voice of opposition and the political influence of the Church steadily increased. Although many Cuban opposition leaders, including some revolutionaries, had left or been imprisoned within Castro's first eighteen months, almost no moderate Nicaraguan leaders had left by January 1981. Though business leaders were reluctant to make significant new investments, they did make some investments, and the economy began to recover. Businessmen also became important political as well as economic actors.

But there were also ominous signs. The Marxist optic of the FSLN prompted them to find enemies where there were only people who disagreed; it prompted them to treat adversaries as if they were "criminals" or "thieves." These attitudes mortgaged the future of the revolution, though few realized it then. The deeply rooted anti-Americanism of the revolution would also bear bitter fruit, but at the beginning, the United States was Nicaragua's most generous donor, providing $118 million in direct aid and encouraging the World Bank and the Inter-American Development Bank to loan $262 million.

The Nicaraguan government successfully cultivated good relations with Latin America and Europe, but from the start, it was clear that its closest relationships would be reserved for Cuba and Soviet-bloc countries. Viewing others with some suspicion, Nicaragua particularly did not want a military relationship with the West. The United States remained at the center of Nicaragua's consciousness, but it had become "the enemy" with limited direct influence.

The decision by the Directorate to aid the Salvadoran insurgents was a major miscalculation, which, in effect, ended the era of support by the United States. It also occurred at a moment when a new Administration was coming into office with a very different perception of the revolution. Under the best of circumstances, it would have been difficult to persuade the Reagan Administration to be patient and forge a long-term relationship with Nicaragua. Unfortunately, it was not the best of circumstances, and the Sandinista support for the Salvadorans was a major contributing factor.

Even without conclusive evidence, the new Administration believed the Sandinistas would try to overthrow its neighbors; the Sandinistas provided the evidence that confirmed their worst suspicions. This new Administration, as we will see, drew very different lessons than its predecessor had from the experience of the Cuban revolution.

Reagan: Mutual Resentment

We are always reacting [to the Soviet Union]. . . . Next time we might
have a few spots of our own in their backyard picked out.

RONALD REAGAN, 1967[1]

We know that our essential responsibility is to work for the building
of the Nicaraguan economy, but it is still more essential to defend
ourselves, to mobilize our people, to prepare an army capable of dealing blows to any other army. It is more essential that our mass organizations are armed to the teeth.

JAIME WHEELOCK, JANUARY 1981[2]

BY THE 1980 Presidential election, according to two public opinion analysts, Americans "felt bullied by OPEC, humiliated by the Ayatollah Khomeini, tricked by Castro, out-traded by Japan, and outgunned by the Russians. . . . Fearing that America
was losing control over its foreign affairs, voters were more than ready to exorcise
the ghost of Vietnam and replace it with a new posture of American assertiveness."[3]
As Carter had reflected America's need in 1976 to restore honesty and integrity in
government, in 1980, Ronald Reagan reflected America's need to take control of its
destiny and the world's.

The Reagan Administration's Lessons

Reagan offered a vision of the world that was uncluttered with the complexities that
had distracted previous Presidents. To him, the problem was Soviet expansion and
the solution was American power. "The inescapable truth," Reagan stated, "is that
we are at war, and we are losing that war simply because we don't or won't realize
we are in it . . . [and] there can only be one end to the war. . . . War ends in victory
or defeat."[4]

Central America, so close to home and seemingly so threatened, became a central part of his campaign. To Reagan, the Panama Canal treaties were not only a "surrender" of vital interests, they were a dangerous invitation to the enemies of the United States. Although some saw the threat to U.S. interests in 1979 as distant or insignificant, Reagan viewed the Communist threat in the region as pervasive, immediate, and dire. He therefore sounded the alarm that "the Caribbean is rapidly becoming a Communist lake in what should be an American pond and the United States resembles a giant, afraid to move."[5]

Reagan carried this perspective into the White House in January 1981.[6] The lesson he learned from Cuba was different from that learned by Carter. Reagan blamed President Kennedy for not saving Cuba when he had the chance: "We have seen an American President walk all the way to the barricade in the Cuban Missile Crisis and lack the will to take the final step to make it successful."[7] Presumably, the "final step" would have been an invasion to remove Fidel Castro. Whereas Carter believed that the best way to prevent Nicaragua from becoming another Cuba was to avoid confronting the new revolutionary regime, Reagan had learned the opposite lesson. Reagan felt the United States must not give Nicaragua time to consolidate its revolution. The time to confront a radical regime was at the beginning.

The Carter Administration had tried to paste "the mask of democracy" on the Sandinistas' face; the Reagan Administration tried to remove the mask and show the world they were really Communists. That is why the Carter Administration hesitated to call the Nicaraguan government Marxist, and why the Reagan Administration relished the use of the term, daring the FSLN to deny it. The Carter Administration offered aid as a first step toward a new, respectful relationship; the Republican Party platform demanded the termination of aid to Nicaragua as a first step toward supporting "the efforts of the Nicaraguan people to establish a true and independent government."[8]

Despite the bellicose rhetoric, the Reagan Administration gave the Sandinistas nearly three months and a second chance before cutting aid. This occurred because the Administration focused on a limited agenda and was slow to place its people in key staff positions and to establish an interagency decision process.[9]

Into the new Administration bounded Alexander Haig as Secretary of State. In his memoirs, Haig said that he wanted to send just two signals abroad at the beginning: first, a warning to the Soviets "that their time of unresisted adventuring in the Third World was over," and second, that U.S. relations would be conditioned not by a government's respect for human rights but by its friendship with the U.S. government.[10] He chose to draw the line against the Soviets in El Salvador, describing the Administration's approach succinctly: "It is our view that this is an externally managed and orchestrated interventionism, and we are going to deal with it *at the source.*"[11]

Haig addressed the problem of Nicaraguan subversion unilaterally and in an East-West framework rather than regionally and as a violation of the Rio Pact. Instead of helping El Salvador use the evidence of Nicaraguan support for the Salvadoran rebels to make its case to the OAS, as Carter had intended to do, Haig released the evidence of Soviet-Cuban involvement in a White Paper in February 1981.

Haig asked Pezzullo to return to Washington in early February for a policy review. The Acting Assistant Secretary of State, John Bushnell, a career foreign service officer, proposed three options for U.S. policy toward Nicaragua, all of them recommended a new certification that would end aid to the Sandinistas. Nicaragua had closed Radio Liberación after Pezzullo's initial démarches in mid-January and had interrupted the flow of arms to the Salvadorans. However, during the first week of the Reagan Administration, the FSLN began moving supplies to El Salvador again. Ironically, the Carter Administration probably would have selected one of Bushnell's options if it had another week. Haig asked for Pezzullo's judgment, and he said that none of the options was any good, which Bushnell called the "zero option."

Pezzullo explained that the aid served as essential leverage to negotiate an end to the arms trafficking. Haig listened, and then said that he chose the "zero option." He asked Pezzullo to return to Managua and tell the Sandinistas that there had been a change in Washington, and the new Administration would no longer tolerate their adventurism.[12] In mid-February, Pezzullo met Daniel Ortega and Sergio Ramírez. Given previous pledges that had been made to him by the FSLN and then broken, Pezzullo specifically identified a number of actions that the Sandinistas would need to take to demonstrate their good faith. He said that in the meantime, the United States would withhold aid. Within one month, the United States would assess the Sandinistas' response and judge whether to renew or terminate aid.[13]

Ortega and Ramírez responded officially on behalf of the Directorate that they understood U.S. concerns about El Salvador, and they would not "risk our revolution for an uncertain victory in El Salvador," although that was precisely what they had done. The Nicaraguans told Pezzullo they had taken a firm decision not to permit Nicaraguan territory to be used for transshipping arms to El Salvador. Ortega admitted that they had been "very permissive in allowing the FMLN [the Salvadoran guerrillas] to mount operations in Nicaragua," but promised that "not a single round" would pass through Nicaragua again.[14]

According to Pezzullo, U.S. intelligence soon found that arms traffic from Nicaragua had stopped, but some Reagan Administration officials claimed that the Nicaraguans had closed "established routes" but were already seeking new ones. Pezzullo felt that the Sandinistas had responded to U.S. concerns and that aid should not be terminated. He acknowledged that Nicaragua might support the Salvadorans again, but to have effective influence in the future, it was necessary for the Administration to demonstrate that it would adhere to its part of the understanding.[15]

Pezzullo was surprised therefore, when the President decided to terminate aid on April 1, 1981. The State Department's announcement was strangely contradictory. It confirmed that Nicaragua had ceased military support for the Salvadoran guerrillas, and because of this "favorable trend," the United States held out the possibility of resuming aid in the future. But aid was ended because "evidence continued to mount that the FSLN was engaged in continuing supply efforts as well as accumulating in Nicaragua arms for the FMLN." Pezzullo was not aware of any such reliable evidence.[16]

Pezzullo was perplexed that the United States had thrown away its only leverage. He had come up against the limits of the new Administration: given Reagan's campaign rhetoric and the Republican Party platform, there was simply no way that the Administration could have renewed aid to Nicaragua. Indeed, compared to the President's campaign rhetoric, the statement was remarkably conciliatory.

Pezzullo had told Haig that he intended to resign and leave Managua in August, but before leaving, he encouraged the new Assistant Secretary of State, Thomas Enders, to meet with the Sandinista leaders and explore whether a bargain was possible.

The Fork in the Road

Beginning with a blunt exchange of views with Nicaraguan leaders on August 12 and continuing through five more meetings ending in October, Enders tried to negotiate an agreement. In response to Enders's principal concern, Daniel Ortega said:

> As for the flow of arms to El Salvador, what must be stated is that as far as we have been informed by you, efforts have been made to stop it. However, I want to make clear that there is a great desire here to collaborate with the Salvadoran people, and also among members of our armed forces, although our Junta and the Directorate have [made] a decision that activities of this kind should not be permitted. We would ask you to give us reports about that flow to help us control it.[17]

Enders was unwilling to provide any additional intelligence, which he feared would compromise U.S. sources and only cause the Nicaraguans to choose alternative routes. Nonetheless, during this period, he developed a proposal composed of five points: (1) Nicaragua would end its support for foreign insurgencies; (2) Nicaragua would cease its military buildup and reduce its armed forces to a level of about 15,000 (down from the existing level of 23,000); (3) the United States would pledge not to intervene in Nicaragua's internal affairs and to enforce U.S. neutrality laws; (4) the United States would renew economic aid; and (5) the United States and Nicaragua would expand cultural relations. Enders also communicated U.S. concerns about political pluralism, a mixed economy, and Nicaraguan relations with the Soviet Union and Cuba, though the proposal did not explicitly cover these points.

As the Nicaraguans considered the proposal, the Administration began the first of a series of large military exercises in the area; this one was off the Caribbean coast of Honduras. The maneuvers and parts of the proposals confirmed the Sandinistas' suspicions of the Reagan Administration. From their perspective, the United States was "merely promising to do what it should be doing already—enforce its laws to stop the paramilitary training of exile groups openly preparing to 'oust the Communists' from Nicaragua."[18] While the United States promised non-intervention, it began military maneuvers. While it promised aid, it publicly canceled $7 million of the economic support funds that the Administration had said it would hold in suspension.

For parallel reasons, Enders was having difficulty gaining Administration-wide agreement on the proposals. Hardliners asked how the Sandinistas could be trusted to stop supporting the Salvadoran guerrillas if they would not even admit to supporting them in the first place. In September, the U.S. Embassy in Managua obtained the text of a speech by Humberto Ortega in which he declared that "we are anti-Yankee, we are against the bourgeoisie. . . . Sandinism without Marxism-Leninism cannot be revolutionary." Another diplomat in Managua overheard Bayardo Arce, one of the most radical leaders, saying "we will never give up supporting our brothers in El Salvador." On October 7, Daniel Ortega again denounced U.S. imperialism at the United Nations. All these events were used to confirm the point that the Sandinistas were not serious about negotiating.

Instead of redrafting the proposal, on October 31, the Nicaraguan government delivered to the Administration complaints about the military exercises, the aid cancellation, and the lack of action against the exile groups. The Administration interpreted this as a rejection of its proposal and the end of negotiations.[19]

The problem was that both governments were constrained by officials who used the events to prove that the other side was untrustworthy. The Sandinistas thus failed to respond specifically to the proposal from Washington, and the Reagan Administration was unable to explore the nature and the depth of the Sandinistas' concerns or to try to negotiate an alternative formulation. Instead of negotiating seriously, each side, for its own reason, preferred to rest on its preconception that the other was not serious.

This was a significant, missed opportunity that some on both sides, but especially the Sandinistas, would regret. In their first meeting, Enders told the Nicaraguans: "There is a fork in the road [in our relationship]. One way leads to accommodation; the other to separation."[20] In fact, the other path led to confrontation.

Ortega responded with his own threat:

We too have seen the crossroads. We have decided to defend our revolution by force of arms, even if we are crushed, and to take the war to the whole of Central America if that is the consequence. . . . We have an historical prejudice towards the United States, because of that country['s] . . . attitudes which makes us fear attack from it, and look for all possible means of defense. We are interested in seeing the guerrillas in El Salvador and Guatemala triumph, when we see that there is no good will in the United States towards us.[21]

The Administration considered that it had "tried" negotiations and found the Sandinistas uninterested. In the future, both sides chose to strike postures rather than negotiate; there is no evidence of any progress in subsequent talks between the two governments. After the fall of 1981, the covert and overt warriors replaced the diplomats.

A sign of the Reagan Administration's predilection to posture rather than communicate can be seen in its choice of ambassadors. Neither of Pezzullo's two successors had experience in Central America. By good fortune, both were intelligent and talented individuals, but that was not the reason they were chosen. The Administration chose individuals whose most recent assignment reflected its picture of Nicaragua. Anthony Quainton, who arrived in Managua in March 1982, had most recently been Director of the Office for Combating Terrorism in the State Department. By the time Quainton was replaced in 1984, the Administration viewed Nicaragua as a Soviet satellite, and it appointed Harry Bergold, then U.S. Ambassador to Hungary. To the disappointment of the ideologues in the Administration, both soon found that their previous experience was of marginal relevance to Nicaragua.

Haig was serious when he talked about going "to the source." In June 1981, Haig submitted a specific proposal to the National Security Council to bring "the overwhelming economic strength and political influence of the United States, together with the reality of its military power, to bear on Cuba" by a blockade and other military actions. Although Reagan had made such a proposal during the campaign, he rejected it as President for four reasons. First, Secretary of Defense Caspar Weinberger feared another Vietnam, and the Joint Chiefs feared that the Soviets might respond with actions in another part of the world. Second, the rest of the Administration doubted that Congress or the public would accept such action without some provocation by Cuba. Third, some in the State Department doubted that a blockade would affect Castro's support for revolutions in Central America. And fourth, the President wanted to keep the public focused on a tax cut. Haig, by his own admission, was "virtually alone."[22]

In a National Security Council meeting on November 16, 1981, two weeks after negotiations with Nicaragua ended, Haig tried again with slightly different proposals, and finally achieved some results, although not what he wanted. The NSC made two pivotal decisions, which were formalized in National Security Decision Document no. 17 signed the next day by President Reagan.[23] First, rather than reject Haig's blockade outright, Reagan ordered contingency planning for the use of U.S. military forces, including "a petroleum quarantine and/or retaliatory air reaction against Cuban forces and installations," but this would only be taken in response to "unacceptable military actions by Cuba" rather than as part of a U.S.-initiated pressure campaign.[24]

The second decision—for the CIA to fund and direct a secret anti-Sandinista guerrilla force—was of greater consequence for the future course of the Administration's policy. The President authorized $19 million for a 500-man Nicaraguan force aimed primarily at the "Cuban infrastructure in Nicaragua that was training and supplying arms to the Salvadoran guerrillas." Ironically, Haig opposed that decision too, but in his words, "was overruled." Haig's reasons for opposing it were, first, that "covert action was a contradiction in terms. There were no secrets." Second, the problem—Cuban-Soviet intervention—was much larger than Nicaragua, and needed a broader response. Third, the contras were a "cop-out," providing the illusion of solving the problem while escalating the level of violence. Finally, Haig felt strongly that the United States ought to address Nicaragua's external behavior rather than "tell others what form of government they must have." He correctly judged that the contra strategy would tempt the Administration to slide toward the goal of trying to change the Nicaraguan government, which he foresaw as unlikely and as a source of problems for the United States in Latin America.[25]

The groundwork for the Presidential finding to support the Nicaraguan resistance had been set earlier in 1981 when the Reagan Administration decided not to enforce the neutrality laws against the Nicaraguan and Cuban exiles who were training in Florida and California to overthrow the Nicaraguan government. The Administration initially saw these camps as bargaining chips in negotiations with the Nicaraguan government.[26] The FSLN saw Reagan's lack of interest in enforcing the neutrality laws as a sign that he supported the exile groups, and although that was not true then, Nicaragua's disinterest in serious negotiations soon made it true.

On March 9, 1981, Reagan signed a "Presidential Finding" authorizing the CIA to undertake covert actions in Central America to interdict arms trafficking to Marxist guerrillas.[27] Using the authority provided by that finding, CIA agents began to organize disaffected Nicaraguans. Edgar Chamorro, who later became a leader of the contras, was first asked in August 1981 to participate in "an important meeting in Guatemala with U.S. officials, the National Guardsmen [the core of the contras at that time], and their Argentine military advisers." As a result of the meeting, those Nicaraguans who had grown disenchanted with the revolution reluctantly decided to unite with the Guardsmen and form the Nicaraguan Democratic Force (FDN).[28]

Although the contras were still small bands of ex-Guardsmen, they had obtained some support from the Argentine military government, which sent military advisers to Honduras in December 1980 to help train them. The U.S. government was unaware of these activities at the time. The reason for Argentine military involvement, according to former Argentine Foreign Minister Oscar Camilión, was that Argentine military intelligence had discovered some Montoneros (Argentine guerrillas) in Managua, and "the Argentine military saw their mission as to fight Montoneros wherever they were."[29] If the FSLN was an ally of Argentina's enemy, then Argentina would help the FSLN's enemy; it is a simple political rule that has led to the connection of other rivalries—Israel vs. the PLO, West vs. East Germany, and of course, the United States vs. Cuba and the Soviet Union— with Nicaragua's.

By November 1981, when the National Security Council decided to support the contras, William Casey, the Director of the Central Intelligence Agency, could argue that the United States was just supporting a program assisted by the Argentines that was already under way.[30] Within a month, Enrique Bermúdez, the former Nicaraguan Defense Attaché in Washington, moved to Honduras and became the most important exile military leader. He remarked that he soon felt the Americans supplant the Argentines, although no real fighting had begun yet.[31] On February 14, 1982, the *Washington Post* disclosed the $19 million covert action program and indicated that the money had been used to support about 1,000 fighters and to help middle-class leaders in Managua.[32] The next month, Enders traveled to Argentina to coordinate policy toward Central America. There, he announced that the Argentine military government had an important role to play in Central America.[33]

Soon after the meeting in Argentina, on March 14, a group of former National Guardsmen, trained in demolition by CIA agents, destroyed two bridges in northern Nicaragua. The attack—the first major assault in Nicaragua—represented a watershed both for the Administration and for the Sandinistas. The Administration had committed itself to the FDN; it had trained and supplied them. Henceforth, abandoning the contras would be perceived as a sign of weakness by the Reagan Administration, and no charge was more fatal. After March 1982, the U.S. strategy came to rely on armed struggle, and U.S. objectives expanded, as Haig had warned, from interdicting arms to El Salvador to demanding internal changes in Nicaragua.[34]

The Sandinistas responded to the news reports and the bombings by declaring a state of national emergency. They imposed direct censorship, increased surveillance, and arrested a number of moderate leaders, including Alfonso Robelo, accusing them of complicity with the contras. At the request of several governments, the Sandinistas released Robelo, who then fled to San José, just as he had done after being released from Somoza's prison three years before. In Costa Rica he met with other Nicaraguans and discussed what to do about the revolution. None wanted to associate with the Guardsmen, but all had lost hope in civil means of influencing the regime.

Edén Pastora had left Nicaragua on July 7, 1981, claiming at the time that like Che Guevara, he wanted to make more revolutions. In fact, he was disillusioned with the revolution, but was uncertain what to do. He went to Panama to consult with his old friend Omar Torrijos, but days later, on July 31, Torrijos was killed in a plane crash. Soon after that, Tomás Borge visited Pastora in Panama and persuaded him to go to Cuba to speak with Castro. The Sandinistas and the Cubans were afraid that Pastora might divide the revolution. When Castro could not persuade Pastora to return to Nicaragua, the Cubans kept him in Havana as a virtual hostage. Only after Martin Torrijos, the General's son who had fought with Pastora during the revolution, invoked his father's memory did Castro permit Pastora to leave.[35]

After meeting with Robelo and Arturo Cruz, who had resigned as Nicaragua's Ambassador to the United States on November 14, 1981, Pastora held a news conference in San José on April 15, 1982. In his colorful style, reminiscent of Torrijos, Pastora castigated the Sandinistas for betraying the revolution to the Cubans: "Fifteen days after the triumph in 1979, I saw Sandinista commanders returning home in Cuban uniforms, and I realized at that moment that our revolution was beginning to lose its originality." He demanded the Directorate return to its pledges of political pluralism, a mixed economy, and freedom of religion and the press, or "I'm going to take them out of those Mercedes [Benzes] at gunpoint." But he also said that he was only "opening fire politically." He hoped the Directorate would change, but he had no intention of associating with the contras.[36]

Two months later, on June 16, 1982, after many of the leaders of his political party (the Nicaraguan Democratic Movement) had left Managua, Alfonso Robelo and Pastora jointly announced in San José the creation of a political-military alliance (ARDE) to fight the Sandinistas. Pastora did not begin armed attacks in Nicaragua until April 1983. Although he resisted CIA pressure to join forces with the FDN and claimed independence from the CIA, he received money from the agency through intermediaries.[37]

The bombings on March 14, 1982, were a crucial turning point not only for U.S. policy and the contras but also for politics in Nicaragua. The Nicaraguan government intensified its repression of suspected sympathizers and drove many Nicaraguans out of the country to join forces with the FDN. Moderate leaders were tempted to believe that the Directorate's days were numbered, and the future was with those outside the country. The strategy to support the contras in 1982, therefore, had the effect of hastening the polarization in Nicaragua and diminishing the possibilities for peaceful change.

The Sandinistas shared the credit for polarizing the country, even before the March bombings. Their heavy-handed attempts to integrate the culturally different Caribbean coast—composed of blacks and Indians who spoke mostly English and disliked the Latins in the west—provoked a bloody clash. Fearful that the Indian groups could be used for counterrevolutionary activities by the United States, the Sandinistas' suspicions and arrogance turned a relatively apolitical people into counterrevolutionaries.

In February 1981, the Nicaraguan government jailed Steadman Fagoth Muller, the most important leader of the MISURASATA (the organization of Indian groups), and released him in May on condition that he go to a socialist country to study. Instead, he fled to Honduras and joined the contras. By the end of the year, the Sandinistas undertook a brutal, forced resettlement scheme to move about 8,500 Indians away from their native homes on the Honduras border. The Sandinistas later acknowledged the terrible human rights abuses that occurred during the evacuation. The result was that the FDN incorporated a potent indigenous group of rebels from the strategically vulnerable east coast of Nicaragua.[38]

In the third year of the revolution, the Sandinista government began to feel the pressure of internal criticism and external aggression, and it moved more rapidly to give the "masses" a greater stake in the revolution. Confiscations of farms increased in order to provide more land for peasants' cooperatives. To solidify Nicaragua's external support, Daniel Ortega flew to Moscow six weeks after the bombings of the bridges to discuss increased aid.

Constraints: Congress and Contadora

The Reagan Administration's proclivity for unilateralism did not mean that it could pursue its objectives without restraint. Actually, the Administration had more difficulty obtaining Congressional and public support for the contra program than the Carter Administration had obtaining aid for the Nicaraguan government in 1980.

Internationally, many of the governments in the area that had helped the Sandinistas to overthrow Somoza had become disenchanted by late 1982, but none was prepared to support the contras. The Administration, therefore, had to cope with two sets of constraints—internal and international—simultaneously.

From the first briefing on the program, both Democratic and Republican members of the House Permanent Select Intelligence Committee expressed concern about the objectives of the contras, the degree of control the Administration could exercise, and whether the strategy might lead to war between Honduras and Nicaragua.[39] Because "neither El Salvador nor its close neighbors possessed the capability to interdict arms," the Committee decided that the United States was justified in undertaking covert actions as long as that was the objective. In April 1982, the Committee adopted an amendment in the classified annex to the bill that affirmed this point.

News reports, which included statements by contra leaders that their goal was to overthrow the Sandinista government, prompted Congress in December 1982 expressly to prohibit the use of U.S. funds for that purpose.[40] Sponsored by Rep. Edward Boland, the Chairman of the House Intelligence Committee, the amendment was adopted unanimously, 411–0, by the House of Representatives.

At the same time, several of Nicaragua's neighbors, led by Mexico and Venezuela, were becoming concerned about the direction of both the Nicaraguan revolution and U.S. policy. As the covert war became a "public secret," Venezuelan President Luis Herrera Campíns criticized Reagan's policy and said that Venezuela would continue its ties to Nicaragua "while there is a possibility that they will realize their pluralistic projects."[41]

Like Venezuela, Mexico lost some of its enthusiasm for the Nicaraguan revolution, but it was not prepared to abandon it. In an important speech in Managua in February 1982, Mexican President José López Portillo offered to try to mediate between the United States and Nicaragua. His proposal resembled Enders', but he tried to make it palatable to the Nicaraguans by putting it in terms of a warning to the United States:

> I can assure my good friends in the United States that what is taking place here in Nicaragua . . . does not constitute an intolerable danger to the basic interests and the national security of the United States. What does constitute a danger for the United States is the risk of history's condemnation as a result of suppressing by force the rights of other nations.[42]

None of these warnings or proposals bore fruit, and the war in the region worsened. In January 1983, the foreign ministers of Mexico, Venezuela, Colombia, and Panama met on the Panamanian island of Contadora to begin a unique negotiating effort. For the first time in history, Latin American governments took the initiative to promote peace negotiations in Central America. For the first time in the twentieth century, the United States was not only not involved in the negotiations; it was excluded.

Both the United States and Nicaragua were skeptical of Contadora's ability to achieve peace, but each tried to steer Contadora to serve its interest while trying to make it appear that the other was the obstacle to peace. The Sandinistas tried to get Contadora to preclude U.S. intervention; the United States hoped it would either demilitarize Nicaragua or isolate it, but it also feared that it would allow Nicaragua the time and space to consolidate its revolution.

In early 1983, opposition to the contras was growing in Congress. Warnings by retiring generals confirmed the fears of the public that the Administration was slipping down the slope toward intervention.[43] To mobilize public support for aid to El Salvador, which needed aid, and to preclude efforts to stop funding the contras, Reagan addressed a joint session of Congress on April 27, 1983. In the speech, he identified Nicaragua as the principal threat to the region and to U.S. interests:

> The government of Nicaragua has treated us as an enemy. It has rejected our repeated peace efforts. It has broken its promises to the Organization of American States, and most important of all, to the people of Nicaragua. . . . Nicaragua's government threatens Honduras. . . . The national security of all the Americas is at stake in Central America.[44]

Independent of Congress, the President raised the costs to Nicaragua of its policies. In May 1983, Reagan sharply reduced Nicaragua's sugar quota, valued at about $18.5 million. Although sugar was not nearly as important to Nicaragua as it had been to Cuba twenty-five years before when the United States cut its quota, the act was widely perceived as a repetition of that decision and another step toward breaking trade relations.

The Fruit of Resentment

While Nicaragua's neighbors were still trying to manage their suspicions of the Sandinistas, the Reagan Administration entered office wearing its distrust on its sleeve. Like its predecessor, the Reagan Administration had a global agenda that had important implications for Nicaragua. The Carter Administration's human rights focus opened Nicaragua to new political forces. The Reagan Administration looked beyond the longstanding policy of containment to a more revolutionary strategy of seeking "targets of opportunity," vulnerable areas where U.S. support for guerrilla movements could overthrow Marxist governments.

The Nicaraguan regime shared with the Reagan Administration a Manichaean view of the world—a world of allies and enemies. The Sandinistas had fought a war, and they had less patience for peace. Their ideology was better suited to mobilizing the masses against a national enemy than providing incentives to increase production of goods and services. Each action by the Reagan Administration prompted the Sandinistas toward a higher level of vituperation against U.S. imperialism, thus justifying and reinforcing the Reagan Administration's strategy.

Both sides were ideologically committed to defeating the other: the Sandinistas sought revolution against imperialism, and the Reagan Administration sought a victory against Communism. Both found it morally indefensible to compromise such objectives.

Reagan: Mutual Obesssions

Reagan has become an obsession for us, and we've become an obsession for him.

TOMÁS BORGE[1]

Curses are like young chickens;
They always come home to roost.

ROBERT SOUTHEY[2]

BY 1983, THE RESENTMENT that the Nicaraguan and U.S. governments felt toward each other had changed to obsession. Each side seemed unaware that the punishment directed at the other harmed itself as much, albeit in different ways. Neither was diverted or deterred by the failure to achieve its goal—the U.S. of overthrowing the Sandinistas, Nicaragua of changing U.S. policy. A symptom of an obsession, of course, is that one stops measuring a policy's effectiveness by whether it achieves its objective. The United States seemed to evaluate its policy in terms of the damage inflicted on Nicaragua; and Nicaragua, in terms of the embarrassment caused to the United States.

Threats maintained the cycle of mutual obsession. The United States threatened Nicaragua if it did not stop helping Salvadoran guerrillas, and Nicaragua threatened revolution throughout Central America if the United States did not stop helping the contras. Nicaragua's threat served to justify the contras, which in turn justified Nicaragua's threat, and thus, the conflict was sustained.

Deepening the Commitment

In September 1983, conceding Congress's point that the contras were not interdicting arms, the Reagan Administration submitted a second Presidential Finding. The finding authorized "material support and guidance to the Nicaraguan resistance groups" for two purposes: inducing the Nicaraguan government "to enter into negotiations with its neighbors, and putting pressure on the Sandinistas and their allies to cease provision of arms, training, command and control facilities and sanctuary to leftist guerrillas in El Salvador."[2]

The new finding not only circumvented the first Boland amendment, which prohibited aid to overthrow the government, but also replaced a specific goal—interdicting arms—with an open-ended, unattainable objective—"putting pressure." The finding symbolized the Administration's deepening commitment to the contras and its growing belief that the only way to stop the Sandinistas from helping other revolutionaries was to change their government or overthrow them. In line with this broader objective, the Administration expanded its military aid, training, and military exercises with Nicaragua's neighbors.

At about the same time, two U.S. aircraft carrier battle groups held naval exercises off each coast of Nicaragua. U.S. forces constructed several airfields in the south of Honduras to support the contras and provide a contingency option for the United States to attack Nicaragua if provoked. Reagan's speeches and his personal involvement emboldened some in his Administration, who began talking openly about military victories in Central America.[3] Sandinista prophecies appeared fulfilled. The imperialists were on their doorstep, and as the House Intelligence Committee concluded, the contras provided an additional reason for Nicaragua to fight back:

> Inflicting a bloody nose on nations achieves a purpose no different with nations than with individuals. It tends to instill a deep desire to return the favor. The Sandinistas are no different. Their policies have not softened; they have hardened.[4]

The Sandinistas were better prepared to deal with the war than with the peace that preceded it. Nicaragua's economy had failed to attain its pre-revolution level by 1983. Investment had stagnated or declined, depending on the sector. The external debt, which was high at $1.5 billion in 1979, reached $3.8 billion in 1983. Agriculture—the dynamic center of the economy before the revolution—declined markedly. In 1982, cotton exports were about half the 1978 level, and meat exports fell from 57 million pounds (1976–77 average) to 32 million pounds.[5] As the war intensified, the economy sank even further.

Tomás Borge acknowledged: "To make war is relatively simple. But to carry on after victory, to make war against poverty and backwardness and egotism and bureaucracy is something else."[6] Nicaragua increased the size of its armed forces from about 5,000 on the date of the Sandinista victory to 15,000 in 1980, 31,000 in 1981, 88,000 in 1983, and 119,000 in 1985; from 3 tanks in 1979 to 50 tanks in 1983; from 2 antiaircraft guns and no missile launchers in 1979 to 150 antiaircraft guns and 30 missile launchers in 1983. With Cuban and Soviet help, the Sandinistas built the most powerful military force in Central American history in a relatively short time.[7]

The contras were estimated to have 5,000–12,000 fighters in late 1983, and 10,000–20,000 by 1985.[8] The Sandinista military buildup preceded the war against the contras, but accelerated as a result of it.[9] The buildup occurred to raise the costs to the United States of an invasion, to defend against counterrevolutionary activity, and to discipline and indoctrinate the youth to be loyal to the revolution. Anti-Americanism was a major element of the nationalism of the Nicaraguan revolution. The contras made the threat from the United States credible, motivating the young and the government to a higher level of dedication than anywhere else in Central America.

The invasion of Grenada in October 1983 enhanced the credibility of U.S. threats and had an immediate impact on the Sandinistas. Borge, the Minister of Interior, assured U.S. Ambassador Quainton that the United States need not worry about protecting U.S. citizens—the alleged reason for the Grenadian invasion. In case of emergency, Nicaragua had a well-organized plan, which designated three hotels and several airplanes for evacuating U.S. citizens. There would be no need for the United States to use any of its own forces to help, Borge told Quainton.[10]

Roger Fontaine, the Latin Americanist on the NSC at that time, subsequently wrote of the invasion's impact on Nicaragua: "In a virtual panic, Managua, among other things, closed down the Salvadoran guerrilla command and control center in Nicaragua and sent most of the FMLN/FDR leadership packing."[11] The Administration was delighted to see the Sandinistas squirm, but it was either unable or unwilling to translate that pressure into effective influence in negotiations. One week after the invasion, President Reagan himself hinted at the reason when he was asked about a recent Nicaraguan proposal. He said: "I haven't believed anything they've been saying since they got in charge."[12] John Horton, a senior CIA official who subsequently retired, later explained that the Administration had stopped seeking a negotiated solution:

> This [Reagan] administration considers agreements with Marxist-Leninists to be risky—as indeed they are—but it also finds them too distasteful and inconsistent with its own tough posturing to be a serious option. The administration did not simply fail to give sufficient hearing to a diplomatic strategy; it ideologically shackled its imagination and so was not free to use the informed pragmatism that enables a skilled diplomat to probe for solutions.[13]

As the United States disengaged from negotiations, Nicaragua became interested. This was probably a ploy; Nicaragua's interest in negotiating only waxed when U.S. interest waned (and vice versa). Alternatively, Nicaragua's ostensible flexibility might have been a response to U.S. threats, contra activities, or to new pressures coming from previously friendly sources, like the Socialist International and the Contadora Group. The latter pursued many of the points on security mentioned by Thomas Enders and others on democracy. By the fall of 1983, Daniel Ortega publicly accepted a "regional declaration of objectives to foster elections and democratic institutions, to remove outside military advisers, and to halt outside military aid to the region."[14]

The Administration was less interested in using its success in Grenada to obtain an agreement with Nicaragua than to gain approval by Congress of $24 million in aid to the contras. In a nationally televised speech, the President called Sandinista rule "a Communist reign of terror," and then said: "Communist subversion is not an irreversible tide. We have seen it rolled back . . . in Grenada. And there democracy flourishes. . . . All it takes is the will and resources to get the job done."[15]

However, Congressional support for the contras, always tenuous, collapsed in the spring of 1984 after a series of disclosures of CIA supervision and involvement in the mining of Nicaragua's harbors and the destruction of the oil storage facility in Corinto.[16] On radio and television, Reagan appealed for more funds for the contras, but he failed to persuade Congress or public opinion. Aid to the contras, which had amounted to $72–$100 million, ended on October 1, 1984. As an acknowledgment of the unpopularity of the program, President Reagan stopped campaigning for the contras and began campaigning for reelection on a peace platform.

A Pause for Elections

On June 1, 1984, Secretary of State George Shultz visited Managua to begin talks with the Nicaraguan government that continued until January 1985. These negotiations proved an effective rebuttal to the argument of Democratic Presidential candidate Walter Mondale that Reagan's reelection would mean U.S. involvement in war in Central America. In the end, Central America played a small part in the voters' calculations, and President Reagan won by a landslide.

Like Somoza, the Sandinistas often looked for opportunities to outsmart the U.S. government. In that spirit, on February 21, 1984, the Nicaraguan government advanced its national elections from 1985 to November 4, 1984—just two days before the U.S. elections. Bayardo Arce candidly explained the reason:

> One by one, we've been eliminating the pretexts used by Washington. The only argument they had left is that we are . . . governing without a popular mandate. By moving the elections date up, we brought a political element into the defense of the revolution. Perhaps if it were not for the aggressions and the possibility of Reagan's re-election, we would have waited until 1985.[17]

In 1984, the opposition, led by the Coordinadora Democrática Nicaraguense, a coalition of moderate political parties, a labor union, and a business association, was divided, although most members agreed to participate if the FSLN permitted a free election. When informed of Nicaragua's announcement to hold elections, Reagan dismissed it as "the kind of rubber stamp that we see in any totalitarian government."[18] A senior Administration official later explained to the *New York Times* that "the Administration wanted the opposition candidate, Arturo Cruz, either not to enter the race, or, if he did, to withdraw before the election, claiming the conditions were unfair." This official said that the Administration feared that if Cruz ran, "the Sandinistas could justifiably claim that the elections were legitimate, making it much harder for the United States to oppose the Nicaraguan government."[19]

Cruz was selected in early July by the Coordinadora to be the united opposition's candidate for the Presidency, but he insisted that the FSLN accept a number of conditions related to the elections as well as a future dialogue with contra leaders before he would participate. Rallies held by Cruz and his supporters were harassed by "turbas," Sandinista mobs, and this hardened the opposition's insistence on certain minimal conditions.

Leaders from the Socialist International (SI) tried to mediate between the two sides on September 30 in Rio de Janeiro at an SI meeting that both Cruz and Bayardo Arce attended. These discussions as well as the elections themselves have been subject to varying interpretations, but it appears that there were elements in the FSLN, notably Arce, and in the Coordinadora, probably in the business community, who did not want the Coordinadora to participate in the elections. When Cruz accepted the SI's proposal, Arce was surprised and rejected it.[20] Cruz nonetheless kept trying to negotiate, but to no avail. Part of the problem was that the opposition conditioned their participation on a number of demands. Some were unrelated to the elections, and all were difficult for the Sandinistas to accept without appearing to be weak. For example, the opposition insisted on the separation of the state and the army from the party. Though a desirable objective, it was impractical to define, let alone resolve, this problem before the election.

On October 19, the U.S. Ambassador was instructed to meet with Virgilio Godoy, the leader of the Independent Liberal Party (PLI) and a Presidential candidate with no direct tie to the Coordinadora. The Ambassador and other groups and governments encouraged Godoy to withdraw, and he did.[21] As had happened six years before and many times before that, the Nicaraguan government and the opposition could not reach agreement on the terms that would permit a free election. One difference was that in 1978, the United States tried to bridge the gap between the two positions; in 1984, it tried to destroy any bridges.

According to the official results of the elections, nearly 1.1 million Nicaraguans voted, representing 75 percent of the eligible voters. Of those who voted, 63 percent voted for Daniel Ortega as President, and 64 percent for Sandinista National Assembly candidates. The opposition parties won 35 of 96 seats in the Assembly. The State Department spokesman dismissed the election as "just a piece of theater for the Sandinistas."[22] The Latin American Studies Association delegation complimented the Sandinistas for a heavy voter turnout and an election that was an "impressive beginning."

Perhaps the best assessment of the elections was made in a letter to Daniel Ortega from Carlos Andrés Pérez, who had participated in the Socialist International negotiations. Pérez opposed the "shameless intervention" of the contras, but he declined to participate in the inauguration, offering the following reasons:

President Ronald Reagan meets with three civilian leaders of the contras (the Nicaraguan resistance): Alfonso Robelo, Arturo Cruz, and Adolfo Calero, April 4, 1985.

Without attempting to play down the importance of the electoral process of November 4, 1984, in which you were elected President, those of us who believe we have done so much for the Sandinista revolution feel cheated, because sufficient guarantees were not provided to assure the participation of all political forces. Sadly, the limiting in this way of true political pluralism weakened the credibility of the elections.[23]

The elections, in short, were another lost opportunity for the Nicaraguan government, its opposition, and the United States to narrow the ever-widening chasm. Arturo Cruz later expressed great regret that he did not participate.[24] Within one month of the election, the FSLN rejected the national dialogue that it had promised the opposition during the campaign.

The Reagan Doctrine on National Liberation

Those who were uncertain whether Reagan's reelection would mean he would pursue peace initiatives or confrontation had their answer on election night. Moments before Reagan's acceptance statement, White House sources told CBS news that the Soviet Union was sending MIG-23 jets to Nicaragua, and that this might provoke an air strike by the United States or even an invasion. A few days later, the Soviet ship docked in Nicaragua, and helicopters—not MIGs—were unloaded. That crisis passed. The Administration sent two other signals. To reassure the contras and the Hondurans of its continued determination, the Administration ended talks with the Sandinistas begun by Shultz the previous June, and withdrew from the World Court's case on Nicaragua.[25]

In his 1985 State of the Union address, President Reagan transformed his contra program into a central theme of his Administration's approach to the world—a doctrine on national liberation movements: "We must not break faith with those who are risking their lives on every continent from Afghanistan to Nicaragua to defy Soviet-supported aggression and secure rights which have been ours from birth. . . . Support for freedom-fighters is self-defense." At a press conference on February 21, 1985, Reagan described his goal as seeing the Sandinista government "removed in the sense of its present structure," or at least, that Ortega would "say uncle."

In his second term, President Reagan probably devoted more time and gave more major speeches on Nicaragua than on any other single issue. He did this because he believed in the contras, and two-thirds of the American people did not. Because of strong Congressional opposition, the Administration initially decided to request humanitarian rather than military aid for the contras, and to pledge to suspend aid if the Sandinistas engaged in a dialogue with the contras under the auspices of the Nicaraguan Bishop's Conference.[26] The Sandinistas rejected the proposal, and so did Congress.

One of the Senate's arguments against aid to the contras was that the United States ought to consider other steps—like economic sanctions—before trying to overthrow a government. The Administration obliged, decreeing a trade embargo on May 1st by declaring Nicaragua "an unusual and extraordinary threat to the national security and foreign policy of the United States."[27]

Daniel Ortega, Nicaragua's President, left for a visit to Moscow days after Congress's vote and unwittingly strengthened the Administration's argument. By June, the Administration found the votes to pass $27 million in humanitarian aid to the contras. This was the first time both branches of the U.S. government openly debated and approved support for a movement whose aim was to overthrow a government with which the United States had diplomatic relations. Congress included an amendment urging the President to use the funds in a way that would advance peace negotiations between Nicaragua and its opposition.

The Sandinistas had received sophisticated military equipment and, by the end of 1985, were using it effectively against the contras. In February, 1986, President Reagan—saying "you can't fight attack helicopters piloted by Cubans with band-aids and mosquito nets"[28]—formally asked Congress to approve $100 million in aid for the contras—75 percent of it military aid. Once again, he combined strident attacks against the Sandinistas and Congressional opponents with a willingness to make symbolic concessions, such as appointing Philip Habib as his Special Envoy for Central America and resuming funding of Edén Pastora.[29] But it was only after vigorous lobbying by the President and a significant Nicaraguan incursion into southern Honduras that the Administration was able to win Congress's approval of $70 million in military aid and $30 million in nonmilitary aid. The law permitted the delivery of the first weapons to the contras on October 1, 1986.

Contadora and Its Offspring

The conflict spurred other initiatives in the region. The foreign ministers of the Contadora Group (Mexico, Venezuela, Colombia, and Panama) and a four-nation support group (Argentina, Brazil, Uruguay, and Peru) met with Secretary of State George Shultz on February 10, 1986, to request that the United States talk with the Sandinistas and stop funding the contras. Reagan refused to meet them and ignored their request.

Nonetheless, by June 1986, the Contadora Group had navigated the Central American states through four drafts of a treaty. The last one was submitted to the Central Americans with a deadline to be signed on June 6, 1986. It mandated an end to support for "irregular forces" (the contras) and "insurrectional movements" (guerrilla groups); a freeze on new arms purchases; the gradual reduction of armaments, foreign military advisers, and foreign military bases; and steps toward national reconciliation.[30]

As the June 6 deadline approached, both Nicaragua and the United States displayed signs of nervousness that the other might win the propaganda war. The Peruvian government proposed that the Nicaraguans sign the agreement but not ratify it until the United States accepted its terms as well.[31] The United States learned of this arrangement, and a fight within and between the State and Defense Departments began on what to do if Nicaragua signed. Philip Habib wrote a letter to Rep. James Slattery on April 11, 1986, pledging that the United States would cease its support for the contras "from the date of signature" of the treaty. But many in the Defense Department and some in State were not prepared to abandon the contras for what they believed would be an ineffective treaty. The Pentagon released a report predicting a "big war," involving over 100,000 U.S. troops and costing more than $9 billion in the first year, if the Contadora Pact were signed. Their argument was that Contadora would delay the day of reckoning with the Communist regime of Nicaragua, and this would be more costly to the United States. The State Department immediately attacked the report as "an internal Department of Defense study written under contract and released without authorization." Defense rejected State's claim, and the White House denied there were any differences. Finally, Assistant Secretary of State Elliott Abrams declared that Habib's letter was mistaken; it should have said that the U.S. would cease support of the contras when the treaty was implemented, not just signed.[32] Reagan's preferences were not evident.

The Nicaraguan government saved the Reagan Administration from tearing itself apart. Ortega rejected any disarmament and insisted that the contras be disbanded *before* they would sign. His Foreign Ministry criticized the treaty for being "close to the U.S. position." [33]

Costa Rica, Honduras, and El Salvador were also not ready to sign. They wanted more talks on verification, arms control (how to reduce each country's armed forces), democratization, and reconciliation. On June 7, 1986, the Contadora Group withdrew the deadline for achieving agreement. On June 20, after it was clear that the treaty needed more work and five days before the U.S. House of Representatives voted on aid to the contras, the Nicaraguan government announced that it would sign the June 6th treaty.[34]

A second set of initiatives emerged from the newly elected democrats in Central America. Guatemalan Christian Democratic President Vinicio Cerezo invited his Central American colleagues to a summit meeting on May 25, 1986, to discuss peace in the region and the possible establishment of a Central American Parliament. The discussion among the Presidents was frank and wide-ranging. Costa Rican President Oscar Arias confronted Daniel Ortega, as he later related: "The difference between you and the rest of us is that we are prepared to become leaders of the opposition, while you are not. You are not prepared to risk political power. And his answer was yes, this is true—our democracy is different."[35] Nonetheless, the Presidents scheduled a second summit for 1987.

Like the rest of his countrymen, Arias disliked the Sandinistas, but he also opposed the contra program and enforced his nation's neutrality.[36] On February 15, 1987, he offered a ten-point peace plan to develop the democratization elements of the Contadora Treaty. His plan would begin with an amnesty, cease-fire, and dialogue between the governments of Nicaragua and El Salvador and the internal opposition. Support for all insurgencies would end, and a "monitoring committee" would help implement the agreement. Nicaragua initially condemned the plan until it learned that the United States had reservations about it; then Nicaragua expressed some interest.[37]

Both the Contadora Treaty and the Arias Plan contained significant innovations for constructing a peace, but they also had flaws, similar to the treaties of 1907 and 1923. Neither had enforcement provisions, and both postponed negotiations on the hardest issues until after the treaties were signed.

The continuing war polarized politics in Nicaragua. Roberto Cardenal, an editor of La Prensa, believed that the contras weakened the internal opposition and reduced the chances of a nonviolent solution: "We are losing strength as our leaders leave. The feeling is that the game is outside, that the possibility of exerting pressure exists only outside the country." Luis Rivas Leiva, a leader of the Social Democratic Party in Nicaragua, criticized the Reagan Administration's strategy: "When they think of the opposition in Nicaragua, they think only of the military opposition."[38]

After the House approved aid to the contras in June 1986, the Sandinistas closed La Prensa and prevented Bishop Pablo Antonio Vega and Rev. Bismarck Caballo, a spokesman for Cardinal Obando, from reentering the country. Daniel Ortega said: "War will be met by war. . . . Those who are against the people and in favor of Reagan have the option of going to Miami. There will be no more tolerance."[39] The Sandinistas harassed an independent press for seven years, but only closed La Prensa in 1986 after Congress passed $100 million aid to the contras.

By calling their opponents class enemies and mercenaries, the FSLN precluded a dialogue that could permit an exit from the war and their national predicament. Instead, the harder they fought, the further they moved from their original aims. The Sandinistas sought independence, but they became more dependent on the Soviet Union. They sought to build a new nation, but they turned their nation into an army. They sought to improve the quality of life for the poor, but the poor were the ones who fought and died. The important advances made at the beginning of the revolution in health care and literacy and their commendable efforts at land reform were jeopardized by the militarization of the country and the diversion of scarce resources to the war.[40]

Home to Roost

The original goals of the Reagan Administration's policy toward Nicaragua were to end Nicaraguan support for Salvadoran guerrillas, reduce Nicaragua's dependence on the Soviet Union and Cuba, and increase the prospects for democracy. Like the Sandinistas, the harder the Administration struggled to achieve its goals, the more elusive they became. Democracy's prospects were lower and Nicaragua's dependence on the Soviet Union was greater at the end of the Reagan Administration than at the beginning.

With regard to Nicaraguan support for Salvadoran insurgents, the evidence was convincing that significant amounts of arms were shipped in 1980 and early 1981. The International Court weighed all of the published documentation, including reports by Sandinista defectors, and concluded that Nicaragua transferred large amounts until early 1981, but after that, the evidence was less certain and, if it occurred, the amounts were small.[41] After its report in 1986, however, shipments of arms to the FMLN seemed to be aimed to discourage the United States from helping the contras, though it usually had the opposite effect.

The Reagan Administration's support for the contras was unprecedented in its scale, duration, and openness. In comparison, the "big stick" of Theodore Roosevelt was more civil and subtle. Roosevelt did not take Panama as he himself boasted, but rather signaled very indirectly to the principal conspirator that he would not be unhappy to see a change in government there. Roosevelt also pressed for international treaties on Central America rather than covert wars. In comparison, from 1982 to 1988, the Reagan Administration provided more military aid to the contras to overthrow the Nicaraguan government than the United States had provided to all five Central American countries from 1962 to 1980.[42] The Administration, by foreclosing negotiations, came to rely on the contras as its only instrument for pursuing U.S. interests.

Of greater consequence, the Administration became so obsessed with Nicaragua that it violated the nation's core precept—respect for the rule of law internationally and at home. Instead of the United States taking Nicaragua to the International Court on charges of subverting its neighbors, Nicaragua took the United States on April 9, 1984, but the United States then withdrew from the case. The World Court, nonetheless, heard the case, and on June 27, 1986, in a report of 546 pages, it found the United States in breach of international law for "training, arming, equipping, financing, and supplying the contra forces" as well as for mining the harbors and attacking various facilities in Nicaragua. The U.S. judge, who tried to defend the United States as acting in "collective self-defense," admitted he was troubled that the United States had not previously sought a collective judgment from either the UN or the OAS.[43]

It was probable, if not logical, that an Administration that showed so little regard for international law would eventually be charged with bending, and perhaps breaking, U.S. law. When Congress prohibited government funding for the contras in October 1984, the CIA sent instructions to its field stations to cease all support for the contras, except for "intelligence-gathering purposes," which was permitted by the law.[44] However, officials in the NSC continued and expanded the operation.

Two years later, on October 5, 1986, the Nicaraguan government shot down a C-123 cargo plane. One of the crew members, Eugene Hasenfus, parachuted to safety, and subsequently told the press that the plane had dropped arms and supplies to the contras and that U.S. officials in Honduras and El Salvador were involved in the operation. Assistant Secretary of State Elliott Abrams insisted that the flight was a "private initiative" and that there was "no U.S. government involvement direct or indirect" in supplying arms to the contras.[45]

In fact, the U.S. government was intimately involved, and as the story unfolded, the Reagan Administration faced its most serious crisis. Administration officials had diverted profits from arms sales to Iran to provide arms to the contras at a time when that was prohibited by law. After receiving a report from the Attorney General, on November 25, 1986, President Reagan admitted that he was "not fully informed" of this activity. Two individuals who did know, National Security Adviser John Poindexter and NSC staff member Lt. Col. Oliver North, were dismissed. A special prosecutor, two Select Congressional Committees, and a Special Review Board, chaired by former Senator John Tower, were appointed to investigate the operation and possible violations of laws.

The reports confirmed that Oliver North had organized and directed a vast covert operation outside the government that involved retired military officers, former intelligence agents, and arms smugglers. Their mission was to assist the contras during the period when Congress prohibited it. [46] North established his private network in 1984 and within two years, his operation acquired more than $4.5 million of assets, including six aircraft, warehouses, and an airfield in Costa Rica.[47]

Congressional hearings tracked the money through fourteen corporations and thirteen bank accounts. Congress established that North solicited funds, and President Reagan helped by meeting with several potential donors. Senior U.S. officials also requested money from the Saudi royal family ($32 million), the Sultan of Brunei ($10 million), Taiwan ($2 million), and possibly Israel. Between 1984 and 1986, when the contras were complaining of a lack of funds, their own records indicated that they received over $100 million.[48] When asked about why the feudal kingdoms of Saudi Arabia and Brunei and the Taiwanese dictatorship provided money for the contras, President Reagan said it was because they "share our feeling about democracy."[49] Although President Reagan denied he knew that the profits from the arms sales were diverted to the contras, after less than three weeks of hearings, only 24 percent of the American people believed him.[50]

The motive for the overall operation was a combination of the President's commitment to the contras and Congress' ambivalence. President Reagan, according to former National Security Adviser McFarlane, "repeatedly made it clear in public and in private that he did not intend to break faith with the contras. . . . People turned to covert action because they thought they could not get Congressional support for more overt activities." Since the CIA and State and Defense Departments would not circumvent the law, which required a Presidential Finding and notification of Congress, the NSC, the President's staff, became, in McFarlane's words, "the agency of last resort."[51]

On November 25, 1986, the day he was fired by the President for possible violations of the law, North was in the hotel room of Richard Secord, a retired Air Force General who had helped manage the operation. The telephone rang. North picked it up and snapped to attention. President Reagan was calling to congratulate North on a job well done. The President called North a "national hero," and then offered the ultimate compliment: "Your work," he told North, "will make a great movie one day."[52]

During Congressional hearings, National Security Advisor John Poindexter said he hid the key decisions from Reagan, thus saving his presidency from impeachment. At his trial after Reagan had left office, however, Poindexter changed his story, with his lawyer saying that Poindexter had told Reagan.[53]

The issue was no longer whether any senior Reagan Administration official had broken the law, but the number of officials and laws that were broken. The chickens that had gone out and broken international law had come to roost.

Despite evident weakness because of the Iran-Contra scandal, President Reagan remained loyal to the contras and sought every opportunity to convince the Congress and the American people. To the hushed delegates at the Organization of American States in October 1987, Reagan said: "I make a solemn vow—as long as there is breath in my body. I will speak and work, strive and struggle, for the cause of the Nicaraguan freedom fighters."[54] And so he did, but in his last two years in office, President Reagan had to contend with a new Speaker of the House, Jim Wright of Texas. Wright spoke Spanish and had considerable experience in the region. Since each vote on contra aid split the Democratic Party on ideological and geographic grounds, Wright tried to negotiate compromises that would prevent repeated votes and keep the party together. Wright believed that the Arias Plan provided the best path toward peace in the region, and he used every opportunity to reinforce it and to respond positively to Arias's request that the U.S. not fund the contras.

When the Sandinistas decided to invade Honduras on March 16, 1988 to destroy the contras' bases, Reagan sent two battalions from the 82nd Airborne and sought additional aid. It was the same day that the Iran-Contra prosecutor handed down indictments against North and Poindexter, and Wright was able to prevent a vote on the aid. The dual signals—the President sending troops, and Congress withhold-ing aid—may have encouraged the Sandinistas and the contras to negotiate a cease-fire in the Nicaraguan town of Sapoa on March 23, 1988. The Sandinistas allowed the contras to keep their arms while negotiations on internal democratization oc-curred. It was a truce without a surrender. Based on this new pact, Congress passed humanitarian aid to the contras on March 30th by a wide margin.

By the summer, the presidential campaign was in full swing, and Michael Dukakis, who opposed contra aid, was ahead of George Bush by ten percentage points in the polls. As in 1984, the Reagan Administration downplayed its support for the contras, and the issue almost disappeared from the public debate. The quiet and the stalemate in the United States actually allowed the space for Nicaraguans and Central Americans to begin to define the parameters of a peace and democracy agreement.

An Assessment of the Politics and the Policy

In many ways, the contra effort resembled a prolonged Bay of Pigs operation, in which the U.S. government organized, trained, and armed Cuban exiles to over-throw Castro. That operation was an embarrassing failure, but different lessons were drawn from it.

Some believed the U.S. should not have supported the exile invasion; and others thought that the U.S. should have followed through with direct military support. In his rhetoric, President Reagan was solidly in the second group, repeatedly asking the American people "to send a message to this brave Nicaraguan [freedom-fight-ers]. Tell them America stands with those who stand in defense of freedom."[55]

But America did not stand united on the contras. Most Americans, preoccupied by other matters, did not even know which side the U.S. supported in Nicaragua. In April 1986, after three years of considerable press coverage and numerous Presiden-tial speeches, only 38 percent of the American people knew that the United States supported the contras. As to whether the U.S. should support them, there was rela-tively little change in public opinion from June 1983 to May 1986: 23 to 31 percent supported aid to the contras, and about 55 to 66 percent opposed it.[56] The 2:1 pub-lic opinion ratio against aid to the contras was the Sisyphean rock that Reagan had to push up Capitol Hill for each vote.

To understand the politics of the issue, however, one needs to look below the sur-face of these surveys and examine the differential impact of the issue on the two po-litical parties. A May 1986 poll showed that only 16 percent of the Democrats sup-ported aid to the contras while 75 percent opposed it; 36 percent of the Republicans supported aid, while 51 percent opposed it.[57] A more revealing poll focused only on the 38 percent of the American people who knew the U.S. supported the contras. Among this better informed group, which is more likely to vote in primaries, 67 percent of the Republicans supported aid, and 64 percent of the Democrats op-posed aid.[58] As both parties became more ideological and different from each other, the contra issue became one of the litmus tests of loyalty.

The contra issue contained an internal contradiction, which was why a consensus was elusive in the United States and why both parties enjoyed raising the issue among their "converted" but were more careful about using it among independents. Simply, Republicans reveled in the patriotic rhetoric of fighting Communists and supporting "freedom fighters," but feared looking too bellicose; and Democrats liked to invoke "Vietnam," but feared looking soft on "national security" issues. These fears were legitimate both politically and from the standpoint of national interest. Americans did not want war, nor did they want their enemies to expand. If the American people feared U.S. involvement in an unnecessary war, Democrats benefited. If the American people feared the Democrats would be ineffective in containing our enemies, Republicans benefited. Americans were interested in Central America not because of what they wanted but because of what they feared. Therefore, Republicans warned of "another Cuba," while Democrats warned of "another Vietnam." In brief, the issue divided the United States, although, of course, not as much as the United States polarized Nicaragua. The two nations' politics remained entangled and stalemated.

In an assessment of the Reagan Administration's strategy, former NSC staff member under Reagan, Roger Fontaine described it as a "qualified failure." He doubted that the Sandinistas could "be dislodged by a guerrilla army,"[59] and since the Administration was not ready to negotiate, the sole point of the contra operation was to increase the costs to the Sandinistas. And, of course, the tragedy of the Contra war was the human toll. The death toll was more than 30,000 people, and the economic cost was estimated to range from $200 million to $2.5 billion. [60]

The mark of a mutual obsession is that it evokes parallel and unproductive behavior. Thus, the Reagan Doctrine on national liberation came to resemble the Sandinistas' "revolution without borders." The difference, according to the Reagan Administration, was that the United States was right, and Nicaragua was not. The Sandinistas, as Borge noted, also became obsessed with Reagan. They were more interested in scoring propaganda points against the United States than in talking with their own people.

The resulting relationship of counterproductive policies and strident name-calling served neither nation. Ramiro Gurdian, a Nicaraguan businessman, tired of listening to the ricochet of rhetoric, said in despair: "There is Sandinista rhetoric; there is Reagan's rhetoric; and then there is reality. They are three different things."[61]

PART FOUR

The Democratic Transition and Nicaragua's Lessons

In few maladies are the pathogenic factors so darkly hidden as the neuroses, and many modes of treatment (e.g. persuasion) can only be described as a blind fight with unseen foes. When the morbid factors are appreciated and precisely defined, our power of managing them is considerably increased.

ERNEST JONES, *Papers on Psychoanalysis*, 1948

The Central American Initiative

[To the two superpowers:] Let Central Americans decide the future of Central America. Leave the interpretation and implementation of our peace plan to us. Support the efforts for peace instead of the forces of war in our region.

OSCAR ARIAS, COSTA RICAN PRESIDENT,
DECEMBER 10, 1987, OSLO[1]

WHILE WASHINGTON DEBATED, and Nicaraguans fought, four newly elected Central American presidents stepped between the United States and Nicaragua and searched for a formula that would restore peace and development to the Isthmus. Although the contra war was aimed at Managua, it was also hurting their countries. This was one of the reasons why they negotiated and signed the peace plan in Guatemala on August 7, 1987, that had been first proposed by Costa Rican President Oscar Arias six months before. They were joined by the Nicaraguan president in an effort to affirm their regional identity, assert control over their destinies, and try to cage the dogs of war.

Because the debate in the U.S. Congress was so evenly divided, Central Americans for the first time in history had an opportunity to influence U.S. policy toward them in a decisive way. The rhetoric of the debate obscured this reversal of the traditional pattern of influence, and thus few recognized or understood its significance, but the effect was unmistakable. From the signing of the peace plan in Esquipulas, Guatemala, on August 7, 1987, until the end of his administration, President Reagan tried to persuade Congress to vote military aid for the contras, but Congress refused because the majority believed correctly that the Central American peace plan would fail if such aid were provided.

Thus, just as the warmakers in Washington and Managua provided a steady flow of provocations to justify each other's belligerence, the peacemakers in Central America and Congress began to help each other. But progress toward peace required more than the conceptual breakthrough provided by Arias and his colleagues; it also needed a practical monitoring system to ensure that the provisions of the peace agreement were implemented, and this had not yet been invented.

Peace Plans

The five Central American presidents arrived in Guatemala on August 6 with the differences between them so deep that there was some question whether they could remain in meetings together for two days. The governments of Presidents Napoleón Duarte of El Salvador and Daniel Ortega of Nicaragua each aided guerrillas fighting the other; they considered each other enemies. Duarte was determined to refashion the Arias Plan so that it would force Nicaragua to recognize his legitimacy and end its support for the Salvadoran rebels.[2] Honduran President José Azcona was squeezed between his military and the United States; U.S. aid kept the military from overthrowing him but also prevented him from being an autonomous president.

The two presidents with the most distance from the Nicaraguan conflict had unquestioned democratic credentials; together they turned the Arias Plan into the Esquipulas Accord. Vinicio Cerezo had been exiled by the Guatemalan military but returned to win election and take office in January 1986. Oscar Arias had taken office in May 1986. Like his predecessor, he pledged Costa Rica's neutrality, but unlike his predecessor, he meant it. He closed the southern front of the contra war, sending Oliver North's operatives into a tizzy. In September 1986, the Costa Rican security forces raided one of the contras' bases in northern Costa Rica, and a secret cable was sent to Washington: "Alert Ollie [that] Pres. Arias will attend Reagan's dinner in New York Sept. 22. Boy needs to be straightened out by heavy weights."[3] Reagan did not prevail upon Arias, and Daniel Ortega began to take notice. Despite deep philosophical differences, Arias and Ortega began to develop a relationship that made the eventual acceptance of the Arias Plan possible.

The Accord contained provisions for democratization—freedom of the press and media, an end to states of emergency, a general amnesty—and regional security, including cease-fire negotiations and the end of support to insurgent groups. The security provisions would be subject to inspections. Some of these steps would have to be implemented simultaneously; all of them, within 150 days. Or at least that was the idea. In addition, the Accord included Cerezo's proposal for a Central American parliament.

By focusing on democratization and internal reconciliation, the Accord proved its genius, slicing through the cord that had tied internal strife to international intervention for 160 years of Central American history. All five presidents had strong reasons to agree to the Accord provided that everyone agreed and implemented it. Their economies were failing; the military and guerrillas threatened several of them; and they knew that, without peace, they could not govern, and their countries could not develop. All wanted to end external support for insurgencies, but only if the provisions were verifiable and effective. Also lurking behind their discussion was the ghost of Central American unity, as well as the pride that an agreement would represent the "coming of age of Central America," in the words of the Costa Rican foreign minister.[4]

Ortega, who sat at the center of the crisis, had additional reasons to sign. He could not afford to antagonize Arias and Cerezo or permit his government to become isolated from the rest of Central or Latin America. The Sandinistas concluded that the U.S. invasion of Grenada occurred for two reasons: internal division and an invitation from Grenada's neighbors. The chances of a U.S. invasion of Nicaragua would increase if its neighbors united in perceiving Nicaragua as a threat to their security. More immediately, the war had grown worse during the year. The contras' strength had increased because of $100 million in U.S. aid. With Red-Eye missiles, the contras were able to limit the effectiveness of Soviet-made helicopters. Moreover, Soviet oil supplies had been reduced, inflation was soaring above 1,000 percent, and the economy was collapsing.

Ortega was practical, but he was also proud. If Arias had not demonstrated his independence from the United States and his willingness to deal respectfully with the Sandinistas, Ortega probably would have played with the Accord without really committing himself to it, much as he had done with the Contadora group. But Ortega not only signed the Accord, he took risks to make it work. In other words, without Arias and his plan, the war in Nicaragua probably would have been unchanged, and the political space and the prospects of democracy would have continued to diminish.

The Accord exacerbated the divisions within the two protagonists. The White House first said it was "encouraged" by the plan, but then the conservative wing of the Republican Party, fearful that the contras would be abandoned, unleashed a terrific campaign that caused the president to flip-flop and reassure his conservative supporters: "I am totally committed to the democratic resistance—the freedom fighters," and he then described the plan as "fatally flawed." Vice President George Bush also criticized the plan for putting too much faith in the Sandinistas.[5]

The discordant sounds were evidence of a battle royal within the administration. Philip Habib, the president's special envoy to Central America, argued that the Accord offered the United States an opportunity to broker an agreement, but others were more concerned that the peace plan was a mirage that would reduce support for the one strategy that could change the Nicaraguan government—the resistance. Habib lost the argument and resigned. Abrams, who prevailed, recalled the U.S. ambassadors from the five Central American countries to discuss why they had been surprised by the Accord and how it could be blocked without the United States getting blamed. With his special flair, Abrams gave the ambassadors copies of the 1973 Paris accords to end the war in Vietnam, reminding them that they had been violated within two years. The ambassadors were instructed to return and "convey doubt" about the plan.[6]

The Sandinistas were also divided, and Ortega confided to Arias and Cerezo that that was why he visited Havana on August 12 and held "an extraordinary meeting of the FSLN National Directorate with the members of the Sandinista Assembly" on August 17. As a result of that meeting, the Directorate backed Ortega and

Ramírez, the only ones supporting the Accord, and the leaders agreed to establish a four-member National Reconciliation Commission with three non-Sandinista members, headed by none other than Cardinal Obando y Bravo, the symbol of the opposition. This was not even conceivable one month before.[7] Two human rights leaders, who had been arrested in the first demonstration after the signing of the Accord, were released, and other demonstrations were permitted.

Tomás Borge, who had arrested the human rights leaders, kept his reservations to himself, refusing to be interviewed by *New York Times* correspondent Stephen Kinzer for nearly four months. He was biding his time, waiting for the Accord to fail, but the other comandantes were serious. On September 15, 1987, Kinzer reported that the repeated public pledges and actions by the Sandinista leadership had created in Managua "a mood of expectation unseen since the Sandinistas swept into power eight years ago."[8]

Arias and Foreign Minister Rodrigo Madrigal oversaw this democratization process in Nicaragua. At their behest, albeit with considerable reluctance, Ortega permitted *La Prensa* to begin publishing without any censorship on October 1. Each time the Nicaraguans took a positive step, Arias called on the United States to suspend its support for the contras and give Central America "political space" to make the negotiations succeed. Arias went to Washington to state his case directly. In a chilling confrontation with Reagan at the White House, Arias recalled telling him: "We agree on the ends but we disagree on the means. You want democracy in Central America by imposing it with bullets. I want democracy by imposing it with votes."[9] Speaker of the House Jim Wright invited Arias to address a joint session of Congress, but Reagan vetoed it.[10]

By the perverse logic that had come to characterize the relationship, every positive step by the Sandinistas upset the Reagan administration, and every negative step was applauded. When the human rights leaders were arrested, the State Department declared: "This shows that one should not place too large a bet on Sandinista good faith." On the same day that Arias asked Washington to stress the positive, the State Department described a series of actions, including *La Prensa*'s opening and the appointment of Cardinal Obando as mediator, as "cosmetic gestures," and Reagan called them "a fraud." When the Nobel Committee announced on October 13 that Arias had been awarded the peace prize, the administration expressed disappointment, and Representative Newt Gingrich of Georgia called the award "saddening."[11]

After much hand-wringing, Ortega finally accepted indirect talks with the contras and promised to declare an amnesty and lift the state of emergency as soon as Honduras dismantled the contra bases. Arias called again for aid to the contras, and the Reagan administration replied in its customary way, asking Congress to renew aid.

Judgment Day

Preparations for the Summit of Central American Presidents in San José on January 15, 1988, followed the rhythm of previous encounters. In advance of the meeting,

President Arias took the one step required of Costa Rica in the plan: He expelled all the contra political leaders from San José. Three of the four Nicaraguan members of the Reconciliation Commission expressed disappointment with the inadequate steps taken by the Sandinista government with regard to internal dialogue or negotiations with the contras. Instead of responding to his people's concerns, President Ortega addressed the American audience by writing an article in the *New York Times*. Reversing a previous position, he pledged that he would "turn over the government" if the opposition won an election, although he said nothing about turning over the military. He also repeated his pledge that "if we receive sufficient security guarantees from Washington, we will not maintain a large army or unnecessary armaments," and within the context of a region-wide agreement, he would accept "a mutual ban on all offensive foreign military bases [and would] actively prevent the use of our territory to threaten or subvert any country in the world."[12]

While the key parties were offering new promises, the Reagan administration repeated an old threat. General Colin Powell, Reagan's sixth national security adviser, traveled to each country in Central America except Nicaragua and told the presidents that if they failed to condemn the Sandinistas in San José, contra aid would probably lose, and so too would aid to their countries. The heavy-handed warning was all the more remarkable because Powell had it published when he returned to Washington.[13]

Prior to the meeting, the Central Americans asked the four Contadora governments to organize an International Verification and Follow-up Commission to prepare a report on the extent of the five governments' compliance. The report was impartial but critical of almost all of the countries, and perhaps for that reason, the Central Americans disbanded the Commission after the meeting. The report was tougher on Nicaragua than on any other country, criticizing it for not including representatives of the resistance on the Reconciliation Commission, for failing to sustain a dialogue with the internal opposition or begin one with the resistance, for continuing its people's tribunals, for offering only a partial amnesty, and for not lifting the state of emergency. It also criticized the United States for not ending its support for the contras. This, it argued, "is an essential requirement for the success of the peace efforts as a whole."[14]

After two days of talks, the five presidents issued a joint declaration calling on all parties to "immediately fulfill" the remaining commitments, especially those related to democratization. The Reconciliation Commission in each nation was given the primary responsibility for compliance, but the presidents also instructed their foreign ministers to meet to discuss "verifying, controlling, and following up on all the commitments."[15]

Daniel Ortega apparently felt most of the heat, and he called a press conference immediately following the issuance of the joint declaration on January 16, 1988. Ortega announced measures that were required by the Accord but that he had previously made conditional on the end of U.S. support for the contras. He ended the state of emergency, agreed to direct talks with the contras, and promised to release 3,000 former national guardsmen from prison if any country would accept them.

These were significant steps, particularly the decision to begin direct talks with the contras, but there was a smallness about these large decisions that revealed Ortega's ambivalence and left his adversaries legitimately uncertain of his intentions. Whereas the joint declaration stressed the need for political dialogue, Ortega sharply circumscribed the talks with the contras, demanding that "the contras must first lay down their arms . . . ."[16]

From the outside, Ortega's approach seemed half-hearted and petty, but from within the Sandinista Party, his reversal on direct talks with the contras probably shocked the cadre, requiring him to preserve some of his previous position. A clash between Ortega and Tomás Borge reflected a life-or-death debate on how the revolution could be preserved, with Ortega characteristically calling for adaptation, and Borge arguing that concessions to the contras would demoralize the party faithful and make the revolution more vulnerable.

Within days of the Accord's signing, Borge's police harshly broke up a demonstration in Managua and arrested several human rights leaders. When Ortega announced direct talks with the contras on January 16 in San José, the police in Managua arrested four opposition leaders. When Ortega returned to Managua two days later to abolish the people's tribunals and end the state of emergency, the police arrested five more opposition leaders. Stephen Kinzer, the *New York Times* correspondent in Managua, was told by "an official close to Mr. Ortega that those reports [that Borge had ordered the arrests without consulting Ortega] were accurate." This was the first time that the private differences among the comandantes were made public.[17]

The Reagan administration, of course, chose to interpret these contradictory events differently, highlighting the arrests as still another reason why the Sandinistas should not be trusted and why aid to the contras was essential. "Without the freedom fighters," said President Reagan, "the hope of democracy in Nicaragua would be lost."[18] The *Wall Street Journal* warned that if the administration reduced its request for aid to the contras, "We may be on the brink of handing over Nicaragua to a communist government. . . . The future of Nicaragua will be decided this weekend in the Reagan White House." The editorial ended sarcastically: "We hope Mr. Reagan will participate in those discussions."[19]

The crucial vote on aid occurred in the House of Representatives on February 3, 1988. To persuade the swing votes, the administration scaled down its proposal from $270 million to just $36 million. Ten percent was for ammunition, and that amount would be suspended until March 31 pending the cease-fire negotiations. The entire package would sustain the contras until July 1988, when the president would make a new request. On the night of the vote, President Reagan addressed the American people on television. He argued that pressure had worked on the Sandinistas, and that this was not the time to let up.[20]

The debate the next day showed the deep polarization that divided America on Nicaragua. One congressperson after another rose either to denounce the Sandinistas as a communist scourge that needed to be excised or to criticize the Reagan administration as the major problem in the region. The White House lost the vote by a narrow margin, 219–211, because of the Accord and because Wright promised a humanitarian aid package for the contras.

President Arias applauded the vote, saying that Nicaragua had "no more excuses" for not complying fully with the Accord. With regard to Wright's proposal, Arias said this "would not be a violation of the peace accord. It is military aid that is prohibited and not humanitarian aid."[21] This was an important but subtle point, suggesting that Arias valued the contras as a lever to move the negotiations forward but opposed military aid as a roadblock that would halt negotiations and preclude acceptance of his plan.

Ortega had previously indicated that "one single additional dollar for the contras, regardless of whether it is termed humanitarian aid or not, would be a dollar used to kill the Central American agreements." But he chose not to repeat that charge after the House vote; instead, he congratulated "the majority of the House" for voting "for a peaceful solution to the . . . conflict." The rest of his comments, however, suggested a perspective different from Arias's. Claiming that Nicaragua was already "complying with each and every point" of the plan, he described how its neighbors—especially Honduras because of the contra bases—were not in compliance. He went further, telling Nicaraguans that they lived "in a complete democracy. Now we do enjoy total freedom of expression."[22]

Ortega's opponents were not prepared to concede that point. Direct negotiations between the contras and the Sandinista government began on January 28 but were deadlocked from the start. The Sandinistas wanted to discuss the technical details of a cease-fire, whereas the contras wanted political guarantees before they gave up their weapons.

Democrats and Republicans in the United States were having no more success in reaching agreement when the Sandinistas attacked the contras in Honduras. Reagan sent U.S. troops to help, but Congress wouldn't approve an increase in aid. The Sandinistas then sent Minister of Defense Humberto Ortega as the head of their delegation to the talks with the contras and allowed them to be held in Nicaragua, but they then dismissed Cardinal Obando as a mediator and scheduled the meeting before the contras were ready.

In these contradictory moves one can still discern a pattern. The battles showed that the Sandinistas were strong but not strong enough to erase the contras. As long as the war continued, the economy, which continued to plummet, could not improve. By denying military aid to the contras, Congress gave the Sandinistas face-saving space to make serious concessions without appearing to surrender. At the same time, after watching U.S. Democrats and Republicans bicker over aid, the contras realized that they could not take U.S. support for granted. In brief, *both sides had compelling reasons to negotiate more seriously than they had before*, and the presence of Humberto Ortega underscored this point. Interestingly, both sides seem to have discovered a common interest in asserting their independence from the United States.

The agreement signed in Sapoá on March 23, 1988 was historic—the first time the Nicaraguan government and its armed opposition faced each other without an

American mediator and reached a compromise that began by recognizing the legitimacy of the other. The agreement's importance was less in what it achieved than in the risks that each side assumed. The contras agreed to move their forces to specified enclaves where they would be vulnerable and their true strength could be ascertained. During the cease-fire period, the contras agreed to reject any military aid. The Reagan administration had rejected efforts by Democrats to channel aid to the contras through "neutral organizations," but the contras accepted that. Most important, the resistance defined a realistic negotiating agenda by accepting the Constitution and President Daniel Ortega's incumbency until 1990. The next round of negotiations would more profitably focus on ways to guarantee the full participation of all Nicaraguans in elections.

In accepting the contras and permitting them to keep their weapons during talks, the Sandinista leadership reversed some sacrosanct positions. The government accepted a gradual but unconditional amnesty, invited the contra leadership to Managua for talks on political issues and not just a cease-fire, and accepted an ongoing role by the Organization of American States (OAS) and Cardinal Obando in verifying the agreement.

The Reagan administration was trapped once again in an awkward position. If it embraced the Sapoá agreement, the administration would have contradicted its argument that military aid to the contras was essential to a good agreement. If it opposed the agreement, it would appear to be even more hard-line and intransigent than the contras. The Reagan administration therefore confessed surprise, officially welcomed the agreement, but privately expressed skepticism and applied pressure to the contras to harden their negotiating posture.

Congress responded warmly to the initiative, as it had to the Guatemalan Accord. Wright assembled a $47 million package of aid that included $17.7 million of food, clothing, and medical aid to the contras to be delivered by "neutral organizations"; an equal amount to finance a special program for the children who were victims of the war; and $10 million for the verification commission. The package passed the House by a vote of 345–70 on March 30, 1988 and the Senate by a vote of 87–7 the next day. By the time that the presidential contest engaged the attention of Americans, the Nicaragua issue had almost disappeared.

New Faces

The election of George H. W. Bush as president and his appointment of James A. Baker as secretary of state placed two men who had had front-row seats to the political turmoil that surrounded the contra issue during the previous eight years in positions where they could change U.S. policy. And both were determined, in the words of Baker, "to remove the issue from the domestic political arena."[23] On November 18, 1988, barely two weeks after his election, Bush visited Jim Wright for a private lunch. Wright brought up Central America. "This has been the most implacable issue of the last eight years. Also the most politically polarizing and personally divisive," said Wright. Without hesitation, Bush agreed. Then, Bush asked:

"Would you be willing to work with Jim Baker in trying to search out the ingredients of a common policy?" It was Wright's turn to agree.[24]

Baker recruited Bernard Aronson, a moderate Democrat, who had helped craft several congressional compromises on the contra issue, as his assistant secretary of state for inter-American affairs. In Baker's view, "Central America was first and foremost a domestic political issue,"[25] and he and Aronson worked with Wright to draft a compromise—the "Bipartisan Accord" announced on March 24, 1989—that offered something to both sides. For conservative Republicans, Bush obtained $49.7 million in humanitarian aid for the contras, and he promised not to abandon them. For Wright and the liberal Democrats, Bush pledged his support for the Arias Plan and vowed not to seek military aid for the contras before the Nicaraguan election. In other words, Bush said he would neither support nor abandon the contras.

This pact not only removed the issue from the domestic political agenda in Washington; it also had the effect of removing the U.S. government from its traditional role as the principal negotiator in Nicaragua. Others were ready and eager to fill the vacuum, and even before the Accord was negotiated, many of them descended on Caracas in February 1989 on the occasion of the inauguration of Carlos Andres Perez as president. The Venezuelan Constitution permitted a president to run for reelection only after two intervening elections. Perez, a genuine democratic leader who played by the rules, waited patiently for a decade to pass before he ran and won reelection. During that time, he continued to play an active role in the region's politics and was often more engaged than the incumbent Venezuelan president. Not surprisingly, then, Oscar Arias, Daniel Ortega, Fidel Castro, and Jimmy Carter were invited to his inauguration, among many others, including Vice President Dan Quayle, and all of them used the opportunity to advance their agendas.

Perez was clearly in the center of all the discussions, and his principal concern was the Nicaraguan peace process, which had stalled. Perez first met with Carter and me privately for one hour, then invited Daniel Ortega to join the meeting. Oscar Arias also met with Perez, Carter, and others. Ortega was seeking support from the United Nations (UN), the OAS, and Venezuela for a plan to disarm and relocate the contras to third countries or integrate them peacefully in Nicaragua. Ortega promised amnesty and land if the international community could provide the aid. Perez, Arias, and Carter endorsed that idea but insisted that internal democratic reforms were critical and needed to be started first. Arias also pressed Ortega to move forward the elections to February 25, 1990.[26]

Ortega responded to the concerns that he heard from Perez, Arias, and Carter at the next Central American Summit Meeting in El Salvador in mid-February. In exchange for his colleagues calling for the dismantling of the contras and the end of aid to them, Ortega promised to move the election forward, invite international observers, and reform the electoral and media laws by April 25, 1989. Vice President Quayle called the agreement a "ruse" to keep Nicaragua under a "Marxist-Leninist dictatorship." Although not all the senior officials in the Bush administration were as negative as Quayle, most did not believe that the Sandinistas would "let themselves lose the elections," in the words of Ambassador Cresencio Arcos. Robert

Zoellick, a close adviser to Baker, later recalled that most senior officials believed that a Sandinista victory was "the most probable outcome" of as clean an election as they thought would be possible. The Bush strategy, according to Zoellick, was to "contain and preoccupy the Sandinistas through the electoral process."[27]

Aronson, however, lent his full support to a free election process and encouraged Baker to consult often with the leaders in the region. On March 30, 1989, Baker visited the Carter Center to give the administration's first address on Latin America and to meet with Carter, former President Gerald Ford, Venezuelan President Perez, Speaker Wright, and several members of the Council of Freely-Elected Heads of Government, a group of leaders from the Americas, chaired by Carter. In his address, Baker promised: "We are committed to work with Latin and Central American democratic leaders to translate the bright promise of the Esquipulas Agreement into concrete realities on the ground."[28]

It was not clear how to accomplish that, however. During the two-day conference at the Carter Center, the senior delegates from Latin America and the United States wrestled with the toughest questions raised, but not answered, by the Esquipulas agreements: verification and compliance.[29] On the external security obligations (demilitarization; prohibiting support for insurgents), the question was whether the OAS and UN would have sufficient authority to verify and ensure compliance. But the challenge was even harder for the democratization obligations. No foreign government or entity had ever negotiated the terms of a free election with a sovereign government, least of all one as nationalistic as the Sandinistas. Arias had been pressing Ortega to implement the pledges of a free press and speech but was frustrated by the half-hearted response.

The first draft of a response to the internal challenge emerged from the most unlikely place: Panama. General Manuel Antonio Noriega, the Panamanian strongman, who gradually assumed power after the death of Omar Torrijos, promised presidential elections on May 6, 1989. At the same time, he reined in the press, intimidated political opponents, and made it difficult for international observers to enter the country. Perez doubted that Noriega would allow a free election, but he joined with Carter and Arias to send a small team to Panama in March 1989 to assess the conditions. Their report was not encouraging. The voting lists were not accurate; there were credible reports of partisan electoral activities by the Panamanian Defense Forces; and the media were not permitted to broadcast freely. By the last week in April, the situation in Panama had deteriorated, and Carter asked me to deliver a letter from him to Noriega and to negotiate the terms for an international mission.

Noriega was in no mood to negotiate when I met with him for a two-hour, brutal exchange on April 26, 1989, but at the end he accepted a mission led by Carter and Ford. In his memoirs, written from his Miami prison seven years later, Noriega blames me for pressuring him to accept international observers: "We had been reluctant to do so . . . . I had argued weeks earlier with Pastor and others, that given the United States' attitude, this would just be another infringement on our rights. . . . We preferred the Mexican political model."[30]

The Carter-Ford mission was organized by the Council led by the Carter Center, the National Democratic Institute for International Affairs (NDI), and the International Republican Institute (IRI). Both NDI and IRI monitored the watershed election in the Philippines in 1986 and the plebiscite on Pinochet's rule in Chile in 1988. In both places, the two party institutes worked with sophisticated local monitoring groups, which used a technique called a "quick count" or a "parallel vote tabulation" by which the group's observers would be stationed at a select sample of precincts at the end of election day. Each observer would listen as the officials counted and added the ballots. Then the observers reported the results. The margin of error could be as low as .5 percent, depending on whether all of the designated sites could be retrieved. In addition to the quick count, observers would visit large numbers of voting sites on a random basis during the election and respond to questions in surveys. The surveys would permit the observers to detect whether a systematic pattern of irregularities was evident. The OAS had sent numerous delegations to observe elections over the years, but they had rarely done surveys or criticized member states. Only with the new techniques did monitors have a capacity to detect systematic fraud. In the Philippines and Chile, the local monitors detected the fraud, and the international monitors gave them a voice—more like a megaphone—to shape world global opinion. Ferdinand Marcos and Agusto Pinochet expected to win the elections. When the results favored their opponents, Marcos tried to ignore them, but the country and the world would not let him. Pinochet's military colleagues let him know that he had no choice but to accept the results.

In Panama, democracy had shallower roots, the military was more oppressive at the time of the election, and the local monitoring groups had much less experience. When I arrived in Panama days before the election to help organize the delegation, I was given a hefty volume of papers by sources I judged to be close to the CIA, describing how Noriega would manipulate the election. It turned out to be completely bogus; Noriega had no plan. However, our group did have one. The Catholic Church would do the quick count, and Carter gave a televised speech in Spanish on the eve of the election urging all eligible voters in Panama to vote. By the early morning after the election, our quick count showed Noriega's candidates losing by a large margin. He tried to shut it down with his usual ruthlessness, and when he failed, he then tried to replace the results with obvious forgeries. Carter tried to meet with him to persuade him to accept the results and gain a face-saving exit, but he refused, so Carter denounced the fraud in a press conference.

Although Carter had not yet considered observing the elections in Nicaragua, the lessons that were learned in Panama proved invaluable when that opportunity arose. First, we learned the necessity of getting involved in an electoral process at the beginning, having an onsite presence, and making regular visits. Second, it was essential to gain and retain the confidence and trust of all sides, but particularly of the government, so that the leader would not reject an advance from Carter on election night. Third, the delegation had to make sure that the vote would be secret and that voters understood that. Fourth, and most important, a parallel quick count was absolutely essential to deter any tampering with the ballots and to provide confidence that the private decisions of the voters would be reflected in the final result.

A successful monitoring mission should also understand how elections are similar and how they are different. The difference between Panama and Nicaragua was so substantial that the monitors had to devise a new and uniquely activist model of "election mediation." This model permitted the parties to close the gap between the concept of Esquipulas and the reality of a democratic election.

The Prospects for Reconciliation

The decision by the five presidents of Central America to sign the Guatemalan Accord on August 7, 1987, was a landmark in Central American history. It changed the terms of the debate within the region and the United States. Before the signing, the region was moving toward militarization and war. Afterwards, one could measure progress toward democracy and peace. The signing was the result of a confluence of events. War, depression, continuing threats of militarization, the Reagan administration's relentless pressure, and the breakdown of the Nicaraguan economy all motivated the presidents to search for an exit and to avoid being blamed for not finding one. During the previous five years, the mutual hostility between the United States and Nicaragua had generated the opposite effect, reducing political space and increasing repression. Two men, Oscar Arias and Vinicio Cerezo, building upon the work done by the four Contadora governments, forged a peace plan and persuaded their colleagues that the alternative was untenable.

By constructing a framework that would require each Central American nation to comply with each principle at the same time, Arias placed the burden on any country that refused to comply. Even Ortega recognized that this approach was a leap beyond Contadora. He could never accept a political dialogue imposed from Washington, but he could accept one that was proposed by Central Americans and accepted as part of a broader regionwide agreement. One measure of the risk he took for peace was the public split that occurred within the FSLN Directorate.

The one crucial piece of the puzzle that the Central Americans could not insert was an end to U.S. aid for the contras, and President Reagan's support was nonnegotiable. Nonetheless, the steps by Nicaragua toward peace convinced the few members of Congress whose minds were still open on this issue. In this sense, Central America had a decisive impact on U.S. policy. Convinced that the region's presidents were serious and making progress, Congress took the political risk that Arias had requested: It suspended military aid long enough to permit negotiations to proceed. The risk was rewarded with the Sapoá agreement, in March 1988, but that was just the first step.

The election of George H. W. Bush as president facilitated a change. Bush, Baker, and Jim Wright negotiated a compromise that provided humanitarian aid to the contras while the electoral process was underway in Nicaragua. Unlike Reagan, Bush wanted the elections to succeed, although his preferences as regards the outcome were no different.

The question, then, was how to create the conditions in Nicaragua that would permit a peaceful election. The negotiators of Esquipulas and Sapoá had not devised a system of monitoring or enforcement that gave confidence that democratic conditions could be injected into the Nicaraguan body politic within the space of a year. The flawed election in Panama provided the lessons from which a new class of mediators could help construct a uniquely democratic peace.

The Second Mediation: Defining the Rules for a Free Election

> It is obviously going to be a very crummy election in Nicaragua.
> President Carter will have the unique historical opportunity to
> lose Nicaragua twice.
>
> ELLIOTT ABRAMS, FORMER ASSISTANT SECRETARY OF STATE
> IN THE REAGAN ADMINISTRATION, FEBRUARY 23, 1990[1]

"ON BEHALF OF THE PEOPLE and government in Nicaragua, I have the great pleasure of inviting you to our Tenth Anniversary festivities." So began the letter, dated June 13, 1989, from Nicaraguan President Daniel Ortega to Jimmy Carter. Ortega also noted that he was inviting Jeane Kirkpatrick and Henry Kissinger, suggesting that the revolution still hadn't grasped the way it was perceived by Americans and particularly Republicans. From Carter's perspective, the invitation was an opportunity, and he asked me to go on his behalf to probe whether Ortega might be inclined to invite the Carter Center's Council of Freely-Elected Heads of Government to observe the elections.

The anniversary was used by the Sandinistas to demonstrate their worldwide support, but, with the exception of myself, the only people who came were sympathizers of the revolution or, more accurately, of its struggle against the United States. The international media were attracted to Nicaragua because of their denunciations of the United States and the epic quality of a contest between a David and a Goliath. Ironically, the only ones deceived by the media coverage were the Sandinistas, who viewed the attention as a sign of the substantial support they enjoyed in their country and the world.

In the course of the anniversary events, the most intriguing presentation was made by Kiva Maidinik of the Institute of World Economy in Moscow. He explained to an uncomprehending audience that the center of their worldview was in the throes of a truly radical transformation. Few in the West and even fewer in those countries that were aligned with the Soviet Union had really grasped the significance of Mikhail Gorbachev's revolution. "Now we understand," Maidinik said, speaking for the new Soviet leadership, "that it was a mistake to separate political democracy from social democracy. *The state and the party must be separated* for there to be a great opening for society. . . . It used to be that Moscow dictated to the people; now we know it should be the other way around, and *the only way to have the leaders listen is by free elections.*" These ideas were the ones that brought me to Managua, but everyone else at the anniversary seemed to be marching to a different drummer.

Since none of the better-known Americans came, my status was elevated beyond what it should have been and certainly beyond what I wanted. I withstood the public ceremony to gain some private time with President Ortega and Vice President Sergio Ramirez. I told them that their defense of Panamanian General Noriega in the OAS was interpreted widely to mean that they intended to manipulate their election, as he had done. "Of course, we know that is not the case," I said, "but the best way to prove your sincerity to the world would be to invite the man—Jimmy Carter—who had denounced the electoral fraud in Panama." Their response left me feeling that I was pushing on a door that was opening.

On my return, Paul Reichler, the Sandinistas' American lawyer, phoned to discuss the language of the invitation, and, to my surprise, he quickly accepted our conditions—specifically, that the Council would "have unrestricted access to all aspects of the [electoral] process" from beginning to end. I told him that the Council was only likely to come if also invited by the opposition and the Supreme Electoral Council (SEC), and that I'd been in touch with both. On August 3, 1989, Ortega's invitation—with the language that I had negotiated with Reichler—arrived, followed the next day by invitations from the Nicaraguan Opposition Union (UNO) and the SEC. Carter officially accepted on August 8.[2]

The exchange of letters represented the crossing of a Rubicon of sovereignty, with significant implications for Nicaragua, the Carter mission, and the future of democracy elsewhere. Up until that moment, most governments—especially the most stridently nationalistic ones, like Nicaragua's—viewed elections as internal matters. The official invitation bestowed potent leverage upon the observers, and Carter would use it to great effect. Having invited him officially, the Nicaraguan government could hardly accuse Carter of interfering in its internal affairs. Carter would distill the key complaints from hours of denunciations by the opposition, and he would then bring them to Ortega, who would find it awkward to reject Carter's advice. A positive response by Ortega compelled the opposition to take the process more seriously. Over time and through numerous iterations, this pattern led both sides to secure a stake in an emerging democratic process.

Thus, with the official invitations, the Nicaraguans transcended conventional definitions of sovereignty. By inviting the international community to monitor and, ultimately, to mediate its election, Nicaragua affirmed that their and other elections had an obligatory international dimension, and that all had a responsibility to defend and support each other's democracy. This universal democratic norm would affect countries all over the world.

Why would the Sandinistas invite international leaders, who could put them on the defensive? The invitation to Carter was not the first time that Ortega had invited the international community to observe Nicaragua's elections, and it was certainly not the first time that countries had welcomed international observers. Indeed, the Esquipulas agreements envisaged observation by both the UN and OAS, among others. The OAS had a long history of observing elections, but their missions were so respectful of incumbents that Ortega may have assumed that other international observers would behave in a similar fashion. Ortega had reason to believe that Carter would be fair and impartial, and he could be forgiven for not anticipating the unprecedented: that the Carter mission would become deeply involved in negotiating the terms of a free election. The last reason for the invitation was probably the most influential: The Sandinistas were convinced by their polls and by their people that they would win a free election, but the war would continue unless they could persuade the international community that the election was fair. International observers could do that.

Even a cursory knowledge of Nicaragua's history would lead one to put aside any illusions that the electoral process would be smooth or, for that matter, free and fair. Nor would one have guessed that the observation missions in Nicaragua would establish a precedent and a new model of "election mediation" that would facilitate other democratic transitions. To accomplish all of that would have required nothing less than a most unusual alignment of the planets.

The Alignment of the Planets

Six months before the election in Nicaragua, the level of suspicion among the political parties was so high and their willingness to compromise so low that those skeptical of a fair election seemed to have a winning hand. Nicaraguan history was littered with electoral farces. The Nicaraguan government—whether Liberal or Conservative, Somoza or Sandinista—viewed the opposition as weak, fragmented, and ineffectual, and did everything to keep it that way. The opposition viewed the government as coercive and corrupt. When elections were called, some opposition groups would participate; others asked the people not to vote, lest they provide a veneer of legitimacy to a dictatorial regime. The elections themselves were often manipulated to assure the incumbent of victory. This was the pattern of the past and the point of departure for the campaign that would culminate with a national election on February 25, 1990. The question was whether history would repeat itself or find a new path.

The early signs were not good. The Nicaraguan government was committed in principle to a free election, but in practice this meant reducing Sandinista control of the state and negotiating with the opposition on the basis of equality and mutual respect. The style of governance in Nicaragua, however, was for the government to decree and the opposition to abstain. This is essentially what occurred when the new election law was considered. Under the terms of Esquipulas, Nicaragua's National Assembly had to approve a new election law by April 25, 1989. The opposition proposed some reforms, and then the government ignored most of these ideas and passed its own law.

The next step was the appointment of election officials. The Sandinistas claimed that the five-member Supreme Electoral Council (SEC) was perfectly balanced, and the opposition complained that it only had one seat. The FSLN then considered fifty-four nominations for regional electoral councils, and the opposition refused to submit a slate of names because the SEC was unbalanced. When a vote was taken, the FSLN said there was a consensus on fifty-three names, but that was because the opposition abstained.

Still, there were other signs that a break with the past was possible. Despite the criticism by the opposition, which was echoed by conservatives in the United States, including Vice President Dan Quayle,[3] the electoral law was not unreasonable, and the differences separating the FSLN and UNO were not as significant as their rhetoric suggested. For example, the FSLN's law permitted the reelection of the president, a voting age of sixteen, the right of the military to vote, and the draft to continue; the opposition wanted "no-reelection," a voting age of eighteen, the military to be prohibited from voting, and the draft to expire.[4] These are reasonable differences, but they do not impugn the legitimacy of the electoral process.

The opposition showed signs that it had learned two critical lessons from the 1984 election: Unite and stay in the race. Invigorated by returning exiles like Alfredo Cesar, encouraged to participate by the Bush administration, and convinced that the collapse of the economy, the continued militarism of the Sandinistas, and the movement toward democracy in Latin America all played to its advantage, the opposition felt that it could win *if* there were a free election, and it counted on Carter, Perez, Arias, and Spain's Prime Minister Felipe Gonzalez to keep the rules fair. At the end of June, fourteen parties united to form the Nicaraguan Opposition Union (UNO), and they pledged to support a single platform and slate of candidates. Perez and Arias also used their considerable influence to persuade UNO to nominate Violeta Barrios de Chamorro as the candidate for president and Virgilio Godoy, the leader of the Liberal Independent Party (PLI), as vice president.

Doña Violeta was the widow of Pedro Joaquin Chamorro, the lifelong rival of Anastasio Somoza. The assassination of her husband in January 1978 left the moderate opposition without a leader and led many youth to believe there was no possibility of change without violent revolution. Indeed, the assassination of her husband was the spark that transformed the Sandinista revolution from extremely implausible to possible. The Sandinistas recruited her for the first junta, but she resigned in the spring of 1980 over the direction they were taking the country. The newspaper, *La Prensa*, which she inherited from her husband, was the voice of the opposition. She was a logical choice to be a unifying presidential candidate since two of her children supported the Sandinistas and two supported the opposition. She proved to be a formidable candidate, supported by an astute group of advisors led by her son-in-law, Antonio Lacayo, and Alfredo Cesar, who had served in the

Sandinista government, then led the contras, and finally returned to Nicaragua to run for the National Assembly.

On the eve of the Summit of Central American Presidents on August 5, 1989, the FSLN finally responded to the concerns of the opposition and negotiated a detailed political accord. In exchange, the opposition called for demobilizing the contras.

Politics in the United States, as we have seen, was also infected by the Central American virus of polarization, and Carter was something of a lightning rod. His involvement reassured most Democrats and enraged many Republicans. Georgie Ann Geyer, a conservative columnist for the *Washington Times,* wrote: "Jimmy Carter is back. . . . Why does this make my heart sink?" Her answer: "The Sandinistas are already cannily spreading his name far and wide . . . as proof of their 'sincerity' about free elections. And that is a smart move. They remember that it was Jimmy Carter who handed them power in 1979." Geyer expected Carter would be fooled by the Sandinistas and would acquiesce in their fraud, and the Bush administration simply wouldn't care.[5]

The relationship between the Carter mission and the Bush administration was a complicated one at several levels. The fact that Carter and Bush were of different parties and had contrary views of the contras strengthened Carter's negotiating hand in Nicaragua, although it also heightened suspicion among some in the Bush administration. Carter could use his opposition to the contras to demonstrate both his distance from Bush and his empathy with the Sandinistas. At the same time, the existence of the contras served to concentrate the minds of the Sandinistas.

At a second level was the personal relationship. During the delicate efforts to negotiate with Manuel Noriega in Panama, Carter was in continuous touch with National Security Advisor Brent Scowcroft. In the end, Carter's denunciation of Noriega elicited a grateful invitation from President Bush to the White House. But there was an unhappy chemistry between the president and the former president that might have stemmed from some unfortunate remarks about Bush's manliness that Carter uttered during the 1988 campaign. Moreover, every gesture by Carter to recognize Sandinista concessions on the elections generated concerns about his partiality among some in the White House. The most productive lines of contact would be between James Baker and Carter and between Bernard Aronson and me. Soon after his appointment, Baker visited Carter in Atlanta, and he returned in March 1989 to give his first formal address on Latin America at the Carter Center. Both gestures were appreciated by Carter. Bernard Aronson was a close friend of mine. We had both worked in the Carter White House, and we maintained a very good working relationship throughout the Nicaraguan electoral process.

Another important factor in the political equation was the Democratic control of Congress. Over the objections of the Bush administration, the Democrats inserted funds for the Carter Center observation into the AID budget, and when the Carter mission needed to confirm that the United States was not engaged in covert actions, we approached the Democratic chairs of the Intelligence Committees directly.

Carter's efforts to improve relations between the Bush administration and the Nicaraguan government were unsuccessful, but that had the effect of further removing administration officials from the negotiations in Managua, leaving Carter as the principal mediator. In the end, Aronson negotiated more with Russians than Nicaraguans. The talks with the Soviets had an ironic effect on Nicaragua. At the level of atmospherics, the two superpowers seemed to be reaching an accommodation, and some thought that Nicaragua might be a gift from the Soviets to the Americans, or it could simply be a casualty of the end of the Cold War.

Actually, Bush and Baker were very frustrated by Soviet behavior in the region. In December 1989, on the eve of the Malta Summit with Mikhail Gorbachev, Baker was so upset by Soviet policy that he publicly warned: "Soviet behavior in Central America remains the biggest obstacle to an across-the-board improvement in United States-Soviet relations."[6] In his memoirs, President Bush describes in some detail his conversations with Gorbachev on Central America. He wrote that he was convinced that Nicaragua was receiving Soviet arms and transferring them to the Salvadoran guerrillas. Gorbachev assured him that the Soviet Union was not responsible, and Bush believed him. The conclusion, then, was that neither superpower had much direct influence on events in Nicaragua.[7] After Chamorro won the election, the Bush administration groped to take credit for the outcome by claiming, ironically given the Malta discussions, that its secret partnership with the Soviets was "behind the Sandinistas' stunning election loss."[8]

The strategic equation was therefore favorable for a positive electoral outcome. The planets were aligned properly, but Nicaragua's history remained the outstanding problem, and the question was whether an outsider could mediate the terms of a free election. If so, who might that be? And how might it be done?

There were three possible candidates for the job: Secretary General Joao Baena Soares of the OAS; Elliot Richardson, the UN secretary general's special representative for the Nicaraguan elections; and Carter. Both Baena and Richardson were very capable, but the OAS and UN Charters and the nature of intergovernmental organizations militated against an active role. The cardinal rule in both the OAS and UN Charters was nonintervention. The UN had only one recent experience in monitoring elections, and that was in Namibia, a trusteeship. The international civil servants who staffed the OAS and UN in Nicaragua were knowledgeable and competent, but they were transparently uncomfortable about negotiating election rules in a sovereign country like Nicaragua.

That left Jimmy Carter, who proved to be well suited for the challenge. Carter's talent as a mediator was displayed most prominently during the Camp David negotiations between Israel and Egypt, and he founded the Carter Center in part to permit him to replicate that experience. Carter was naturally drawn to the developing world because of his ideals and his concerns about alleviating poverty, disease, and conflict. He identified with the underdog and wanted to help, and he knew how to listen to and speak with Third World leaders. In a conversation with Carter in February 1986, Nicaraguan Minister of Defense Humberto Ortega told Carter: "We are very pleased that you have come here to try to understand our revolution better. The Reagan Administration has never tried to understand us."[9] Few, if any, senior statesmen in the world would devote as much time and energy as Carter did to the most remote areas of a small, poor country, and this affected Third World leaders in ways that Washington analysts and policymakers rarely understood or recognized.

Carter's skill as a mediator derived from two sources: a politician's charm and an engineer's mastery of technical details. He could empathize with his interlocutor and had a special ability to make unsavory leaders feel respected. Some interpreted this trait as a kind of naivete, but that critique missed the man. Carter was sincere, but he was also a risk-taker, prepared to go to great lengths to accomplish something that most people of his stature would never even contemplate. That characterized his defining odyssey for the presidency in 1976, and even after losing his quest for reelection, he continued to reach for the stars. Failures—and there were many in his post-presidency—did not deter him partly because he constantly redefined his goals to adapt to what he could accomplish.

Carter's negotiations with authoritarian leaders, particularly those who were anti-American, dismayed conservatives and confused liberals, who knew him as the president who placed human rights at the center of his foreign policy. What neither group understood was that Carter was always less interested in criticizing violations of human rights than in ending the violations. As president, he was the one who insisted on trying to reinforce Somoza to make good on his pledges to improve human rights. He was eminently practical. In the midst of delicate negotiations in Nicaragua in 1989—and subsequently in North Korea, Haiti, and elsewhere— *Carter did not judge his interlocutor on past behavior but on whether the leader would reach an agreement with him.* One of his techniques of gaining trust was an almost inexhaustible capacity to listen but not to be diverted by provocative digressions. Instead, he would repeat the essence of the argument, proving that he had listened, and then he would distill from all the rhetoric and anger a few pertinent points. He always kept focused on reaching agreement, and with his mastery of detail and his calm persistence, he would drive toward closure, which he would then announce and move on to the next point. Although his public demeanor seemed soft and, to some, weak, few negotiators were as tenacious and persistent as he was. After watching him negotiate with the Haitian military leaders in September 1994, Colin Powell acknowledged with surprise: "There was such power in his presentation. He was tougher and more dogged than I had thought."[10]

After a decade of war and virtually no communication with the United States, Daniel Ortega remembered nostalgically his meeting with Carter in September 1979 in the White House to discuss U.S. aid to his government. Ortega mentioned that meeting several times during the negotiations in the fall of 1989. What he recalled most vividly was the respect that Carter had shown. Nothing in Ortega's experience had prepared him for that, and as he looked back across a bloody decade, he realized he had missed an opportunity. Now Ortega and his colleagues did not want to miss a second one.

In February 1986, Carter, his wife, and I helped build Habitat for Humanity houses in the northern part of Nicaragua. We also had extensive discussions with the leaders in the government and the opposition. The actual purpose of the trip was to try to mediate a peace plan between the government and the opposition, including contra leaders Arturo Cruz and Alfredo Cesar. The contra leaders were prepared to ask the U.S. Congress to cut military aid in half if Carter persuaded Ortega to engage in serious direct talks. One sign of Ortega's sincerity would be if he asked the UN secretary general to request a mediator, who Carter hoped would be himself.

Carter presented this proposal while Ortega drove his Jeep Cherokee for an eight-hour ride north from Managua. Ortega listened, and on the return he rejected the idea. Carter lit into him with such force that Ortega quickly retreated and promised to pursue it. He didn't, in part because he thought he was winning the war, and he doubted Congress would approve any more aid. This proved a colossal mistake because Reagan soon persuaded Congress to approve $100 million for the contras, intensifying the war. Carter and Ortega's memories of this exchange were selective. Both recalled struggling to find a formula for peace at that time, and even though that was only true of Carter, the fact that they shared that memory was helpful as they embarked on a second journey.

The Parameters of the Election

In a memorandum to Carter in August 1989, I made the case for his leading a monitoring mission, and I defined the goals in three parts: the elections, democratization, and normalization of relations with the United States.[11] The first goal would be to help both sides define the parameters of a free election in a manner that would establish durable electoral institutions and would give both sides a stake in the election's success. Rather than encourage all the parties to approach us to solve the problems, we would back-stop the process and insist that they use existing institutions—the SEC, the courts—to register voters, adjudicate complaints, and ensure a secret vote and a public count. By watching—with an onsite presence and high-level delegations each month—we would encourage Nicaraguan officials to be responsive and the opposition to participate.

In addition to securing a free election, we wanted to construct a foundation for a democratic transition. We encouraged both sides to communicate with each other directly and build enough trust to permit the next administration, whether Ortega or Chamorro, to govern and democracy to take root.

Carter would also try to use the electoral process to narrow the distance between the Sandinistas and the U.S. government. The FSLN saw the election as a chance to unlock European aid and end the U.S. embargo. To the extent that Ortega understood that this was only possible if the election were free, the United States and Europe could use their leverage effectively. To the extent that the United States and Europe pledged to help if the election were free, that would provide a positive incentive.

To be effective, the Carter Center mission had to be multinational, and it would need to convince each side that it was meticulously impartial, intent on helping resolve serious complaints with the process, and absolutely dedicated to making the election free and fair. *In brief, this would not be an observation mission; it would be a mediation project to define the terms that would allow all sides to accept the process and respect the election results.*

The first visit would set a precedent for subsequent ones, so preparations were intense. Carter asked Raul Alfonsin, who had been president of Argentina, to be his co-chair. Alfonsin was one of the most respected democratic leaders in Latin America, and he had special appeal to the Sandinistas because he was a Social Democrat, had been very critical of the contras, and exhibited a touch of anti-Americanism. At the same time, Chamorro's coalition liked him because he was a courageous anti-militarist who had stood up to the military in Argentina and elsewhere in Latin America and was a committed democrat. In addition, Carlos Andres Perez sent a senator who was a close ally of his. Mrs. Carter and I accompanied Jimmy Carter. Prior to the visit on September 16–18, 1989, I went to Washington to brief administration officials and leaders from Congress and to discuss a coordinated approach with the OAS secretary general and with Elliot Richardson.

We had a full agenda.[12] Based on our experience in Panama, we agreed that our most important specific objective was to secure agreement from the Nicaraguan government to undertake a quick count and reach an understanding with the OAS and the UN missions to coordinate our efforts to do it. None of the actors in Nicaragua or the international organizations had heard of a quick count, let alone understood its significance, so we needed to pitch it so that each would view it as serving its interests.

The second objective was to begin a process that would reduce the tensions and the possibility of conflict during the elections. Although a cease-fire was technically in place, there were many violent incidents in the north of the country and some on the Atlantic coast. Ortega and the other Central American presidents had called for the demobilization of the contras by December 5, but the lack of any progress toward this goal frustrated Ortega and heightened tensions in Nicaragua. Based on talks with Aronson, I did not expect full demobilization to occur before the elections, so I proposed that we aim to enlist some high-profile contras to return and participate in the political process. This would send a message of peace to a people who had become inured to war.

The best candidate was Brooklyn Rivera, a leader of Yatama, a Miskito Indian group from the Atlantic coast that had been fighting the Sandinistas. He approached me and asked for assistance to return to Nicaragua to participate in the election. Since the Miskitos were much less of a threat to the Sandinistas than the contras in the north and west, this seemed like a good place to start.

The people on the Atlantic coast of Nicaragua were predominantly Indian, Black, or mixed race and spoke mainly English or Miskito. Somoza had largely left the region alone, but the Sandinistas brought their revolution to it. Many rebelled and joined Yatama. I found Rivera quite flexible and negotiated some language on the conditions for his re-entry into Nicaragua that we would try with Ortega.

In addition to using Rivera to find an incremental approach to integrating the contras into a peaceful political process, we wanted to establish a precedent for other election-monitoring missions by visiting a region outside of Managua. In this case, we would travel to the Atlantic coast.

The third objective for the trip was to identify steps to normalize U.S.-Nicaraguan relations. The two governments had recalled their ambassadors, and we decided to propose that they dispatch new ambassadors and increase their embassy staff. In addition, we would suggest that Ortega not target the United States in his campaign activities and ask him what he would need to assure himself that the U.S. government was not undertaking any covert activities. Those were the goals; the next step was the reality.

On his arrival, Carter publicly explained the purpose of the mission: "We were invited. . . . We are here to listen and to learn. . . . We are neutral with regard to all the political parties and candidates in Nicaragua, but we are partial to the democratic process." At the end of the trip, he held a press conference in which he described his evaluation of the state of the electoral process and specific agreements that had been reached. In between, he and his team held non-stop private meetings, first with the opposition and those who had complaints with the process, then with the SEC, and finally with Daniel Ortega and the other leaders.

The first meeting with the leaders of the fourteen opposition parties that made up UNO was an eye-opener. For about four hours, the leaders complained in the harshest language that a free election was not possible under the Sandinistas. Carter listened patiently. Then he tried to lower the temperature of the discussion by calmly probing for specific problems. He then distilled the issues and promised to raise the following with the SEC and Daniel Ortega: conscription of youth, unequal access to the media and campaign resources, political prisoners, and the right of contra and Miskito leaders to participate in the elections.

"Let me urge you," Carter said, "to document your complaints and submit them directly to the Supreme Electoral Council with copies to the observers. It is not our role to take the place of the government or the SEC. If they don't take action, however, then we will raise our voices."

We then assembled a group of economists from the government, the FSLN, the business community, and the opposition to discuss the state of the economy. One of the leaders said: "Nicaraguans talk to everyone who visits from abroad, but Nicaraguans do not talk among ourselves. This is the first time that we have begun to talk to each other."

The Sandinista Directorate had given Minister of the Interior Tomas Borge responsibility for the Atlantic coast, and the group flew with him to Puerto Cabezas in an old Soviet plane. Borge, the last survivor of the first generation of Sandinistas, was the most transparently authoritarian of the Directorate, but he was also an engaging cynic with a wry sense of humor. Although an atheist, he had a meeting room filled with crosses and Christian symbols that he used just for foreign visitors. He also could be quite candid, as when he told me in private: "We have committed ourselves to free elections, but we have not committed ourselves to losing."

We asked to meet with the local people on the Atlantic coast in private, and they described for us the horror of the civil war and the indignities perpetrated by the

Former President Jimmy Carter, Robert Pastor, and Tomas Borge, Nicaraguan Minister of the Interior (on the right).

Sandinistas, who displayed little or no respect for the cultural differences of the people. The Sandinistas acknowledged their errors, and Borge said he wanted Brooklyn Rivera to return. We went through dozens of drafts of an agreement. In the end, Carter closed the talks with a letter to Daniel Ortega, which summarized the points of agreement: The Yatama leaders could return if they renounced the armed struggle and promised to participate in legal political activities and encourage their followers to disarm.[13]

Alfonsin was unable to stay until Sunday evening when Carter and Ortega worked systematically through the entire agenda of issues for two hours in Carter's hotel room. Ortega invited Carter to describe his concerns. Ortega's response followed a familiar pattern. At first, he tried to demonstrate that Carter's concerns were not justified; failing that, he conceded almost everything. Ortega promised there would be no more conscription into active military service and that he would consider releasing numerous political prisoners after receiving a list of names from the opposition. He admitted that if Enrique Bolaños, a leading opponent, had not given a political speech, his land would not have been expropriated, but he also said that there wouldn't be any further confiscations of land before the elections, although land reform would continue afterwards.

On the critical elements needed to complete an accurate "quick count," Ortega and the SEC agreed to permit the main groups of international observers—the

Former President Jimmy Carter begins his mediation of the Nicaraguan election, September 1989. From the left: Carter, President Daniel Ortega; Alejandro Bendaña, Secretary General of the Nicaraguan Foreign Ministry; Raul Alfonsin, former president of Argentina; Robert Pastor; and David Morales Bello, senator and representative of President Carlos Andres Perez of Venezuela.

OAS, UN, and the Council—to receive and transmit the *actas* (the vote tally sheets from each precinct) to their communications headquarters. The observers would be permitted to release that information or a selected sample at a fixed time, perhaps at noon on February 26, the day after the election. (A week later, however, Reichler called, saying that Ortega had not fully understood this issue.)

Carter then addressed U.S.-Nicaraguan relations:

> I would like to do what I can to prevent the issue of covert aid from the CIA from becoming an issue because I know in the heat of the campaign it would be beneficial to the FSLN to allege that CIA money was coming to UNO. I wonder what I could do to convince you that this isn't the case. I would like to get a commitment from President Bush.

Ortega said that he was prepared to accept overt aid coming from the United States to UNO provided that it was in accordance with Nicaragua's law, which required that half of the funds be given to the SEC to conduct the election. "There is absolutely no problem," Ortega said, "with this kind [overt] of aid. What we fear is that . . . an even greater sum of aid would be approved covertly. . . . Covert aid would create a lot of tensions in Nicaragua and in our relations with the United States. We would feel obliged to strike against the conduits here. We already have concrete information that $250,000 has been introduced—and this was crucial in getting the opposition groups to unite. . . . We have not yet taken steps to prosecute."

Carter replied: "I expected complaints from the opposition about violations of the laws, but invite you to call upon us for the same purpose." I added that if Ortega attacked the United States, "there is no possibility of improving the relationship." I then asked Ortega: "Would Carter's assurance convince you that there was no covert aid?"

"It would be a positive contribution, but the problem is the campaign," Ortega responded: "We will gear ours to the opposition's tone, and we will not be on the defensive."

We continued to press him. Ortega responded that "the only way is for President Bush to receive me and say he would respect a free and fair election." Carter promised to "convey the message, but I cannot write the response."

"You seem to be suggesting that the politics of the campaign will compel you to attack the CIA regardless of whether or not there is any covert action," I said. "If that is so, then I presume that nothing or no one—not even President Carter— would convince you there were no covert actions."

"No," Ortega insisted. "If President Carter's proposal works, I would trust him, and we would not attack the CIA." That was our opening.

Carter then asked Ortega whether he'd be prepared to exchange ambassadors.

"We could do that," Ortega said, "but we would like to hear the results of your conversation with George Bush first because if you have a negative response, then I would not want to do it as I would expect the opposition to say, 'we were rebuffed, . . . that only UNO's Ambassador would be accepted. Therefore, for normal relations, vote UNO.'" Carter promised to explore the issue privately with Bush.

The discussion moved to the issue of whether Sandinistas were supporting the guerrillas in El Salvador (the FMLN). Carter asked if Ortega would permit independent monitors to verify that they were not providing weapons to the Salvadorans. Ortega's response implied that he viewed the FMLN as his bargaining chip: "We will comply [with Tela, prohibiting support for insurgents] in so far as others comply. If demobilization of the Contras occurs, then we would comply." When Carter modified the question and posed it a second time, Ortega dodged it by claiming that the FMLN got its arms from Americans and other sources. He then acknowledged that Nicaragua told the FMLN: "Insofar as our relations improve with the United States, and that is the logic of the peace plan, then we won't accept anything that gets in the way of that. In our territory, we will exercise utmost control." When Carter asked him again about the possibility of observers verifying arms transfers, Ortega repeated: "This could be an outcome of a meeting with President Bush."

Ortega then insisted that any aid to the contras should be sent through the UN/OAS authority (CIAV) responsible for disarmament. When I asked if he would accept a proposal whereby 75 percent of the funding would be used to encourage the contras to return to a peaceful life in Nicaragua (the rest would be for food), Ortega said "the channel of the assistance is critical. If it were CIAV, and it took longer than December 5 to implement, fine. But if the funds are transferred from the CIA covertly, then the objective is to keep the contras alive."

Despite the intensity of the exchange, and the fact that Carter was the demandeur for most of it, the conversation ended cordially, with Ortega thanking Carter "for your sustained and constructive interest in our country and your efforts to improve relations."

The Washington Connection

A few days later, on September 21, Carter and I stepped into a world far from Managua: the Oval Office. Despite the distance, our hour-long discussion with President Bush, Secretary Baker, and their teams resembled the meetings in Nicaragua in their intensity and awkwardness. Carter began with a crisp summary of his trip, and Baker immediately asked whether the Nicaraguans would accept exit polls. I explained that they objected for all the right reasons: In a transitional country, voters would be suspicious and would probably not tell the truth, and so they would be unreliable. I explained that we preferred a quick count and described why it is the "best measure and guarantee of a genuine outcome." In the room were people who had run the most expensive and important political campaigns in the world, but no one knew or understood—until that moment—why a quick count was a far better instrument to guarantee a fair election in a country like Nicaragua than an exit poll.

Carter understood that he needed to persuade Bush that he was not soft on the Sandinistas. "Both sides are confident of victory," Carter explained, "and I am trying to use this moment to establish barriers against fraud or manipulation that will be almost insurmountable if the Sandinistas begin to lose their confidence."

Bush and Baker peppered us with rapid-fire questions, displaying an unusual degree of interest in and knowledge of the election: on access to the media, foreign funds for UNO, and the balance of power on the SEC. "The Sandinistas are very sensitive to international condemnation from me, the UN, and the OAS," said Carter, "and they will try to avoid such denunciations."

Carter told Bush that Ortega was ready to exchange ambassadors, but Bush said that he wasn't ready. "If they hold certifiably free elections, we might be ready."

"Ortega is ready to meet with you," said Carter, "if that would help."

"I bet he would," laughed Bush, and that was the end of that subject.

Baker asked several times whether the Nicaraguans would accept congressional observers. Carter said that would depend on whether they felt the United States was complying with the Tela agreement to disarm the contras by December 5, and he mentioned that Ortega would consider it a very positive step if we channeled our humanitarian aid to the contras through CIAV. The administration did not respond initially, but when pressed a second time, Baker said: "It would be better to separate elections from the repatriation/contra issue." He did not want Congress to "pull the chain" on the money to the contras, but he added: "We are willing to use some of that to repatriate those who want to return voluntarily if they get some assurances from the Sandinistas." Carter said he had no disagreement with that.

Carter then abruptly posed the most sensitive question: "Are you intending any covert actions in Nicaragua during the campaign?" The president responded: "No, but I can't rule it out in the future if the Sandinistas were to try to overthrow the process." Carter said that congressional delegations would be possible if he could commit to Ortega that all U.S. money would be spent in accordance with their law. "If money came through other channels, it would be embarrassing," Carter said.

"Would it be equally embarrassing if the Soviets were discovered to have given covert funding to the FSLN?" Bush asked rhetorically. Carter responded calmly, as he had done to such fusillades in Managua, that he viewed his job as including the monitoring of the use of state resources by the FSLN.

"The administration has no intention of sending covert aid to Nicaragua; it would be counterproductive," Baker said. "But in January, if the National Endowment were unable to transfer overt aid, if the Nicaraguans did not permit congressional observers, or if the system were breaking down, then I don't know." The president said it also depended on how the Sandinistas were getting their funds.

"I will tell Ortega," Carter summarized, "our government intends to fund the opposition in accordance with Nicaraguan law, and I will encourage him to approve a congressional delegation."

From there, we briefed the OAS secretary general and Elliot Richardson, and all agreed to work closely with each other in the months ahead. Then we met with Brooklyn Rivera, who agreed to return to Nicaragua within a week with many of his followers. Finally, we went to Capitol Hill for a full discussion and briefing with congressional leaders. They were very supportive, and several provided additional assurances about covert actions.

On the same day, September 21, Bush asked Congress for aid related to the election: a total of $9 million, of which UNO would receive roughly $1.8 million. Exactly one month later, Congress passed the bill, and the president signed it.

Just four days after leaving Managua, on September 22, Carter wrote a long letter to Ortega, summarizing all of the meetings and nailing down the outstanding issues. He wrote that he had "absolute assurances from U.S. officials, both in the executive and legislative branches" on covert funding, and he asked Ortega to "refrain from any attacks" on the United States on this issue and to inform him of any evidence to the contrary. He also conveyed Bush's principal concern: "I would like for you to assure me that the FSLN will abide by the same restrictions concerning compliance with your country's election laws: that any foreign funding to the FSLN be disclosed and distributed in accordance with Nicaraguan law."

He asked Ortega to ensure that the return of Rivera and his colleagues be handled smoothly, and he said that the U.S. government would comply with its interpretation of the Tela agreement, meaning that it supported "voluntary demobilization"—but would not insist on it until after the elections. He wrote that an exchange of ambassadors wasn't possible then, but a private, step-by-step increase in embassy personnel would be "well-received." Finally, he reminded Ortega of his agreement on the quick count, and said that the OAS and UN would work with us on that.

The next week, on September 28, I returned to Capitol Hill with letters from Carter for the chairs of the House and Senate Intelligence Committees. He wanted to receive firm written assurances that there would be no covert aid for the electoral process, and they so promised. On October 1, Congress passed a secret law barring "any funds for covert assistance to opposition parties or candidates in the February 1990 elections."[14]

This concluded the first phase. Carter had been honest and direct with all parties, and he had gained their trust. He identified clearly the conflicting and the overlapping interests and sought to use the areas of agreement to build confidence in the electoral process. Considering how rancid the relationships had been and how ominous the campaign appeared, the September meetings in Managua and Washington emitted a hopefulness that the election might actually succeed. The international community had finally begun to reinforce the democratic process, not the belligerent process, but the electoral race had just begun.

Registering Voters and Political Earthquakes

After the meetings in Washington, the Carter Center established an office in Managua, recruited an office director, Jennifer McCoy, who had been associate director of the Latin American Program at the Carter Center, and began to assemble a multinational delegation. Because of the Bush administration's preoccupation with congressional observers, we sought Baker's advice for a Republican co-leader of the delegation and for other members. Baker proposed Daniel Evans, who had been governor of the state of Washington and subsequently senator. Moderate in demeanor, a quick study, and a natural leader, Evans proved an effective channel to the Republicans and a good interlocutor with the Nicaraguans. In addition, we decided to incorporate a number of congressional leaders of both parties in our delegation.

Nicaragua's electoral focus shifted to the second stage of the electoral process, the registration of voters. This may seem like a simple task, but it is not, even in advanced democracies, as Americans learned during the election in November 2000 when many complained that they were disenfranchised by an obsolete voters' list. The process of registering voters is one of many administrative tasks that compose the entire electoral process. Poor countries, like Nicaragua, with no experience in democracy, begin an electoral process with two heavy burdens. First, they have weak administrative systems with few educated personnel. Therefore, they are likely to make numerous mistakes. Second, the opposition generally assumes that the electoral administrators serve the government, and it will interpret every mistake as deliberate.

During registration, the opposition viewed every mistake as part of a conspiracy to disenfranchise their supporters, and the government interpreted the opposition's complaints as aimed to discredit the election and the government. Electoral accidents—some almost fatal—occurred at the intersection between incompetence and distrust.[15]

The purpose of a registration list is to enroll all eligible citizens and make sure that only those who register can vote, and that they do so only once. Nicaragua did not have a permanent registration list. In each national election, the Election Commission "called" citizens to register on one of four successive Sundays. With the international community watching the process closely, the SEC established 4,394 registration sites in the country and advertised for the people to register at one of the sites closest to their homes. Since most Nicaraguans did not have documents, local people had to verify their domicile. The list was administered by people, some of whom were partisan, in each town, but the other party usually observed the process.

In Nicaragua, the opposition filed numerous complaints. One was that soldiers were registered at their barracks and their homes, and the opposition feared that they were very loyal to the FSLN (a myth, as it turned out); their vehicles would permit them to vote in multiple places. The government, on the other hand, claimed that registration problems were due to contra violence and intimidation. The Carter/Council sent a mission in late October 1989, led by Rafael Caldera, the former (and future) president of Venezuela, and former Arizona Governor Bruce Babbitt, to assess the registration process. They visited fifty-nine different registration sites in three regions and concluded that the process had gone well but that there was inadequate time or facilities to register all those who applied. They recommended an extension. The UN and OAS teams, and numerous members of the U.S. Congress, all made a similar proposal, and the SEC agreed to re-open five sites on November 12 and twelve additional sites on February 11.

With this extension, the SEC and UNO verified the registration list, and *La Prensa* praised the process. A total of 1,752,088 Nicaraguans registered, representing 89 percent of the estimated voting population. Neither side's fears came true.

However, while the SEC was registering voters, seismic tremors under the political landscape could be felt, and on October 21, 1989, an earthquake erupted, registering high on the political Richter scale. On that day, the contras ambushed two army trucks in Matagalpa. The cease-fire was never very effective, and the army felt they had been unduly restrained because of international public opinion. The ambush finally compelled Ortega to react, but he chose the worst possible time and place—the Centennial Celebration of Costa Rican democracy on November 1—to announce an end to the cease-fire and an offensive against the contras.

Ripples from Nicaragua's earthquake could be felt in El Salvador, where the FMLN launched an offensive against the government in El Salvador, and a plane registered in Nicaragua crashed with twenty-four Soviet-built SA-7 surface-to-air missiles onboard. Salvadoran President Alfredo Cristiani broke diplomatic relations with Nicaragua, accusing Ortega of trying to provide "a smokescreen for his internal problems." Referring to the recent killing of six Jesuit priests in San Salvador, Ortega said he felt "proud that this murderous government [in El Salvador] has cut relations."[16] The other Central and Latin American presidents pressed Ortega and the contras to negotiate a new cease-fire, but the talks stalled. At the same time, on a grander scale, President Bush met with Gorbachev to heal the divisions in Europe but warned the Soviet leader that if he didn't stop the arms transfers in Central America, U.S.-Soviet relations would deteriorate.

Why, at this moment when the belligerents seemed to be untying the Gordian knot around Central America's throat, did they decide to tighten it? The exercise of untying the knot is a meticulous one, requiring skills that the protagonists in Central America had never learned and had little patience to acquire. In comparison, it was much easier to accuse, defy, and fight. One side's attack provoked the other to retaliate in part because each assumed that the other was unified, but the problem stemmed from the opposite premise. Each actor was beset by its own internal struggle between those advocating war and those counseling patience. By the time of the contra ambush, the Sandinistas were near the end of their rope. From their perspective, they had made one concession after another to the international community. To them, each concession signaled weakness and strengthened their opponents. At the same time, there was no movement on the one item that the FSLN most wanted and had been promised twice: demobilizing the contras by December 5.

The Sandinistas had also asked for a sign of accommodation from the Bush administration, and although the administration had given Carter much of what he sought, Carter could not deliver on that or on contra demobilization. The FSLN's implicit threat ("we will comply to the extent that others are complying"), meaning that if the contras weren't demobilized, then they would help the FMLN, was ignored. Bush would not demobilize the contras before the elections because he thought the contras were helpful to compel the Nicaraguans to hold free elections, and also because the right wing in his party would have crucified him if he had. Moreover, Bush might have thought that the Soviets would stop arms transfer to the FMLN. The truth was that both superpowers had moved to the margins of the Central American game. The Sandinistas came unstuck as a result of the contra ambush, and they chose a desperate way to gain the world's attention: They ended the cease-fire, attacked the contras, and armed the Salvadoran guerrillas.

The Sandinista actions strengthened the extremists in the other arenas. Virgilio Godoy, Chamorro's very conservative vice presidential candidate, warned that if a cease-fire were not renewed, the "electoral process will be seriously affected since the Government of the Ortega brothers will have a pretext to adopt a hardening position. Already, we have begun seeing incidents of violence provoked and promoted by the Sandinistas."[17] In the U.S. Congress, Senator John McCain called for military aid to the contras, and after the administration denied visas to several Sandinista leaders to attend a symposium at the Carter Center, the Sandinistas reciprocated by denying visas for a congressional delegation organized by the White House, and they began to hold up the money to UNO.

The FSLN and UNO had been holding rallies for months, but the campaign officially began on December 4. UNO accused Ortega of trying to wreck the elections by restarting the war, and the FSLN responded by associating UNO with Somoza's

National Guard. The harsh rhetoric exchanged by both sides provoked a rash of bloody incidents. Even the normally sedate UN mission began to fear the possible outbreak of "armed conflict."[18] The prospects for a free election were diminishing.

When Carter returned from a trip to Africa, I urged him to go to Nicaragua, and we hurriedly assembled a delegation that included Senator Daniel Evans and former Costa Rican President Daniel Oduber. We left on December 13 and visited two cities in the north—Matagalpa and Esteli—where the most violent clashes had occurred. On December 16, we returned via Costa Rica where we stopped for talks with Venezuelan President Carlos Andres Perez and Costa Rican President Oscar Arias. On the eve of the trip, another tremor unsettled the country.

A group of young militants disrupted a UNO rally in Masatepe, twenty-five miles south of Managua. One person was killed and several were injured. As always, there were dozens of versions of the events, with UNO blaming Sandinista militants, and the FSLN claiming that it was all prearranged by UNO to happen in front of international observers. The truth, to the extent that it could be located, was more complicated. At previous rallies, UNO had complained that the police would swagger through the crowds, trying to intimidate UNO's supporters. They asked the police to keep their distance from the rallies, and the police complied. When the thugs attacked the rally at Masatepe, the police did not try to stop it because they feared their involvement could be misinterpreted or, worse, could lead to more violence.

The Center for Democracy, an American NGO directed by Dr. Allen Weinstein, had brought a delegation to the rally. The Center held press conferences in Nicaragua and Costa Rica, blaming the Sandinistas for the violence.[19] The country was on a knife-edge, and many felt that the election was in grave danger.

Carter's arrival a few days later gave both sides an opportunity to step back from the precipice. Vice President Sergio Ramirez met Carter on his arrival to inform him that the FSLN was planning to issue a decree to stop any further violence. That was the old way of doing things. Carter urged an alternative approach—to ask Mariano Fiallos, the chair of the SEC, to assist all parties in formulating a set of police procedures that would prevent future incidents.

Ramirez agreed, and then Carter's group embarked for the north. Matagalpa produced about 65 percent of the country's coffee, and its farmers were strong supporters of UNO. The village leaders described in considerable detail the arbitrary behavior of the Sandinista police and the military. The police blamed most of the problems on the contras, who had returned to the area during the cease-fire. The situation was tense there and also in Esteli, near the Honduran border, where there was considerable contra activity and violence.

After returning to Managua and consulting with leaders from UNO and the FSLN, Carter asked me to prepare a set of specific guidelines to prevent violence at rallies. I gave them to Fiallos, but his efforts to forge a consensus failed. The FSLN Commission members insisted on adding a paragraph condemning the contras and on omitting the specific guidelines that we had suggested. UNO's objections were ignored, and the SEC approved the decree. At that point, Carter picked up the baton, met with Ortega and Chamorro, and gained acceptance of our modified guidelines. The decree would be specific and practical. It instructed the police to seize all weapons or anything that could be used for aggressive purposes within a 200-meter radius of a campaign event. It also identified a number of other tasks that the police would do together with campaign organizers to ensure that there would be no violence or, if it occurred, that it could be brought under control very quickly. Carter and Fiallos announced the decree at their press conferences.

While both sides in Nicaragua predicted more violence, and many conservatives in the United States viewed Masatepe as the beginning of the end of a democratic electoral process, the result was almost the opposite. The event compelled both sides in Nicaragua to recognize the cost of violence, and the mediated decree gave each side room to retreat without losing face. Most important, the police used the decree in a very professional manner, and UNO cooperated fully. UNO's leaders later described the decree on violence as a watershed event, and in fact, Masatepe would be the last significant burst of violence in the campaign.

Reconciling Nicaraguans and Observers

Still, the confrontation between the Sandinista armed forces and the contras in the north left Carter extremely worried and determined to try to fashion a private channel between Ortega and Chamorro and their principal advisers. The idea was to bring "wise men" from both sides together to consider how the country's divisions could be healed after the election. Frankly, it was my idea, but it was impractical. Despite Carter's herculean efforts, the rhetoric of the campaign was driving the rivals farther apart. Moreover, many of Chamorro's advisors thought that her distance from Ortega was an asset, and most of Ortega's advisors believed that tying Chamorro to the contras was to their advantage.

We tried another approach: to persuade the major governments in Europe and Latin America to promise to help Nicaragua regardless of who won, but conditional on a free election. Although the U.S. chargé d'affaires was not thrilled with the idea, at Carter's request he invited the ambassadors from fifteen governments, including the Soviet Union, to a reception. Carter told them he would be writing to their presidents and prime ministers urging their countries to provide aid to Nicaragua if the elections were fair.

The only negotiation that was more difficult than the one on the decree was with the UN and OAS on the quick count. This issue illuminated another recurring syndrome: the unraveling of a decision that had seemed solid. By the end of the first trip in September 1989, Carter thought he had persuaded all the major parties. He told the Sandinistas that a quick count was the best way to prevent UNO from declaring fraud. He told Chamorro that it was the best instrument for preventing the Sandinistas from stealing the election. The two arguments, of course, were not incompatible. Indeed, they were both true. The next negotiation was with the UN and OAS. To obtain a good sample, it would be desirable for the observers to retrieve results from roughly 8 to 10 percent of all the polling sites (4,383 in all nine electoral regions). This would require a large delegation, and the Carter/Council only had funds for thirty-five observers. The OAS and the UN had most of the money and had brought into Nicaraguan large numbers of competent personnel, so we turned to them for help. None of the senior officials from the OAS or UN was aware of the quick count idea. When we first broached the issue in September, they appeared to be agreeable to a cooperative and unified approach.

As soon as we returned to Atlanta, the agreement began to unravel. Chamorro told a press conference that Carter had promised her he would do an independent poll to make sure the Sandinistas could not steal the election. Daniel Ortega was naturally unhappy to hear Chamorro's remarks, and he told Carter through Paul Reichler that he had never approved an independent poll. I explained to Reichler what we had in mind, and he promised to try to sell it to Ortega. It would take many more efforts, but all the Nicaraguans realized that the quick count could be an invaluable tool to calm both sets of militants on election night and to ensure that any serious fraud in counting would be detected. The Nicaraguans did not have a problem with it. In fact, both UNO and the FSLN decided to do their own quick counts as well.

The problem was with the UN and OAS. Carter and I spoke with UN Secretary General Javier Perez de Cuellar and Elliott Richardson, his personal representative to the election; OAS Secretary General Joao Baena Soares; Iqbal Riza, who directed the UN office in Managua; and Mario Gonzalez, who coordinated the OAS observers. Most of the conversations were pleasant; the problem came when we talked specifics about how to do the quick count. Then they retreated, and despite almost twenty different drafts of an agreement among the three organizations, negotiated over a three-month period, we seemed to be marching in place. To be able to announce an agreement on this issue at the Carter Center's Nicaraguan Symposium in November 1989, Carter phoned the UN and OAS secretaries general, but both refused to sign a letter.

Prior to the December trip, Carter tried again. This time, Perez de Cuellar was candid in his response. In a letter to Carter on December 5, he expressed his agreement in principle to cooperate informally with Carter's group, provided that the OAS also agreed. He then expressed his reservations about the idea of monitoring an election in a sovereign country—"an exceptional undertaking which breaks new ground in our 44-year history"—and indicated that he had no desire to allow Nicaragua to be a precedent. Then, he concluded on a typically ambiguous note: "It should now be possible to initiate discussions . . . on the feasibility and modalities of cooperation between the two missions and your group."

What was going on? The mission of all three groups was, at the most general level, the same: to observe and report on the electoral process. In practice, however, each group initially defined its role in very different ways. The OAS had the longest history in observing elections, but it was ineffectual, rarely issuing a statement, let alone a critical one. The UN, as Perez de Cuellar noted, had never observed an election in a sovereign country and did not want to do it. Intergovernmental organizations, like the OAS and UN, faced an awkward dilemma because the Nicaraguan government was one of their members and also one of the parties competing in the election. The OAS and UN had to treat their members differently, and the opposition noticed that from the beginning.

Jimmy Carter and the Carter/Council did not suffer from those inhibitions. The Council defined its mission not just as observing and reporting but assisting the parties and the electoral officials to make the election successful. This lifted the Carter mission up two steps above passive observation. First, it would use techniques—such as surveys and a quick count—that would permit it to detect fraud and thus to deter it. And second, it would not sit back passively while disputes among the parties endangered the electoral process. It would mediate among the parties and try to resolve the disputes in a manner that would strengthen democratic institutions and habits. With each visit and each problem solved, the parties gained greater confidence that the election might actually succeed. At the same time, watching Carter, the OAS and the UN also gained more confidence and began to pursue issues more aggressively. Elliot Richardson explained part of the reason for the evolution in the UN's role: "The very fact that the future of Nicaragua literally depended on the fairness and freedom of the elections would have made a purely passive role for ONUVEN [the UN group] morally unacceptable."[20]

The other part of the equation was simply competition. Not only were Ortega and Chamorro competing for power, so too were Carter, Richardson, and Baena competing, albeit in a more subtle and perhaps subconscious way, for attention and credit. The competition was more intense between the OAS, which regarded Latin America as its sphere of influence, and the UN, which happened to be led by a Latin American. The comments shared by officials from each organization with us about the other were almost as vitriolic as the ones exchanged between the FSLN and UNO. The only feeling shared by officials in the OAS and UN was the professional's disdain for the politician's ability to grab the world's attention, even though that politician, Carter, was a different breed.

Like many contests, the one between the observers served a wider purpose. In fact, the international monitors were used as wedges, prying political space between the Sandinista party and the state, just as Maidinik proposed, permitting UNO to bring its positions to the Nicaraguan people and giving the people a choice. In the end, the different observer groups, playing complementary roles, helped make Nicaragua's electoral process more democratic and responsive. The OAS supplied 435 observers, mostly in the field. Some performed brilliantly, mediating between groups, as did some of the UN observers. The UN mission had 237 observers and wrote crisp analyses and reports. Riza would go to the SEC and tell its chairman: "Wouldn't it be better if our next report were to describe how you are correcting a problem?" The professionals in both organizations naturally preferred quiet and private diplomacy, and their efforts were often effective. The competition among the observers spurred them to do more.

The quick count was a different matter. In that case, both Perez de Cuellar and Baena Soares feared this would cross the line into more direct involvement in the electoral process. We rebutted that argument by noting that both sides in Nicaragua welcomed this technique. In classic diplomatic fashion, the UN and OAS never said "no" to the idea, but they also never said "yes." Finally, in the December visit to Managua, we sat down with the OAS and UN representatives for two of the most difficult hours of negotiations during that trip. Both repeated their interest in cooperating and then dodged the two specific issues on the table: the quick count and formulating a single uniform survey for all of our observers to use. Finally, they surprised us by both admitting that they were considering doing a quick count, but by themselves. Neither would cooperate with the other or with the Carter/Council. This worried us even more because we weren't sure of the quality of their efforts, and if the two came up with very different results, then they could add to the chaos rather than calm the waters.

In a convoluted way, they also seemed to be telling us that they would not share the information with anyone! We agreed that the information had to be handled in the most delicate and confidential manner, but if it were held so tightly that no one knew the information or used it properly, it would contribute to rumors and thus instability. The officials also expressed their interest in cooperating on a single form, but by this time we doubted their sincerity. We had not given up on cooperating, but we also decided to explore ways to do our own count.

After leaving Managua, we flew to San Jose and spent four hours with Arias and Perez. They had the most at stake and were as eager to learn Carter's perceptions as we were to learn their strategies. Arias also briefed Carter on the Central American Summit that had occurred several days before. All the Central American presidents had pressured Ortega to stop shipping arms to the FMLN and to condemn the FMLN for terrorism. This was hard for Ortega, but he agreed after the others reaffirmed their support for the demobilization of the contras.

We returned to Georgia and then a few days later we flew north to consult with Secretary of State James A. Baker and brief him on the trip. We arrived in Washington on the same morning that 13,000 American troops parachuted into Panama.

The Invasion and Its Aftermath

The invasion came as a complete surprise to everyone. Even Noriega, who had spent the two previous years accusing the United States of planning to invade Panama, was literally caught with his pants down and escaped to, of all places, the Papal Nuncio, where he undoubtedly prayed a lot, before the mother superior persuaded him to give it up.[21]

President Bush had been embarrassed in October 1989 by his administration's failure to assist Panamanian military officers who tried to overthrow Noriega. Bush came to feel that Noriega "was thumbing his nose at him," rejecting every compromise, defying the United States at every turn.[22] In mid-December, Noriega had himself declared "maximum leader," and Panama's rump legislature declared that a state of war existed with the United States. Then, an American soldier driving past a roadblock was shot and killed, and another serviceman and his spouse were beaten and harassed. To protect American citizens, restore democracy, and capture Noriega, Bush authorized an invasion of 26,000 soldiers, the biggest military operation since Vietnam and the largest parachute drop since World War II.[23]

The invasion hovered like a dark cloud over our talks with Baker. Carter barely mentioned it. He was preoccupied with trying to persuade Baker to negotiate a cease-fire between the Sandinistas and the contras. Like many with whom he had spoken in the north of Nicaragua, Carter feared that the election hung in the balance. In a letter that he sent to Baker the next day, he summarized his arguments and the main points of a proposed agreement. Carter described the contras as "a serious political handicap for the UNO campaign" because they "are condemned by an overwhelming majority of Nicaraguans, and the FSLN is taking full and effective advantage of the opportunity." The deal that he proposed would allow the contras to stay where they were, but funding to them would be channeled through the UN/OAS peacekeeping mission. The United States would agree to lift the embargo "provided that the election is certified to be honest," and he proposed that Humberto Ortega meet with Deputy Secretary Lawrence Eagleburger to cement the deal.

Baker did not want to pursue these issues before the election, nor did he want to get into a debate with Carter over the utility of the contras. To Baker, the Sandinistas' preoccupation with the contras was proof enough of their utility. Baker had a point, but he did not adequately appreciate Carter's. The war was a continued threat to the election, and it proved a serious mistake to postpone the beginning of the process of demobilization until after the election because it would consume so much time that it would endanger the transition as well.

This debate, like others, was rendered moot by the next crisis. United States troops entered the Nicaraguan embassy in Panama looking for Noriega, and Ortega responded by dispatching Nicaraguan tanks to surround the U.S. embassy in Managua. Minister of Defense Humberto Ortega issued a communiqué outlining steps that would be taken in the event of a "Yankee intervention," one of which was "neutralization, judgment, and execution of all those recalcitrant traitors . . . that had advanced the intervention." Having been previously accused of such activities, UNO leaders viewed this as a direct threat. The international observers strongly criticized the communiqué, and the SEC, which had increasingly played a responsible and professional role, asked publicly for a clarification. Humberto Ortega did not rescind the communiqué, but he did pledge that the armed forces would defend a free and fair election.

The Christmas holidays, a knee injury that hospitalized Violeta Chamorro, and the next wave of problems soon overshadowed the crisis of December. Senator Christopher Dodd led one of our delegations in early January, and Carter led a larger one at the end of the month. Both observed the technical preparations for the election, tried to stop the intimidation that had led to the resignation of UNO poll watchers and candidates, and sought a formula for uncorking UNO's funds.

The last issue—funds to UNO—returned with a vengeance in mid-January when official Washington awoke to discover that practically none of the $9 million that Congress had approved on October 21 had been received by UNO. There were signs of problems before then. Even before Congress approved aid, the newspapers reported that UNO was receiving millions of dollars, but there were no signs or posters for UNO; their rallies did not have loud speaker systems. By late January, the *Washington Post* reported that UNO had been "outsmarted and outspent." The ninety-three vehicles purchased with U.S. funds could not get through customs. "UNO's campaign is virtually invisible. By contrast, billboards featuring Ortega are over nearly every major intersection" in Managua.[24] Washington was furious, and many hinted that if the Sandinistas did not permit UNO to get the funds, covert actions would be essential. To find the truth, as always, required a more patient search.

Although Congress had authorized $9 million, only $1.8 million was for UNO—with a matching $1.8 million for the SEC, as required by law. Another $1.5 million was for a nonpartisan group, IPCE, which was associated with UNO but would spend the money only on training poll workers and verifying the registration list. The rest of the money would be spent on international observation missions, including $400,000 for the Carter Center. Congressional requirements were so severe that nearly $1 million would be spent on auditing and management of the transfers. Unfortunately for UNO, the frequent reference to $9 million chased away any other funds that they might have attracted, and so they were left practically bankrupt going into the final month of the campaign.

The delays were not all the fault of the Sandinistas. Although the law was signed on October 21, 1989, the grantors—national Democratic and Republican institutes—and the grantees—UNO and IPCE—did not complete their grant agreements until the second week of December because of the time needed to prepare budgets, retain personnel, hire outside auditors, and so forth. Only at that point—a few days before the Christmas holidays—did UNO and AID begin the bureaucratic procedures in Nicaragua, which were complex and difficult to manage even before the United States had imposed a complete economic embargo and then invaded Panama, where Nicaraguan funds were frozen in banks.

Suffice it to say that even if the Nicaraguan government had wanted to be helpful to UNO, it would have had to bend or break a number of its own laws and work without rest through the Christmas holidays. And needless to say, the government was in no mood to be helpful until Carter and the Republican members of his delegation drew the line, drafted an agreement, and compelled Ortega to implement it.

During our delegation's long negotiations in Managua, perhaps the most interesting element was that Panama was never mentioned, although it was just one month after the invasion. The invasion's impact, however, was felt in other ways. The Nicaraguan government expelled some U.S. embassy officials and rejected the Bush-sanctioned congressional delegation led by Senator Richard Lugar because they viewed the group as biased. I spoke with the government and asked whether we could absorb in our group another eight senators and congressmen, and they accepted that. Senator John Danforth, who was a member of our delegation, insisted on the importance of the funding to ensure that UNO could field its election observers throughout the country. He was absolutely right to insist on it, and the Sandinistas accepted the point.

On the eve of the January visit, Carter and I met with four comandantes of the contras at the Carter Center. Several CIA agents accompanied them. The Sandinistas were extremely upset by the meeting, but its purpose was simply to gain the contras' agreement that they would not disrupt the election in any way. Carter later announced that point in his press conference in Managua, concluding: "So I believe that there will be minimal violence and interference in the electoral process by them."

In that same press conference, as in previous ones, Carter described succinctly the complaints that he had heard, his judgment about their seriousness, and the response that he had received from the authorities. For example, he said: "The report that has been very disturbing to us has been of intimidation against supporters, candidates, and poll watchers of opposition parties. We have brought these matters to the attention of the government and leaders of the FSLN. President Ortega informed me that he discussed this with Cardinal Obando y Bravo and that he and all members of the government and the FSLN campaign were determined to eliminate any possible future intimidation, and that they would do this, and I quote President Ortega 'with the firmest private instructions and also public declarations.'" The trip had cleared away a number of issues, including improved access to the media by UNO and the release of political prisoners. Carter reported that technical preparations for the election were going well, but he stressed to the press and to James Baker that Ortega had made numerous concessions. Fortunately, some conservative newspapers, like *The Washington Times*, reported that point: "Sandinistas Yield To Carter, Will Give Election Aid to Foes."[25]

Ortega was prepared to be very responsive to requests by Carter and other leaders whom he viewed as either fair or sympathetic to him in large part because he was increasingly convinced that he was going to win. All of his party's polls showed him with a considerable lead, and in mid-January, he hired Stanley Greenberg, a major Democratic Party pollster, whose survey showed Ortega with a commanding and growing lead: 51 to 24 percent. I had met with Greenberg before he went to Managua and had tried to explain to him in a careful and indirect way that his experience in polling would be of limited use and could be seriously misleading in a country where people knew that the best defense of their freedom was to conceal their views. This warning had no impact on Greenberg.

The great irony of Greenberg's poll, of course, was that it fooled Ortega and many in the United States, and that, of course, was what the Nicaraguan people—or rather about 30 percent of the people—aimed to do. Ortega was so confident that he firmly curbed the excesses of his militants and continued seeking accommodation with the United States. In background briefings, some in the Bush administration seemed resigned to Chamorro's loss. "U.S. Bracing for Ortega Win in Nicaraguan Election" was a headline in *The Miami Herald*.[26] Believing the polls, conservatives and many moderate Republicans were distressed and criticized the lack of a level playing field.

The senior leadership of UNO were just as confident as the Sandinistas that they would win. Arias and Perez sponsored their polling firms in Nicaragua, and their results showed Chamorro winning by 37 to 30 percent in the Costa Rican poll and 41 to 33 percent in the Venezuelan poll. Of course, both polls found about one-third of the electorate undecided or not responding to the question, and their decisions would make the difference between victory and defeat. The Sandinistas, however, were far more expert in getting their polls publicized, and the Greenberg poll therefore set the tone and began to shape expectations.

The next strategic move was to inform and try to capture the moderate Republicans on Capitol Hill. On February 7, we traveled to Washington to meet with bipartisan groups from the House and the Senate. We also met with the editorial board of the *Washington Post* and with Baena Soares and Elliot Richardson. The last meetings broke the ice, and they agreed to share the results of their quick counts with us. The UN also decided to focus on the presidential count and the OAS on a more comprehensive review of all the votes.

The meetings on Capitol Hill proved very productive. By that time, no one knew the issues better than Carter, and he was able to dispel rumors and some of the fears that had grown up during the past months. We also identified eight additional members of Congress to join our team.

Senator Dodd told his colleagues that Bayardo Arce, the campaign manager of the FSLN, had announced that his party would respect a UNO victory, and if the FSLN lost, they would transfer control of the armed forces and state security. Dodd was concerned, however, with rumors that UNO might cry fraud if they lost. At Carter's request, I spoke with Alfredo Cesar, who said that those rumors were completely unfounded. Cesar said that Chamorro felt that the electoral process could not be considered completely fair because the Sandinistas had used the power of the state in unfair ways. Nevertheless, she was "willing to accept the results if the vote count is honest," and she would make her judgment based on the international observers' determination. She also told our delegation that if she lost, she would be the first to extend her hand to Ortega. Those were the two key statements we had been nurturing: Both sides said they would accept the results, and Chamorro promised to follow the judgment of the international observers.

In the closing weeks of the campaign, the government released 1,190 political prisoners, the culmination of six months of negotiation. The SEC took additional steps to increase the confidence of the opposition, for example, by extending the deadline to designate poll watchers, opening registration at a few sites that had been closed for security reasons, and reducing the number of voters at each site.

The last rallies of the campaign were large and peaceful, confirming in the minds of the two camps that they would win. The law required that the campaigns end three days before the election, and this helped to bring the political temperature down in Nicaragua, even though rumors of fraud were rife. The SEC also negotiated an agreement among the parties to prohibit the disclosure of any vote projections or opinion polls until midnight on February 25.

From the invitations to the international observers in August 1989 to the eve of the election, few would have predicted Nicaragua's journey. The high degree of suspicion on both sides would have been sufficient to derail the process even if there had not been a bitter civil war, a breakdown of the cease-fire, a poor administrative system, a guerrilla war next door, and the largest unilateral invasion by U.S. forces in Latin America since the return of the marines to Nicaragua in 1927. Each of these events unleashed nervous tremors in a body politic that could not be easily quieted by patient international observers.

Nicaragua's democrats, however, could not have reached their destination without the active involvement of the international community. The story of Nicaragua during the Cold War is a story of how foreign rivalries exacerbated divisions within the country. Nicaragua's democratic transition is a story of how nongovernmental actors could reinforce the fledgling democratic instincts in the country. The hardest part of a journey is always the last steps. On the eve of the election, both sides agreed to accept the results even if they lost. That was a good omen, but few believed it.

16

The Transfer

A transition is the period between two transitions.

JACOB VINER

NO COUNTRY'S ELECTIONS have been witnessed by more international observers from more diverse groups than was Nicaragua's on February 25, 1990. On election day, 278 organizations from around the world deployed 2,578 accredited foreign observers to observe Nicaragua's election. Fifteen hundred foreign correspondents followed en masse, most of them chasing the story of a Sandinista victory. On the eve of the election, Forrest Sawyer of NBC News interviewed Jimmy Carter and Antonio Lacayo, Chamorro's principal advisor, and told them that he was "absolutely certain" the Sandinistas would win, and asked what they would do. Lacayo was so angry he almost stomped out of the interview. But this was a sideshow.

The main event was at 4,383 polling sites on Sunday morning, February 25, beginning at 6 A.M. Some 1.5 million Nicaraguans—86 percent of all eligible voters—went to the polls. In the days preceding the vote, the SEC broadcast television and radio advertisements encouraging people to vote, and Carter and Cardinal Obando promised Nicaraguans that the international community would make sure that their vote was secret and would count. Observers from the UN traversed the country with signs painted in Spanish on the sides of their sparkling white Toyota Landcruisers: "Your Vote Is Secret" and "Your Vote Counts."

Did the people believe it? Waiting in lines, Nicaraguans were calm and subdued. In response to friendly questions about their preferences, a few would sheepishly raise a single finger, signifying support for UNO. But most did not respond, believing that their votes should remain secret.

UNO managed to field poll watchers in 96.5 percent of the polling sites, and the FSLN at all of them. Representatives of some of the eight small parties were present at nearly half of the sites. The observers reported no serious irregularities and only a few problems where polling sites started late or did not have adequate materials.[1]

Then, at 11:30 A.M., a Venezuelan working with the OAS reported to me that the indelible ink in which the voters' thumbs were dipped could be washed off with bleach. The purpose of the ink was to prevent people from voting more than once, but if it could be removed easily, that would pose a serious challenge to the entire election. A simple experiment confirmed the report, and Carter and I informed the OAS and UN and went directly to report to Mariano Fiallos. The indelible ink was just one of more than 100 technical issues that had been raised during the campaign. UNO operatives believed the ink was doctored so that the military would be able to wash it away and vote multiple times. To test that suspicion, the observers undertook several public experiments. The ink passed the tests, although bleach was never used, and of course, one could not experiment with every one of the thousands of ink containers.

When Carter told Fiallos, the SEC chairman turned white, as if the blood in his face had disappeared. This was a man who had navigated a weakened ship of state to the port of elections. He was a Sandinista, but he was also a former rector of the Leon branch of the National University and a man of great integrity. Ortega had allowed him autonomy to make the election work, and he had done a professional job. I had told Carter that I wasn't certain what Fiallos would do if the election were close and Ortega decided to tighten the leash on him, but until that moment, his work had been exemplary, and it was clear from his physical reaction that the news came as a huge surprise. We decided to call the leaders of the OAS and UN missions and the campaign managers of the FSLN and UNO. This was the ultimate test: to see whether all the parties could reach agreement on how to handle this bomb that had been thrown into the electoral process. It had not exploded, but we were unsure whether it could be deactivated. No one could ignore this potentially grave challenge to the integrity of the electoral process, and as observers, we feared that if both sides did not reach agreement on how to handle the issue, the loser might later use the ink problem to cry fraud.

Carter let the discussion meander for a while to allow both parties to understand the gravity of the issue and the need to reach some understanding. At one moment, the group seemed inclined to call off the vote and hold it in two weeks after the ink could be certified, but after months of such intense pressure, the mere thought of suspending the election for that long and starting again was more than anyone in the room could accept. Luckily, the two campaign managers, Bayardo Arce of the FSLN and Antonio Lacayo of UNO, were each confident of victory, and both decided to go ahead. They agreed that they would respect the outcome of the election unless signs of multiple voting were witnessed by poll watchers or observers. This was the best of all outcomes. Everyone congratulated each other, took deep breaths, left the meeting, and prayed that this would be the last incident.

Before the election I had consulted with a group of experts—including Jennifer McCoy, the director of our Managua office, Richard Millett, who had written an influential book on Somoza, and Ambler Moss, who had been U.S. ambassador to Panama—about how we should respond to a variety of contingencies. We were determined to avoid a repetition of what had happened in Panama, where Noriega avoided talks and eventually annulled the election. Most of us thought that Chamorro would win, and if that occurred, we wanted Carter to meet immediately with Ortega to persuade him to accept an undiluted transfer of power. To do so would require some assurances that the transfer would not be vindictive.

Carter's intense negotiations with Ortega had drawn him close, and I suspected that Carter thought Ortega would win, although I did not ask him about this until many years later, when he confirmed my guess. Similarly, he never asked me who I thought would win. Interestingly enough, Baker, relying on Greenberg's and other polls, also thought that Ortega would win. Aronson and I were confident of a Chamorro victory.[2] At two polling sites, Carter and I witnessed a surprisingly one-sided victory for Chamorro. Carter sensed the ground moving under us, and he told me that he was prepared to set our plan in motion. We went directly to two places where we expected Ortega to be, but he wasn't there. We therefore asked senior officials in his government to pass a message to him that Carter wanted to see him urgently.

We returned to the hotel for dinner and to consult with our delegation, and then at about 9:30 P.M. we left for the UN headquarters, where Richardson and Iqbal Riza escorted Carter, Mrs. Carter, and myself into a small room and handed us the results of the quick count. Slightly more than one-third of the UN sample had been received, and Mrs. Chamorro was decisively ahead by a margin of about 55 to 40 percent. The statisticians were as certain as people in their profession could be. The margin was so wide and the returns coming in were so consistent that there was no question about her victory. Richardson suggested that the two teams go to the National Vote Counting Center to brief the OAS secretary general and to see the SEC's results. He then said that Carter, in a private capacity, should meet with Ortega.

Richardson understood the importance of the quick count but also the role that only Carter could play in influencing Ortega to step down. It was inappropriate for the representative of an intergovernmental organization to play that role. Baena Soares understood that and made himself virtually inaccessible that evening.

The National Vote Counting Center was not announcing the results, and Fiallos found himself in an awkward situation, trying to make excuses when, in fact, his leash had been pulled taut. At about 11:30 P.M., Daniel Ortega finally sent word to the Vote Counting Center that he wanted to meet with Carter, Richardson, and Baena Soares. Fiallos was relieved, and we knew that the moment of truth had arrived. We spoke quietly in the car on the way to the meeting. I whispered to Carter that he would have to do everything he could to make Ortega comfortable in accepting the loss. Carter knew that and was prepared.

Midnight Meeting

The three leaders and their assistants filed into a room in the bowels of the grandiose Sandinista Party Headquarters at 12:20 A.M. The OAS secretary general arrived last and acknowledged that he did not know why he had been called. Carter and Richardson did not need to ask. Daniel Ortega walked into the room with Sergio Ramirez, Bayardo Arce, Foreign Minister Miguel D'Escoto, and their American lawyer, Paul Reichler. Ortega, Ramirez, and Arce were ashen-faced; not the bloodless glaze of Fiallos's face when he learned about the ink: Their faces were gray, sad, and stunned.[3]

Daniel Ortega sat across from Carter and began: "We've been reviewing our quick count. We know that you've done yours as well. The current trend is favorable to UNO, by perhaps a 5–6 percent margin, but we do not discount the possibility that the trend will reverse." Then, he got to the point of the meeting.

"I wanted to talk to you about what could be an eventual triumph of UNO and take steps to ensure that if this occurred, it would not produce a bad outcome." He said that the Sandinista military were very worried that the contras might take offensive action. "There is a section within UNO who would be so encouraged by a UNO victory that they might want to provoke acts of violence against the FSLN. . . . There could be a civil war. The conduct of the U.S. government would be decisive."

"When we took up the challenge, I was fully confident that we would win," Ortega spoke in almost a monotone. "But I knew that we could lose, and I made up my mind that I would comply with the popular will. If the people decide to give the opportunity to UNO, I will respect that, but the Sandinista base, the grassroots, must be protected from a Pinochetazo. The difference is that the people here are armed. But I still think it might be possible to reverse the trend."

This last thought hung there as a reminder that he had not yet accepted defeat.

"The delay by the SEC will generate nervousness," Ortega continued. "It's important to keep calm and allow the people to know the results. I also think it's important to talk to UNO right away, starting from the possibility that they might win. But even if 15 percent of the vote is received, I still want to wait because of the delicate nature of the information."

Ortega had grasped the possibility, not the inevitability, of defeat. It sounded as if he was still trying to leave a little room to double back.

But Ortega then stared at Carter and implored: "If UNO does win, I will ask you to play the kind of role that you played during the election—to achieve reconciliation of the country until April 24[h] and perhaps beyond that—to ensure that what has been agreed upon can be guaranteed. And with your support, we can engage Cardinal Obando."

Carter listened intently. The room was quiet and somber, but outside, a rock band was playing loudly, waiting apparently for Ortega to announce his victory. It was an incongruous juxtaposition of serene defeat inside the room and boisterous celebration on the outside, but it permitted the "wise men" to recognize that Ortega faced the agonizing problem of informing his minions that they had nothing to cheer about.

Instead of debating Ortega's reservations or consoling him, Carter instinctively used the background music to try to lift his spirits and provide arguments that he could use with his party to relieve any lingering doubts. Carter congratulated him: "What has been done in this country in the last five to six months deserves tremendous worldwide credit, reflecting such a full commitment to democracy and freedom. It was one of the finest campaigns and elections I have ever known. It is very important that my country respond to this with generosity and reconciliation—perhaps even more than UNO—but both are important."

He then focused on Ortega's principal preoccupation: "I would like to call Secretary Baker before sunrise to talk about what is needed from Washington to restrain the contras until April 24. During this time, the Ministry of Interior and the army would be under your control. It would be a deadly mistake for UNO to precipitate any violence. We would be glad to work with UNO to make sure their statements and actions are fair, accommodating, and generous."

"In my opinion," Carter said, "the FSLN can come out as heroes, having triumphed in a revolution against an oppressive dictator, survived a war against an enemy that was financed abroad, and at the end of ten years, brought democracy."

"You have a united front. Initially, UNO will be divided in victory or defeat. You are all young men. Six years may seem like a long time, but it's not. The next six hours will make a difference as to how the people of Nicaragua will look on you."

After Ortega's initial remarks, none of us were sure whether he had accepted defeat. His comments about the "tendency" of the polls and the narrow margin he cited left us uncertain, so Carter bore down on this point next: "Our information is very accurate. UNO's margin is 55–40 percent, and it remains stable. . . . It would be a serious mistake for the SEC to delay its results. The information should come out tonight. When people wake up, they should be convinced that the election was fair and honest. If you have special concerns, especially about the army, these can be discussed with the top levels of UNO to make sure they are treated fairly. That's not our place, but in a quiet, unpublicized fashion, we would be glad to help—and not just for a few days."

"My feelings for you are very deep," Carter said with genuine affection. "Like you, I have won a presidential election, and I have lost one, but losing the election wasn't the end of the world."

"But I thought it was," Rosalynn Carter interjected, breaking the tension, and everyone laughed. It would be the Sandinistas' last laugh, but it was a necessary release for everyone in the room.

Carter completed his thought: "If the world sees in you what I and others have seen, they will know you as a leader of pride, dignity, and generosity. We are here to help you."

Elliot Richardson then offered his support: "I wholly share all of President Carter's views. I have great respect for how you have invited international observers. I would like to underscore the point that you are in a position to make a unique contribution to the history of this country by demonstrating generosity. For that, you will always be remembered. This will assure you a position of leadership. I hope you will not delay a statement to the people of Nicaragua. That would help prevent anything bad from materializing."

Carter urged Ortega to draft a positive statement that also took credit for the fact that the election was free, fair, and democratic.

Baena Soares then brought the weight of the OAS to the table: "I am in agreement with all your declarations, and we would help to make a peaceful, democratic transition."

Bayardo Arce explained that his principal concern was that once the SEC began to announce results, supporters of the Sandinistas and UNO would go into the streets. He recommended that Ortega ask the people to be calm and to wait for the final verdict.

Richardson suggested that the international observers should also call on the people to remain calm. Arce asked if they could speak with UNO before Ortega called for calm. "They can express their joy, but they shouldn't say that the results are all in, that it's over."

Carter was concerned about any delays. He said that the SEC should make an announcement immediately that UNO was in the lead. Then UNO should urge calm and ask the people to wait for the final results.

Ortega then summarized the discussion: "We must conclude now in order to minimize tension and distrust. The FSLN is willing to have the SEC share its information, but UNO needs to refrain from announcing its victory. Then, the SEC will release returns at intervals of about 5 percent of the vote, until they reach 90 percent of the results, and then everything will be certain. Let us not say victory before that."

The last formulation sounded as if the Sandinistas were seeking to delay the inevitable, and Richardson interjected: "We don't have to wait for 100 percent of the results."

Arce then responded by saying that all the previous polls had apparently been incorrect, and we needed to wait.

This last point caught our attention, and some of us worried that the Sandinistas were seeking some wiggle-room. President Carter asked me to explain the difference between the polls before the elections and the quick count. With few words, I tried to put a stop to the two lines of argument that seemed the most potentially dangerous: that the results were still in doubt and that the process of accepting them should be delayed.

"The polls," I told Ortega, "were *attitudes.* They reflected what people wanted to tell the pollsters, and the people apparently weren't always truthful. The quick count is *the results of the election.* It is conclusive. The margin is wide and consistent. The quick count will be very close to the final outcome."

I emphasized the difference between attitudes and results. Ortega heard what I said and did not dispute my statements. Instead, he turned to Carter and the future and said: "Faced with the hypothetical triumph, I ask you to continue your work as guarantors of the transition. We will plan it jointly."

"We will do what you say," Carter responded, "but I hope you consider the advantage you will gain if you make the first, positive statement."

"When the trend is fixed, then I can make the statement," Ortega answered.

"I think you're right, but you need to do it before the morning news goes out."

Ortega: "I'm not going to bed. Tomorrow, we can do it."

The meeting broke up at 1:10 A.M. It was already tomorrow.

The historical weight of the meeting seemed to transform the fifty minutes into several hours. Everyone in the room had a great deal invested in the meeting's outcome. Everyone had developed so much respect for the others that the points exchanged were gentle and indirect, but they were nonetheless clear. At the beginning of the meeting, and at several points during it, some of us had our doubts whether Ortega had accepted defeat or would accept it. But by the end of this most fascinating exchange between revolutionaries and elder statesmen, there was little doubt that Ortega would concede. He just needed some time to prepare his people, and he needed Carter to restrain UNO until he had done that.

We shook hands, quietly filed out of the room and into our cars, and went directly to Mrs. Chamorro's home, arriving at 1:30 A.M.

Chamorro's house was crowded with her supporters. The atmosphere as we entered was a mixture of nervousness and concealed celebration. The eyes of her supporters fixed on the wise men and their aides as we entered the house; they sought some assurances that the Sandinistas had lost, and that Violeta would be president. They were not certain because they had had problems collecting their quick count and suspected that the Sandinistas had created those problems. The anxiety was palpable.

Carter summarized the previous meeting: "Daniel wants to know how to concede with dignity and without violence. They would like you to restrain your supporters so Daniel can convince his supporters that they should concede."

Richardson restated the point with his characteristic deliberateness: "In allowing him to concede with a degree of magnanimity and grace, that will contribute to the possibility of a smooth transition, that will . . . "

Carter interrupted: "He cannot concede with just 15 percent of the vote in, but I think he's convinced that before daybreak, he is prepared to do so."

"The word is about that we are winning," Violeta finally said. "We are preparing a very responsible speech that will include congratulations to Daniel Ortega for allowing an electoral process like a statesman."

Alfredo Cesar worried whether Ortega was holding up the results and whether they would be accurate when they came out. Carter said that if the results were not accurate, "we would denounce them." Richardson said that Ortega wouldn't have asked them to their headquarters if he intended to do that. Cesar said that if the results released were partial and accurate, that wouldn't be a problem, but for how long should they hold off making an announcement? Richardson said: "You don't have to delay immeasurably if he refuses to concede, but it's much better if he goes forward first."

As we were leaving, Cesar and Lacayo pulled me aside. I had known Cesar for more than a decade and had become very close to him and to Lacayo because I liked them, but also because I sensed a need to balance the special affinity that had grown up between Carter and Ortega.

"Will they accept defeat?" They asked me, but it was more than a question. The moment of truth had arrived, and they did not trust the Sandinistas to accept it.

They knew I shared their views of Ortega. I answered firmly: "It's over. They know it, but it's sinking in slowly. You've won. Take your time. They cannot take it from you if you handle your victory with patience and statesmanship. Don't claim victory yet!"

Then I raced for the door to get in Carter's van. Later that morning, when I returned to Chamorro's house, Lacayo and Cesar told me that when Carter, Richardson, and Baena left, the house erupted into a ferocious debate. Virgilio Godoy insisted that Violeta claim victory immediately and that they organize their people to defend it in the streets. A draft of her speech had been written and included several paragraphs proclaiming her victory, but Lacayo and Cesar fought back. Violeta listened and then told Lacayo to modify the paragraphs claiming victory. It was a wise move, but it was just one of many instances where a different decision could have sidetracked the democratic process.

We drove back to the National Vote Counting Center, and at 2:50 A.M. Fiallos released 30 percent of the results, which showed Chamorro ahead by 54 to 42 percent. I passed a message to Ortega through his aide that the meeting with Chamorro had gone well.

Then we returned to the hotel, and Carter phoned Secretary Baker at 3:10 A.M. I suggested waiting a few hours to let Baker get a good night's sleep. Carter said that he was sure that Baker would want to receive the call at that moment, and Baker later confirmed that he was glad to have been awakened.[4]

Carter told Baker that, based on the quick count, Chamorro had won a substantial victory, but the results wouldn't be announced for a few hours. He said that UNO would wait for the results and that Ortega would make a concession statement by daybreak. He urged Baker and the president to make very positive, congratulatory statements not just to Violeta but also to Ortega for allowing a free electoral process. Baker asked if Ortega had really accepted the outcome. "There is not any doubt at all. Both sides want an orderly transition, but it won't be easy." Carter insisted, as he had done many times before, on the need to restrain the contras and lift the embargo. "Everyone is hanging on the words of the State Department," he concluded, and handed the phone to Dan Evans and John Danforth to speak to Baker as well.

Reichler then stopped by to tell us that Ortega would give his speech at 6:00 A.M., and Carter asked me to tell Violeta about his conversation with Baker and the news that Ortega would speak at that time. It was about 3:45 A.M., and Violeta was about to speak to her supporters, so I commandeered a taxi to go to the UNO rally. I arrived just as she began. She keyed her remarks to the release of results by the SEC, and although she didn't proclaim her victory, she left no doubt as to the outcome:

"After having heard about the first electoral results, I would like to tell you that I am certain that this constituency's tendency in favor of UNO is irreversible . . . ." She then asked her people "to be calm and abstain from displaying any signs of victory." She repeated her determination "to achieve national reconciliation" and congratulated everyone for "the first election in our history won by the opposition." She did not quite get to the point of mentioning Ortega, but then, he had not quite gotten to his concession yet either. The crowd was excited but also a little uncertain. In most democratic countries in Latin America, on the night of the election as the results become clear, one can hear the continuous bleating of horns beeping wildly from a cavalcade of cars. This, of course, was Managua's first election, and the early morning was quiet.

After Violeta concluded her speech, Antonio Lacayo and Alfredo Cesar invited me into their van to return to her house, where I briefed them on Baker's call, and then we moved to the television set to watch the returns come in and await Ortega's speech. At 5:45 A.M., Fiallos announced that 61 percent of the polling sites had reported, and that Chamorro was ahead by 55 to 41 percent—exactly the margin that I had predicted to Mark Uhlig of the *New York Times* eight months before, and virtually the same as the UN's quick count.

Then, at 6:20 A.M., Daniel Ortega arrived at Olaf Palme auditorium. His face had regained its color, but he looked dazed, almost as if he had been drugged or crying. He gave his speech in a low monotone and covered the points that Carter had suggested the night before: praising the Sandinista Front for the revolution against Somoza, for defending Nicaraguan sovereignty against U.S. intervention, and for conducting an historic free election.

Referring to the announced results, Ortega then made a convoluted statement that reflected complex feelings and his difficulty in admitting defeat: "These numbers and these percentages mark a tendency that possibly could be changed by breaking all mathematical calculations, as I believe that here all the suppositions of the public opinion polls have been broken, but the fact remains that there is a marked tendency."[5] This was not exactly a straightforward concession, but the point was clear from his face and from his next statement. He pledged to "recognize and respect the popular will."

At this moment, Violeta popped the corks on the champagne bottles in her living room, and UNO officially celebrated.

In her statement to her supporters earlier that evening, she had not proclaimed victory, a concession to the wise men and Ortega, but she had announced that the opposition had won, a concession to her supporters. She didn't gloat, and she urged calm and restraint. Similarly, Ortega spoke after the returns were announced and as he had promised, but he could not quite bring himself to concede in so many words. Nonetheless, his message was unmistakable. The two, in brief, did not fully adhere to the understanding mediated by the wise men, but their statements acknowledged each other's needs, and they followed the agreed sequence. Considering the country's history, Daniel and Violeta traveled a long distance that night and opened a new path for their country.

The First Days of the Transition

The tension of the previous weeks almost evaporated with the bubbly. Violeta, who had been talking back to Daniel on the television screen, also relaxed in her own way. Her leadership qualities were not self-evident, and indeed, many people dismissed her as simply the widow of a martyr. But Pedro Joaquin Chamorro also had able sons and daughters and strong and articulate brothers and cousins, and before one underestimated Violeta, one would have to explain why she, rather than the others, inherited his mantle.

A tall, handsome woman with a distinguished profile, she was both approachable and distant at the same time. She had strong feelings, particularly about the Sandinistas, but she also knew the necessity of controlling those feelings. She was almost "Reaganesque" in her leadership in the sense that it was easier to recognize her impact if you watched her from a distance than if you engaged in conversation with her. For these reasons, I relied much more on her two advisors, Lacayo and Cesar. Both were very intelligent and also knew her mind.

I had not slept for days, but my adrenaline was working overtime, and so sipping champagne for ten minutes seemed like I had taken the day off. At about 7:30 A.M., I decided it was time to go back to work. I asked Cesar and Lacayo to come with me to meet Carter. They asked why, and I said that it was time to plan the transition. They had been so busy preparing for the election, they had not begun to think about that. I had prepared a paper, and when we arrived in Carter's hotel suite, I briefed them on it. The principal objective was a simple one: Chamorro would have full authority on April 25, but to get to that point and to govern effectively, they needed to find ways to reassure the Sandinistas that they would not be persecuted and that the contras would be completely dismantled. They agreed completely on these issues and also understood that they would have to address several other issues, such as property and the armed forces, during the transition and beyond.

The country did not go to sleep on the night of the election; by the time of Ortega's address in the morning, people had adjusted calmly to Chamorro's victory. Managua was tranquil and exhausted during the day of February 26.

In the late afternoon, at about 5:45 P.M., Carter and I visited Daniel Ortega to discuss our talks with Cesar and Lacayo and their interest in a smooth transition without any retribution. Carter asked Ortega whether he had any specific issues to raise, and Ortega answered that he needed to consult with his brother, Humberto, before responding. Carter also asked about the unity of the FSLN, and Daniel said that all agreed to accept defeat, but the Directorate was focused on the contras and feared they might use this moment to attack.

It was now time for the public concession. Carter, Richardson, and Baena accompanied Ortega to Violeta's house for a brief thirty-minute meeting. As we walked into the study, she received a phone call of congratulations from Ronald Reagan, but her assistant asked him to return the call the next day. The conversation was awkward but polite. Chamorro felt a need to restate the obvious—that she had won—and they exchanged pleasantries and a stiff embrace. Then both Chamorro and Ortega agreed that they wanted Carter, Richardson, and Baena to serve as guarantors of the transition; that there would be no hate or vindictiveness; that the contras should be demobilized quickly; and that the military should be sharply reduced in size.

Former President Jimmy Carter accompanied Daniel Ortega to the home of Violeta Chamorro on February 26, 1990.

The symbolism of Ortega visiting Chamorro in her house was as important as any event in those historic days. The actors in the room seemed a bit shell-shocked, but Richardson roused them by saying that he felt "a sense of privilege" witnessing this occasion. It represented a decisive break from the conflicts of the past. In this case, the guerrilla leader of a violent revolution was accepting defeat by a woman whose popularity derived in substantial part from her husband and his murder.

Although it would take a few more days for all the results to be counted, the election shattered many myths. There were ten presidential candidates, but two alone captured 96 percent of the vote. Chamorro won 54.7 percent of the vote and Ortega 40.8 percent. This was, in brief, a binary election in which the majority voted against the incumbent. Given the war and the state of the economy, it was not a surprise that the government would lose the election, except, as this book testifies, that this was no ordinary election. In the legislative elections, UNO won an absolute majority with fifty-one of ninety-two seats, but not enough to change the Constitution. The FSLN won thirty-nine. UNO also swept 102 of 131 municipal elections. In the two Atlantic coast autonomous regions, Brooklyn Rivera's coalition did exceptionally well, and Brooklyn himself was elected to the Assembly.

In the areas of the country where the contra war was fiercest, UNO enjoyed the most support, suggesting that the contras were not as much of a liability as Carter, Ortega, and some in UNO thought. Another interesting outcome was that UNO did very well in Managua, which had the heaviest concentration of government employees, and in polling sites that had a large proportion of soldiers voting. Chamorro's promise to end the war and conscription and restart the economy undoubtedly helped. While people were uncertain whether the election would be fair, the international observers gave them confidence, and they voted as if their vote counted, as it did. Under the circumstances, perhaps the most surprising result was the strong support of 40 percent of the population for the FSLN.

The transition was unprecedented in so many ways that it dawned only slowly on the key actors that managing it would be immensely complicated and at least as risky as the election itself. The Sandinistas had constructed a huge armed force and police that were instruments of their party as much as of the government. What would happen with that armed force? There were some who thought that UNO should rely on the contras as their army, but that would be a recipe for civil war. Chamorro and her principal advisors did not hesitate during the campaign or afterwards to accept the Central American pledge that the contras should be completely dismantled, but people in her coalition and in the United States thought she should not rely on the Sandinista army. In addition, although the FSLN lost the election decisively, they lost to a fourteen-party coalition whose only unifying thread was their opposition to the FSLN. Keeping the coalition united after the election proved even harder than assembling it in the first place.

Our next meeting, at 7:10 P.M. on Monday, February 26, was with Humberto Ortega. He was clearly the shrewdest of the Sandinistas. Although he enjoyed the role of being the senior military commander, his mind was not a soldier's. He was much more of a political strategist and an intellectual. Without his strategy to incorporate middle-class leaders, the Sandinistas would never have won the revolution. Daniel relied on his advice, and it was therefore not a surprise when he asked him to help navigate the uncharted waters of the transition.

The Nicaraguans were thinking about a transition that went from February 26 to the inauguration on April 25, but Carter wanted to return to Georgia in two days. He saw no reason why all the agreements could not be negotiated by then. Humberto did not want to hurry, but he was a great improviser.

A typical presentation by Humberto Ortega would begin with a set of general principles; then he would trace them logically to the specific policies he was proposing. But on this evening, his mind was focused on a single issue, the contras, and his presentation was sharp and to the point: "The army and the Ministry of Interior are obligated by the Constitution and by our spirit of reconciliation to serve the commander-in-chief, and we will do so when Violeta Chamorro takes office, but we cannot accept another armed body that is not a legal institution."

"We feel threatened insofar as the contras remain militarized," he admitted. "The first condition is that they demobilize exactly as contemplated in the Central American Accords. As long as that does not occur, we are obligated to our friends, who died, to demand it." Humberto was intelligent enough to understand that it would not be advantageous for him to threaten Carter or the incoming administration, but he also suspected that he would not be able to deliver his own army to the new government in the absence of such a clear understanding.

He was very precise in his expectations: "First, we will offer a cease-fire so that the demobilization can proceed. Second, President Ortega would make a public statement asking the United States to rechannel contra funds through CIAV. Third, Violeta would make a statement supporting Daniel Ortega's call on the contras to comply, and would assure them guarantees of peace in resettling in Nicaragua. If this occurs, that would help me to control the forces in the military or any radical elements, and it would permit us to create a basis for dealing with other issues."

Having spent the previous six months trying to persuade the Bush administration to rechannel the funds, Carter said that he could not disagree with the points made and that he would convey them to Lacayo and Cesar. Carter asked if Humberto also spoke for Tomas Borge, and Humberto responded that he spoke for all those "with responsibility" for the army and police. In response to Carter's question about any other issues, Humberto admitted that he hadn't had time to address any others. It was clear that they couldn't address any others until this issue was satisfactorily disposed of.

We returned to the hotel and invited Cesar and Lacayo for another round of talks. Cesar said that he didn't like the "conditionality" of Humberto's proposal, but he agreed that the contras should be demobilized. Carter said that at this time a clear statement of intent was needed; the demobilization would take more time. Cesar and Lacayo both believed that Chamorro's government would be threatened if there were two armies, and if this issue were not resolved by April 25, her government would be unstable. Lacayo promised to secure her agreement on a statement along the lines that Humberto had requested. Lacayo would soon be appointed to head her transition team, while Cesar, who had been elected to National Assembly, would try to secure a leadership position in that body.

That same day, President George H. W. Bush issued a statement congratulating Chamorro and also Ortega "on the conduct of the election and on his pledge to stand by its results." Bush also said that "given a clear mandate for peace and democracy, there is no reason at all for further military activity from any quarter, and we hope the cease-fire will be re-established without delay and respected by all sides."[6]

Would Bush have accepted the results if Ortega had won? The answer came in the midnight meeting on election night between the wise men and Ortega. By the time of the election, the wise men had accumulated so much credibility that if they reached an unequivocal consensus on the fairness of the election, it would have been very hard for anyone to contest that. Ortega, Chamorro, and Bush all understood that point even though they might not have articulated it in that way. The Bush administration had no wish to restart the contra war. In the event of an unequivocally free election, Bush would have accepted the results and phased out his support for the contras, but that does not mean that the contras would have surrendered or given up their war.

In his next meeting with Humberto Ortega on the morning of February 27, Carter began by referring to Bush's statement and other assurances he had received about the process of implementing the steps that Humberto had outlined the day before. He had sent a note to Mariano Fiallos asking him to complete the count and declare Mrs. Chamorro the president-elect. Until Fiallos announced Chamorro's victory, Lacayo said she would not issue her statement on the contras. After Chamorro called for demobilizing the contras, Carter would seek to elicit a comparable statement from the Bush administration. Carter aimed to get the SEC to confirm Chamorro's victory first, and he was applying the same back-and-forth techniques to reassure each side of a peaceful transition. He was anxious to tie up all the loose ends, but Nicaragua was not accustomed to moving at his pace.

Humberto had regained his balance and returned to his old style. He spoke about a new "correlation of forces" in Nicaragua as a result of the election and the need for both sides to respect the adjustment. "All of the army and security forces will take the oath of loyalty to Violeta, but we are worried that some right-wing sectors might start death squads or try to destabilize the process. . . . In order to generate confidence in the Sandinistas, it is indispensable to assure our cadres that there won't be a risk of the past coming back." Through a long and meandering presentation, Humberto began to target his goal, which was that the new president "should not demand any change in the army or the Ministry of Interior."

I sensed where he was going with his argument and scribbled a note to Carter: "Transition is between now and April 25. After that, V must be Pres and choose her own Cabinet. Unacceptable to keep Humberto and Borge!"

"We are willing to bring both into a new political-ideological setting compatible with the other Central American governments, and to reduce the size of the army," Humberto continued, "but . . . ."

Carter had heard enough: "If I understand you, this is more serious than the contras. In fact, it sounds like you will be the new contras, and the president will not have the authority to appoint her own cabinet . . . ."

Humberto slumped down awkwardly in the seat as if he were a schoolboy trying to put something over on his teacher, who had caught him in the act. Before he could recover, Carter hammered him: "She has to have authority to choose her minister of defense and make instructions to the army and the Interior Ministry."

Humberto shifted awkwardly and tried to agree: "Correct. These are special circumstances. We need to proceed step-by-step because of the degree of distrust. To generate confidence, it would be best for her to name Tomas Borge and me as new ministers, and within that framework, we would act in conformity with her instructions. This would generate new confidence. If a right-wing minister of defense is appointed to dismantle the army and to change everything the army stands for, it will generate distrust in the officer corps and chain of command and would create instability. Our goal is to preserve stability. Another area that could generate instability is if someone decides to take back all the land . . . . We must recognize that there is a new correlation of forces and to have a viable process, we need to generate confidence. This is the general framework."

Carter would have none of this. He had been trying to find a way to deal with the property issue, but he was sure that Humberto's was not the way: "If a house is owned by the government, it does not mean that a Sandinista leader has a right to keep the property. If a campesino has land or a home, it can only be handled according to the law and the constitution."

The central issue remained the military, and Carter did not conceal his anger over Humberto's presentation: "It is highly unlikely that Violeta will allow you and Tomas Borge to stay on as ministers of defense and interior. I haven't spoken to her about it, but this would be a demand that would be unacceptable. She has to have the right to choose her own cabinet. I have no preference, but you cannot make such a demand as a prerequisite to a transfer of authority."

Carter leaned toward Humberto to underscore the depth of his feelings on this issue: "This is of paramount importance—even more than the contras. Unless the Sandinista leadership is prepared to recognize her, and she will truly command the army and police, the election is a waste of time. . . . She has to have full authority. It is possible to negotiate the honoring of certain career offices, land, or homes, but you need to clarify this issue before I convey it to Lacayo and UNO, because if this demand is made public, it would create a situation of consternation and chaos . . . in the country."

Humberto had tried to renegotiate the entire election, and Carter stopped him in his tracks and reminded him that the essence of democracy was civilian control of the military. Humberto tried to recover his balance and minimize his embarrassment; in the end, he agreed to withdraw his proposal or to raise it privately with Lacayo. One thing was clear, however: Carter would never approve any bending of the Constitution to serve the interests of the Sandinistas.

Carter then shuttled back to Lacayo, told him of the exchange on the military, and urged Lacayo to proceed with caution on the appointments. I suggested that an informal vetting of candidates for the Defense and Interior Departments with Humberto might be the best way to proceed. I advised that he first work with them and try to get to know them, then listen to their views on prospective candidates before making a final judgment but not give them the decision. On property, Carter said that his position would be to follow the existing law. "My biggest concern," Carter counseled Lacayo, "is how the revolution can give it up."

He now had enough to bring Humberto and Lacayo together to negotiate a set of principles that would guide the transition. The small Carter Center Office was the site, and the meeting ran from 5:20 to 6:30 P.M. on Tuesday, February 27, 1990. At its end, Baena Soares, Richardson, and their aides joined to seal the agreement and decide on its implementation. It was the first time that Humberto Ortega and Antonio Lacayo had met, a truly remarkable fact in a country as small as Nicaragua.

Carter summarized the positions on the three sets of issues:

- *Contras:* Daniel Ortega and Violeta Chamorro would both call for a cease-fire and the full implementation of the Central American agreements on demobilizing the contras, and Carter would ask Bush to support the process.
- *Security:* On April 25, President Chamorro would become commander-in-chief and would have "the unquestioned right to choose her own ministers, including of Interior and Defense." Because of the sensitivity of the positions, Carter said that it would be desirable if the people chosen were trusted by the Sandinistas. Humberto Ortega and the armed forces pledged to help implement Chamorro's campaign promises of reducing the size of the military.
- *Property:* The existing law would govern the disposition of property, and the Supreme Court would make final decisions in the case of disagreement. However, the peasants who were living on the land of large landowners would be permitted to stay. With the exception of those associated with the Somoza family, the others whose homes were expropriated by the Sandinistas would get them back or be compensated. Any new laws passed by the Assembly during the transition would have to be approved by UNO or risk the chance of being reversed after the transfer of power. (This last point confirmed the obvious: FSLN could legislate before and UNO after the transition, but it was intended to encourage both sides to use the transition to reach some longer-term understandings.)

Both Humberto Ortega and Antonio Lacayo accepted these points and used the opportunity of the meeting to express their desire to work out all of the transition problems in a spirit of reconciliation. Elliot Richardson and Joao Baena Soares, the OAS secretary general, then arrived to witness the agreement and to explain what their two organizations would do to implement it. The UN would receive the weapons of the contras and would assist in their demobilization, and the OAS would work with the Inter-American Development Bank to assist the contras in resettlement.

Carter was moved by the exchange between Lacayo and Ortega and by the support of the OAS and the UN, but he understood that the pivotal figure, who would determine whether the agreement endured, was not in the room. That man was Cardinal Miguel Obando y Bravo, and we went from that meeting directly to the cardinal's home.

The cardinal was not in Managua in September when Carter made his first visit, but Carter saw him on subsequent visits, and it slowly dawned on him that Obando was Nicaragua's fulcrum. As an archbishop, Obando had stood up to Somoza and returned the presents that the dictator had given to try to compromise him. The Sandinistas initially tried to ignore him, then defy him, and finally, Daniel Ortega asked him to mediate the civil war. The cardinal was probably the most revered Nicaraguan, and his sermons greatly influenced the mass of religious

Nicaraguans. Carter arrived to ask for the cardinal's blessing for the agreement and his help in convincing the contras to demobilize. After Carter had summarized the agreement, the first question the cardinal asked was: "Will they turn over the Ministry of Interior and the armed forces to Violeta?" Carter responded affirmatively, but said that it would depend on assurances to protect the professional integrity of the organizations.

The cardinal was the most astute politician in the country. To persuade the contras to demobilize, he said, "we have to put ourselves in their shoes, and guarantee the security of their lives." He understood what others would soon learn: that the contras were not controlled by the United States, UNO, Violeta, or anyone. Their leaders wanted to be treated with respect, and they had to have a seat at the table if full demobilization were to occur.

Early the next morning, Carter and I flew to Washington to see Baker, National Security Advisor Brent Scowcroft, Deputy Secretary of State Lawrence Eagleburger, and Aronson. We arrived in time for lunch, and the conversation could not have been more cordial or complimentary of Carter's role. After hearing Carter's summary of the previous days' events, Baker said: "Although you may be disappointed with our policies, the election would not have happened if we hadn't changed policies last March [the bipartisan accord]. I believe that we have always pursued the same end and do so now: to assure a peaceful transition and a change of power." Carter had received most of the credit for the election, but Baker was undoubtedly correct. It was his change in policy that made a free election possible.

Carter was focused on securing a clear statement of intent from the administration to demobilize the contras immediately and to show respect for the Sandinistas during the transition. Baker agreed that the contras would have to be demobilized, but he was not in quite such a hurry as Carter. He was more intent on their need for assurances, particularly in the light of a comment by Daniel Ortega that the Sandinistas intended "to govern from below." This was obviously intended to raise the morale of his defeated followers, but such comments continued to be interpreted by the United States in a more cynical light. Baker and Scowcroft remained very worried that the Sandinistas would continue to control the armed forces and the Interior Ministry. Carter tried to persuade them this would not happen if the process of demobilization were expedited. After nearly a year of dueling, the Carter Center and the Bush administration were finally on the same side of the table, but the two sides continued to see the main challenges differently.

Two days later, on March 2, the Department of State issued a press release that touched on most of the points agreed to by Carter and Baker. The State Department complimented the two sides for the cease-fire and the transition talks and indicated that it was "convinced that immediate steps should be taken to encourage demobilization and repatriation of the Resistance Forces." Also, the United States promised aid to the UN and OAS missions to oversee the process. Everyone was marching in the same direction, but the pace was different, and it was not clear whether they would reach their goal by the inauguration.

The Wayward Path to the Transfer

Nicaragua's leaders were exhausted, but there was no time to rest. With barely two months before the official transfer of power, Lacayo and Humberto Ortega organized teams to work on the long agenda delegated by Carter. Two different worlds—of revolutionary nationalism and of democratic politics—had to find a way to connect.

Both sides agreed that the contras would need assurances to return to Nicaragua, but neither UNO nor the FSLN wanted to negotiate with them directly for fear that they would open new issues. Carter, Obando, and the Bush administration all encouraged the contras to reach agreement, but they insisted on negotiating with both the outgoing and the incoming administrations. In the end, they signed four agreements. On March 23, Chamorro's representatives and the resistance signed an accord whereby the latter agreed to demobilize and disarm in Honduras no later than April 20, to be monitored by CIAV (OAS), ONUCA (the UN group), and Cardinal Obando. On April 18, one week before the transfer, three additional accords were signed in Managua: (1) between the resistance and the Sandinista government to begin a cease-fire on April 19 to be verified by ONUCA and Cardinal Obando and the entry of contras into designated security zones in Nicaragua; (2) between the resistance and the president-elect to disarm the contras voluntarily in Nicaragua between April 25 and June 10, also under the auspices of ONUCA and CIAV; and (3) between the Sandinista government and the Yatama resistance to permit the entry of Yatama troops on April 19 into designated zones and to begin a cease-fire the next day. The cardinal witnessed all three agreements, and Governor Mike O'Callaghan, a member of the Carter delegation, accompanied the Yatama resistance fighters from Honduras to Managua. The Bush administration moved promptly to lift the economic embargo and on March 13 requested a supplemental aid appropriation of $300 million for Nicaragua.

Lacayo and Humberto Ortega also signed a Protocol of Procedure for the Transfer of Power on March 27. It reaffirmed the points negotiated by Carter a month before and added several more on the depoliticization of the armed forces and employment of public servants. All of these agreements were punctuated by clashes between contras and the Sandinista army and frequent threats from both sides.

The Sandinista-dominated National Assembly was also busy passing laws during the transition. Some of them were negotiated and accepted by UNO, as Carter had recommended, but others were simply approved in the standard way. The Assembly passed laws granting general amnesty to all Nicaraguans—both contras and army—who had committed crimes against the public order since July 19, 1979 and immunity for the highest officials of the government. Since the Sandinistas were leaving the government, they decided to repeal the media law that had given the government control of television. To repay their followers, the FSLN passed housing laws that granted legal rights to those who occupied government houses, and it finally approved a compensation fund for the previous owners of some of the houses. UNO accepted the first two laws—on amnesty and immunity—as unavoidable, but they opposed the others and hoped to repeal them in the next session.

In a press conference reported in *La Prensa* on April 5, Antonio Lacayo, who was named the minister of the presidency by Chamorro, said that the new government would try "to break the violent cycle" of Nicaragua's past. To do so, UNO would have "to respect the 41 percent minority": the Sandinistas. This seemed merely to state the obvious, but in fact, Lacayo's view was not shared by most of UNO's leaders. The split within UNO that had been concealed during the campaign was breaking into the open as the inauguration approached. As the leader of the more conservative group, Vice President-elect Virgilio Godoy accused Lacayo of being too solicitous of the FSLN and of going behind the backs of UNO to strike deals with Humberto Ortega.

Partly as a result of this rupture, the Political Council of UNO, led by Godoy, voted against Alfredo Cesar becoming president of the National Assembly. Cesar then collaborated with the FSLN to assure that two FSLN representatives and more liberal UNO leaders would be included in the Assembly's leadership. Godoy interpreted Cesar's move as a further sign of betrayal.

Lacayo and Cesar admitted that UNO leaders had become so conservative and vindictive that they felt they had no choice but to depend on the Sandinistas. Indeed, Lacayo and Humberto struck a bargain that divided both coalitions. Violeta would name herself defense minister, and Humberto would remain chief of the army, where he would help Violeta dismantle State Security and much of Tomas Borge's fiefdom in the Ministry of Interior. When Lacayo told me that Violeta would keep Humberto, I was shocked and reminded him that Carter had blocked Humberto on this issue and would gladly do it again, but Lacayo said he favored it. He had become convinced that only Humberto—not his second in command, Joaquin Cuadra Lacayo, who was white and related to Cesar—could control the Sandinista militants. "The problem," Lacayo confided, "was that the Sandinistas got very nervous because of a lack of progress on demobilization, and they insisted that until that was completed, Humberto would need to lead the army."

A decade later, Lacayo acknowledged that Chamorro had struck a deal with Humberto. In a curious twist, the Sandinistas claimed that if the new president dismissed Humberto, that would politicize the military since there was no cause under the military law to do so. They wanted respect for the military law, and Chamorro wanted the FSLN to respect civilian control of the military. At a practical level, Chamorro wanted to reduce the military by half, recover the tens of thousands of weapons that had been given to Sandinista militants, and transform the Sandinista army into a national army. Humberto promised to do all of that, and he kept his word.[7]

Aronson visited Managua on April 20 to preside over the demobilization accords. He met with Chamorro and, according to Lacayo, "hammered" her on this appointment. Two days later, I was invited by Chamorro to witness a meeting of the Political Council and Cabinet of UNO. At the end, they voted 56–3 against the appointment. The three in the minority were Lacayo, Cesar, and Carlos Hurtado, the new interior minister. Two other newly designated cabinet ministers—Jaime Cuadra and Gilberto Cuadra—resigned before officially taking office. Chamorro, sitting quietly as her own coalition voted against her decision, paid a high price. The next day, I talked with Humberto about reducing his tenure to six months, and he seemed agreeable to the idea, but Lacayo wanted to keep him there. At the time I thought he was making a mistake, but subsequent events proved the wisdom of his decision.

The inauguration on April 25, 1990, was unlike any I had ever seen. The National Stadium was as divided as the country, with half filled by supporters of Chamorro and the other half by Ortega's supporters. Each would alternate cries of support for their leader with cat-calls aimed at the other. Despite that, when Daniel Ortega said that all Nicaraguans voted for peace, there was unanimous applause, and that occurred a second time when he gave the presidential sash to Mrs. Chamorro, who defined her principal task as creating "a spirit of reconciliation present in all of our actions." When Chamorro said, "Here we have neither victors nor vanquished," she was referring to Humberto, but still, regrettably, speaking for a small minority. But everyone stood and cheered when she concluded: "I am your president. I do not want to rule. I want to serve."

A new day had dawned, although there were still clouds in the sky.

Trading Places

On that beautiful inaugural day, one could be tempted to think that all of the old problems had disappeared, but alas, the economy was in ruins, the contras were still armed, and the hopes of retrieving homes were mixed with the fears of being displaced. Still, Nicaragua had achieved the first peaceful transfer of power in its history, and it was the first country in the world where a government that had come to power by violent revolution was replaced as a result of a free election. Moreover, in the difficult two months of transition, both UNO and the Sandinistas had begun to "do politics": to bargain with each other even at the risk that each would divide its own coalition. This was not possible before the election. The moderates in both camps—Lacayo and Humberto Ortega—reached agreement on awkward issues like the contras, amnesty, and shutting down state security at the cost of provoking Virgilio Godoy and Tomas Borge. And they did this on their own; Carter, Baena Soares, and Richardson had left the scene.

One year later, President Chamorro invited the international community to return to Managua to celebrate the anniversary of the election, and almost no one came. A small country with huge problems of poverty did not generate one iota of the international media attention attracted by Daniel Ortega defying the United States. Nicaragua was one of those really important stories that was no longer covered. Chamorro had accomplished a great deal in one year: As many as 22,000 contras had been disarmed and many had been given government land; the Sandinista army had been reduced by two-thirds, and 5,000 officers were laid off; and there were no restraints on the press. Resolving the security and political problems, however, had a cost.

The transfer of power: President Daniel Ortega places the presidential sash on the newly inaugurated president, Violeta Barrios de Chamorro, on April 25, 1990.

When Chamorro was elected, the Nicaraguan economy had been in free-fall for nearly a decade. The gross domestic product was about half of the pre-1980 level, inflation was 4,700 percent in 1989, international reserves were depleted, and debt had risen from $1.7 billion when Somoza left to about $9 billion. Before leaving office, the Sandinistas had doubled wages, and the resulting deficits accelerated inflation.[8]

Every effort to bring the budget under control evoked strikes and seizures of public buildings by labor unions that exercised their new freedoms. To secure peace, the Chamorro administration promised jobs and raised wages. Daniel Ortega understood that the future of the Sandinista Party required that he stay in front of, or at least alongside, the unions, and in his competition with the new union leadership, the government and the economy kept losing. In October 1990, the government was compelled to accept a "concertacion" agreement with labor that led to still another bout of hyper-inflation.

By early 1991, inflation had reached 13,500 percent, and virtually all the leaders asked for Carter to return. Other than the considerable aid provided by the United States, the international development banks and other donors had refused to give any aid unless the government restored some fiscal integrity. The objective of Carter's visit was to secure support—primarily from Daniel Ortega and the labor unions—for a new austerity agreement. A few days after Chamorro announced a new economic plan, in early March 1991, Carter visited Managua and persuaded Daniel to support the agreement in exchange for a new emphasis on some social programs.

Carter's role in 1991 was very different from what it had been during the election, and the difference defined the country's political progress. During the election he was an active mediator, listening to both sides, defining compromises, and then gaining agreement. A year later, his role was to provide Daniel Ortega and the main labor union with a face-saving retreat from their opposition to a plan developed by the government and the IMF. In his long talk with Carter, Ortega recognized that "there was no alternative" to austerity; he just needed some political cover, and Carter provided that. The international community, in brief, moved from the center of the negotiations to the side. Nicaraguans were beginning to define their own future.

But it was not easy for any of them. In confidence, several Sandinista leaders acknowledged that they were suffering an identity crisis and trying to find a way to be a constructive opposition. Some were having an easier time than others, and Daniel Ortega seemed to be having the most difficulty. UNO was having a similar problem finding its place in the firmament of governance, although Alfredo Cesar personally had recovered and was elected the new president of the Assembly.

The austerity plan stopped the inflation, but unresolved problems on property inhibited any new investment. A repolarization of politics in Nicaragua and with the United States also occurred because of the new dependence on U.S. aid and the tangled ambitions of Antonio Lacayo and Alfredo Cesar. As each positioned himself for the next presidential election, they clashed and looked for allies in Washington.

In August 1991, under Cesar's leadership, the Assembly passed Law 133, which revoked three decrees on property secretly passed by Daniel Ortega during the transition. Although Carter had advised against it, the Sandinistas had changed the laws to legalize the transfer of property to their supporters. Most controversial was the decree that allowed senior-level Sandinistas to purchase their homes at below-market value. While some in UNO accused Lacayo of secretly approving these "piñata" decrees, that was not true. "I never knew of the decrees until I read them in the paper, and I would never have approved them since they were inconsistent with the 'Protocol of Transition,'" Lacayo later recalled.[9] With Cesar's law, the Sandinistas would have to pay the "real value" for the houses, or former owners would receive compensation. Chamorro vetoed Cesar's law in September 1991 because she feared it would involve a massive confiscation of property from so many poor people that it could be destabilizing.

After a year of stalemate on the issue, Lacayo introduced another property law, but UNO and Cesar rejected it. At this point, Cesar established a new alliance with the Godoy faction of the Assembly, and Lacayo worked with the Sandinistas. In September 1992, Cesar used a moment when the Sandinistas had walked out of the Assembly to elect a new slate of leaders. The Sandinistas brought the issue to the Supreme Court, which ruled against the vote. When Cesar refused to accept the Court's judgment, Lacayo sent the military to supervise new elections in the Assembly. Lacayo's supporters won the election, and Cesar refused to accept the result. He went to Washington to ask Congress and the administration to suspend aid.

It was sad that the politicians in Nicaragua who tried to draw the United States back into the center of Nicaraguan politics were the two smartest and most modern, Lacayo and Cesar. Worse than that, they appealed to the two sides of the old Cold War divide. Cesar spoke to the Republican leadership and helped them draft a letter to the secretary of state insisting on detailed conditions before aid should be released, and Lacayo appealed to the Democrats and Carter. The Clinton administration entered the fray with little knowledge of the past, but its senior officials were easily intimidated by the Republicans. Secretary of State Warren Christopher dodged the issue, and Deputy Secretary Clifton Wharton was drawn into talks with Lacayo on very specific topics, including mechanisms to judge charges of corruption, a fixed term for Humberto Ortega to step down, and specific human rights abuses and crimes. These should not have been in America's portfolio at this time.[10] Just before leaving office, Bush had released about half of the $108 million in aid. A phone call from Carter to President Clinton finally unlocked the remainder on April 2, 1993.[11]

The most intractable problem remained the issue of property, partly because it continued to distinguish the Sandinista revolution from the counterrevolution. At its most fundamental, the Sandinista victory in 1979 had transferred power and property from an old wealthy elite to a new one that came from the lower middle class. During the 1980s, the new leadership gradually took some of the homes and property of the old guard. With the transfer of power to Violeta Chamorro, many of the old families wanted their homes and land back, and they found ready allies in Congress, particularly among those, like Senator Jesse Helms, who were still fighting the Cold War.

The property issue was so large and multifaceted that genuine peace and sustained development were not possible without a solution. The Nicaraguan government identified 171,890 beneficiaries of agrarian and rural reform and other expropriated property. On the other side were 5,288 former owners of homes and about 25 percent of the cultivable land area of the country. The estimated cost of compensating the former owners was $650 million, or 35 percent of the GDP and twice the country's exports in 1995.[12]

Soon after taking office, the Chamorro government established two mechanisms to resolve the claims. By July 1995, nearly 108,000 occupants of land and property—out of 112,000 who had applied—had received approval for titles, although the titles would not be received until surveys were completed (possibly in four years). The government made less progress in resolving the claims of former owners. By June 1995, 1,800 people (or 31 percent of 5,288 claimants, representing 19 percent of the parcels of property) had had their claims approved for compensation. The difficulty in sorting out these claims was compounded by Nicaragua's extremely poor titling system, which the revolution only made worse; a completely inadequate court system; and no money to compensate owners.

As if the problem of sorting out these claims were not difficult enough, the United States made it worse. An amendment by Senator Helms to the 1994 Foreign Assistance Act required the secretary of state to certify by July 30 each year that Nicaragua was promptly and fairly compensating U.S. citizens for their property. If not, the U.S. government would suspend aid and vote against multilateral bank loans to Nicaragua. There were two mischievous features to the bill. First, any Nicaraguan whose property had been expropriated would be eligible for special help from the United States, provided the person became a U.S. citizen. International law only applied to people who were citizens of a foreign country at the time of expropriation. Needless to say, the law encouraged Nicaraguans, including many associated with the Somoza family, to become U.S. citizens. The Somocistas owned the most property that had been expropriated, but most Nicaraguans, including the Chamorro government, agreed with the 1979 expropriation of their property. The United States compelled the Chamorro government to change its approach. Second, and more serious, Helms insisted that U.S. citizens receive fair compensation at "full value." Although most Nicaraguans were willing to accept a lower value for their property, no one would accept such a compromise if Americanized Nicaraguans received more money. Moreover, Nicaraguans resented the fact that those who abandoned the country would get priority. Thus, Helms's intervention made the resolution of the property issue much more difficult and dangerous; it was, in a sense, the peace time equivalent of the contra war.

The United Nations Development Program asked Carter to help solve the property issues, and he went to Nicaragua in June 1994 and then returned in July 1995 to chair high-level meetings with the country's leaders. Together, they reached a consensus on basic principles, including that poor families could remain on their land until they received titles and that fair compensation would be given to former owners. To pay for the property, the government agreed to privatize the National Telephone Company.

The most encouraging aspect of the meeting was the interaction between former guerrilla leaders and right-wing property owners as both searched for a compromise despite the complex issues and the heated emotions.[13] In the fall, the Assembly passed two property laws based on the consensus with enough modifications to leave each side somewhat dissatisfied. The Telephone Company would not be fully privatized, the property issue would remain a problem, and foreign investors remained wary.[14]

The Struggle Among Brothers and Branches

The personal dispute between the two brothers-in-law, Lacayo and Cesar, was transformed into a titanic struggle between the two branches of the government. Maneuvering between conservatives of the UNO and radicals of the FSLN, Cesar helped steer constitutional reforms through the Assembly in June 1995, which reduced the power of the presidency, shortened the term from six to five years, and required that any candidate serving in the cabinet or as a mayor resign one year before the election. In addition, as a final arrow aimed at Lacayo, who was the president's son-in-law, no presidential candidate could be related to the incumbent.

In December 1995, the Assembly passed a new electoral law that was supposed to democratize election administration but in fact made it so chaotic as to endanger the integrity of the elections. The country's administrative divisions were increased from nine to seventeen, and the number of individual polling stations doubled to 8,995. The SEC would choose new polling officials based on nominations from more than twenty political parties. In addition, all SEC members were replaced, except for two. People would vote for six different races from a ballot that was three feet long, and they would be identified by a mixed voter registration system. In February 1996, Dr. Mariano Fiallos, who had been chairman of the SEC since 1983 and did a remarkable job in 1990, formally resigned, protesting that the new law would make it almost impossible to conduct an effective election or train officials by October 1996. He was proven correct.

In 1996, the incumbent did not run for election, nor did she support any candidate, but she left a much more solid foundation than she found. Since the 1991 economic plan, the Chamorro government had conquered inflation. With the exception of two years—in 1993 and 1998 when inflation averaged about 18 percent—the consumer price index was mostly in single digits throughout the rest of the decade, and the growth rate after 1995 averaged above 5 percent. Chamorro had privatized some 350 state enterprises, and although the property issue was not solved, all parties had come close to an agreement. In 1995 Humberto Ortega stepped down from the army, but by then he had shrunk the armed forces to one of the smallest in Central America, and for the first time in the country's history, the army was professional and nonpolitical.

Doña Violeta had struggled through some of the most difficult circumstances imaginable. She started out with a bankrupt economy and a civil war and two large politicized armies. She confronted hyper-inflation, droughts, low prices for coffee, an alienated base of support, and an American government policy led by Senator Helms that tried to undermine her. Despite all of this, she successfully led her country through three transitions: (1) from war to peace to reconciliation, (2) from a ruined command economy to a market economy, and (3) from an authoritarian system to democracy. These were remarkable achievements, but having said that, the poverty rate was still very high, and Nicaragua remained one of the poorest countries in the hemisphere.

Twenty-four candidates ran for president, but two would win 88 percent of the vote: Arnoldo Aleman, the heavyset mayor of Managua, heading the Liberal Alliance, and Daniel Ortega. Among the fourteen party candidates who received less than .5 percent of the vote were three who had once seemed likely contenders: Sergio Ramirez, Ortega's vice president, who headed the Sandinista Renewal Movement; Virgilio Godoy, who led the Independent Liberal Party; and Alfredo Cesar, who was the candidate of the Alianza Uno 96. Each of those three won fewer than 8,000 votes from the 1,849,362 Nicaraguans who voted on October 20, 1996.

The campaign was polarized but peaceful. Both major candidates moved toward the center during the campaign, Aleman promising the poor would receive land titles, and Ortega recruiting a businessman as his running mate and committing himself to a market economy. Few feared that the SEC would manipulate the election, although some were concerned that it would not conduct it well.[15]

The international observers were also more relaxed. Carter asked James Baker and Oscar Arias to co-chair the Council/Carter Center delegation, and Bernard Aronson and I worked together to staff them. Most of the pre-election visits were technical and found problems that were manageable. The major irregularities witnessed during the count stemmed from the length and complexity of the six ballots and the lack of carbon paper, which required the officials to copy the results twenty times to give to each poll watcher. Needless to say, numerous mistakes were made.

Still, compared to six years before, the election almost seemed routine, and without the political electricity that kept us working without sleep through several nights, the observers went to bed early in 1996. The candidates stayed up, however, and at 4:30 A.M., with fewer than 10 percent of the results announced, Aleman proclaimed victory. The FSLN reacted with outrage. It was, of course, just such a dynamic that the observers had interrupted six years before, but we had lost our edge and anticipated that Nicaragua had graduated as well. We were mistaken.

The quick counts coincided with the early returns—roughly 50 percent for Aleman to 40 percent for Ortega—but they were not used effectively. Again, the Sandinista count showed a difference of only one or two points, and they alleged that thousands of votes had not been counted. The FSLN's quick count—as in 1990—was not accurate, probably because their militants were more likely to report the "good" results. This occurs in many transitional elections.

By the next afternoon, the reports of problems in the elections finally activated the observers. Carter and his delegation persuaded Aleman to postpone his victory party, and President Chamorro asked Carter to delay his departure to try to secure Ortega's acceptance of the results.

A core group of international observers caucused with the SEC and launched an intensive, three-week post-election review of the ballots and tally sheets in all of the regions of the country. The most serious disputes occurred in the two most populous departments: 14 percent of the poll sites were annulled in Managua, and 11 percent in Matagalpa. The first "official" results were announced on November 8, and Aleman was declared the winner in the first round with 51 percent of the vote

For the election of 1996, former President Jimmy Carter invited former Secretary of State James A. Baker III and former Costa Rican President Oscar Arias to be co-leaders of the monitoring mission.

to Ortega's 37.8 percent. About a dozen parties filed appeals, and the Sandinistas submitted a collection of documents totaling nearly 650 pages. On November 22, the SEC announced the results of the appeals. It remedied some of the concerns but rejected the Sandinista demand for regional annulments on the grounds that the law only applied if the problems affected at least half of the registered voters in a district.

The Liberals won forty-two seats in the Assembly, and the FSLN won thirty-five seats plus one for Ortega as a losing presidential candidate with more than 1.5 percent of the vote. Liberals also captured 91 of the 145 mayorships, including Managua, and the FSLN won 52. On November 24, Daniel Ortega denounced the election as fraudulent and insisted on a run-off. The Carter Center mission did a systematic analysis of the annulled votes and found many irregularities. Still, it concluded that even if Aleman had received none of the votes, an unlikely prospect in those areas, he would still have won the election without the need for a run-off. Carter called Ortega and urged him to concede. After deliberations, the Sandinistas decided to acknowledge the Aleman government as the country's legal authority but not as a legitimate one—a distinction that permitted them to save face and also participate in the new Assembly.

In 1990, the election seemed like such a sharp departure from Nicaragua's political past that many thought that the country had escaped its history. The tangled vines of its past, however, tripped up the fragile democracy. In some ways, the 1996 election revealed more clearly than even the one in 1990 both the progress that Nicaragua had made toward democratic politics and the distance it still had to travel. The progress was evident in the patience that the Sandinistas and the other parties demonstrated during a three-week period of reviewing the ballots and assessing the irregularities. Moreover, no one accused the national electoral authorities of a political motive for the technical problems, even though the problems in two departments were plausibly related to partisan control at the local level. The failure on the part of Ortega to accept the results showed how far Nicaragua still needed to go before its democracy established firmer roots. Overall, however, perhaps the most dramatic evidence was the silence: the absence of any violence or street protests and the willingness to accept the legal procedures as the vehicle for deciding the outcome.

Politics remained a serious sport in Nicaragua, but by the time of Aleman's inauguration on January 10, 1997, the international media had lost interest in the country. Ortega refused to attend Aleman's inauguration, but within hours of the transfer of power, Ortega met privately with the new president to discuss a common agenda for the years ahead. During the next four years, both men secured control of their parties. This was easier for the president, who had a clear economic program that was enjoying some success. Aleman also concentrated on strengthening his party around the country.

Ortega faced a far more difficult challenge. During the Chamorro years, the FSLN had split with Sergio Ramirez, who founded a new party. The FSLN had given up control of the armed forces and the police as well as the courts and the SEC. Even their union base was divided and weakened. Worst of all, Daniel Ortega was accused by his stepdaughter of years of abuse, and Humberto publicly urged him not to run again for president. Despite all that, and very high negative poll numbers, Daniel Ortega was nominated to be the FSLN candidate for the presidential election in November 2001.

Although Aleman and Ortega seemed to be at the two ends of the political spectrum, they led their parties to a pact in January 2000 that altered the powers of three key institutions—the comptroller general, the Supreme Court, and the SEC—and placed their people in charge of all three. Other constitutional reforms would have the effect of making it more difficult for the two major parties to be challenged by new ones. Some believe that a two-party system would be good for Nicaragua, but others have argued that the two will collude to prevent competition from other parties and oversight into corrupt activities.[16]

Although the international media were not watching Nicaragua, the international development banks were working closely with NGOs to build institutions that would monitor the transparency of governance and would make their loans conditional on acceptance of global standards. Aleman understood that investment was essential to achieve economic development, and that would only occur if the international community certified his government as clean. He took some steps in that direction, but not enough to persuade the banks or prospective investors.

The presidential election of November 4, 2001, pitted Daniel Ortega against an inveterate enemy of the Sandinistas, Enrique Bolaños. In 1989, Ortega had expropriated his farm because Bolaños had given a speech critical of the Sandinistas. In his seventies, Bolaños was not tainted by corruption as many others in Aleman's party, which may explain why he was not Aleman's first choice. Ortega's campaign was designed to reassure voters that he was a European-style Social Democrat. He chose Agustin Jarquin, the former incorruptible Comptroller General, as his running mate, and Antonio Lacayo, the minister of the presidency under Chamorro, as his prospective foreign minister. Ortega pledged his support for a free-market economy and for the U.S. war against terrorism. The polls once again suggested that the race would be very close. Bolaños resurrected the old fears that people had of the Sandinista years, and the Bush administration reverted to an earlier era by campaigning alongside him and in strong opposition to Ortega. Jimmy Carter once again monitored the polls, and the result was similar to the two previous elections: 54 to 45 percent. The margin was large, and the quick counts were professional. Ortega quickly and graciously conceded. Indeed, he promised his support to Bolaños's efforts to improve the economy. Bolaños also displayed a higher degree of political maturity in congratulating the Sandinista Party and Ortega "with all my heart. Nicaraguan brothers, I invite you to accompany me in building a new Nicaragua."[17]

At one level, history seemed to be repeating itself, with Ortega struggling against Bolaños, who was backed by Bush, but the result and the behavior of the candidates confirmed that politics in Nicaragua had changed. The rhetoric might disorient those who remembered the years of revolution, but there were other signs—notably, the immediate concession speech by Ortega and the generous words from Bolaños—that Nicaragua was finally on a different road.

Lessons from Three Challenges:
Succession, Revolution,
and Democracy

For what is the value of going to the trouble of remembering the past
which cannot become a present.

SOREN KIERKEGAARD

Only by reaching across to your adversaries could you bring them
back into the Nicaraguan family. National reconciliation was your
message, and because of that, Nicaragua's future will improve on its
past.

LETTER FROM JIMMY CARTER TO
VIOLETA BARRIOS DE CHAMORRO,
SEPTEMBER 27, 1990

JOSE FIGUERES, the former president of Costa Rica, once complained that U.S.
foreign policymakers often view the countries of Central America as "pilot projects," as laboratories for experimenting with new policies. That explains how some
in the region think the United States views them, but from the U.S. perspective,
Central America looks very different. It is viewed as a small, poor region, which
has been peripheral to America's global interests and yet preoccupied almost
every U.S. president during the twentieth century. Nicaragua, more than any of its
neighbors, has confounded U.S. policymakers and has been at the center of the
three most intractable security challenges faced by the United States in the developing world:

1. *Succession crises:* how to deal with a weakened dictator who supported U.S. foreign policy but was repressive and unpopular among his people and was facing a threat from anti-American revolutionaries;
2. *Revolutionary governments:* how to deal with an anti-American revolutionary government that allied with the enemies of the United States, challenged the values of liberal democracy, and sought to undermine its neighbors' regimes; and
3. *Democratic transitions:* how to facilitate a democratic transition in a poor developing country with very little, if any, experience with democracy.

The first edition of this book told the story of the first two challenges. It explained how and why the nightmares feared by all the actors in the story—Nicaraguans and Americans of all ideologies—came true. Somoza feared losing power and being assassinated. The United States feared that Marxists could capture Nicaragua. The Sandinistas feared that the United States would make war on their revolution. The tragedy of Nicaragua is that the behavior of all the actors helped make their fears—not their dreams—a reality.

The first edition of this book also suggested that it might be possible to change counterproductive policies and escape those fears. This edition maps the escape route to a democratic transition, and the lessons from that experience are many and rich. In the previous three chapters, I showed how the democratic path opened but also how it almost closed. Lessons and life do not always require a fine appreciation of details. In reviewing the first two challenges—succession crises and revolutionary governments—one could conclude that the details of decisions were less important than the broad strokes of policy. That was not the case for the democratic challenge. One can only appreciate the difference between the correct and the mistaken path if one sees the details. At almost every stage in the democratic transition, there were forces that almost derailed it, and groups that tried to reinforce the better instincts of the Nicaraguans. A slight change in the balance of those forces could have defeated the democratic transition and sucked Nicaragua back into its authoritarian past. To understand the success of the democratic transition, therefore, I have provided precise maps of the road.

In this chapter, I begin by summarizing the seven stages of U.S. policy toward Nicaragua through the succession crisis and the revolutionary confrontation, then explain the patterns of behavior. Finally, I extract lessons from each of the three challenges that might help future policymakers profit from the past rather than pay its price.

The Patterns of Policy

What is uncanny about the U.S. government's policy toward Nicaragua from the onset of the succession crisis through the confrontation with the revolutionary government is how it followed virtually the same pattern as it did with Cuba two decades earlier. There were seven stages, discussed in the following paragraphs.

1. IDENTIFICATION. The power of Anastasio Somoza García and his two sons rested first on their control of the National Guard, second on a united Liberal Party, and third on their identification with the United States. The United States sometimes protested or rejected that identification, and in 1945, 1947–1948, 1963, and 1978–1979 encouraged Somoza to step down or not to seek reelection. Nevertheless, at critical periods during the Cold War and during the tenure of two U.S. ambassadors, Thomas Whelan and Turner Shelton, the United States identified its interests with those of the Somoza family. It was a shortsighted policy for which the United States paid a heavy price.

2. DISTANCE AND DISSOCIATION. In 1975, after the resignation of Richard Nixon and his ambassador, the Ford administration began to distance itself from Somoza. The Carter administration withdrew U.S. support from Somoza, but it initially rejected the opposition's request to mediate because it wanted to separate itself from a past in which the United States had been the pivotal political actor in Nicaragua. The administration altered this preferred policy in September 1978, when Somoza tried to eliminate the moderate option and leave Nicaraguans and Americans with a simple but unacceptable choice between himself and the Sandinistas. There was a consensus in the administration that the longer Somoza remained in power the more likely it was that the Sandinistas would win a violent revolution. The issue became how to prevent that worst-case scenario without harming other interests.

The United States reluctantly decided to mediate, but it did so in small steps that permitted policymakers to think that the change did not weaken the administration's commitment to nonintervention and that it reinforced other principles like regional cooperation. Carter's first decision was to support a Central American mediation effort, and when that failed, he insisted that U.S. mediation be undertaken within a multilateral framework under the auspices of the OAS.

To those inside and outside the administration who had a different view of the appropriate U.S. role, each decision by the administration was frustrating and inadequate. Pragmatists, like Assistant Secretary of State Viron Vaky, recommended that the United States force Somoza's departure. Although President Carter's aversion to mediation was overcome, he was reluctant to accept a unilateral strategy because he believed a multilateral approach was in the best long-term interests of the United States, and he would not approve overthrowing Somoza. Instead of forcing Somoza's resignation, the Carter administration tried to negotiate the terms that would permit a free plebiscite. That effort failed, and the United States blamed Somoza, imposing sanctions in February 1979.

3. THE LEFT LEGITIMIZED BY THE MIDDLE. Between February and July 1979, the moderates drifted toward the Sandinistas, as the United States had feared they would. Having failed to secure Somoza's resignation, Nicaragua's moderates despaired. They did not have the patience or the leadership to wait; they thought the Sandinistas were more moderate than they actually were; and they ignored the United States and listened to Costa Rica, Panama, and Venezuela, all of whom had

decided that the only way to displace Somoza was by helping the Sandinistas. Alfonso Robelo later explained that he joined the junta of the revolutionary government "because the support of Torrijos, Carlos Andrés Pérez, and Carazo gave me confidence that it was the right thing."[1]

The intrinsic weakness of a policy of "distance and dissociation" is that it ultimately depends on the blind man seeing the light. Having decided not to overthrow Somoza and having been unable to encourage his departure through sanctions, the United States lacked a policy during this period. All it could do was hope that the blind man, Somoza, would see. Instead, the blind man was struck by lightning. In the month of June, as the Sandinistas' "final offensive" gathered military equipment and assembled political support, the United States came to recognize that its nightmare was coming true.

4. THE SEARCH FOR A THIRD FORCE. The United States searched desperately for an executive committee of credible moderate leaders that would assume power after Somoza's departure and call for a cease-fire. That would have allowed time for the Guard to stabilize and for the committee to negotiate a modus vivendi with the San José junta.

The strategy failed. After the sanctions, the U.S. embassy in Managua had few officers to maintain contacts with the opposition, and the State Department failed to provide guidance to encourage embassy officials to support an independent moderate opposition. Even worse, the Pentagon had no independent contacts with the National Guard, which would have permitted a military base under a post-Somoza government. It may have been too late by the time that Ambassador Pezzullo arrived, or he may have had only a day or two to construct the "third force." It's hard to know, but it's clear that he did not have the personnel in the embassy or the knowledge of the personalities to achieve that mission in such a short time, particularly because of the bitterness of the moderate opposition and the fact that so many had gone to San José and allied with the junta. When the moderates were ready, Somoza was intransigent, and the United States did not move him; when Somoza was ready to go, and the United States was ready to facilitate a new government, most of the moderates were not. The actors were out of sync.

Those few moderates who were prepared to consider an executive committee wanted unequivocal assurances from the United States. But because of Latin America's growing support for the junta, the widening insurrection in the country, and the atrocities committed by the Guard, Carter made his support conditional on multilateral cooperation, which did not materialize. The executive committee idea died. Working with other leaders in the region, the administration negotiated a final arrangement that precluded a bloodbath and permitted a relationship to be developed with the incoming junta.

5. RELATING TO THE REVOLUTION. After the Sandinistas' victory, the administration sought good relations. The United States provided aid to the revolution, denied it an enemy, and hoped the new government would become more pragmatic and less

ideological. The relationship was awkward, but the Nicaraguan government showed that it was not impervious to either internal or outside Western influence. There were signs of arbitrariness and tyranny but also of political space and pluralism. Independent institutions and the press were harassed but permitted to exist and criticize. The government seemed willing to share some power, but not all of it. The Sandinistas were interested in diversifying their relations with Europeans and Latin Americans, but reserved as their principal relationships those with Cuba and the Soviet Union. There was enthusiastic support for health and education, but these services were delivered in a Marxist, anti-American package. And there was moral solidarity with other revolutionaries, but the FSLN restrained their impulse to provide material support.

6. DISTANCE AND NEGOTIATION. In November 1980, despite its promises, the Nicaraguan government decided to provide massive aid to the Salvadoran rebels. On receiving the evidence in its last days, the Carter administration suspended aid to Nicaragua. The Reagan administration entered office with a pledge to end aid and a perception that Nicaragua and Cuba were major threats to U.S. interests. Nonetheless, the administration negotiated with the Nicaraguan government, which halted its arms transfers to the Salvadorans. For political and ideological reasons, the Reagan administration did not resume aid.

A second round of negotiations in August 1981 tested the ability of two extremely resentful governments to reach an agreement on security issues. Neither side passed the test. The Reagan administration then walked away from the bargaining table, convinced that the Sandinistas were not serious. The Sandinistas did not read the United States any better; they were unaware that this was their last chance to negotiate peacefully with the administration.

7. CONFRONTATION. President Reagan's decision in December 1981 to support exiles whose goal was to overthrow the Nicaraguan regime was a fateful one, which led to a gradually deepening American commitment to the rebels and an escalation of the war. On March 15, 1982, the Sandinistas declared a state of emergency in response to military attacks by the contras and the disclosure of the U.S. covert program. Prior to that date, no important Nicaraguan leader, except Pastora, had left the country for exile. Subsequently, there was a steady stream of moderate leaders joining the violent opposition.[2] With the intensification of the war, the political space in Nicaragua grew smaller and the dependence on Cuba and the Soviet Union increased.

The pattern of U.S. policy toward Nicaragua's succession crisis and revolution followed not only its policies toward Cuba but also those in many other similar cases. In addition to Cuba and Nicaragua, I have reviewed U.S. policy toward five other high-profile succession crises: Iran (1978–1979), the Dominican Republic (1960–1961), Haiti (1961–1963 and 1985–1986), the Philippines (1983–1986), and Chile (1988–1989).[3] All seven crises began with a key event that shook the dictator and ended with his death, exile, or a transfer of power. In each case, the United

States had played a large role in the country's internal affairs and, with the exception of Chile, had at some point occupied the country with troops.

The objectives of the United States were defined precisely by President John F. Kennedy as he surveyed the Dominican Republic after the assassination of Rafael Trujillo in 1961: "There are three possibilities in descending order of preference: a decent democratic regime, a continuation of the Trujillo regime, or a 'Castro' regime. We ought to aim at the first, but we really can't renounce the second until we are sure that we can avoid the third."[4] The worst outcomes for Washington occurred in Cuba, Iran, and Nicaragua, where anti-American, undemocratic regimes took power. The best outcomes occurred with the democratic transitions in the Philippines and Chile. The Dominican Republic and Haiti were ambiguous outcomes because a fragile democracy eventually emerged, but only after years of instability and major U.S. interventions. How to explain the different outcomes?

The four stages of U.S. policy toward succession crises identified above were landmarks for navigating all of the succession crises. *United States policy does not explain the different outcomes because U.S. policy—whether directed by a conservative Republican or a liberal Democratic president—was almost the same in all the cases.*

The difference in outcomes in the seven cases can be explained as follows:

- If the guerrillas stayed independent of the moderates, they failed.
- If the guerrillas allied with the moderates and friendly regional governments, and if the military remained united until the dictator fled, anti-revolutionary regimes triumphed.
- If the military divided and some or all of its leaders defected from the dictator, and if there were no elections, then a military takeover occurred.
- If the moderates supported elections, and if the military divided but did not collapse, then democracy won.

The middle sectors played the pivotal roles in every case. Indeed, from the U.S. perspective, the crisis began when middle-class opposition to the dictator became militant. From the beginning to the end of the crises, the moderate groups stimulated, guided, and defined the parameters of U.S. policy, although they were often unaware of their influence. Indeed, the worst outcomes occurred because signals were misunderstood between the moderates, who thought they were following the United States but were actually leading it, and the United States, which was a step behind. Because U.S. policy alone cannot explain the different outcomes does not mean that U.S. policy was irrelevant, only that the decisive factors were indigenous.

Comparing the evolution of U.S. policy toward the three revolutionary governments of Cuba, Grenada, and Nicaragua, one also finds the same pattern in all three cases. Policy evolved from tentative cooperativeness to cool distance to tense confrontation.[5]

The revolutionary regimes' policies invariably evolved from pledging democratic elections to repressing political opponents, from professing an interest in good relations with the United States to forging close alliances with its enemies. The revolutionaries viewed Washington as bent on controlling and undermining their revolutions. The United States viewed these governments as Marxist-Leninist efforts to expand Soviet influence in the hemisphere. Each side exaggerated negative and discounted positive information about the other. By a mutually reinforcing process, the preconceptions, which were not originally accurate, became true. The self-fulfilling prophecy works most effectively when it works both ways. Richard Welch referred to this dynamic as the "cross fertilization of animosity."[6]

Explaining Continuity and Change in U.S. Policy

What explains the continuity in U.S. foreign policy over the course of such different administrations? Primary U.S. interests in Nicaragua and the region do not stem from a desire to extract resources or to implant a political philosophy, although the history of U.S. policy is replete with examples of both, but from fear, a rather unseemly fear for such a large nation facing such a small one, but a fear nevertheless that a hostile group could come to power and ally itself with a rival of the United States. Some U.S. policymakers exaggerated the threat; others underestimated it; but few denied it.

The security motive helps to explain why and when the United States became exercised about developments in Nicaragua, and it partially explains why the United States identified with Batista and Somoza and confronted the Cuban and Nicaraguan revolutionary governments. But it does not adequately explain why the United States dissociated itself from Batista and Somoza and why it initially respected the two revolutionary governments. Nor does it explain the repetitive pattern of U.S. policy.

To explain the entire pattern of U.S. policy, one should start with the premise that the U.S. government draws its policies from a reservoir of national experiences, a kind of collective political subconscious. "Foreign policy," Arthur Schlesinger Jr., wrote, "is the face a nation wears to the world."[7] All nations project their style, political culture or character, and interpretations of recent history onto the international landscape. The less a nation knows about the world, the more its policy resembles its character rather than that of the nation that is the target of the policy. This is not just true of the United States. Mexico's policy toward Nicaragua, for example, stemmed more from its own revolutionary history than from Nicaragua's.

Because each national experience is unique, one would expect that different countries, even those with similar interests, would pursue different policies toward the same crisis. The United States, for example, repeatedly proposed elections as the strategy for resolving conflict in Central America; Mexico never did. Mexico supported revolutions; the United States opposed them.

"Political culture," as one element of the national experience, may also help to explain why a nation's decisions that are separated by a generation may be so similar—for example, the similarities between the Bowdler Mission to Nicaragua in 1978 and the Stimson Mission fifty years before. But in implying an immutable, predetermined inheritance, the term "political culture" unnecessarily constrains.[8]

For that reason, "national experience" might be a more useful concept because it includes the concepts of style, character, and culture. It also suggests that the sources of foreign policy can be found in national roots but also in the way each generation adapts to the changes in the world and revises its perception of its nation's history.

In the case of Nicaragua, the question of why the United States "so often supports dictators"[9] is easily answered: it mostly didn't. Most U.S. administrations were uncomfortable with the Somoza regime and particularly with its attempts to identify with the United States. When did the United States support him? President Nixon shared Somoza's fervently anti-communist view of the world, and others thought the Somozas hardly the worst dictators in an area that appeared to have no aptitude for democracy. When the United States needed Nicaragua's support either for specific actions in Guatemala or Cuba or for a global objective, the United States subsumed its dislike for the regime. This, of course, is the traditional way in which states have related to each other.

Given this tradition, what is most surprising in U.S. policy toward Nicaragua is not the moments when it treated Somoza well but the historically longer-lasting periods of detachment from and distaste for the regime. After the first Somoza took power in 1936, the United States spent much less time debating whether to support him than it did trying to decide what to do about him. The explanation for this resides in the political values and experience of the United States, which has always given more attention to the character and internal behavior of regimes than have most other governments.

North Americans identify with the "middle" abroad, meaning not just the middle class or businesspeople but rather all people and groups in favor of gradual and peaceful change. In a 1974 poll, nearly three-fourths of the American people agreed that it was "morally wrong" to support a military dictatorship even if that government provided military bases for the United States.[10] Because North Americans dislike dictators, U.S. policymakers are generally defensive about charges of supporting them. For example, when Luis Somoza visited the United States in 1959 as Nicaragua's president, he was surprised and upset that the administration "shied away" from him. The Eisenhower administration was worried, according to an internal memorandum, that official contact with Somoza would confirm "accusations that the U.S. favors dictatorships."[11]

When the "middle" delegitimizes a dictator, U.S. officials are compelled to follow the "middle." Even a conservative administration cannot sustain a policy of supporting a dictator if the moderate groups in that country have rejected him. That explains the distancing from both Batista and Somoza. It also explains why the Reagan administration, which had originally embraced Philippine President Ferdinand Marcos and Haitian President Jean-Claude Duvalier, kept its distance when the middle openly opposed both leaders.

The United States is uncomfortable about supporting dictators but is also averse to overthrowing them. In response to the question whether the United States should ever consider overthrowing a Latin American government, 63 percent of the American public said no; 24 percent said yes.[12] For an American, elections are the natural "middle path" between dictators and revolutionaries. An election is often the last idea considered by people trying to remove a dictator, but it is generally the first thought of U.S. policymakers.

An important debate during the Nicaragua crisis that illustrates this tension in the national style was whether to force Somoza's resignation. The pragmatic argument was very powerful: No one could force out Somoza but the United States; failure to do so would lead to a Sandinista victory. The analysis was accepted, and it proved correct. Yet the administration did not follow the analysis to its logical conclusion. Why? First, Somoza was an indirect, not a direct, threat to U.S. interests. The administration disliked Somoza's regime, but the only threat that it posed was that its continuing in power increased the chance of a Sandinista military victory, which, it was believed, was more likely to threaten U.S. interests.

Second, the principle of nonintervention was a fundamental element of Carter's approach toward Latin America, but it was not sacrosanct. As Carter stated: "We have no inclination to interfere in the internal affairs of other nations *unless* our direct security interests are threatened." Because Somoza did not directly threaten those interests, the United States would not intervene. A third reason for not overthrowing Somoza stemmed from a concern with the consequences of the action. If the United States had forced out Somoza, it would have had to assume responsibility for the consequences, which would almost certainly have been a period of instability. It was also possible that the National Guard, which was so closely tied to Somoza, might collapse on his departure, leaving a clear path for the Sandinistas to come to power. In short, deposing Somoza could produce the very outcome the United States wanted to avoid.

A fourth reason was uncertainty and a lack of information. A nation, like an individual, infrequently takes undesirable actions unless it has no other choice. As late as one month before Somoza fled Nicaragua, the United States thought a "third force" could assume power because it was unaware that the Sandinistas had accumulated an arsenal and logistics network sufficient to defeat Somoza. Nor did the United States know that the FSLN's political support from Latin American democratic governments was so deep that it would preclude a third option. Even Daniel Ortega, who knew that, later admitted he was uncertain that Somoza's end was near.

Fifth, the decision to force the resignation of a foreign head of state is, as Speaker Jim Wright said, "extreme." Somoza was despised with good reason, but compared to several other military dictators in Latin America, like Pinochet of Chile, Stroessner of Paraguay, or Castro of Cuba, he would hardly qualify as the most ruthless. If one started by overthrowing Somoza, then where would one stop?

In sum, the United States chose not to overthrow Somoza because of a national experience that seeks "middle options" abroad as well as at home and because of a mixture of principle and pragmatism, a tension that has long shaped U.S. foreign policy. What is most illuminating is how this reluctance to overthrow a right-wing dictator in the midst of a succession crisis also characterized the policies of Eisenhower and Kennedy in the Dominican Republic (1960–1961), Kennedy

(1961–1963) and Reagan (1985–1986) in Haiti, and Reagan (1985–1986) in the Philippines. In every case, the president rejected the option of pushing out a rightist dictator. In the one case where an administration did force out a dictator—Diem of South Vietnam—the Kennedy administration soon regretted it.[13]

Because the broad sweep of U.S. policy was unchanged between administrations does not mean that the presidents had no choices, or that they all agreed on every policy. When faced with the prospect of Somoza taking power or being reelected, the administration of Franklin Roosevelt remained silent, that of Harry Truman broke diplomatic relations, and that of Richard Nixon helped him secure another term. When faced with a leftist Sandinista regime, Jimmy Carter lobbied Congress to give it economic aid, and Ronald Reagan lobbied Congress to provide its enemies with weapons.

The United States is motivated by security concerns, but its choices of how, when, and in what ways to respond to a threat require a richer explanation. Each administration reacts to its predecessor and makes it own judgment about which U.S. interests matter most. Moreover, a new administration, particularly one that represents a different party from its predecessor, tends at the beginning to overstate differences with its predecessor to justify its mandate for change. William Howard Taft condemned the "big stick" of Theodore Roosevelt and announced "dollar diplomacy," which in turn was criticized even more sharply by Woodrow Wilson, who offered a ringing defense of liberty and democracy. Similarly, Jimmy Carter criticized the covert acts to destabilize governments by his predecessors and identified his administration with human rights, and Ronald Reagan rebuked Carter for opening the Caribbean to communism and enunciated a doctrine aimed at overturning leftist governments.

Republicans have been more conservative and anti-communist, giving higher priority to security and stability and less to human rights and social reform. The choice of instruments reflects these different priorities, with Republicans giving greater weight to military aid, covert actions, military maneuvers and shows of strength, private investment, and bilateral aid, and Democrats stressing diplomacy and negotiations, economic aid, and multilateral institutions. Fundamental debates almost never occur within an administration. Nixon's policy of supporting Somoza because of his anti-communism and Carter's of withdrawing support because of human rights violations were so fundamental to each administration that the United States could only change direction when either it changed administrations or events compelled a change in policy.

Perhaps the most important single variable explaining why administrations choose different policies is a president's perception of the nature and intensity of the threat that the United States faces. The more distant the threat the more likely it is that an administration will adhere to its initial principles; the more immediate the threat the more likely it is that the administration's policy will adapt its approach to respond to the threat. As the Cuban and Nicaraguan crises reached a climax, the Eisenhower and the Carter administrations began contemplating options—such as forcing the dictator's resignation—that they had rejected before.

Threat perception not only explains changes during a single administration, it also helps to explain the differences between administrations. The Carter administration was headed for a cool and difficult relationship with the Sandinista government after finding evidence of its arms transfers to the Salvadorans, but as Carter himself confirmed, he would not have organized and supported a covert war, as Reagan did.[14] The two administrations had sharply divergent perceptions of the nature and intensity of the threat. To Reagan, the Sandinistas represented an immediate, grave, Soviet-inspired threat that was testing the will and jeopardizing the interests of the United States. His policies flowed from that definition. To Carter, the Sandinistas represented a Central American revolution; the United States should try to contain it.

In addition to a president's ideology and perception of threat, a third factor that is important in explaining why a policy changes is the period in which it occurs. The way policymakers perceive an issue like the Nicaraguan revolution is affected by the general swings in the public mood and by significant international events, such as the Iranian revolution or the Soviet invasion of Afghanistan. Moreover, the concern of U.S. policymakers and others quickens after traumatic events like the Cuban or Nicaraguan revolutions, but it usually peters out in a few years. Compare, for example, U.S. policy immediately after the Cuban revolution toward Haiti and the Dominican Republic from 1960 to 1964 to its policy after Nicaragua toward the Philippines and Chile in 1985–1986.[15] These other crises ended differently than those of Nicaragua and Cuba, but as we saw, U.S. policy toward these and other succession crises was similar. In almost every case, the president feared a power vacuum and rejected the option of pushing the dictator out. Because U.S. policy was similar, the explanation for the different outcomes must reside in the decisions of local actors, who were influenced even more by the previous trauma.

Democratic Latin American governments played important roles in Nicaragua, partly because of the historical distance from Cuba but mostly because of their hatred for Somoza. They saw the Sandinistas as the main lever for displacing Somoza, and they did not consider the consequences, in part because they thought the United States would not permit the revolution to turn to Cuba. Yet their decisions prevented the U.S. from limiting Cuban influence.

This explains why the Sandinistas came to power, but it does not explain the radicalization of the revolution, which was not inevitable. Because of the Sandinistas' preconceptions of imperialism, the United States was limited in its ability to influence them positively. The most it could do was not make the situation worse. The Nicaraguan government wanted to diversify its relations, and thus the major opportunities for positive influence rested with Latin American and European governments.

By 1983, however, most of these governments either were disillusioned with the Marxism of the Sandinista leadership or had serious economic problems of their own. The decline in the price of oil and the rise in debt turned Mexican and Venezuelan policy inward. Many of these governments had their own reasons for lowering their profile and reducing aid to Nicaragua; U.S. pressure gave them an additional reason. The Contadora group wanted to play a role but was disregarded by two increasingly intransigent actors, the Reagan administration and the Sandinistas, who seemed determined to collide.

Both sides claimed they wanted to avoid confrontation, yet both contributed to it. Each had a fearful prophecy about the other that connected and came true. The suspicions that each harbored about the other led them to interpret the behavior of the other in the worst possible light. Therefore, each felt the need to take defensive measures, which were interpreted as provocations by the other side. This, in turn, led to deliberate provocations.

By 1983, the Reagan administration deliberately sought to transfer legitimacy from the Sandinistas to the contras and to isolate Nicaragua from the rest of Central and Latin America. To achieve this goal, moderate leaders in Nicaragua needed to leave and join the armed opposition outside the country. In four years, hardly a long time, U.S. policy had shifted from trying to avoid polarization in Nicaragua to promoting it.

Having committed itself to the contras, the Reagan administration could neither retreat nor change direction. In response to a question from Congress about whether he had ever contemplated proposing an alternative approach to the president on Nicaragua or telling him the policy was wrong, Robert McFarlane confessed: "To tell you the truth, probably the reason I didn't is because if I'd done that, Bill Casey, Jeane Kirkpatrick, and Cap Weinberger would have said I was some kind of commie."[16] Inhibited by the fear of looking soft or pink, the administration was locked into a strategy that could not succeed in Nicaragua or be sustained in the United States; all it could do was hurt Nicaragua and diminish the president's credibility.

What about the Sandinista strategy? The Sandinistas viewed negotiations and tolerance of criticism as signs of weakness. Either the government was unaware of, or it did not care about, the effect of its actions on the congressional debate over funding the contras. At crucial points in the debate, in May 1985 and then in March and May 1986, the Nicaraguan government took actions that strengthened President Reagan's case for aid to the contras. Why? Because as Omar Cabezas, a Sandinista leader, explained: "The only thing they are debating in Washington is how and when to destroy us." Nicaraguan government radio echoed this point: "Nothing good will come from Congress. We must be prepared."[17]

In short, both governments were insecure and distrusted each other so completely that they believed force was the only method of influence, although the evidence on that was hardly clear. Nicaragua's moderates, who were squeezed to the left during the revolution, were then squeezed to the right by both the Sandinistas and the Reagan administration. By leaving Nicaragua to join the contras in the mid-1980s, the moderates contributed to the polarization of the country.

The Democratic Option

Despite its efforts, Washington's ability to influence developments in Nicaragua during the succession crisis and the revolutionary government was limited. While both Carter and Reagan pursued a strategy aimed at bringing democracy to Nicaragua, both failed. There seemed little chance that Nicaragua would evolve democratically until 1989. It turns out that Jimmy Carter could not mediate a democratic election when he was president, but one decade later as the head of a NGO, he could. What explains the difference?

Because of administrative inadequacies and political suspicions, the prospects are small that a poor country with little or no experience with democracy could conduct free and fair elections and establish a representative democracy. If a regime is in the midst of a war or threatened by one, the prospects are diminished even further. This was Nicaragua's handicap. The odds of a democratic transition, however, improved as a result of two initiatives: the Arias Plan of 1987 and the Bipartisan Accord negotiated by Secretary of State James A. Baker and Speaker of the House Jim Wright in March 1989.

The Arias Plan offered a way to untie the Gordian knot that had connected internal conflict in Nicaragua with external intervention. All of Central America became responsible for ending the civil wars by securing democracy and promoting national reconciliation in each of the countries. It was a brilliant idea that turned the security problem on its head. *Instead of trying to secure democracy by negotiating peace, Central America decided to secure peace by promoting democracy.* To succeed, however, two other ingredients were essential. The United States had to accept the Central American agreement calling for the demobilization of the contras, and mediators or verifiers were needed to ensure a free election.

President Reagan called the Arias Plan "fatally flawed" and requested more aid for the contras, insisting that democracy was not possible unless Congress approved his request.[18] The Iran-contra scandal, however, weakened the president, and Congress disapproved the request. The Bush administration came into office the next year determined to put this divisive issue aside. The Bipartisan Accord stressed its support for the Arias Plan and provided humanitarian, not military, aid to the contras. The Bush administration also supported free elections not just in principle but in its policies. Whereas the Reagan administration had encouraged moderates to leave Nicaragua and discouraged the opposition from participating in the 1984 election, the Bush administration did the opposite, helping the moderates to return and insisting that they unite and participate in the 1990 election. The suspension of the threat from the United States gave the Sandinistas the political space to organize an election; the continued existence of a possible threat gave the Sandinistas an incentive to have a good election.

The problem was how to ensure that the terms of the election would be free and fair. Arias and Perez devoted much time and energy to persuading the Sandinistas to liberate *La Prensa* and free political prisoners, but their two governments could not negotiate the many other issues necessary to permit a free election. Moreover, the opposition was a substantial part of the problem, and they required constant nurturing if they were to remain in the race. The opposition was suspicious of the Sandinistas and the entire electoral process, and their proclivity was to withdraw rather than offer constructive proposals. Some in the Bush administration, notably

Vice President Dan Quayle, who called the entire electoral process "a sham" and "a fraud," reinforced those in the opposition who were skeptical of the process. By the summer of 1989, the probability was that Quayle would be right. Given the history of the country and the absence of trust between the Sandinistas and UNO, something new was needed for the election to be free, but no one knew how to square the circle, how to design a fair election supported by both sides without intervening in Nicaragua's internal affairs.

The answer arrived with a new actor: international election mediators. When the Nicaraguan government invited the international observers in August 1989, no one expected that their role would go beyond observation, and of course, the OAS and the UN were constitutionally ill-suited for playing any other role. Carter had the advantage of representing a NGO while also being an ex-president, an adept mediator, and someone who was known and trusted by both sides. Carter also defined his mission expansively: He was less interested in grading the electoral process than in ensuring that the election would be free and fair. A free election would not happen automatically in Nicaragua, and if one watched passively, it definitely would not happen. What was needed was a leader who would mediate among all the parties and the SEC to ensure that the rules were fair.

There are many reasons why Carter failed in 1979 and succeeded a decade later. In 1979, the government and the moderate opposition each feared that the other might win an election; the opposite was the case a decade later. The opposition believed that Somoza would manipulate the election, and Somoza feared he might not be able to do that. A decade later, the opposition was united and determined to participate, and the overall climate had changed. But there is a more generic reason why the U.S. government could not mediate an election but an NGO could. No issues are more sensitive "internal" matters than the rules for choosing one's leaders. No government wants to allow a foreign government to assist in this process. Nongovernmental organizations do not have armies or any coercive instruments of influence. Their rights are clearly prescribed in a foreign country. In the case of Nicaragua, Carter could stretch the boundaries, but he never constituted a threat to Nicaragua. He also zealously guarded his relationships with government officials, even as he insisted on his impartiality. All these factors help to explain why mediation was more effective in 1989–1990 than a decade before.

The mediation relied on improvisation and trial-and-error. It had some successes and some failures, but in the end, the specific agreements were less important than the momentum that Carter generated and the optimism he transmitted that the election would be free and fair. His readiness to address every problem also gave the opposition the sense for the first time that someone was paying attention to their concerns, and the government was responding to their legitimate complaints. This was the first time in Nicaraguan history that the opposition felt that they were having an effect on government policies, and that gave them a stake in the electoral process that permitted it go forward. Moreover, two monitoring techniques—survey forms to monitor the electoral process on election day and the quick count to estimate the final result within hours of the polls closing—added confidence and stability in a country that feared announcing results could cause chaos. Soon after the election count was completed, the international mediators were ready and well-positioned to negotiate the acceptance of defeat by Ortega and the terms of the transition from a revolutionary government to its opposition.

Carter's skills were helpful, but his success was also due to the fact that he was not acting alone, and the external strategic equation—the Bush administration's passive support for the contras—reinforced his approach. As the OAS and the UN came out of their shell during the electoral process, their officials often did similar mediation at lower levels, in other regions, and on a continuing basis, as Carter and his teams did during an intense burst of activity for a few days each month.

The long-term effect of the election was as great on the international community as on Nicaragua. The successful outcome provided an impetus for both the UN and OAS to establish permanent election units, an idea that would have been completely implausible before the election. The OAS has gone further, gradually expanding the norms of cooperation to defend democracy in the hemisphere.

Missed Opportunities and Lessons of Nicaragua

The world is not a laboratory that will hold still while a social scientist changes a single variable to see if that would produce a different outcome. Nevertheless, as one reviews the history of U.S.-Nicaraguan relations, there appear to be certain turning points when different decisions—by Somoza, the moderate Nicaraguans, the Sandinistas, and the United States—might have led to different outcomes. Let us briefly identify these missed opportunities and then turn to the lessons to be drawn from them.[19]

Although no single actor is responsible for the Nicaraguan revolution and its aftermath, Anastasio Somoza Debayle is more responsible than any other. If he had chosen to step down from power or, even better, accept the terms for a free and fair plebiscite, he would have saved his country from the bloodshed and trauma of a decade. If, after the death of Pedro Joaquin Chamorro in January 1978, the moderates had been able to unite behind a single leader and risk an election or remain independent of the Sandinistas, they might have used their leverage to construct a transitional government when Somoza departed.

From the U.S. perspective, one could identify three moments between 1978 and 1984 when a different policy might have advanced U.S. interests more effectively. In December 1978, Somoza sent three questions to the Department of State regarding the possibility of his being permitted to go into exile in the United States. The State Department answered affirmatively in a routine manner rather than using the request as the leverage that it had been desperately seeking to gain Somoza's consent on a plebiscite or departure from power. The second missed opportunity occurred between March and June 1979 after the imposition of sanctions. Exhausted and frustrated from the previous negotiations, the U.S. government turned to other issues instead of redoubling its efforts to establish an "executive committee" of moderates, who could be positioned to assume a role in a transitional government. By the time that the United States began pursuing this option in late June, most of the moderates had aligned with the Sandinistas.

A third, critical turning point occurred in December 1981 when President Reagan signed a presidential finding to support the contras. Some believed this would be useful leverage in future negotiations with the Sandinistas, and although that idea was not incorrect, it proved politically impractical. The contra strategy had a political logic of its own in the United States that prevented the more pragmatic members of the administration from using the leverage to attain realistic negotiating objectives. For example, in late 1983, after the invasion of Grenada, the Sandinistas began to pay very close attention to America's security concerns, but they did not have anyone with whom they could negotiate because the ideologues thought they were in sight of victory, and the pragmatists were afraid of being perceived as soft on communism. The logic of the contras also prevented the administration from taking the election of 1984 seriously.

The Sandinistas also had three turning points where a different decision might very well have led in a happier direction. In November 1980, they decided to provide massive support to the Salvadoran guerrillas despite a clear warning by the Carter administration and the determination of the incoming Reagan administration. Having crossed this line once, despite pledges that it would not do so, the Sandinistas would not ever again be trusted by any U.S. administration on this basic security goal. The second turning point occurred in the negotiations with Assistant Secretary of State Thomas Enders in August 1981. He tried to negotiate a deal with the Sandinistas that would have met the security concerns of the United States in exchange for letting the Sandinistas define the political and economic character of their regime. He also implied that a failure to achieve a security deal might lead to an insurgency, as it did. The Sandinistas would later regret their failure to take this offer. The final turning point occurred in 1984–1986 when the Contadora countries and also Jimmy Carter proposed a negotiating framework that would have ended contra aid in exchange for a serious dialogue between the Sandinistas and the opposition. The Sandinistas missed this opportunity because they thought that the Democratic Congress would prevent any further aid to the contras, and they thought they had defeated them. In fact, the Reagan administration was able to obtain the largest ever amount of military aid to the contras, who purchased "stinger" missiles and other equipment that neutralized the Nicaraguan government's helicopters and deepened the war dramatically. This third turning point may have been illusory, however, because the Contadora group had not developed a precise enough security plan, and the Reagan administration had been captured by ideologues uninterested in negotiation.

These mistakes or missed opportunities are clearer, of course, in retrospect than they were at the time, but they also underscore how history could have been written differently. So what lessons should one draw from each challenge?

The best strategy for dealing with a succession crisis turns out to be the same as that for a democratic transition: a mediated negotiation aimed at defining the terms of a free and fair election. We learned a great deal more about how to do this during the 1990s than we knew a decade before. The mediators have to be of sufficient stature and with the right abilities to be able to gain the trust and confidence of the major parties. They need the firm support of the international community and especially of the closest neighbors and most interested powers. They must be meticulously impartial, continuously engaged with both sides, able to focus on the larger issues and the legitimate complaints, resolve problems, and develop a capacity for detecting and denouncing fraud.

The lessons to be drawn from dealing with revolutionary governments are difficult for democracies like the United States to learn. The first lesson is that confronting a Third World nationalistic regime is usually a mistake when it is not just plain counterproductive. Most such regimes rely on stoking nationalistic timbers to gain the support and suppress the dissent necessary for the regime to install its revolution. Some revolutionary leaders would identify the United States as an enemy even if the United States were trying to be friendly. Of course, the United States rarely exhibits the kind of patience and perseverance necessary to avoid being trapped into a confrontation.

The second lesson is that U.S. policymakers should try to do the opposite of what usually comes to mind. Instead of withdrawing diplomatic personnel to express its displeasure toward a hostile revolutionary government, the United States should send more officials to engage the population. Instead of identifying the similarities between revolutionary regimes, the U.S. government should spend more time trying to understand how different they are. The U.S. government saw the Sandinistas and the Grenadians as mirror-images of Castro's revolution, when in fact the Sandinistas were consciously more pragmatic and pluralistic, Castro was more defiant and revolutionary, and the Grenadians were more eccentric. By focusing on the differences, policymakers would be better equipped to design a nuanced strategy. The third lesson is the easiest to conceptualize but the hardest to implement. The best way to preclude a hostile relationship is to recognize the shared responsibility of both sides. Each can retain a policy that exaggerates the negative and provokes the worst in the other, or each can try to bring out the best. *The problem is that each side usually tries to get under the skin of the other rather than into the other's shoes.*

In a post-Cold War world, one might question the relevance of the revolutionary challenge. With the exception of Castro's Cuba, and two Colombian Marxist groups, communism, for all practical purposes, is dead in Latin America, or at least it does not pose a threat to the United States. The challenge of how to deal with revolutionary governments, however, preceded the Cold War, and although it does not constitute a contemporary problem, it is probable that it will return in some guise in the future.

The problem occurs when there is a leader or a government that steps outside international norms, defies the United States, and searches for allies among America's enemies. Whether the leader's decision is justified by the country's poverty and inequalities or by personal ambition is impossible to establish and therefore not a firm basis for U.S. policy. The challenge is particularly acute in Latin America because of its proximity, and especially in the Caribbean Basin, but it occurs in other areas, as the cases of Libya, Iraq, and North Korea testify. In the post-Cold War era, the United States viewed General Noriega of Panama largely from this frame of reference: Not only was he a repressive drug-trafficker, he also was too friendly with too many pariahs.

One can see the continued resonance of this line of argument in the reaction to the election of Hugo Chavez as president of Venezuela and to Daniel Ortega during his fourth campaign for the presidency in 2001. Chavez's well-publicized friendship with Fidel Castro and Ortega's visits to Libya and Iraq raised concerns among U.S. officials. The fact that both Chavez and Ortega were playing by the rules of democracy did not appear to influence conservatives in Washington, although the concern was lower than during the Cold War, and the fact that both governments are democratic mitigates the concerns. But again, if a new leader steps off the democratic train, seeks alliances with America's enemies, and is perceived to be trying to subvert its friends, the United States will soon find itself dealing with the same three phases of the revolutionary challenge.

Two lessons stand out above all the rest. First, the successful response to the third challenge of a democratic transition reminds us that *learning is possible in international relations. We are not condemned to repetition.* The mediation of 1989–1990 profited from the failure of a decade before and, even more, from the failure in Panama the year before. The election of 1990 became possible because the moderate opposition in Nicaragua learned the lessons from their experience with the 1984 election. And America began to learn that the "contras" were a blunt instrument and probably counterproductive to key U.S. interests.

In his massive volume on Nicaragua, Robert Kagan, who had served in Ronald Reagan's State Department, argued that the contras did play an important role in the outcome of the 1990 election. But he admitted that "President Reagan's policies, if continued unchanged, would probably not have led to fair elections in February 1990." Reagan would never have accepted the electoral process, and the Sandinistas knew that. "Reagan's policies, unmodified by the Arias plan or by Congress," in Kagan's words, "would probably have meant many years of inconclusive struggle in Nicaragua."[20]

The role played by the international mediators in 1990 not only secured the first free election in Nicaragua's history, it also defined a transition arrangement that precluded violence and instability. The fact that the Nicaraguans—an intensely nationalistic people—would ask the leaders of the international community to forge such an agreement was unlikely, and yet it occurred. Some viewed the invitation as an infringement on sovereignty or a sign of weakness, but it was actually the opposite: It permitted Nicaragua to become stronger and more autonomous. And there was much less intervention in the country's internal affairs after the election than before. Moreover, the awareness of that lesson—that Nicaragua is not condemned to repeat a pattern of authoritarian behavior—is empowering and ought to encourage us to intensify our search for dysfunctional patterns in history so that policy can be improved.

The second lesson is almost the antithesis of the first: *Old habits do not disappear easily or entirely.* As one reflects on the transformation of Nicaragua in the last three decades, it is easier to see the authoritarian connection between Somoza and his revolutionary successors and to see that the democratic successors to Daniel Ortega did not always behave democratically. History has tugged at contemporary actors. An entire generation sometimes must pass from the scene before one can see real change.

Nicaragua is not condemned to repetition, but it is also not completely free of its authoritarian past. Nor is the United States free from its past policies of trying to manage the country's affairs. Neither country has mastered the rhythm that would permit a new twenty-first century equilibrium, but there is no doubt that the 1990 election constituted a genuine watershed. Since then, Nicaragua has been learning and practicing democratic politics, for the first time in the country's history.

NOTES

Preface

1. At the time, the polls showed Daniel Ortega ahead of all of the other opposition leaders by at least 2:1, but that meant 30 percent–15 percent. The "undecided" represented 50 percent of eligible voters. A closer look at other questions besides the one on the candidates suggested that the Sandinistas had a bedrock of support of 30 to 40 percent, but the rest of the population was deeply dissatisfied, as one would expect after eight years of civil war, hyper-inflation, and high unemployment. I guessed that if the opposition remained unified behind Violeta Chamorro, she would attract the "residual"—virtually all but the hard-core Sandinistas—and that's what happened.

2. Sandinista Comandante Dora María Tellez held a press conference in Panama that day. It was published by the Foreign Broadcasting Information Service, *Daily Report* [hereafter *FBIS*], September 2, 1978, pp. N4–5, annex 2. Somoza's interview with ACAN-EFE was republished in *FBIS*, September 5, 1978, p. P2.

3. Charles A. Krause, "Nicaraguan Rebels Losing Key Support," *Washington Post*, March 17, 1979, p. A20.

4. Lenin's prediction is cited by Hans J. Morgenthau, *Politics among Nations* (New York: Alfred A. Knopf, 1973), p. 22; Daniel Ortega's is in his interview with WGBH in Managua, June 4, 1984.

Chapter 1

1. Few books or articles written about Nicaragua since the 1960s in English or Spanish fail to mention some variation of this comment. Some authors have modified the comment, and some have suggested that Roosevelt used it to refer to Dominican dictator Rafael Trujillo. The most commonly used story is that Roosevelt said this of Somoza on the eve of Somoza's visit to Washington in 1939.

2. I did my own search of the published documents of FDR before interviewing Donald Schewe, former Assistant Director of the Franklin D. Roosevelt Library, October 10, 1986, Atlanta. Arthur M. Schlesinger, Jr., one of the foremost historians of the Roosevelt era, wrote me that he has "never been able to find any source for the alleged FDR statement, and I suspect it is apocryphal" (letter to the author, March 30, 1987).

3. Visiting Americans commented about the Somoza family's use of "quaintly antiquated American slang which they laced with obscenities portraying a 1930s B-picture tough-but-nice-guy image." Bernard Diederich, *Somoza and the Legacy of U.S. Involvement in Central America* (New York: E. P. Dutton, 1981), p. vii.

4. This story is recounted by Diederich, *Somoza*, p. 212. Transcendental meditators believe they emit "positive unity force fields," which can, among other things, reduce crime rates, traffic accidents, and global tensions. Andrew Malcolm, "Iowa Town Contemplates Pitfalls of Being Meditators' Utopia," *New York Times*, January 1, 1984, p. 14.

5. *FBIS*, September 5, 1978, p. 1. Also published in *Washington Star*, September 4, 1978.

6. Jeane Kirkpatrick, "U.S. Security and Latin America," *Commentary*, January 1981, p. 36. Her other article was "Dictatorships and Double Standards," *Commentary*, November 1979.

7. William LeoGrande, "The Revolution in Nicaragua: Another Cuba?" *Foreign Affairs* (Fall 1979): 28; Tom Farer, "At Sea in Central America: Can We Negotiate Our Way to Shore?" in *Central America: Anatomy of Conflict*, ed. Robert Leiken (New York: Pergamon, 1984), pp. 282–83; Shirley Christian, *Nicaragua: Revolution in the Family* (New York: Random House, 1985). Three other books argue the United States should have overthrown Somoza and might have, if it had understood the situation better: Thomas G. Walker, *Nicaragua: The Land of Sandino* (Boulder: Westview Press, 1981); John A. Booth, *The End and the Beginning: The Nicaraguan Revolution* (Boulder: Westview Press, 1982); and George Black, *Triumph of the People: The Sandinista Revolution in Nicaragua* (London: Zed Press, 1981). All are sympathetic to the revolution and critical of U.S. policy.

8. Richard R. Fagen, "Dateline Nicaragua: The End of the Affair," *Foreign Policy,* no. 36 (Fall 1979): 188.

9. LeoGrande, "Revolution in Nicaragua," pp. 37–38.

10. Fulgencio Batista y Zaldivar, *Cuba Betrayed* (New York: Vantage Press, 1962); Anastasio Somoza, Jr., as told to Jack Cox, *Nicaragua Betrayed* (Boston: Western Islands, 1980).

11. Castro advised the Sandinistas not to repeat the mistakes he made at the beginning of his revolution. *New York Times,* July 9, 1980, p. 10.

12. Bryce Wood, *The Making of the Good Neighbor Policy* (New York: Columbia University Press, 1961), p. 64.

13. The following chronology on the Cuban revolution and the U.S. response to it has been reconstructed from many sources, but the following have been most useful: Richard E. Welch, Jr., *Response to Revolution: The United States and the Cuban Revolution, 1959–61* (Chapel Hill: University of North Carolina Press, 1985); Hugh Thomas, *Cuba: The Pursuit of Freedom* (New York: Harper and Row, 1981); Cole Blasier, *The Hovering Giant: U.S. Responses to Revolutionary Change in Latin America* (Pittsburgh: University of Pittsburgh Press, 1979); and Philip W. Bonsal, *Cuba, Castro, and the United States* (Pittsburgh: University of Pittsburgh Press, 1971).

14. Thomas, *Cuba,* p. 958.

15. Blasier, *Hovering Giant,* p. 22.

16. Thomas, *Cuba,* p. 965.

17. Figueres's involvement is documented in a Senate hearing. See U.S. Senate, Committee on the Judiciary, *Communist Threat to the U.S. through the Caribbean: Hearings before the Subcommittee to Investigate the Administration of the Internal Security Act and Other Internal Security Laws, Part 8,* January 22, 23, 1960, pp. 447–54. Pérez noted his help in his interview with WGBH, May 2, 1984, New York City.

18. WGBH interview with José Figueres, June 8, 1984, San José.

19. Thomas, *Cuba,* p. 1005.

20. Cited in ibid., pp. 1015–16.

21. Thomas, *Cuba,* p. 1018.

22. Ibid., p. 1028.

23. Welch, *Response to Revolution,* p. 62.

24. Some correspondents also noted the similarities. Don Bohning, "Nicaragua 1978, Cuba 1958—Parallels Are Striking," *Miami Herald,* September 6, 1978.

25. For one example, see "Forum: Why Are We in Central America? Can the U.S. Live with Latin Revolution? The Dilemmas of National Security," *Harper's,* vol. 268, no. 1609, June 1984, pp. 35–48.

26. Walter LaFeber, *Inevitable Revolutions* (New York: W. W. Norton, 1983), p. 15.

27. For a perceptive essay on the nature of revolution, see Chalmers Johnson, *Revolutionary Change,* 2d ed. (Stanford: Stanford University Press, 1982).

28. Both theses—that revolutions are inevitable and resisted by the United States and the bourgeoisie—are developed by Walter LaFeber in *Inevitable Revolutions.*

29. I have examined the issues related to how events in Central America could affect the national security of the United States in several other papers. See "Our Real National Interests in Central America," *The Atlantic,* July 1982, pp. 27–39; and "U.S. National Security and Latin Revolutions: Imprismed," in *Alternatives to Intervention: A New U.S.-Latin Americana Security Relationship,* edited by Richard J. Bloomfield and Gregory F. Treverton (Boulder: Lynne Rienner Publishers, 1990), pp. 57–79.

30. Even in the case of "revolutionary" Grenada, U.S. policy was not negative at the beginning. See Robert Pastor, *Exiting the Whirlpool: U.S. Foreign Policy Toward Latin America and the Caribbean* (Boulder: Westview Press, 2001), Chapter 9.

31. LaFeber, *Inevitable Revolutions*, p. 230.

Chapter 2

1. Carlos Fonseca Amador, *Nicaragua: Hora Cero*, first published in *Tricontinental*, no. 14, 1969; excerpts reprinted in Tomás Borge et al., *Sandinistas Speak* (New York: Pathfinder Press, 1982), p. 29.

2. David Richard Radell, *An Historical Geography of Western Nicaragua: The Spheres of Influence of León, Granada, and Managua, 1519–1965*, cited in Walker, *Nicaragua: The Land of Sandino*, pp. 10–12.

3. Franklin D. Parker, *The Central American Republics* (New York: Oxford University Press, 1971), pp. 219, 66.

4. Thomas L. Karnes, *The Failure of Union: Central America, 1824–1975* (Tempe: Arizona State University, 1976), p. 94. The civil wars in Nicaragua were typical of the entire region. In the same period, El Salvador had 40 battles and 23 different Presidents; Honduras, 27 battles and 20 Presidents; Guatemala, 51 battles and 18 Presidents.

5. Richard Millett, *Guardians of the Dynasty: A History of the U.S.-Created Guardia Nacional de Nicaragua and the Somoza Family* (Maryknoll, N.Y.: Orbis Books, 1977), p. 16.

6. For a description of the U.S.-British competition in Central America, see Karnes, *Failure of Union*, ch. 5, pp. 96–125; Parker, *Central American Republics*, pp. 234–35; and Samuel F. Bemis, *The Latin American Policy of the U.S.: An Historical Interpretation* (New York: Harcourt, Brace and Company, 1943), pp. 103–108.

7. Proclamation of President Franklin Pierce, December 8, 1855, in *Messages and Papers of the Presidents, 1789–1897*, ed. James D. Richardson (Washington, D.C.: GPO, 1897), pp. 388–89.

8. William O. Scroggs, *Filibusters and Financiers* (1916; reissued New York: Russell and Russell, 1969), pp. 166–67.

9. See Laurence Greene, *The Filibuster* (New York: Bobbs-Merrill, 1937), pp. 137, 200–201; Scroggs, *Filibusters*, pp. 166–72.

10. See Dana G. Munro, *The Five Republics of Central America: Their Political and Economic Development and Their Relations with the United States* (New York: Oxford University Press, 1918), ch. 4.

11. Millett, *Guardians*, pp. 19–22.

12. Munro, *Five Republics*, p. 90.

13. "Letter transmitted from the Nicaraguan Minister to Secretary of State Richard Olney," 1895, cited in Wilfrid Hardy Callcott, *The Caribbean Policy of the United States, 1890–1920* (Baltimore: The Johns Hopkins Press, 1942), p. 77.

14. Bemis, *Latin American Policy*, p. 145.

15. For a good description of the Washington conference and an evaluation of the effectiveness of the treaties on peace in the region, see Karnes, *Failure of Union*, pp. 188–203; and Munro, *Five Republics*, pp. 206–226.

16. Millett mentions the Canal negotiations (*Guardians*, p. 23). Karl Berman doubts these occurred, but notes the railroad contract. *Under the Big Stick: Nicaragua and the United States Since 1848* (Boston: South End Press, 1986), p. 150.

17. Actually, Estrada provoked U.S. intervention with a clever use. As governor of the province, Estrada informed the U.S. Consul that his efforts to resist an attack by Zelaya's soldiers prevented him from protecting U.S. citizens in the area. Though self-serving, the statement was credible, and given the norms of the times, the Consul was compelled to ask the Marines to provide the protection. See William Kamman, *A Search for Stability: United States Diplomacy toward Nicaragua, 1925–1933* (Notre Dame: University of Notre Dame Press, 1968), p. 10.

18. Dana G. Munro, *Intervention and Dollar Diplomacy in the Caribbean, 1900–21* (Princeton: Princeton University Press, 1964), pp. 176–86.

19. Harold Norman Denny, *Dollars for Bullets: The Story of American Rule in Nicaragua* (New York: Dial Press, 1929), p. 7.

20. Callcott, *Caribbean Policy*, pp. 280–85; Millett, *Guardians*, pp. 26–30.

21. For a description of the extensive involvement by the United States in restructuring the finances of the Nicaraguan government, see Department of State, *The United States and Nicaragua: A Survey of the Relations from 1909–1932*, Latin American Series no. 6 (Washington, D.C.: GPO, 1932), pp. 12–28.

22. Dana G. Munro, *The United States and the Caribbean Republics, 1921–33* (Princeton: Princeton University Press, 1974), pp. 159–66. The United States was so involved in Nicaragua's affairs that an American refused to reimburse the Nicaraguan President for his expenses ($446) in hosting a reception.

23. Ibid., p. 162.

24. The United States tried to follow this formula even when it was not in its interests because it did not want to contribute to undermining the treaties (as it had done with the Central American court established by the 1907 treaties). Ibid., pp. 118–19, 193. See also Thomas M. Leonard, *U.S. Policy and Arms Limitation in Central America: The Washington Conference of 1923* (Los Angeles: California State University, Occasional Papers no. 10, 1982).

25. Munro, *United States and the Caribbean Republics*, p. 218.

26. Calvin Coolidge, *Message to Congress: The Conditions and the Actions of the Government in the Present Disturbances in Nicaragua*, January 27, 1927.

27. Henry Stimson, *American Policy in Nicaragua* (1927; reprint New York: Arno Press, 1970), p. 42.

28. Ibid., p. 57.

29. See Stimson, *American Policy*, pp. 84–87; Munro, *United States and the Caribbean Republics*, p. 247.

30. See Neill Macaulay, *The Sandino Affair* (Chicago: Quadrangle Books, 1967); Gregorio Selser, *Sandino* (New York: Monthly Review Press, 1981); Millett, *Guardians*, pp. 63–65, 87.

31. In a study of this and other U.S.-supervised elections in Latin America, Theodore Wright argues that an election might be fair but could not be considered completely "free" when it is supervised by a foreign military presence. See his "Free Elections in the Latin American Policy of the United States," *Political Science Quarterly* 74 (1959).

32. Millett, *Guardians*, p. 136.

33. Ibid., pp. 137–38, 183.

34. Secretary of State Cordell Hull initially rejected the request for a statement because he did not want to "dignify such absurd stories by issuing a denial," and because the United States wanted to remove itself from Nicaraguan internal affairs. See U.S. Department of State, *Foreign Relations of the United States* [hereafter *FRUS*], 1934, vol. 5, "Policy of the U.S. Not to Interfere in Nicaraguan Internal Affairs," pp. 526–58.

35. Millett, *Guardians*, pp. 146, 153, 155.

36. *FRUS*, 1934, vol. 5, "The Secretary of State to the Minister in Nicaragua [Lane]," February 26, 1934, pp. 538–39.

37. *FRUS*, 1935, vol. 4, "Memorandum by the Assistant Chief of the Division of Latin American Affairs [Beaulac]," reporting on conversation with Dr. Sacasa," October 1, 1935, pp. 877–79.

38. *FRUS*, 1935, vol. 4, "The Minister in Nicaragua [Lane] to the Secretary of State," May 14, 1935, pp. 855–61.

39. This part of the historical record captures the ambiguity and hesitancy of U.S. policy in its title, "Efforts to Discourage President Somoza's Bid for Re-Election in 1947, While Maintaining a Policy of Non-Interference in Nicaragua's Internal Affairs," *FRUS*, 1945, vol. 9, p. 218.

40. The opposition urged the State Department to protest the fraud, but to no avail. *FRUS*, 1947, vol. 8, "Telegrams from Secretary of State to Embassy in Nicaragua and from Embassy to the Secretary of State," April 8 and 23, 1947, pp. 846–47.

41. Author's telephone interview with Maurice Bernbaum, Washington, D.C., July 24, 1985. Bernbaum was the Chargé at the time.

42. *FRUS*, 1947, vol. 8, "Telegrams from the Chargé in Nicaragua to the Secretary of State," May 9, 24, and 26, 1947, pp. 848–53.

43. *FRUS*, 1947, vol. 8, pp. 40, 589, 859–65.

44. *FRUS*, 1947, vol. 8, "Memorandum of Conversation, by Assistant Secretary of State Armour," August 24, 1947, pp. 871–72. During this time, U.S. Chargé Maurice Bernbaum is reported to have called Somoza's son (Tacho II) and asked when his father would leave. The elder Somoza returned the call, enraged: "This is my country. Where do you want me to go? You come and take me out!" Cited in Diederich, *Somoza*, p. 30.

45. Two decades before, on January 2, 1947, Undersecretary of State Robert Olds wrote that Central American "governments which we recognize and support stay in power, while those which we do not recognize and support fall." Cited in Millett, *Guardians*, p. 52. The failure to unseat Somoza by nonrecognition was one of several cases that ended the nonrecognition policy. See Thomas M. Leonard, "The Decline of the Recognition Policy in United States–Central American Relations, 1933–49," Occasional Paper 49, Florida International University, July 1985.

46. Charles Ameringer has examined the rise of democrats in the Caribbean area in three works, from which the next sections of this chapter borrow: *The Democratic Left in Exile: The Antidictatorial Struggle in the Caribbean, 1945–1959* (Coral Gables: University of Miami Press, 1974); *Don Pepe: A Political Biography of José Figueres of Costa Rica* (Albuquerque: University of New Mexico Press, 1978); "The Thirty Years War between Figueres and the Somozas," *Caribbean Review* 8, no. 4 (Fall 1979).

47. *FRUS*, 1952–54, vol. 4, *The American Republics* (Washington, D.C.: GPO, 1983), September 29, 1952, pp. 1372–75. In light of the Eisenhower Administration's decision in 1953 to overthrow the Arbenz government, the State Department's reasons for rejecting the idea in 1952 are interesting: it violated international law, and "we would find it difficult to fight aggression in Korea and be a party to it in this hemisphere" (p. 1374). Actually, one of Truman's aides thought the plan had merit, and persuaded the President. Truman instructed the CIA to proceed with the conspiracy, but when Secretary of State Acheson learned of it, he convinced the President to abort the mission. Stephen Schlesinger and Stephen Kinzer, *Bitter Fruit: The Untold Story of the American Coup in Guatemala* (Garden City, N.Y.: Doubleday, 1982), p. 102.

48. *FRUS*, 1952–54, vol. 4, "Memorandum by the Secretary of State to the President," May 1, 1952, pp. 1369–71.

49. Ibid., "The Ambassador in Nicaragua [Whelan] to the Department of State," March 6, 1953, pp. 1375–77. Whelan, a former Republican Party chairman from North Dakota, was appointed by President Truman in 1951 as part of a deal with Senator William Langer, Chairman of the Judiciary Committee, who threatened to delay the Administration's legislation until Truman appointed a North Dakotan to an Embassy. Albert M. Colegrove, "Nicaragua: Another Cuba?" *The Nation*, July 1, 1961, pp. 6–9.

50. For the negotiation and signing (April 23, 1954) of the military aid agreement, see *FRUS*, 1952–54, vol. 4, p. 1378. On the Guatemalan chronology, see Schlesinger and Kinzer, *Bitter Fruit*, p. 113.

51. *FRUS*, 1952–54, vol. 4, p. 1389; Ameringer, *Don Pepe*, pp. 119–22; Millett, *Guardians*, pp. 213–14.

52. Cited in John D. Martz, *Central America: The Crisis and the Challenge* (Chapel Hill: University of North Carolina Press, 1959), p. 199.

Chapter 3

1. Millett, *Guardians*, p. 225; Ameringer, "Thirty Years War," p. 40. Chamorro and Lacayo were released in 1960.

2. Interviews (both author's and WGBH) with Edén Pastora (November 14, 1983 [author]; July 1, 1984 [WGBH]; both Washington, D.C.) and Tomás Borge (August 4, 1983 and February 8, 1986 [author]; June 3, 1984 [WGBH]; all Managua). The origins of the FSLN are not clear. Pastora predictably tends to enlarge his role, and Borge and the Ortegas omit or discount Pastora's role. A Senate Foreign Relations Committee study in 1969, however, indicated that the Frente Liberación Nacional had been founded first in Havana, giving some credibility to Pastora's claim that he inserted the word "Sandino" into the Frente's name. U.S. Senate Committee on Foreign Relations, *Survey of the Alliance for Progress*, April 29, 1969, p. 233.

3. Carlos Fonseca Amador, "El Aporte Revolucionario de Sandino," from *Escritos*, in *Nicaragua: La Estrategia de la Victoria* (Mexico: Editorial Nuestro Tiempo, 1983), pp. 71–72.

4. Millett, *Guardians*, p. 227.

5. See the description in his memoirs of his trip to South America in 1958, where he attributes the demonstrations against him to Communist agitators. Richard Nixon, *RN: The Memoirs of Richard Nixon* (New York: Grosset and Dunlap, 1978), pp. 186–92.

6. Author's conversation and correspondence (December 3, 1982) with James Cheek, who was political counselor in the U.S. Embassy in Managua at the time. Cheek risked the Ambassador's displeasure by sending his reports to the State Department by the dissent channel. He later received a special award from the department for these reports.

7. Author's interview with Max Kelly, Somoza's friend, February 13, 1984, Miami.

8. Cited in Diederich, *Somoza*, p. 24.

9. Somoza, *Nicaragua Betrayed*, p. 58.

10. Diederich's book is an excellent portrait of the two sides of Anastasio Somoza—a man who was relaxed with Americans and authoritarian to Nicaraguans who were not members of his family. A similar characterization of the man was made by two Nicaraguans who worked closely with Somoza, but who asked not to be identified.

11. The book was published in English by the John Birch Society just before the Presidential election in 1980. In a press conference on August 24, 1978, in Managua, Somoza was asked whether he viewed Carter's policy as a betrayal. He answered: "I am a politician, and I recognize that every adminstration has different attitudes. Therefore I do not consider a change in the attitude of the United States government a betrayal. We both have to adjust to our new relations." Unclassified Cable from U.S. Embassy, Managua to Secretary of State, 26 August 1978, Managua 3997, "Somoza's Press Conference."

12. Somoza, *Nicaragua Betrayed*, p. 55.

13. Ibid., p. 209. Although the human rights situation in Nicaragua was not as bad as in many countries of the Southern Cone, Amnesty International's Annual Report for 1975–76 noted "many reports of arbitrary arrest, torture, and disappearance." Cited in *Human Rights Reports*, prepared by the Department of State, submitted to the U.S. Senate Committee on Foreign Relations, March 1977, p. 134.

14. Somoza, *Nicaragua Betrayed*, p. 58.

15. This and subsequent information on the Ford Administration's policy toward Nicaragua was obtained in an interview with William D. Rogers, Assistant Secretary of State for Inter-American Affairs (1974–76) and Under Secretary of State for Economic Affairs (1976), May 22, 1985, Washington, D.C.

16. Interview with William D. Rogers, May 22, 1985, Washington, D.C.

17. Somoza, *Nicaragua Betrayed*, p. 58. Somoza also noted the award to James Cheek and the Congressional hearings on human rights in Nicaragua as other signs that public opinion in the United States might be beginning to turn against him.

18. Stephen Kinzer, "Sandinistas Mark Raid That Presaged Victory," *New York Times*, January 7, 1985, p. A4.

19. WGBH interview with Tomás Borge, June 3, 1984, Managua. Humberto Ortega agrees that this was "the most important operation carried out by the Front. . . . For the first time, the Sandinistas' revolutionary views were broadcast on TV and radio." "Interview with Humberto Ortega," in Borge et al., *Sandinistas Speak*, p. 55.

20. Author's interview with Alfredo César, April 9, 1984, Washington, D.C.

21. Many of the original Sandinista leaders were writers and poets, and there is ample literature to identify their world view. In English, the most accessible compendium is the short book *Sandinistas Speak* (New York: Pathfinder Press, 1982), which includes the translated and edited speeches and writings of Carlos Fonseca and others. In particular, see the 1969 program of the FSLN and excerpts from Fonseca's *Zero Hour*, pp. 13–42. For a discussion of the significance of U.S. interventions in the history of Nicaragua, see the excerpt from Fonseca's book and the speech by Daniel Ortega also in that volume. For a discussion of the importance of U.S. imperialism in defining Nicaragua's economic problems, see Jaime Wheelock Román, *Imperialismo y Dictadura: Crisis de una Formación Social*, 6th ed. (Mexico: Siglo Veintiuno Editores, 1982), originally published 1975. For an overall analysis, see David Nolan, *The Ideology of the Sandinistas and the Nicaraguan Revolution* (Coral Gables: University of Miami, 1985).

22. This early history is recounted by Carlos Fonseca, who excused this "grave error" by suggesting that "the Marxist leadership [in Nicaragua] did not possess the necessary clarity" of thought at the time. In Borge et al., *Sandinistas Speak*, pp. 31–32.

23. Cited in Selser, *Sandino*, p. 97. Neill Macaulay describes the break between Sandino and the Communists in *The Sandino Affair*, pp. 158–60.

24. WGBH and author's interviews with Edén Pastora, November 14, 1983 (author), Washington, D.C.; July 1, 1984 (WGBH), Washington, D.C.

25. WGBH interview with Daniel Ortega, June 4, 1984, Managua.

26. Humberto Ortega Saavedra, *50 Años de Lucha Sandinista* (Managua: Ministerio del Interior, 1980), but originally published in 1976. At the conclusion of his book, the Sandinistas are confronting the combined forces of Central America, plus advisers from the United States, Brazil, Colombia, and exiles from South Vietnam (p. 120). Also, see Humberto Ortega in Borge et al., *Sandinistas Speak*, p. 57.

27. WGBH and author's interviews with Tomás Borge, August 4, 1983 (author), Managua; June 3, 1984 (WGBH), Managua.

28. The interviews were with Henry Ruiz from the GPP, Daniel Ortega from the Terceristas, and Jaime Wheelock Román of the TP, in *Latin American Perspectives* 6, no. 1 (Winter 1979): 108–128.

29. Cited in *The Central American Crisis Reader*, ed. Leiken and Rubin, p. 154.

30. *Latin American Perspectives*, p. 115.

31. Ibid., p. 118.

32. This is Jaime Wheelock Román's conclusion at the end of his study of the Nicaraguan economy. See his *Imperialismo y Dictadura*, 6th ed., pp. 195–96.

33. The Nicaraguan case offers an almost classic fit with the thesis developed by Samuel P. Huntington that revolution "is most likely to occur in societies which have experienced some social and economic development and where the processes of political modernization and political development have lagged behind the processes of social and economic change." *Political Order in Changing Societies* (New Haven: Yale University Press, 1968), p. 265.

34. U.S. Agency for International Development, *U.S. Overseas Loans and Grants*, July 1, 1945–September 30, 1978, p. 56.

35. All of the statistics in this section are from World Bank, *World Development Report, 1980* (New York: Oxford University Press, 1980); this from pp. 112–13.

36. Harry W. Strachan, *Family and Other Business Groups in Economic Development: The Case of Nicaragua* (New York: Praeger, 1976), p. 116.

37. Richard Feinberg and Robert Pastor, "Far From Hopeless: An Economic Program for Post-War Central America," in *Central America*, ed. Leiken, p. 195. Nicaragua's development progress during this period was typical of most of Central America.

38. Robert W. Fox and Jerrold W. Huguet, *Population and Urban Trends in Central America and Panama* (Washington, D.C.: Inter-American Development Bank, 1977), pp. 53, 160.

39. *New York Times*, July 22, 1979, p. III, 1.

Chapter 4

1. Cited in U.S. House Appropriations Committee, *Foreign Assistance and Relations Programs Appropriation Bill, 1978*, Report no. 95-417, June 15, 1977, p. 65.

2. For a description and analysis of Carter's policies, see Robert Pastor, *Exiting the Whirlpool: U.S. Foreign Policy Toward Latin America and the Caribbean* (Boulder, Colo.: Westview Press), Chapter 3.

3. For the Congressional origins of the human rights policy, see Robert Pastor, *Congress and the Politics of U.S. Foreign Economic Policy* (Berkeley: University of California Press, 1980), pp. 301–321. Also see Congressional Research Service, Library of Congress, *Human Rights and U.S. Foreign Assistance: Experiences and Issues in Policy Implementation (1977–78)*, for the U.S. Senate Committee on Foreign Relations, November 1979 [hereafter, Senate Human Rights Report].

4. Author's interview with Alfonso Robelo, May 3–4, 1983, San José, Costa Rica. Curiously, Somoza himself acknowledges this side of Solaun: "I'll say this for Mr. Solaun, he did his best. However, he was

not forceful enough and he didn't have the clout to impress his superiors in the State Department." Somoza, *Nicaragua Betrayed*, p. 70.

5. WGBH interview with John Murphy, May 15, 1984, Danbury, Connecticut.

6. Author's interview with Alan Riding, May 13, 1983, Washington, D.C.

7. Alan Riding, "Nicaraguan Bishops Accuse Government of Resorting to Widespread Torture," *New York Times*, March 2, 1977, p. 1.

8. *Human Rights Reports*, prepared by the Department of State, submitted to the U.S. Senate Committee on Foreign Relations, March 1977, pp. 133–34.

9. For more detail on Somoza's lobbying activities, see Lars Schoultz, *Human Rights and U.S. Policy toward Latin America* (Princeton: Princeton University Press, 1981), pp. 58–64; and Diederich, *Somoza*, pp. 130–35. Both authors tend to exaggerate the importance of the lobbyists, taking their self-promotional boasts at face value.

10. WGBH interview with John Murphy, May 15, 1984, Danbury, Connecticut. Murphy, who had served nine terms in the House, was indicted on June 18, 1980, and subsequently convicted for conspiracy and bribery charges resulting from the FBI's ABSCAM investigation. He served sixteen months in Federal prison.

11. My conclusions about Wilson's motivations are based on numerous conversations with him, as well as an interview on July 31, 1985. When asked by a reporter whether Somoza was too corrupt and repressive to receive military aid, Wilson said: "I think that's real bullshit, and you can quote me." "Charlie Wilson: What's He Done for Nicaragua Lately?" *Texas Observer*, September 23, 1977, pp. 1–2, 22.

12. Amnesty International was extremely critical of the abuses of the National Guard from 1974 to 1977. However, by the release of the report in August 1977, the Catholic Church in Nicaragua acknowledged that Somoza had ended the abuses. One of Riding's sources said: "Since March, we haven't received any reliable report of a massacre. The National Guard has definitely been told to clean up its act." *New York Times*, August 16, 1977, p. 6.

13. Diederich, *Somoza*, pp. 136–38. Somoza claims his attack occurred while doing his daily Canadian Air Force exercises. Somoza, *Nicaragua Betrayed*, pp. 72–73.

14. Somoza, *Nicaragua Betrayed*, pp. 72–73; Diederich, *Somoza*, p. 139. Somoza, who was never accused of spending his own money extravagantly, complained in his memoirs that the flight cost him $30,000 and took seven hours.

15. Author's interviews with Max Kelly, Somoza's personal aide, February 13, 1984, Miami, Florida; and with Luis Pallais, October 16, 1985, Miami.

16. This account is based on an interview with Daniel Oduber, May 19, 1984, Falmouth, Massachusetts. In his memoirs, Somoza alleges that I told Oduber in June 1977: "When are we going to get that son of a bitch up to the north out of the presidency?" Oduber confirmed that I had not said that, but Oduber also acknowledged that he tried to use my remarks as a lever to get Somoza to leave.

17. John Goshko and Karen DeYoung, "U.S. Aid to Nicaragua: 'Garbled' Human Rights Message," *Washington Post*, October 24, 1977, p. A1; and Karen DeYoung, "Nicaragua Denied Economic Aid, Gets Military," *Washington Post*, October 5, 1977, p. A10.

18. Chilean writer Marta Harnecker did an extensive interview with Humberto Ortega that was first published in *Granma*, January 27, 1980, entitled, "La Estrategia de la Victoria." It is a remarkably candid and credible description of the Sandinistas' political-military strategy to gain power. I cite from the English translation in Borge et al., *Sandinistas Speak*, p. 56 [hereafter H. Ortega, "Strategy"].

19. Author's interview with Tomás Borge, August 4, 1983, Managua.

20. H. Ortega, "Strategy," p. 59.

21. These raids were later described by several of the Sandinista combatants in a book of interviews by Pilar Arias, *Nicaragua: Revolución, Relatos de Combatientes del Frente Sandinista* (Mexico: Siglo Veintiuno Editores, 1981), pp. 134–39. The attacks involved very few Sandinistas but were judged a success by one, José Valdivia, "because it received great international news."

22. Somoza, *Nicaragua Betrayed*, p. 86.

23. Alan Riding, "Nicaraguan Rebels Deny Marxist Aim: Guerrillas Seek Broad Support and Vow Free Elections If Bid to Topple Somoza Succeeds," *New York Times*, October 26, 1977, p. 9.

24. Cited in Luigi Einaudi, ed., *Beyond Cuba: Latin America Takes Charge of Its Future* (New York: Crane, Russak, and Co., 1974), p. 30.

25. The statement was circulated in Washington the day of the announcement. A variation on the statement can be found in *The Central American Crisis Reader,* ed. Robert S. Leiken and Barry Rubin (New York: Summit Books, 1987), pp. 172–73.

26. Sergio Ramírez explains the origin of the Group of Twelve in an interview in Arias, *Nicaragua: Revolución,* pp. 129–33, supplemented by an interview with the author, February 8, 1986, Managua.

27. Author's interview with Arturo Cruz, October 2, 1986, Atlanta.

28. WGBH interview with Edén Pastora, July 1, 1984, Washington, D.C.

29. WGBH interview with José Figueres, June 8, 1984, San José, Costa Rica.

30. Author's interview with Alfonso Robelo, July 29–30, 1983, San José, Costa Rica.

31. That was the conclusion of Gary Sick, *All Fall Down* (New York: Random House, 1985), p. 34.

32. Author's interview with Pedro Joaquín Chamorro Barrios, July 26, 1983, San José, Costa Rica. The Sandinista government held a trial, and in June 1981, found a Miami-based Cuban exile, Pedro Ramos, and eight Nicaraguans guilty of Chamorro's murder. *La Prensa* had published a series of articles exposing Ramos for corruption shortly before Chamorro's murder. *Latin America Weekly Report,* June 26, 1981, p. 12.

33. WGBH interview with Carlos Andrés Pérez, May 2, 1984, New York City.

34. *Public Papers of the Presidents of the United States, Jimmy Carter, 1977,* vol. II, p. 1296.

35. See, for example, Robert G. Kaiser, "Brzezinski, Vance Are Watched for Hint of a Policy Struggle," *Washington Post,* March 28, 1977, p. A2.

36. Zbigniew Brzezinski, *Between Two Ages: America's Role in the Technetronic Era* (New York: The Viking Press, 1970), p. 288.

37. Zbigniew Brzezinski, "America in a Hostile World," *Foreign Policy,* no. 23 (Summer 1976): 96.

38. In October 1976, Vance prepared a detailed memorandum for Carter setting out specific goals and priorities for U.S. foreign policy. The memorandum is reprinted as Appendix I in Vance's memoirs. The section on Latin America resembles the comments of Brzezinski and the reports of the Linowitz Commission on U.S.-Latin American Relations. See Cyrus Vance, *Hard Choices* (New York: Simon and Schuster, 1983), pp. 451–52.

39. For the two views on this issue, see Vance, *Hard Choices,* pp. 84–88; and Zbigniew Brzezinski, *Power and Principle: Memoirs of a National Security Adviser, 1977–1981* (New York: Farrar, Straus, Giroux, 1983), pp. 178–85.

40. Author's interview with Alfonso Robelo, July 29–30, 1983, San José, Costa Rica.

41. In retrospect, the last comment was revealing, because both the moderate opposition and Somoza were then seeking U.S. involvement in Nicaragua, albeit on different sides. Only the Sandinistas, who viewed the United States as the enemy, wanted it to be neutral.

42. Author's interview with General José Antonio Olavarría, Deputy Director of Venezuela's National Security Council (1977–81), December 14, 1986, Casa de Campo, Dominican Republic.

43. WGBH interviews with Edén Pastora, July 1, 1984, Washington D.C.; and with Carlos Andrés Pérez, May 2, 1984, New York City.

44. The Administration did request $150,000 for military training, but this is separate from military aid. For the first time since the military program began, Somoza's government did not officially request military aid for the 1979 fiscal year budget. Senate Human Rights Report, pp. 193–95.

45. John M. Goshko, "U.S. Frees Aid to Nicaragua in a Policy Reversal," *Washington Post,* May 16, 1978, pp. A1, 18.

46. In a speech he gave to the OAS on June 21, 1978, Carter himself had written the italicized part of the following sentence: "*We prefer to take actions that are positive,* but where nations persist in serious violations of human rights, we will continue to demonstrate that there are costs. . . ." *Public Papers of the Presidents, Jimmy Carter, 1978,* vol. I, pp. 1141–46.

47. Somoza devotes an entire chapter of his book to the letter, which had an extraordinary roller-coaster effect on him. He first saw it as a sign he had won over Carter, but on reflection, saw it as another attempt to undermine him. Somoza, *Nicaragua Betrayed,* ch. 10. The letter is reproduced on pp. 276–77.

48. Author's interview with Max Kelly, a Nicaraguan adviser to Somoza since his graduation from West Point in 1970, February 13, 1984, Miami, Florida. Murphy confirmed this point in his interview with WGBH, May 15, 1984, Danbury, Connecticut.

49. Somoza, *Nicaragua Betrayed*, pp. 137–38.

50. Both Pérez (WGBH interview) and Somoza (*Nicaragua Betrayed*, pp. 138–44) have described the meeting in ways that add to the other's account without contradicting it. I have also been able to confirm other aspects of the conversation with Manolo Reboso, a Cuban-American who accompanied Somoza on the trip; Max Kelly; and with Carlos Andrés Pérez on September 22, 1982.

51. Somoza, *Nicaragua Betrayed*, pp. 137–38.

52. WGBH interview with Carlos Andrés Pérez, May 2, 1984, New York City.

53. Correspondence with the author from Jimmy Carter, August 19, 1985.

54. These are the words used by Vance's special assistant, who called Goshko to try to identify the leaker. Author's interview with John Goshko, June 24, 1985, Washington, D.C.

55. "Somoza Letter Called Joint Effort," *Washington Post*, August 2, 1978, p. A7. The literature on U.S. policy toward Nicaragua has, without exception, used the first Goshko article, rather than the clarification, and has described it as "congratulatory." For example, Booth, *The End and the Beginning*, p. 130; Walker, *Nicaragua: The Land of Sandino*, p. 112. Lars Schoultz suggested it undermined Carter's entire human rights policy; see Schoultz, *Human Rights and U.S. Policy toward Latin America*, p. 117.

56. Somoza, *Nicaragua Betrayed*, pp. 146–47. See also Diederich, *Somoza*, pp. 172–73. Diederich cited a Somoza aide, who said that Somoza's final reaction to the letter was that "Carter was telling Tacho he ran a dictatorship."

57. Diederich describes how. *Somoza*, pp. 177–83.

58. Diederich, *Somoza*, p. 184. This was the consensus of virtually all the reporters who covered the event.

59. Tad Szulc, "Rocking Nicaragua: The Rebels' Own Story," *Washington Post*, September 3, 1978, p. C1.

60. Author's interviews with Edén Pastora, November 14, 1983, Washington, D.C.; Tomás Borge, August 4, 1983, Managua; and Rafael Solís, Secretary to the Council of State, August 2, 1983, Managua.

61. H. Ortega, "Strategy," in Borge et al. *Sandinistas Speak*, p. 69.

62. Karen DeYoung, "Nicaragua Reports It Has Suppressed Anti-Somoza Plot," *Washington Post*, August 29, 1978, p. A12.

63. Diederich, *Somoza*, p. 197. Richard Millett's sources in Nicaragua led him to conclude that Somoza had Allegret killed (author's interview, Atlanta, February 23, 1987), but both Lt. Col. James McCoy, the U.S. Military Attaché, and Luis Pallais insisted that Allegret was not plotting against Somoza, and Somoza did not have him killed. Author's interviews with McCoy and with Pallais, both October 16, 1985, Miami, Florida.

64. "Church in Nicaragua Urges Somoza to Quit to Quell Civil Unrest," *New York Times*, August 5, 1978, p. A22.

65. Luis Pallais, the President of the Nicaraguan Congress, revealed the existence of this special force in an interview with WGBH, May 17, 1984, Miami, Florida.

66. H. Ortega, "Strategy," in Borge et al., *Sandinistas Speak*, pp. 66, 62.

67. Somoza's interview was with ACAN-EFE, but republished in *FBIS*, September 5, 1978, p. P2. The interview with Dora María Tellez was published by *FBIS*, September 5, 1978, pp. N4–5, annex 2.

68. Alan Riding, "In Nicaragua, This May Be the Twilight of the Somozas," *New York Times*, October 30, 1977, p. IV, 3.

Chapter 5

1. Cited in Murray Marder, "Panel Predicted Shah's Ouster," *Washington Post*, December 23, 1984, p. A11.

2. Harold Milks, "'Somoza or Communism,' Nicaraguan Leader Warns," *Arizona Republic*, September 5, 1978, reprinted in *Congressional Record*, House, September 6, 1978, p. H9068.

3. These characterizations of Vaky's views are the result of years of conversations with him, a long interview on July 24, 1985, Washington, D.C., and his comments on a draft of this manuscript.

4. For a good description of the way the NSC was organized under President Carter, see Brzezinski, *Power and Principle*, pp. 57–63.

5. *Public Papers of the Presidents of the United States, Jimmy Carter, 1978*, vol. II, p. 1521.

6. Correspondence with the author from Jimmy Carter, August 19, 1985. Carter's recollection is based on his diary.

7. Author's interview with Rodrigo Carazo Odío, July 30, 1983, San José, Costa Rica.

8. Correspondence with the author from Viron Peter Vaky, September 8, 1986.

9. His speech is in the *Department of State Bulletin*, January 1979, pp. 57–58.

10. Author's telephone interview with William Jorden, March 12, 1987.

11. This is an excerpt from Carter's diary, which he sent to the author August 19, 1985. These events were reconstructed from the author's interviews with Gabriel Lewis Galindo (many occasions), Viron Peter Vaky (many occasions), and Zbigniew Brzezinski (July 17, 1985, Washington, D.C.).

12. The President's statement is in *Public Papers of the Presidents of the United States, Jimmy Carter, 1978*, vol. II, pp. 1596–1602.

13. White House transcript of "Interview with Zbigniew Brzezinski for Latin American Editors," September 22, 1978.

14. For a brief biographical sketch of Torrijos, see my article, "Remembering Omar Torrijos: Ode to Omar," *The New Republic*, August 15, 1981.

15. Author's interview with Carlos Andrés Pérez, Washington, D.C., September 22, 1982. Gabriel Lewis also filled in some of the gaps of this story in an interview in Panama on December 28, 1982.

16. Author's interview with Gabriel Lewis Galindo, December 28, 1982, Panama.

17. The entire published record of the mediation and its origins is compiled in the *Report to the Secretary of State on the Work of the International Commission of Friendly Cooperation and Conciliation for Achieving a Peaceful Solution to the Grave Crisis of the Republic of Nicaragua*, 1979.

18. Excerpts from the meeting are reproduced in Somoza's memoirs, *Nicaragua Betrayed*, pp. 313–24. The meeting, however, is incorrectly dated as occurring in November.

19. Author's interview with William D. Rogers, May 22, 1985, Washington, D.C. Christopher does not recall these points, nor does he remember whether he or Vance spoke to Carter about it (letter to the author, December 10, 1986). Carter also does not recall this exchange. I would judge that only Rogers focused on these conditions, which went considerably beyond the Administration's position at that time. Rogers had also set a stiff condition when he assisted negotiations on Panama, and then he had acquiesced when it was violated. See William Jorden, *Panama Odyssey* (Austin: University of Texas Press, 1984), p. 579.

20. Somoza, *Nicaragua Betrayed*, p. 318.

21. Correspondence with author from Viron Peter Vaky, September 8, 1986.

22. *New York Times*, September 26, 1978, p. 56.

23. *FBIS*, October 5, 1978, p. 9.

24. Somoza, *Nicaragua Betrayed*, p. 216.

25. Author's interview with Edén Pastora, November 14, 1983, Washington, D.C.

26. Alfonso Robelo said in an interview printed in the *Washington Star*, September 25, 1978: "Somoza's resignation is the solution."

27. H. Ortega, "Strategy," in Borge et al., *Sandinistas Speak*, p. 72.

28. Interview with Sergio Ramírez, in Arias, *Nicaragua: Revolución*, p. 169.

29. Author's interview with Tomás Borge, August 4, 1983, Managua.

30. Gale McGee recounted this conversation for me on September 5, 1978. It was the only bright spot that day.

31. See, for example, the testimony of Stanford University Professor Richard Fagen before the Senate Foreign Relations Committee, *Latin America*, October 4–6, 1978, pp. 35–36. Church groups in the U.S. were reflecting the changes occurring in the churches in Latin America. See James R. Goff, "Latin American Churches Want Somoza to Resign," *Washington Post*, October 13, 1978.

32. William P. Bundy, "Who Lost Patagonia? Foreign Policy in the 1980 Campaign," *Foreign Affairs* (Fall 1979): 6.

Chapter 6

1. Author's interview with Alfonso Robelo, July 29–30, 1983, San José, Costa Rica.

2. Sergio Ramírez described this in an interview with Arias, *Nicaragua: Revolución,* pp. 170–71.

3. Ramírez interview in Arias, *Nicaragua: Revolución,* p. 171.

4. Correspondence with the author from Viron Peter Vaky, September 8, 1987.

5. After the IMF vote on November 1, Somoza communicated a message to me through Reboso that he considered the vote "an act of hostility," and if we kept behaving like that, he would "no longer consider the U.S. a friend."

6. Richard Millett reports considerable unhappiness among junior officers when Somoza first assigned Gutierrez abroad. *Guardians,* pp. 227–28.

7. Somoza, *Nicaragua Betrayed,* pp. 219–20.

8. This is Vaky's recollection of what Bowdler told him.

9. Career officials are sometimes accused of "clientilism"—defending the positions of foreigners—rather than advancing the positions of the United States, and political appointees are often accused of "tunnel vision"—projecting U.S. values abroad where they don't fit. Both charges have some validity, but miss the pivotal question of *which* foreign interests a career official chooses to defend—a dictator, the middle class, the poor?—and which U.S. values a political appointee attaches highest priority to.

10. It is significant that Vance's decision to omit a State Department recommendation because he disagreed with his line officers occurred in the middle of Carter's term. The longer an Administration is in office, the more the Cabinet Secretaries are drawn to their department's institutional perspective, widening the gap between the department and the President and the NSC.

11. Correspondence with the author from Jimmy Carter, August 19, 1985. Though Shirley Christian did not speak with either Carter or Bowdler, she reports that Carter asked Bowdler whether Somoza was a "moral man." (*Nicaragua: Revolution in the Family,* p. 77). Carter does not recall asking such a question, and Bowdler would not comment on the conversation.

12. Author's interview with Luis Pallais, October 16, 1985, Miami, Florida.

13. Author's interview with Viron Peter Vaky, July 24, 1985, Washington, D.C. On reflection, Vaky thought he might have missed the significance of Pallais' questions at the time because of the "noise" of other events and distractions.

14. "Communiqué to the Nicaraguan People from the National Directorate of the FSLN-GPP, PC of the FSLN-TP, General Staff of the War Resistance, FSLN-Insurrectional," December 9, 1978, published in *Latin American Perspectives* 6 (Winter 1979): 127–28. Ramírez later said: "If the plebiscite had occurred, it would have been an opportunity—imperialism's last—to unseat Somoza and preserve Somocismo." In Arias, *Nicaragua: Revolución,* p. 170.

15. Author's interview with Edén Pastora, November 14, 1983, Washington, D.C.

16. Author's interview with Luis Pallais, October 16, 1986, Miami, Florida. Pallais' account that Somoza was serious about a plebiscite until the third week in December is credible because he was the only one of Somoza's entourage to admit that Somoza deliberately decided against the plebiscite at the time of the Cabinet meeting.

17. Somoza, *Nicaragua Betrayed,* p. 328. Citations come from the transcript of the tape that Somoza took of the conversation.

18. Somoza wanted to change the simple question of whether he should remain in office to a two-part question: Should Somoza complete his constitutional term? Should a national constituent assembly be convened? Other than the fact that the relationship between the two questions is uncertain and confusing, particularly for a barely literate campesino, the second question leaves open the possibility that Somoza could manipulate and control the constituent assembly if he were to fail to win approval on the first question. For that reason, the FAO rejected this question.

19. Author's interviews with Jimmy Carter, January 28, 1982, Plains, Georgia, and October 11, 1984, Panama; WGBH interview with John Murphy, July 31, 1985, Danbury, Connecticut. Several writers, such as Shirley Christian (*Nicaragua: Revolution in the Family*, pp. 87–88) and William LeoGrande ("Revolution in Nicaragua," p. 35), have suggested that Murphy's influence on the Canal legislation constrained Carter on Nicaragua. Christian even insinuates that there might have been a deal on the two issues between the two men. She offers no evidence, however, and both men deny it.

20. Author's interview with Jimmy Carter, October 11, 1984, Panama; correspondence dated on August 19, 1985. Carter also said that he never saw any evidence that Murphy was successful in convincing Somoza. Somoza, *Nicaragua Betrayed*, p. 226.

21. Somoza, *Nicaragua Betrayed*, p. 226.

22. Letter from Rep. John Murphy to President Jimmy Carter, January 22, 1979; response from Secretary of State Cyrus Vance on February 10, 1979. Carter Presidential Library, Atlanta.

23. The announcement is in the *Department of State Bulletin*, April 1979, p. 66. It was a mistake to include the Peace Corps in the announcement. Although the rationale for withdrawing them was that we feared for their safety in another round of violence, inclusion of the Peace Corps unintentionally politicized an organization whose strength remains its neutrality and autonomy.

Chapter 7

1. H. Ortega, "Strategy," in Borge et al., *Sandinistas Speak*, pp. 77–79.

2. Author's interview with Viron Peter Vaky, July 24, 1985, Washington, D.C.

3. Author's interview with Alfonso Robelo, July 29–30, 1983, San José, Costa Rica. Pastora was referring to the FSLN's unity agreement in December in Havana.

4. Cited in Diederich, *Somoza*, pp. 235–36.

5. Cited in Diederich, *Somoza*, pp. 230–31.

6. *Washington Post*, March 17, 1979, p. A20

7. Karen DeYoung, "Sandinistas Try Pulling Together to Bring Down Somoza," *Washington Post*, April 5, 1979, p. A22.

8. Author's interview with Alfonso Robelo, July 29–30, 1983, San José, Costa Rica.

9. Author's interview with Rodrigo Carazo Odío, July 30, 1983, San José, Costa Rica.

10. For an excellent summary of the involvement of international organizations in the Nicaraguan crisis, see Dennis R. Gordon and Margaret M. Munro, "The External Dimension of Civil Insurrection: International Organizations and the Nicaraguan Revolution," *Journal of Inter-American Studies and World Affairs* 25 (February 1983): 59–81.

11. H. Ortega, "Strategy," in Borge et al., *Sandinistas Speak*, p. 77

12. Author's interview with Rodrigo Carazo Odío, July 30, 1983, San José, Costa Rica.

13. Asamblea Legislativa, San José, Costa Rica, Comisión de Asuntos Especiales, *Informe Sobre el Trafico de Armas, Primera Parte, Epe 8768*, 14 Mayo 1981, pp. 16–18, 5 [hereafter Costa Rican Arms Report]. The commission was established on June 25, 1980, after some of the arms originally imported for the Sandinistas were discovered to have been sent to the Salvadoran guerrillas. The principal concern of the commission, which was modeled on the Watergate investigation, were allegations that high officials in the Carazo Administration may have made money as middlemen for the arms shipments. The final report condemned Carazo for *not informing* the Costa Rican people, but he was not condemned for aiding the Sandinistas, because in 1981 Costa Ricans were still proud of their nation's role in overthrowing Somoza.

14. Author's interview with Viron Peter Vaky, July 24, 1985, Washington, D.C.

15. WGBH interview with Carlos Andrés Pérez, May 2, 1984, New York City.

16. Ibid., and confirmed in Pallais interview with WGBH, May 17, 1984, Miami Florida.

17. Carlos Andrés Pérez recounted his view of the conversation in an interview with the author, January 28, 1987, Atlanta.

18. Author's interview with Arístides Calvani, January 22, 1985, Washington, D.C.

19. Author's interview with General José Antonio Olavarría, December 14, 1986, in Casa de Campo, Dominican Republic. Olavarría was Deputy Director of Venezuela's National Security Council, which was responsible for shipping the arms.

20. Author's interview with Carlos Andrés Pérez, January 28, 1987, Atlanta.

21. This information was confirmed by the Costa Rican Legislative Commission. See Costa Rican Arms Report, pp. 10–11.

22. Costa Rican Arms Report, pp. 19–20. Edén Pastora said he received several large shipments of arms that Jaime Wheelock purchased in Portugal. Cited in Claribel Alegría and D. J. Flakoll, *Nicaragua: La Revolución Sandinista* (Mexico: Serie Popular Era, 1982), p. 372

23. Author's interview with Rodrigo Carazo Odío, July 30, 1983, San José, Costa Rica.

24. Walker, *Nicaragua: The Land of Sandino*, p. 38.

25. The report was later leaked and reprinted in the *Congressional Record*, Senate, May 19, 1980, pp. 11653–55. Whether the Cuban assessment was disinformation or simply wrong is not known.

26. The following account is a composite taken from many sources. Most important were the author's interviews with Santiago Roel, Mexican Foreign Minister (1976–79) and José Juan De Olloquí, Under Secretary of Foreign Relations of Mexico (1976–79), both on June 13, 1986, Mexico City; interview with Jorge G. Castañeda, a former adviser to the Foreign Ministry (August 25, 1986, Mexico City), and his article, "Don't Corner Mexico," *Foreign Policy* (Fall 1985); and many other interviewees, who asked to remain anonymous.

27. Alan Riding, "Castro, Citing Blockade, Lays Poor Relations to the United States," *New York Times,* May 19, 1979, p. 2.

28. The irony of the juxtaposition of that decision with the Castro visit was that Mexico had rejected the decision by the OAS to break diplomatic relations with Cuba in 1964 because of Mexico's adherence to the Estrada Doctrine, which calls for relations with all regimes regardless of ideology.

29. Cited in Marlise Simons, "Mexico Leads Major Regional Effort to Isolate Somoza," *Washington Post,* May 23, 1979. p. A17.

30. Cited in *New York Times,* May 30, 1979, p. A3.

31. See, for example, two articles by Alan Riding in the *New York Times:* "Nicaraguans Brace for Fresh Violence: Rebels Plan New Offensive as Bid to Set Up a Vote on Somoza's Rule Appears to Collapse," January 17, 1979, p. 7; and "Nicaragua on Edge as Rebels Prepare," March 21, 1979, p. 2.

32. "Nicaragua's Military Says It Broke Rebel Offensive," *New York Times,* June 1, 1979, p. A7.

33. The key elements of both letters were reprinted in Fred Barnes, "Royo Assures Carter Panama Won't Intervene in Nicaragua," *Washington Star,* June 10, 1979.

34. Shirley Christian's sources told her that was the case (*Nicaragua: Revolution in the Family*), pp. 95–96. In addition, the Costa Rican Legislative Commission confirmed that by late May, Pastora was receiving arms in Costa Rica directly from Cuba.

35. Graham Hovey, "Panama Is Accused of Aiding Sandinistas," *New York Times,* June 7, 1979, p. 3.

36. Office of the White House Press Secretary, "Remarks of the President at a Briefing for Members of Congress on the Panama Canal Implementing Legislation," June 11, 1979.

37. Declassified cable from the U.S. Secretary of State to all American Republic Diplomatic Posts, 15 June 1979, State 153522, "OAS Action on Nicaragua."

38. A démarche is an official request to a foreign government to take a specific action.

39. Somoza acknowledged the symbolic and real importance of the recall of the Israeli ship. *Nicaragua Betrayed,* p. 239.

40. Carter's popularity sank to a rating lower than Nixon's had been two months before he resigned. Political instability in Iran and the strengthening of OPEC led to a shortage of gasoline, a rise in prices, and the beginning of hyperinflation in the United States.

41. Author's interviews with Alfonso Robelo, July 29–30, 1983, San José, Costa Rica; and with Tomás Borge, August 4, 1983, Managua.

42. For a description of these events, see Karen DeYoung, "Andean Nations Provide Sandinistas a Diplomatic Opening," *Washington Post,* June 18, 1979, p. A20.

Chapter 8

1. Tomás Borge told me this was the reason he opposed an OAS meeting. He admitted his surprise with its outcome. Author's interview with Tomás Borge, August 4, 1983, Managua.

2. *Public Papers of the Presidents of the United States, Jimmy Carter, 1979,* vol. II, p. 1092.

3. Alan Riding, "Rebels in Nicaragua Name Five to Form Provisional Junta," *New York Times,* June 18, 1979, p. 1.

4. Quoted in William Long, "Key Rebel Dreams of New Nicaragua with 'Democracy,'" *Miami Herald,* June 23, 1979.

5. Quoted in Bernard Diederich, "New Nicaragua Front: Rebels Deny Cuba Tie," *Washington Star,* June 24, 1979.

6. Author's interview with Carlos Andrés Pérez, January 28, 1987, Atlanta.

7. Author's interview with Viron Peter Vaky, July 24, 1985, Washington, D.C.

8. For his speech and the final resolution, see *Department of State Bulletin,* August 1979, pp. 56–59.

9. Portions of the secret session on June 20 were published in the *Congressional Record* on July 17, 1979, pp. H6054–6064. Wright's statement was on p. H6059. On June 21, the House voted narrowly to keep the two issues separate, and to pass Murphy's bill to implement the Canal treaties by a vote of 224 to 202.

10. "A Painful Decision for Carter: President's Belief That Disaster May Be Imminent in Nicaragua Overturns Nonintervention Resolve," *New York Times,* June 22, 1979, p. 1.

11. Author's interview with Jorge Castañeda G., son and adviser to the former Foreign Minister. August 25, 1986, Mexico City.

12. That "creeping intervention" culminated in a Soviet invasion in December 1979. For Brzezinski's views, see his *Power and Principle,* p. 426.

13. These quotes are from Zbigniew Brzezinski's diary—as read to me—in an interview on July 17, 1985, Washington, D.C. For the meeting on June 22, and others that I did not attend, his recollections are the only ones available. I interviewed three other participants—Carter, Vance, and Brown—and they do not recall what was said.

14. For the resolution, see *Department of State Bulletin,* August 1979, p. 58. The Inter-American Human Rights Commission later described the resolution in the following terms: "For the first time in the history of the OAS and perhaps for the first time in the history of any international organization, [the resolution] deprived an incumbent government of a member state of the Organization of legitimacy, based on the human rights violations committed by that government against its own population." Organization of American States, Inter-American Commission on Human Rights, *Report on Nicaragua,* June 30, 1981, p. 2.

15. Diederich, *Somoza,* p. 281.

16. Somoza, *Nicaragua Betrayed,* pp. 263–67.

17. Cable from U.S. Embassy, Managua, to the Secretary of State, 24 June 1979, Managua 2787, "Message to the FAO." This is one of a number of secret cables that have been declassified. They offer a clearer view of developments during this period than was possible to reconstruct from the memories of several of the participants. These cables are available at the National Security Archive in Washington, D.C.

18. Somoza had the tapes of four of his conversations transcribed and included in his book. Pezzullo said they appear accurate but "doctored"—portions put in different order, some of Pezzullo's questions read as if they were his statements, and vice versa. Author's interview with Lawrence Pezzullo, July 30, 1985, New York City; Somoza, *Nicaragua Betrayed,* pp. 333–82.

19. The parallels are striking. In Cuba, Batista blocked the release of Col. Barquín—a comparable figure—from prison in 1958 for the same reason. More recently, the Shah of Iran prevented the return of General Jam, who could have been a credible transitional Minister of Defense. Sick, *All Fall Down,* pp. 120–21.

20. Author's telephone conversation with Ambler Moss, Jr., August 1, 1985.

21. The account of the Embassy and Managua is a composite based on declassified cables and the author's interviews with Lawrence Pezzullo, July 30, 1985, New York City, and several staff members from

the Embassy in Managua. Also see Lawrence and Ralph Pezzullo, *At the Fall of Somoza* (Pittsburgh: University of Pittsburgh Press, 1993).

22. Author's interview with James L. McCoy, October 16, 1985, Miami, Florida.

23. Declassified cable from U.S. Embassy, Managua, to Secretary of State, 28 June 1979, Managua 2861, "FAO Communique."

24. Declassified cable from U.S. Embassy, Managua, to Secretary of State, 28 June 1979, Managua 2870, "The Current Scene."

25. Declassified cable from U.S. Embassy, Managua, to Secretary of State, 28 June 1979, Managua 2876.

26. Declassified cable from U.S. Embassy, Managua, to Secretary of State, 29 June 1979, Managua 2887, "Meeting with Red Cross President."

27. Declassified cable from Secretary of State to U.S. Embassy, Managua, 29 June 1979, State 167430, "Discussion with G-12 Member Arturo Cruz."

28. Author's interview with Jimmy Carter, October 11, 1984, Panama.

29. Declassified cable from U.S. Embassy, Managua, to Secretary of State, 30 June 1979, Managua 2914, "National Guard Survival."

30. Declassified cable from U.S. Embassy, Managua, to Secretary of State, 30 June 1979, Managua 2919, "Nicaraguan Scenario."

31. Author's interviews with Alfonso Robelo, July 29–30, 1983, San José, Costa Rica; and Alfredo César, April 9, 1984, Washington, D.C. The statements that follow are based on those interviews as well.

32. In San José and Managua, the public learned of the *New York Times* disclosure of the "U.S. Plan" on June 29, and Washington learned of their reaction on June 30, 1979, the same day that Pezzullo's two cables on the ExCom and the Guard arrived.

33. Torrijos told me this at the time.

34. For much of Torrijos' thinking during the trip, and also for his behavior, I rely on my own impressions at the time and interviews with Ambassador Gabriel Lewis, who accompanied Torrijos, and Ambassador Ambler Moss, Jr.

35. Gabriel Lewis later told me this story, which sounded more credible than the one he had told me that evening when I received his phone call in the White House.

36. This is my interpretation of the meetings.

37. This, like the other references, is directly from Brzezinski's diary.

38. WGBH interview with Lawrence Pezzullo, May 15, 1984, New York City.

Chapter 9

1. Author's interview with Tomás Borge, August 4, 1983, Managua. Interviews with Borge, Robelo, and Alfredo César were helpful in reconstructing the negotiations with the Junta at this time. Carlos Andrés Pérez, who was involved in the negotiations, recalled that Robelo said "he would resign if the Junta is enlarged because the idea originated in the White House. Then, Borge rejected Robelo's statement . . . [and] Ortega supported Borge." Pérez explained that an article in the *Washington Post* that had been reprinted in Central America, indicating that the expansion of the Junta was a U.S. idea, made the moderates more intransigent. Author's interview with Carlos Andrés Pérez, January 28, 1987, Atlanta.

2. Interview with Sergio Ramírez in Arias, *Nicaragua: Revolución,* p. 201.

3. Declassified cable from U.S. Embassy, Managua, to Secretary of State, 6 July 1979, Managua 3633, "Negotiations with FSLN."

4. These negotiations are the composite of interviews by the author with Ambler Moss, Jr., U.S. Ambassador to Panama, telephone conversation, August 1, 1985; William Bowdler, July 23, 1985, Sharps, Virginia; Marvin Weissman, U.S. Ambassador to Costa Rica, July 17, 1985, Washington, D.C.; and Lawrence Pezzullo, December 16, 1982, Washington, D.C.

5. Author's interview with Rodrigo Carazo Odío, July 30, 1983, San José, Costa Rica.

6. Author's interviews with Gabriel Lewis and Ambler Moss, Jr. Each used the cited words to describe Torrijos's often-stated belief.

7. Karen De Young, "Somoza agrees to Quit, Leaves Timing to U.S.," *Washington Post*, July 7, 1979, pp. A1, 3. Most people in Nicaragua and most of the leadership of the Guard were unaware of this report. Author's interview with Col. Carlos Agurto, October 22, 1985, Miami, Florida.

8. Cited in *New York Times*, July 14, 1979, p. 2; and *Newsweek*, July 23, 1979, p. 56.

9. Karen De Young, "Nicaraguan Rebels Call for Military Including Guardsmen," *Washington Post*, July 12, 1979, p. A21; also see *New York Times*, July 12, 1979, p. 14.

10. Author's interview with Carlos Andrés Pérez, January 28, 1987, Atlanta. Carazo confirmed this was Pérez's idea.

11. For the full text of the Junta's letter to the OAS, see Organization of American States, Inter-American Commission on Human Rights, *Report on the Situation of Human Rights in the Republic of Nicaragua*, June 30, 1981, pp. 4–6.

12. Carazo wanted the United States to rely more on Pastora, as he was doing, but at the same time he recognized that Pastora didn't trust the United States. Author's interviews with him (July 30, 1983, San José, Costa Rica) and Pastora (November 14, 1983, Washington, D.C.).

13. Stephen Gorman and Thomas W. Walker, "The Armed Forces," in *Nicaragua: The First Five Years*, ed. Thomas W. Walker (New York: Praeger, 1985), p. 100.

14. Military contacts between U.S. and Latin American officers have always been subject to the widest divergence in perceptions because both sides project their own institutions onto alien landscapes. The U.S. military avoids politics at home and abroad. U.S. officers are aware that their Latin counterparts often play pivotal political roles, but they still relate to them in the direct, matter-of-fact manner that they relate to each other. Latin military officers similarly assume that their U.S. counterparts are as powerful in the United States as Latin American officers are in their countries. Leaders as different and as politically sophisticated as Omar Torrijos and Anastasio Somoza Debayle both thought the Pentagon played a much larger, if not the only, role in the policy process.

15. Defense Attaché James L. McCoy denied this was the case, although he also mentioned that he knew of one case—described below—when Somoza personally called the U.S. Army Chief of Staff. Author's telephone conversation with McCoy, August 15, 1985.

16. Author's interviews with James L. McCoy, August 15, 1985 (telephone conversation), and October 16, 1985, Miami, Florida.

17. Author's telephone conversation with James L. McCoy, August 15, 1985.

18. The following account of the conversation is based on the author's interview with Lawrence Pezzullo, July 30, 1985, New York City.

19. Karen DeYoung, "Somoza Agrees to Quit, Leaves Timing to U.S.," *Washington Post*, July 7, 1979, p. A1.

20. Author's interview with James L. McCoy, October 16, 1985, Miami, Florida.

21. This is Pezzullo's explanation for why he gave lower priority to the Guard. In a cable he sent on July 7 (Managua 3039), Pezzullo acknowledged that he had left to Somoza the responsibility for preserving the Guard, but Somoza "had not yet done so."

22. Author's interview with Lawrence Pezzullo, July 30, 1985, New York City.

23. "Nicaraguan Rebels Say U.S. Is Ready to Back Regime Led by Them," *New York Times*, July 16, 1979.

24. Author's interview with Col. Carlos Agurto, who commanded three battalions of the Guard at the time. October 22, 1985, Miami, Florida.

25. Luis Pallais described the purpose of the trip in an interview with the author, October 16, 1985, Miami, Florida.

26. From the nature of the request, it appeared that the other Central American generals were going through the motions and were seeking to elicit a negative reply.

27. Author's interview with Lawrence Pezzullo, July 30, 1985, New York City.

28. WGBH interview with Francisco Urcuyo Maliaños, May 18, 1984, Miami, Florida, and his book, *Solos* (Guatemala: Editorial Academica Centro Americana, 1979).

29. Author's interview with Lawrence Pezzullo, July 30, 1985, New York City.

30. This is Urcuyo's account (in WGBH interview, May 18, 1984, Miami, Florida). Pezzullo does not recall this conversation. He also does not recall that the Sandinista delegation had even reached Urcuyo.

The Urcuyo account is plausible if one believes that Somoza, or someone else, translated Pezzullo's comment that the plan was "unrealistic" into a suggestion that it was a fabrication.

31. Author's interview with Lawrence Pezzullo, July 30, 1985, New York City.

32. Ibid.

33. This represents a composite interpretation of what happened. Author's interview with Pezzullo (July 30, 1985, New York City) and McCoy (October 16, 1985, Miami, Florida), and WGBH interview with Pezzullo (May 15, 1984, New York City).

34. Transcript of WGBH Public Television series, "Nicaragua."

35. This is a composite interpretation based on my interviews, Urcuyo's book (*Solos*), Shirley Christian's book (*Nicaragua: Revolution in the Family*), and WGBH interviews with Pezzullo (May 14, 1984, New York City) and Urcuyo (May 18, 1984, Miami, Florida). There is a considerable amount of inconsistency on the details—for example, who called whom and when. But on the central points of trading insults, and Mejía's aborted trip, there is no disagreement.

36. Author's interview with Lawrence Pezzullo, July 30, 1985, New York City.

37. Interview with Nuñez, cited by Black, *Triumph of the People*, p. 179.

38. Author's interview with Lawrence Pezzullo, December 16, 1982, Washington, D.C.

39. Christian, *Nicaragua: Revolution in the Family*, p. 115.

40. Shirley Christian's interview with Col. Smith (ibid., p. 114), confirmed and developed further in the author's interviews with Pezzullo (July 30, 1985, New York City) and McCoy (October 16, 1985, Miami, Florida).

41. WGBH interview with John Murphy, July 31, 1985, Danbury, Connecticut.

42. Somoza, *Nicaragua Betrayed*, pp. 390–91. Also WGBH interview with Luis Pallais, May 17, 1984, Miami, Florida.

43. WGBH interview with Francisco Urcuyo Maliaños, May 18, 1984, Miami Florida.

44. Author's interviews with Alfonso Robelo (July 29–30, 1983, San José, Costa Rica) and Alfredo César, April 9, 1984, Washington, D.C.

45. *New York Times*, July 20, 1979, p. 1.

46. Cited in Bernard Diederich, *Somoza*, p. 37.

Chapter 10

1. In his conversation with the Nicaraguan Junta in the White House, September 24, 1979.

2. Cited in Black, *Triumph of the People*, p. 196. Castro's advice was also reported in the *New York Times*, July 9, 1980, p. 10; and *Washington Post*, November 9, 1980, p. A1.

3. See, for example, Maurice Zeitlin and Robert Scheer, *Cuba: Tragedy in Our Hemisphere* (New York: Grove Press, 1963).

4. For a sophisticated variation on this thesis, see Jorge Domínguez, *Cuba: Order and Revolution* (Cambridge: Harvard University Press, 1978).

5. For a fuller development of all three lessons and a test of one case, see Robert Pastor, *Exiting the Whirlpool: U.S. Foreign Policy Toward Latin America* (Boulder, Colo.: Westview Press, 2001), Chapter 9. Also see W. Anthony Lake, "Wrestling with Third World Radical Regimes," in John W. Sewell, ed., *U.S. Foreign Policy and the Third World: Agenda, 1985–86* (New Brunswick, N.J.: Transaction, 1985).

6. Cited by Blasier, *Hovering Giant*, pp. 208, 300 n. 178; and for an elaboration of this point by Bonsal, see *Cuba, Castro, and the United States*, chapter 17.

7. Kissinger's analysis was reported in an NBC documentary, "The Castro Connection," in September 1980. The left also argues that the middle is illusory, and that the United States should support leftist guerrillas because revolutions will inevitably succeed. For example, See Marlene Dixon and Susanne Jonas, eds., *Revolution and Intervention in Central America* (San Francisco: Synthesis Publications, 1983), and LaFeber, *Inevitable Revolutions*.

8. The United Nations study was cited by Viron Peter Vaky in his testimony before the Subcommittee on Inter-American Affairs of the Senate Foreign Relations Committee, *Central America at the Crossroads*,

September 11, 1978, p. 3. Also see Inter-American Human Rights Commission, *Report on the Situation of Human Rights in the Republic of Nicaragua,* June 30, 1981, p. 155.

9. White House Announcement, "Emergency Aid to Nicaragua," July 27, 1979, reprinted in *Weekly Compilation of Presidential Documents,* July 30, 1979.

10. Reprinted in the *New York Times,* July 26, 1979, p. 14.

11. Author's interview with Edén Pastora, November 14, 1983, Washington, D.C.

12. The FSLN later acknowledged that they did not know how many rebels fought Somoza, but they estimated that at the end there were 3,000–5,000 fighters with some 10,000 muchachos (young boys who joined the fighting). Robert Matthews, "The Limits of Friendship," in North American Congress on Latin America (NACLA), *Report of the Americas,* May-June 1985, p. 25.

13. For conservative fears, see Cleto DiGiovanni, Jr., and Alexander Kruger, "Reports: Central America," *Washington Quarterly* 3 (Summer 1980); for fears from the left, see James Petras, "Whither the Nicaraguan Revolution?" *Monthly Review* 31 (October 1979). For a disappointed Mexican perspective, see Jorge Castañeda, *Contradicciones en la Revolución* (Mexico City: Tiempo Extra Editores, 1980).

14. Gobierno de Reconstrucción Nacional, *1979: Año de la Liberación,* June 18, 1979, Algun lugar de Nicaragua. The document was actually issued in San José, Costa Rica.

15. Author's interview with Alfonso Robelo, July 29–30, 1983, San José, Costa Rica. Arturo Cruz, who became president of the Central Bank, was called to the Junta a couple of weeks after the victory to discuss an issue. To his surprise, he saw "some guys in fancy uniforms" alongside the Junta. "It had not dawned on me," Cruz later said, "until then, that the National Directorate was going to run the country." Christian, *Nicaragua: Revolution in the Family,* p. 122. Cruz had evidently forgotten what he had told the State Department official in his conversation on June 29, 1979. See Chapter 9.

16. Pastora told this story to Christopher Dickey, *With the Contras: A Reporter in the Wilds of Nicaragua* (New York: Simon and Schuster, 1985), pp. 31–32. In late August, the Directorate sent a Comandante to Peñas Blancas to assume command of the forces under Leonel Poveda, one of Pastora's closest friends. Poveda asked the Comandante to wait while he went to Managua and asked Pastora "three times if you are sure you want me to do this." Pastora said yes each time, and Poveda returned home to transfer power and retire from the army. Christian, *Nicaragua: Revolution in the Family,* p. 123.

17. Borge describes the chaos at the beginning of the revolution, and the difficulty that the FSLN had in asserting control. Tomás Borge, "On Human Rights in Nicaragua," in Borge et al., *Sandinistas Speak,* pp. 88–90, 102.

18. "Sandinista Staff Discusses National Security, Defense," *FBIS,* news conference on July 28, 1979, published July 30, 1979, pp. P2–5.

19. The Directorate noted that "we cannot divulge [as much] as we would like" because they recognized the "72-Hour Document" could leak, as it did several months later. Nonetheless, it is an authentic glimpse of the Sandinista perspective. The Department of State translated and published it in February 1986 as "Analysis of the Situation and Tasks of the Sandinista People's Revolution." The following quotes are from this translation.

20. For an analysis of this debate by a former Sandinista official, see Arturo Cruz Sequeira, "The Origins of Sandinista Foreign Policy," in *Central America: Anatomy of Conflict,* ed. Leiken.

21. See Stephen M. Gorman, "Power and Consolidation in the Nicaraguan Revolution," *Journal of Latin American Studies* 13 (1981): 133–49; and Richard Fagen, *The Nicaraguan Revolution: A Personal Report* (Washington, D.C.: Institute for Policy Studies, 1981).

22. Inter-American Development Bank, *Economic Report: Nicaragua,* July 1983, Washington, D.C., p. 3.

23. Tomás Borge, "On Human Rights in Nicaragua," a presentation to the Inter-American Human Rights Commission, October 10, 1980, reprinted in Borge et al., *Sandinistas Speak,* p. 95.

24. Author's interview with Tomás Borge, August 4, 1983, Managua. I discussed the self-fulfilling prophecy with him, noting that if he kept calling Yankees imperialists, they might behave like imperialists. He said *his* words would not be responsible.

25. Pastora's remark is also cited in the article, though my question was omitted. See Warren Hoge, "Nicaraguan Official Warns U.S. on Arms," *New York Times,* August 12, 1979, p. 17.

26. *New York Times,* August 13, 1979, p. 3.

27. Torrijos' views were related to me on July 17, 1979, by a senior U.S. military officer who had just spoken with him.

28. Cruz Sequeira, "The Origins of Sandinista Foreign Policy," in *Central America: Anatomy of Conflict*, ed. Leiken, p. 104.

29. William D. Rogers had several long conversations with Torrijos at this time, and recalls how Torrijos' initial exuberance dissipated as he received reports of the number of Cubans in Nicaragua and the disrespectful way the Panamanians felt they were treated by the Sandinistas. Author's interview with William D. Rogers, May 22, 1985, Washington, D.C.

30. Author's telephone conversation with Lawrence Pezzullo, March 19, 1987. Daniel Ortega was incorrect when he said, "We tried to get weapons from the United States, but our efforts were completely blocked," interview with *Playboy*, September 1983, p. 196.

31. The author learned about this for the first time in an interview with General Olavarría on December 14, 1986, in Casa de Campo, Dominican Republic.

32. U.S. House of Representatives, Subcommittee on Inter-American Affairs of the Foreign Affairs Committee, *Central America at the Crossroads*, September 11–12, 1979, pp. 3–4.

33. Ibid., pp. 28–31.

34. An additional $5–10 million was requested for military aid and training for the Caribbean and a similar amount for Central America. The Administration also sought approval for reprogramming $10 million in aid to the Caribbean.

35. Michael Wormser, "Emergency Nicaraguan Aid Bill Survives House Test," *Congressional Quarterly Weekly Report*, March 1, 1980, p. 594.

36. Ibid.

37. *Congressional Record*, February 11, 1980, p. E496. The Administration had deliberately exceeded the level of U.S. support after the earthquake.

38. Cited in *Congressional Quarterly Weekly Report*, May 31, 1980, p. 1519.

39. Republican National Convention, *Republican Platform* (Detroit, July 14, 1980), pp. 68–69.

40. *FBIS*, March 10, 1986, p. P15.

41. *FBIS*, "Security Chief Discussed CIA Activities in Country," March 10, 1980, p. P16.

42. Author's interview with Alfonso Robelo, July 29–30, 1983, San José, Costa Rica. Also, see Shirley Christian's excellent description of this crisis (*Nicaragua: Revolution in the Family*, pp. 147–60).

43. Cited in Christian, *Nicaragua: Revolution in the Family*, pp. 149–50.

44. The discussion of this 1980 mediation is from the author's interview with Lawrence Pezzullo, July 30, 1985, New York City.

45. Robelo's speech is in Fagen, *The Nicaraguan Revolution*, pp. 30–32.

Chapter 11

1. Alan Riding, "Reality Transforms Nicaragua's Revolutionists into Pragmatists," *New York Times*, July 20, 1980, p. E5.

2. For Castro's statements, see Alan Riding, "Castro, in Nicaragua, Chides U.S. But Meets Officials," *New York Times*, July 20, 1980, pp. 1, 13. Messages similar to mine were also passed to Castro by other visitors.

3. For an analysis of the Literacy Crusade and the statistics used here, see Leonor Blum, "The Literacy Campaign: Nicaragua Style," *Caribbean Review* 10, no. 1 (Winter 1981), and Valerie Miller, *Between Struggle and Hope: The Nicaraguan Literacy Crusade* (Boulder: Westview Press, 1985). According to Blum, the teachers' manuals were openly ideological. Even mathematical problems gave examples based on "Yankee imperialist exploitation" and an idealized, equitable Communist system.

4. Ameringer, *Don Pepe*, pp. 153–55. Figueres particularly angered Castro by suggesting that he should give more attention and consideration to U.S. concerns.

5. The speech is reprinted in Robert Leiken and Barry Rubin, eds., *The Central American Crisis Reader* (New York: Summit Books, 1987), pp. 227–29.

6. Robert D. Tomasek, *The Deterioration of Relations between Costa Rica and the Sandinistas* (Washington, D.C.: American Enterprise Institute for Public Policy Research, September 1984).

7. For a description of Mexican foreign policy during this period, see Jorge G. Castañeda, "Don't Corner Mexico," *Foreign Policy*, no. 60 (Fall 1985): 75–90; Bruce Bagley, "Mexican Foreign Policy: The Decline of a Regional Power," *Current History* (December 1983).

8. Christopher Dickey describes the beginnings of the conspiracy to overthrow the Sandinistas and the murder of Bravo in *With the Contras*, pp. 62–67.

9. In a letter to the *Times of the Americas* published on March 25, 1987 (p. 8), Jimmy Carter wrote, "my Administration provided no funding or support of any kind to any contra group fighting against the Sandinista government." Admiral Stansfield Turner, the CIA Director during the Carter Administration, also denied these reports. See Joseph Lelyveld, "The Director: Running the C.I.A.," *New York Times Magazine*, January 20, 1985, p. 25.

10. International Court of Justice, *Case Concerning Military and Paramilitary Activities in and against Nicaragua*, Nicaragua v. United States, Judgment of 27 June 1986, p. 54. [Hereafter ICJ *Judgment.*]

11. Reported in *FBIS*, July 30, 1979, p. P3.

12. Author's interview with Edén Pastora, November 14, 1983, Washington, D.C.

13. The article in *Time* was actually published on September 15, 1980 (p. 55), three days *after* Carter signed the certification.

14. Presidential Determination No. 82-26 of September 12, 1980. *Federal Register*, vol. 45, no. 185, September 22, 1980, p. 62779.

15. The Argentine People's Revolutionary Army (ARP), a small Trotskyite group, later took credit for the assassination. Some ARP leaders had lived in Nicaragua after the revolution, but there was no evidence of direct Sandinista involvement.

16. U.S. House of Representatives, Subcommittee on Inter-American Affairs of the Foreign Affairs Committee, *Hearing: Review of the Presidential Certification of Nicaragua's Connection to Terrorism*, September 30, 1980.

17. An account of the U.S. démarches and the Nicaraguan reaction can be found in Department of State, *"Revolution beyond Our Borders": Sandinista Intervention in Central America*, no. 132, September 1985, pp. 20–21. Author's and WGBH interviews with Lawrence Pezzullo were also helpful in expanding the case.

18. Department of State, *"Revolution beyond Our Borders,"* p. 21.

19. This account is based on the guerrilla documents (this quote is from document "J") in "Communist Interference in El Salvador: Documents Demonstrating Communist Support of the Salvadoran Insurgency," U.S. Department of State, February 23, 1981. The White Paper that was issued with the documents was criticized for its exaggerations and for some errors, but the documents themselves appear authentic. [Hereafter "Guerrilla Documents."]

20. The State Department cited a report that the Salvadoran left had accumulated $50–100 million through kidnappings in 1977–79, and that some of this was passed on to the Sandinistas. Department of State, *"Revolution beyond Our Borders,"* p. 5. Alan Riding told me he had witnessed the delivery of money from Salvadoran guerrillas to some Sandinistas during the revolution. Author's interview, March 13, 1983, Washington, D.C.

21. "Guerrilla Documents," "G," "Informe sobre Viaje."

22. Costa Rica's Special Commission traced at least three plane shipments of arms in 1980 and 1981 from Cuba through Costa Rica to El Salvador, using the same network originally developed by Costa Rica's Minister of Public Security Echeverría. See Costa Rican Arms Report cited in chapter 7; also Alan Riding, "Arms Scandal Is Charged in Costa Rica," *New York Times*, May 21, 1981, p. A3.

23. "Guerrilla Documents," "I" and "J."

24. Department of State, *"Revolution beyond Our Borders,"* p. 7.

25. Cited in Borge et al., *Sandinistas Speak*, p. 103.

26. The story of the Jorge Salazar conspiracy, which began on May 4, 1980, and ended with his murder on November 16, 1980, is told by Shirley Christian, *Nicaragua: Revolution in the Family*, pp. 170–85, and Christopher Dickey, *With the Contras*, pp. 76–82. The account here focuses on the U.S. role, which they do not.

27. *New York Times,* November 10, 1980, p. 5; November 19, 1980, p. 11; December 10, 1980, p. 6.

28. See Flora Lewis, "Except for Latin America, Most Allies and Enemies Are Only Mildly Interested Bystanders," *New York Times,* October 26, 1980. Lewis reported that Central America was "almost paralyzed awaiting the result" of the election, with rightists viewing Reagan as "a kind of savior" and the democratic opposition hoping for Carter. "Only the extreme left say that Carter and Reagan are the same."

29. WGBH interview with Lawrence Pezzullo, May 15, 1984, New York City.

30. Cited in Robert Kagan, *A Twilight Struggle* (N.Y.: Free Press, 1996), p. 164.

31. "Guerrilla Documents," "K," letter of November 1, 1980.

32. Some of the information gathered at the time was published by the State Department on February 23, 1981, in *Communist Interference in El Salvador.* The most convincing information, however, including the imagery on the Papalonal airstrip, was not revealed until September 1985 in Department of State, *"Revolution beyond Our* Borders," pp. 7–8. The International Court of Justice accepted the conclusion of Nicaraguan support for the Salvadorans at that time in its *Judgment* of June 27, 1986, p. 86.

33. The principal findings of this intelligence report were declassified and published in Department of State, *"Revolution beyond Our Borders,"* p. 8.

34. This, and other diplomatic correspondence, is summarized in ibid., pp. 21–22, 7 (on Radio Liberación).

35. Ibid., p. 9.

36. See Robert Pastor, "Continuity and Change in U.S. Foreign Policy: Carter and Reagan on El Salvador," *Journal of Policy Analysis and Management* 3 (Winter 1984): 175–90. Among the conditions that the Salvadoran military accepted in January 1981 were steps to investigate the murders of the Americans, including involvement by the FBI; greater authority to Napoleon Duarte over military affairs; and the transfer or dismissal of a dozen military officers associated with the repression, including Vice Minister of Defense Carranza.

37. Department of State, *"Revolution beyond Our Borders,"* p. 22.

38. Press conference of Jimmy Carter, February 9, 1986, Managua.

Chapter 12

1. Cited by Ronnie Dugger, *On Reagan: The Man and His Presidency* (New York: McGraw-Hill, 1983), p. 357. Reagan made this remark in 1967 in a speech on Vietnam. Ward Just reported on the speech and wrote that Reagan implied "that the United States should consider promoting wars on Communist territory."

2. Jaime Wheelock, "Nicaragua's Economy and the Fight against Imperialism," speech given to the First International Conference in Solidarity with Nicaragua, Managua, January 26–31, 1981, reprinted in Borge et al., *Sandinistas Speak,* p. 126.

3. Daniel Yankelovich and Larry Kaagan, "Assertive America," *Foreign Affairs: America and the World, 1980,* p. 696.

4. Cited by Dugger, *On Reagan,* p. 351.

5. Ibid., pp. 518–19.

6. For an analysis of the origins, ideology, and policy of the Administration, see Robert A. Pastor, *Exiting the Whirlpool: U.S. Foreign Policy Toward Latin America and the Caribbean* (Boulder, Colo.: Westview Press, 2001), Chapter 4.

7. Cited by Dugger, *On Reagan,* p. 360.

8. Republican National Convention, *Platform* (Detroit, July 14, 1980), p. 68.

9. In his memoirs, Haig laments the time it took (nearly one year) for President Reagan to decide on National Security Decision Document no. 1, which established the organization and procedures for the National Security Council. Alexander M. Haig, Jr., *Caveat: Realism, Reagan, and Foreign Policy* (New York: Macmillan, 1984).

10. Haig, *Caveat,* pp. 96–97.

11. Cited in John Goshko and Don Oberdorfer, "Haig Calls Arms Smuggling to El Salvador 'No Longer Acceptable,'" *Washington Post,* February 28, 1981, p. A12. Emphasis added.

12. Interviews with Lawrence Pezzullo by WGBH (May 15, 1984, New York City) and by the author (December 16, 1982, Washington, D.C.).

13. Pezzullo's conversations were summarized by the Department of State from diplomatic correspondence and published in Department of State, "*Revolution beyond Our Borders*," p. 22. Citations reflect the department's summary.

14. In January, when the State Department announced that U.S. aid had been suspended to Nicaragua, Daniel Ortega categorically denied his government's involvement in aiding the Salvadoran guerrillas. *New York Times,* January 23, 1981, p. 3.

15. Author's telephone conversation with Lawrence Pezzullo, March 9, 1987.

16. For the announcement, see *Department of State Bulletin,* May 1981, p. 71. Pezzullo's views were conveyed to me in a conversation on March 9, 1987.

17. This quote is from the Nicaraguan government's record of the conversation, which was submitted to the International Court of Justice. ICJ *Judgment,* pp. 76, 488–95. In addition, the U.S. proposal and record of the conversations can be found in Department of State, "*Revolution beyond Our Borders*," pp. 21–23.

18. The description of the Sandinista perspective is from Nicaraguan sources in an article summarizing the negotiations by Don Oberdorfer, "U.S., in Secret Dialogue, Sought Rapprochement with Nicaragua," *Washington Post,* December 10, 1981, pp. 1, 12. Department of State, "*Revolution beyond Our Borders*," pp. 21–23, describes U.S. positions. Additional sources include the author's interviews in Managua in July–August 1983 with Minister of Interior Tomás Borge, officials from the FSLN International Relations Department, and U.S. Embassy personnel.

19. These references are from Oberdorfer, "U.S., in Secret Dialogue." Shirley Christian cites Humberto Ortega's speech, which was given on June 23, 1981, but only became available in September. *Nicaragua: Revolution in the Family,* pp. 191–92.

20. Cited in Oberdorfer, "U.S., in Secret Dialogue." In August 1983, several senior Sandinista officials told me they were prepared to accept a variation on the Enders proposal, which they had previously rejected. That was no longer sufficient for the Reagan Administration.

21. This is from the Nicaraguan record of the conversation. See ICJ *Judgment,* p. 490.

22. The sources for this summary of the debate are: interviews with Administration officials; Haig, *Caveat,* pp. 98–100, 117–40; Don Oberdorfer, "Applying Pressure in Central America," *Washington Post,* November 23, 1983; Roy Gutman and Susan Page, "Central America: The Making of U.S. Policy," *Newsday,* July 31, 1983; and Leslie H. Gelb, "Haig Is Said to Press for Military Options for Salvadoran Action," *New York Times,* November 4, 1981. The Oberdorfer article describes three separate occasions in which Haig tried to persuade the NSC to accept a blockade of Cuba.

23. The authoritative reference to National Security Decision Document no. 17 of November 17, 1981, is in the NSC document "U.S. Policy in Central America and Cuba through FY '84," which was written in April 1982, but leaked and published in the *New York Times* on April 7, 1983. [Hereafter NSC document (April 1982).] Haig's memoirs (*Caveat*) refer to the discussion. A credible account of the meeting is by Don Oberdorfer, who interviewed other senior officials. See his "Applying Pressure in Central America," *Washington Post,* November 23, 1983, p. A1.

24. One official told Oberdorfer that the decision was "a way of letting A1 [Haig] down easily." There is no evidence that the group agreed on what constituted "unacceptable" actions by Cuba. ("Applying Pressure in Central America.")

25. Haig described his views in testimony before the U.S. Senate Foreign Relations Committee, *Commitments, Consensus, and U.S. Foreign Policy,* February 7, 1985, pp. 223–24, 242–43.

26. Department of State, "*Revolution beyond Our Borders*," p. 23. Hector Fabian the leader of an exile training camp in Florida, confirmed the Reagan Administration's decision not to enforce the law in an interview in December 1981. Jo Thomas, "Latin Exiles Focus on Nicaragua as They Train Urgently in Florida," *New York Times,* December 23, 1981, pp. 1, 14.

27. A Presidential Finding is required for a covert action. The reference to the March 9, 1981, finding is in the NSC document (April 1982). That document noted that $19.5 million had been allocated for the covert interdiction program, and recommended an increase to $22 million to cover an expanded program in Guatemala to begin in 1982.

28. Edgar Chamorro and Jefferson Morley, "Confessions of a 'Contra': How the C.I.A. Masterminds the Nicaraguan Insurgency," *The New Republic*, August 5, 1985, pp. 18–23.

29. Author's interview with Oscar Camilión, Argentine Minister of Foreign Relations (1980–81), December 14, 1986, Casa de Campo, Dominican Republic.

30. Cited by Dickey, *With the Contras*, p. 112. On November 1, Casey met in Washington with General Galtieri, then Argentine Army Chief of Staff (p. 123). Dickey's book and the following are the best sources on the origins of the contras: Nina Serafino, "U.S. Assistance to Nicaraguan Guerrillas: Issues for the Congress," Congressional Research Service, Library of Congress, January 21, 1987.

31. Dickey, *With the Contras*, p. 127.

32. Don Oberdorfer and Patrick E. Tyler, "Reagan Backs Action Plan for Central America: Political, Paramilitary Steps Included," *Washington Post*, February 14, 1982, p. 1. For a history of Congressional objections, see U.S. House of Representatives Permanent Select Committee on Intelligence, "Report 98–122: Amendment to the Intelligence Authorization Act for Fiscal Year 1983," May 13, 1983. [Hereafter Select Committee 1983 Report.]

33. Jackson Diehl, "State Department Official Sees Role for Argentina in Central America," *Washington Post*, March 10, 1982, p. A18. On March 10, the Administration presented aerial photographs of Nicaraguan military bases as "formal proof" of the threat of Cuba and Nicaragua. *New York Times*, March 10, 1982.

34. Christopher Dickey describes the CIA training of the contras, the bombing of the two bridges, and the views of the senior Administration official. *With the Contras*, pp. 131–32.

35. The story of Pastora's journey from Nicaragua through Panama to Cuba and back was reconstructed from the author's interviews with Pastora (November 14, 1983, Washington, D.C.); Haroldo Monteleagre, former Sandinista Minister (December 4–6, 1981, Washington, D.C.); and members of Panama's National Guard and friends of General Omar Torrijos (in Panama, January 30–31 and December 28, 1982).

36. Shirley Christian, "Rebel Hero Rips Sandinista 'Terror,'" *Miami Herald*, April 16, 1981, pp. 1, 22. Christian includes a copy of Pastora's statement in *Nicaragua: Revolution in the Family*, pp. 319–22.

37. Dickey claims that both the CIA and Pastora understood the value of Pastora's independence, and therefore, the Agency did not press the latter too much in the early period to join the FDN. *With the Contras*, p. 149.

38. For a survey of the alienation of the Atlantic Coast communities from the Sandinista government, see Martin Diskin, Thomas Bossert, Salomon Nahmad S., "Peace and Autonomy on the Atlantic Coast of Nicaragua: A Report of the LASA Task Force on Human Rights and Academic Freedom," *LASA Forum* 16, no. 4 (Spring 1986): 1–18.

39. This quote and subsequent citations are from the Select Committee 1983 Report, pp. 7–8.

40. In a cover story, *Newsweek* reported that the contras were trying to topple the Sandinistas rather than interdict arms. "America's Secret War," November 8, 1982. For a summary of Congressional action, see Nina Serafino, "Summary and Chronology of Major Congressional Action on U.S. Aid to the Anti-Sandinista Guerrillas," Congressional Research Service, Library of Congress, January 28, 1987.

41. Barbara Crosette, "Venezuelan Warns U.S. on Nicaragua," *New York Times*, November 18, 1981, p. A3; Jackson Diehl, "Venezuelan Criticism," *Washington Post*, March 24, 1982. "Public secret" was a phrase used by José Figueres. Author's interview, February 6, 1986, San José, Costa Rica.

42. Excerpts of the speech were reprinted in the *New York Times*, February 22, 1982.

43. 78% of the U.S. public opposed overthrowing the Nicaraguan government while only 13% favored it. A majority viewed the prospect of becoming entangled in Central America as a greater danger to the United States than the spread of Communism there. See Barry Sussman, "Poll Finds a Majority Fears Entanglement in Central America," *Washington Post*, May 25, 1983, pp. A1, 20.

44. The speech was reprinted in the *New York Times*, April 28, 1983, p. 12.

Chapter 13

1. "Interview," *Playboy*, September 1983, p. 67.

2. See *The Tower Commission Report* (New York: Times Books, 1987), p. 450. Senator Barry Goldwater also discussed the finding in a Senate debate (*Congressional Record*, April 4, 1984, p. 3766).

3. See, for example, the speech by Under Secretary of Defense Fred Iklé, Baltimore Council on Foreign Relations, September 12, 1983; Fred Hiatt, "Weinberger Calls Military Effort in Central America Vital to U.S.," *Washington Post*, September 7, 1983; and especially, "Heat on Central America: The Three Big Words around Washington These Days Are 'Whatever Is Necessary,'" *Newsweek*, June 20, 1983, pp. 18–19.

4. Select Committee 1983 Report, pp. 10–11.

5. Inter-American Development Bank, *Economic Report: Nicaragua*, DES–13, July 1983 (p. 19 for agricultural statistics). For debt statistics, see United Nations Economic Commission for Latin America and the Caribbean, "Preliminary Overview of the Latin American Economy, 1986," Santiago, Chile, December 1986, p. 21.

6. "Interview," *Playboy*, September 1983, p. 64.

7. James P. Wootten, "The Nicaraguan Military Buildup: Implications for U.S. Interests in Central America," Congressional Research Service, Library of Congress, December 18, 1985. "Armed forces" include all active personnel, reserves, militias, and Ministry of Interior forces. In 1985, he estimated there were 62,000 active soldiers.

8. The lower estimate is from the Nicaraguan Ministry of Defense, cited in Agencia Nueva Nicaragua, "The Defeat of the Counter-Revolution," April 1987. The higher estimate is from U.S. Departments of State and Defense, *The Challenge to Democracy in Central America* (Washington, D.C., June 1986), p. 38.

9. CIA analyst Peter Clement concluded that the Sandinistas' military buildup "seems to be tied to the growth of contra activity." "Moscow and Nicaragua: Two Sides of Soviet Policy," *Comparative Strategy* 5 (1985): 78.

10. Interview with Ambassador Anthony Quainton, February 11, 1984, Miami, Florida.

11. Roger Fontaine, "Choices on Nicaragua," *Global Affairs* 1 (Summer 1986): 113. The FMLN/FDR is the combined military and political leadership of the Salvadoran guerrillas.

12. The President's press conference was published in the *New York Times* the next day, November 4, 1983, p. A16.

13. John Horton, "The Real Intelligence Failure," *Foreign Service Journal* (February 1985): 24.

14. In my interviews in Managua in the summer of 1983, I found progress in the Nicaraguan positions, and the Administration also described it as "encouraging," even while it condemned the continued military buildup (Hedrick Smith, "Arms Aid to Nicaragua Still Rising, U.S. Says," *New York Times*, October 5, 1983, p. A11).

15. The speech was delivered on May 9, 1984, and reprinted the next day in the *New York Times*, p. A16.

16. David Rogers and David Ignatius, "How CIA-Aided Raids in Nicaragua in '84 Led Congress to End Funds," and "CIA Internal Report Details U.S. Role in Contra Raids in Nicaragua Last Year," *Wall Street Journal*, March 6, 1985. The latter article cites an internal CIA report that documents direct CIA involvement in nineteen separate operations from January 1 to April 10, 1984. National Security Adviser Robert McFarlane later testified that President Reagan personally approved the mining of Nicaragua's harbors. David E. Rosenbaum, "McFarlane States He Briefed Reagan on Contras Often," *New York Times*, May 14, 1987, pp. 1, 7.

17. Arce's remarks were published in *Barricada*, and cited by William I. Robinson and Kent Norsworthy, "Elections and U.S. Intervention in Nicaragua," *Latin American Perspectives* 12, no. 2 (Spring 1985): 84.

18. Statement to the press, reprinted in the *New York Times*, March 29, 1984.

19. Philip Taubman, "U.S. Role in Nicaragua Disputed," *New York Times*, October 21, 1984, p. 12.

20. Two accounts of these talks and the elections themselves tend to attribute the failure to different sides, though both agree that the Reagan Administration reinforced those who wanted to boycott the election. Robert Leiken ("The Nicaraguan Tangle," *New York Review of Books*, December 5, 1985, pp. 55–64) blames the Sandinistas; the Latin American Studies Association argues that the Coordinadora did not participate "by their own choice, not because of government exclusion" (see Latin American Studies Association, "Report of the Latin American Studies Association Delegation to Observe the Nicaraguan General Election of November 4, 1984," *LASA Forum* 15, no. 4 (Winter 1985).

21. Leiken recounts the meeting. "Nicaraguan Tangle," p. 61.

22. For the results and the State Department's reaction, see Alexander H. McIntire, Jr., *Political and Electoral Confrontation in Revolutionary Nicaragua* (Miami: University of Miami North-South Center, July 1985). For the reaction of the LASA delegation, see LASA, "Report."

23. The letter was reprinted in the *Wall Street Journal*, January 11, 1985.

24. Author's interview with Arturo Cruz, October 2, 1986, Atlanta.

25. Robert J. McCartney, "McFarlane Ends Trip to Five Nations," *Washington Post*, January 20, 1985, p. A19; Philip Taubman, "U.S. Says It Has Halted Talks with Nicaragua," *New York Times*, January 19, 1985, p. 4; "Text of U.S. Statement on Withdrawal from Case before the World Court," *New York Times*, January 19, 1985, p. 4.

26. Reagan made this proposal on April 5, 1985, and it was reprinted in the *Washington Post* that day.

27. For a description of the embargo's origins, see Joanne Omang, "Sanctions: A Policy by Default," *Washington Post*, May 8, 1985. For the Executive Order, see Bernard Weinraub, "Reagan, Declaring 'Threat,' Forbids Nicaraguan Trade and Cuts Air and Sea Links," *New York Times*, May 2, 1985.

28. Gerald M. Boyd, "Reagan Asks Arms Aid for Nicaraguan Rebels," *New York Times*, February 19, 1986, p. 7.

29. Gerald M. Boyd, "Reagan Sees a 'Moral Obligation' by U.S. to Aid Nicaraguan Rebels," *New York Times*, March 11, 1986, p. 1; Doyle McManus, "U.S. Resumes Funding for Rebel Leader Pastora," *Los Angeles Times*, March 12, 1986, p. 1. The Administration discontinued aid to Pastora again after it lost the House vote. Stephen Kinzer, "Nicaraguan Rebel Chief Gives Up Fight," *New York Times*, May 17, 1986, p. 3.

30. A very good analysis of the changes made in each draft of the agreement was done by Nina M. Serafino, "The Contadora Initiative: Implications for Congress," Congressional Research Service, Library of Congress, May 18, 1987.

31. Author's interview with a senior Peruvian diplomat, May 5, 1986, New York City.

32. Leslie H. Gelb, "Pentagon Predicts Big War If Latins Sign Peace Accord," *New York Times*, May 20, 1986, pp. 1, 6; and Bernard Gwertzman, "State Department Assails the Pentagon over Study of Latin Peace Talks," *New York Times*, May 21, 1986, pp. 1, 6.

33. "Nicaragua Rejects Proposal for Arms Limits in Region," *New York Times*, May 20, 1986, p. 6; Stephen Kinzer, "Nicaragua Balks at Latin Peace Accord," *New York Times*, May 12, 1986, p. 3.

34. For a good analysis of these negotiations, see Bruce Bagley, "Contadora: The Failure of Diplomacy," *Journal of InterAmerican Studies and World Affairs* 28 (Fall 1986): 19–21.

35. "An Interview with Oscar Arias: In the Eye of the Storm," *Newsweek International*, October 6, 1986, p. 52.

36. James Lemoyne, "Costa Rica's Return to Neutrality Strains Its Ties with Washington," *New York Times*, March 22, 1987, p. E2.

37. Stephen Kinzer, "Nicaragua Warms to Latest Peace Plan," *New York Times*, February 22, 1987, p. 10.

38. Stephen Kinzer, "Sandinistas' Foes Fault Role of U.S.: Opposition in Managua Urges Washington to Do More to Support Its Cause," *New York Times*, June 25, 1986, p. 6.

39. Cited by Reid G. Miller, "U.S. Aid to Contras Triggers Increase in Repression by Managua," *Mexico City News*, June 29, 1986, p. 10.

40. Inter-American Development Bank, *Economic Report: Nicaragua*, July 1983, p. iii.

41. Cited in Philip Taubman, "The C.I.A.: In from the Cold and Hot for Truth," *New York Times*, June 11, 1984, p. B6; also see Don Oberdorfer and John M. Goshko, "Ex-C.I.A. Analyst Disputes U.S. Aides on Nicaragua," *Washington Post*, June 13, 1984, pp. A1, 28; Select Committee 1983 Report, pp. 10–11; and ICJ *Judgment*, p. 86. In 1984, Senator Daniel Patrick Moynihan said: "It is the judgment of the [Senate] Intelligence Committee that Nicaragua's involvement in the affairs of El Salvador, and, to a lesser degree, its other neighbors, continues. . . . [and as compared to 1983, it] has not appreciably lessened." *Washington Post*, April 10, 1984, cited in ICJ *Judgment*, p. 485. On the other hand, Col. Humberto Vallatta, Salvador's Naval Commander, explained at a press conference in 1986 that the last arms interdiction that he knew about was in 1981. "Arms Flow Largely Stopped," *The Times of the Americas*, December 10, 1986, p. 7.

42. A conservative estimate of military aid to the contras totals $142 million ($72 million from 1982 to 1984, $70 million in 1986 and 1987) as compared to $131.6 million in military aid to the five governments of Central America from 1962 to 1980. This does not take into account the $57 million in "non-lethal" military aid to the contras, the fact that all military aid to the contras has been grants (only 60 percent of the aid to Central America has been in the form of grants), or the considerable amount of money that the Administration solicited from foreign governments and private donors. For the data on aid to Central America, see Agency for International Development, *U.S. Overseas Loans and Grants*, July 1, 1945–September 30, 1984, pp. 43, 47, 49, 52, 55.

43. For the judgments, see ICJ *Judgment*, pp. 146–50, and for the reservations of the U.S. judge, Stephen Schwebel, p. 269. Although the key judgments were negative for the United States, the Court also rejected two important Nicaraguan arguments: that it had not supported Salvadoran insurgents and that the contras were solely an instrument of the U.S. government.

44. *Tower Commission Report*, p. 451.

45. David Shipler, "U.S. Again Denies a Nicaraguan Role," *New York Times*, October 16, 1986, p. 4; Stephen Engelberg, "Supply Upsurge to Contras Reported," *New York Times*, October 12, 1986, p. 6. In testimony before Congress, Abrams later admitted he was wrong, but he said that at the time he did not know of NSC involvement.

46. *Tower Commission Report* (February 26, 1987), esp. pp. 51–61, 450–79; U.S. Senate Committee on Intelligence, "Report to the Select Committee on Secret Military Assistance to Iran and the Nicaraguan Opposition," January 29, 1987, pp. 42–63.

47. Ibid., p. 58.

48. Joel Brinkley, "Spotlight Falls on the Secret World of a Master Operative," *New York Times*, May 10, 1987, p. IV, 1.

49. This is an excerpt from President Reagan's statement on Taiwan's help, reprinted in the *New York Times*, May 16, 1987, p. 6. President Reagan said Saudi Arabia helped "because they shared our interest in securing democracy in Central America." Gerald M. Boyd, "Reagan Denies Asking Saudis for Contra Aid," *New York Times*, May 13, 1987, pp. 1, 9.

50. "24% Believe Reagan on Contras," *New York Times*, May 24, 1987, p. 10.

51. Excerpts from statement by Robert McFarlane to Congressional Committee, reprinted in *New York Times*, May 12, 1987, p. 6.

52. General Secord told this to the Congressional Committee. Cited in David E. Rosenbaum, "Secord Recounts Being Told Reagan Knew of His Work," *New York Times*, May 7, 1987, pp. 1, 6, 7. Secord was told by Poindexter that "not only was he pleased with the work that I had been doing, but the President was as well."

53. Poindexter told Congress: "The buck stops here with me. I made the decision." At his trial, his lawyer said that "the President was the driving engine behind his [Poindexter's] actions" and that his client was a victim of a "frame-up." David Johnston, "Poindexter is Found Guilty of All Five Criminal Charges for Iran-Contra Cover-Up," *New York Times*, April 8, 1980, p. 1.

54. The address was reprinted in the *New York Times*, October 8, 1987, p. 8.

55. President Reagan's address to the nation, June 24, 1986.

56. See Adam Clymer, "Poll Finds Americans Don't Know U.S. Positions on Central America," *New York Times*, July 1, 1983, p. 1; David Shribman, "Poll Finds Fewer Than Half in U.S. Back Latin Policy," *New York Times*, April 29, 1984, p. 1; and "Opinion Outlook," *National Journal*, May 17, 1986, p. 1224. I also looked at various Harris surveys from this period.

57. *National Journal*, May 17, 1986, p. 1224.

58. "Poll: Americans Divided on Nicaraguan Intervention," *Miami Herald*, March 31, 1985, p. 4A.

59. Roger Fontaine, "Choices on Nicaragua," *Global Affairs* 1 (Summer 1986): 101–114.

60. Peter Kornbluh, "U.S. Role in the Counter-Revolution," in Thomas W. Walker, ed., *Revolution and Counter-Revolution in Nicaragua* (Boulder, Colo.: Westview Press, 1991), based on statistics from the Nicaraguan government in 1990.

61. Cited in "Business Dissent: It's Out Front in Nicaragua," *New York Times*, March 31, 1985, p. 6.

Chapter 14

1. Excerpts of Arias's address on receipt of the Nobel Peace Prize are in the *New York Times*, December 11, 1987, p. 3.

2. For Duarte's views, see his interview of August 11, 1987, printed in *FBIS*, August 13, 1987, pp. F1–2.

3. The cable appears to be from the CIA station chief. It is reprinted in Joint Hearings Before the House Select Committee to Investigate Covert Arms Transactions With Iran and the Senate Select Committee on Secret Military Assistance to Iran and the Nicaraguan Opposition, *Testimony of Richard V. Secord*, Vol. 100–1, May 5–8, 1987, p. 435.

4. Luis Solis-Rivera, "Peace and the Future of Central America: A Costa Rican Viewpoint," paper prepared for a conference sponsored by the Friedrich Ebert Foundation, Washington, D.C., October 19, 1987, p. 2.

5. For Reagan's address, see *New York Times*, August 13, 1987, p. A8; his comment on the plan as "fatally flawed" was in the *New York Times*, September 13, 1987, p. 8; Bush's comment was in Elaine Sciolino, "Latin Peace Plan Is Said to Set Back Help for Contras," *New York Times*, August 11, 1987, pp. 1, 6.

6. Michael R. Gordon, "Habib Quits Post As Special Envoy," *New York Times*, August 15, 1987, pp. 1, 5; Neil A. Lewis, "U.S. Envoys Told to Convey Doubt Over Latin Plan," *New York Times*, August 18, 1987, pp. 1, 4; Neil A. Lewis, "U.S. Aide Calls Contras Crucial to Region's Peace," *New York Times*, August 19, 1987, p. 4.

7. As he was leaving for Havana, Ortega told the press that he had called "Presidents Arias and Cerezo this afternoon, and informed them about this trip; they reacted positively." The interview is printed in *FBIS*, August 13, 1987, p. I1. The FSLN Communiqué of August 17 is printed in *FBIS*, August 18, 1987, p. I1.

8. Stephen Kinzer, "Nicaraguans and the Winds of Peace," *New York Times*, September 15, 1987, p. 3.

9. Arias's comments are in a radio interview he gave on October 27, printed in *FBIS*, October 29, 1987, pp. 6–7. He also said that he did not believe that Reagan could impose sanctions against his country because of "the prestige we now have in the U.S. Congress."

10. Neil A. Lewis, "Arias Asks U.S. to Give Latin Peace Plan a Try," *New York Times*, September 23, 1987, p. 8.

11. Serge Scheman, "Costa Rica Leader Wins Nobel Prize for Peace Plan: Blow to Contra Aid Seen," *New York Times*, October 14, 1987, pp. 1, 8.

12. Daniel Ortega Saavedra, "More Contra Aid, More Suffering," *New York Times*, January 14, 1988, p. 27; James LeMoyne, "Contras Are Given Costa Rican Edict," *New York Times*, January 14, 1988, p. 8.

13. Neil A. Lewis, "Four Latin Presidents Cautioned by U.S. on Contras' Fate: Security Adviser Tells Leaders Rebel Failure Could Hurt Their Countries Badly," *New York Times*, January 13, 1988, pp. 1, 6.

14. The text of the report is reprinted in *FBIS*, January 19, 1988, pp. 20–24.

15. The declaration issued on January 16 was printed in *FBIS*, January 19, 1988, p. 4.

16. His comments of January 16 were printed in *FBIS*, January 19, 1988, pp. 16–20.

17. See the following three articles by Stephen Kinzer in the *New York Times:* "Nicaragua Detains Five More Leaders of the Opposition," January 20, 1988, p. 1; "Sandinista Strains: Ortega's Effort to Comply with Peace Pact Points up Differences Among the Leaders," January 21, 1988, p. 6; and "Ortega Is Said to Face Challenge from Borge in Sandinista Regime," January 24, 1988, p. 7.

18. Joel Brinkley, "Contra Aid Foes Given a Scolding," *New York Times*, January 22, 1988, p. 1.

19. *Wall Street Journal*, January 22, 1988, p. 26.

20. Excerpts of both addresses were in the *New York Times* on February 3, 1988, p. 6.

21. Cited in "Arias: It's Soviets' Turn to Cut Military Aid," *Atlanta Journal-Constitution*, February 7, 1988, p. 3A.

22. Ortega's comment about humanitarian aid was made at his press conference in San José on January 16 (*FBIS*, January 19, 1988, pp. 16–20); his latter comments were printed in *FBIS*, February 5, 1988, pp. 17–24.

23. James A. Baker III, *The Politics of Diplomacy* (New York: G. P. Putnam's Sons, 1995), p. 50.

24. Jim Wright, *Balance of Power: Presidents and Congress from the Era of McCarthy to the Age of Gingrich* (Atlanta: Turner Publishing, Inc., 1996), pp. 479–480.

25. Baker, *Politics of Diplomacy*, p. 50.

26. The summary of the discussion is based on notes that the author took at the time and memoranda of the various conversations. See also Ann Devroy and Julia Preston, "Quayle Irked at Carter's High Profile," *The Washington Post*, February 3, 1989; and Alan Riding, "Quayle in Caracas to Hail New Chief," *New York Times*, February 2, 1989.

27. Cited by Robert A. Kagan, *A Twilight Struggle: American Power and Nicaragua, 1977–90* (New York: Free Press, 1996), pp. 633–637.

28. Transcript of address to the Carter Center, Atlanta, Georgia, March 30, 1989, reprinted by U.S. Department of State.

29. Latin American and Caribbean Program, The Carter Center of Emory University, "The Hemispheric Agenda Conference: Final Report," March 29–30, 1989, pp. 2–4.

30. Manuel Noriega with Peter Eisner, *The Memoirs of Manuel Noriega: America's Prisoner* (New York: Random House, 1997), p. 145.

Chapter 15

1. Quoted in *Stanford Magazine*, June 1990. Abrams had left the government the year before. He made this statement during a speech that he gave on the eve of the Nicaraguan election.

2. The letters are reproduced in the final report of the Council. See The Carter Center of Emory University, The Council of Freely-Elected Heads of Government, *Observing Nicaragua's Elections, 1989–1990*, Special Report # 1, May 1, 1990, pp. 46–49.

3. Robert Pear, "Quayle Calls Managua Vote Plan a Sham," *New York Times*, June 13, 1989, p. 3.

4. Mark A. Uhlig, "Managua and Its Rivals Sparring Over Vote Rules," *New York Times*, May 14, 1989, p. 4.

5. Georgie Anne Geyer, "Is 'Good' What the Mission Calls for?" *Washington Times*, September 14, 1989.

6. Andrew Rosenthal, "Bush Hoping to Use Malta Talks to Speed Strategic Arms Pact," *New York Times*, November 30, 1989, pp. 1, 11.

7. George Bush and Brent Scowcroft, *A World Transformed* (New York: Alfred A. Knopf, 1998), pp. 163–166.

8. Michael Kramer, "Anger, Bluff—and Cooperation: Behind the Sandinistas' Stunning Election Loss in Nicaragua Is the Secret Story of U.S.-Soviet Partnership in Central America," *Time*, June 4, 1990, pp. 38–45.

9. Memorandum of conversations between Jimmy Carter and Nicaraguan officials, February 6–9, 1986. These memoranda are in the Carter Library.

10. Cited by Douglas Brinkley, *The Unfinished Presidency: Jimmy Carter's Journey Beyond the White House* (New York: Viking, 1998), p. 427. Brinkley's book is the best study of Carter's activities after he left the White House.

11. "Memorandum: Background on Nicaraguan Elections," from Robert Pastor to Jimmy Carter, August 4, 1989. Much of this chapter is based on policy memoranda, memoranda of conversations, and other documentation, which is available in files at the Carter Library.

12. "Memorandum: Trip to Nicaragua, September 16–18, 1989, Strategy," from Robert Pastor to President and Mrs. Jimmy Carter, September 16, 1989.

13. The agreement, dated on September 22, 1989, after a meeting in Washington as well, is in the Carter Center's Final Report, p. 61.

14. *Newsweek* published a story, "The CIA on the Stump," on October 21, 1991, reporting that Carter's assurance was violated by a $600,000 program to help some contra leaders return to Managua during the elections. A subsequent investigation by the Senate Intelligence Committee concluded that the law and the assurance had not been broken. None of the money was spent on the election; all of it was spent in amounts averaging about $12,000 for assistance or resettlement of families of several hundred contra leaders. In fact, in the meeting between Bush and Carter in September 1989, when the latter pressed the administration to channel some of the humanitarian aid for the contras through the

OAS/UN teams, Secretary Baker responded that "we are willing to use some of that to repatriate those who want to return voluntarily if they get some assurances from the Sandinistas." Carter said that he had no disagreement with that.

15. For an analysis of how administrative irregularities can derail elections, see Robert A. Pastor, "The Role of Electoral Administration in Democratic Transitions: Implications for Policy and Research," *Democratization* 6, no. 4 (Winter 1999): 1–27.

16. Lindsey Gruson, "El Salvador Suspends Relations with Nicaragua," *New York Times*, November 27, 1989, pp. 1, 4.

17. Cited in Larry Rohter, "How a Plane Crash Upended Peace Plans for Central America," *New York Times*, December 3, 1989, p. E2.

18. United Nations, *Second Report to the Secretary General by the UN Observer Mission to Verify the Electoral Process in Nicaragua*, December 7, 1989, p. 28.

19. William Branigan, "U.S. Team Says Violence Imperils Managua Vote: Melee at Rally Sunday Laid to Sandinistas," *Washington Post*, December 12, 1989. In the article, Center for Democracy delegates were blunt in blaming the Sandinistas, and the Nicaraguan government was equally clear in blaming UNO. A more careful account of what occurred was in the Center for Democracy's report, *Violence at Masatepe: An Eyewitness Report by a Center for Democracy Observer Delegation to the Nicaraguan Election*, December 14, 1989.

20. Letter to the UN Secretary General from Elliott Richardson, March 22, 1990.

21. Noriega was with his mistress in a hotel near the airport when the United States invaded. For the acknowledgment of surprise, see Manuel Noriega and Peter Eisner, *The Memoirs of Manuel Noriega: America's Prisoner* (New York: Random House, 1997); and for the identification of the hotel and other facts surrounding the invasion, see Margaret E. Scranton, *The Noriega Years: U.S.-Panamanian Relations, 1981–90* (Boulder: Lynne Rienner, 1991), pp. 202–205.

22. Maureen Dowd, "Doing the Inevitable: Bush Reportedly Felt That Noriega 'Was Thumbing His Nose at Him,'" *New York Times*, December 24, 1989, p. 5. For an analysis of the background and motives for the invasion, see Robert A. Pastor, *Exiting the Whirlpool: U.S. Foreign Policy Toward Latin America and the Caribbean* (Boulder: Westview Press, 2000), pp. 95–98.

23. Margaret Scranton, *Noriega Years*, p. 202. Thirteen thousand troops were already deployed in Panama, and they were joined by 13,000 coming from the United States.

24. Lee Hockstader, "Nicaraguan Opposition: Outsmarted and Outspent," *Washington Post*, January 25, 1990. See also "Money Isn't Everything: Despite U.S. Funding, Nicaragua's Opposition Lags," *Newsweek*, October 9, 1989.

25. *The Washington Times*, January 29, 1990, p. A8.

26. Martin McReynolds, "U.S. Bracing for Ortega Win in Nicaraguan Election," *The Miami Herald*, January 28, 1990.

Chapter 16

1. Most of the elections that the Carter Center observed between 1987 and 2000 had more problems on election day regarding the opening of polling sites and the inadequacy of election materials than Nicaragua had in 1990.

2. Carter told me on June 29, 2001, in Atlanta, Georgia. Baker and Aronson revealed their preferences in October 1996.

3. Recognizing the historic moment, I kept extremely detailed notes of this conversation as well as the others that followed. The memoranda of conversation are in my files at the Carter Library.

4. Six years later, in November 1996, Baker co-chaired the election observation mission to Nicaragua with Carter, and he, Carter, Aronson, and I reviewed the events of that evening from our various perspectives.

5. "Text of the Speech delivered by the President of Nicaragua, Daniel Ortega Saavedra to the People of Nicaragua on February 26, 1990," distributed by the Nicaraguan Embassy to the United States.

6. "Bush's Remarks on Nicaragua," *New York Times*, February 27, 1990.

7. E-mail messages from Ing. Antonio Lacayo, July 23, 2001 and August 5, 2001.

8. The World Bank, *Report and Recommendations of the President of the International Development Association on a Proposed Economic Recovery Credit to the Republic of Nicaragua* (Washington, D.C., September 3, 1991), Report No. P-5598-NI, pp. 1–4.

9. E-mail message from Ing. Antonio Lacayo, July 23, 2001.

10. Correspondence between Lacayo and Wharton was extraordinarily detailed, with the U.S. government insisting on micro-managing Nicaragua's affairs. For example, in response to a single-spaced, six-page latter from Lacayo detailing all of his government's problems and proposing solutions, Wharton responded by demanding even more specific steps and advancing the timetable for Humberto Ortega's departure by one year, appointing an impartial comptroller general, and calling for joint investigation of corruption charges. See Lacayo's letter of March 30, 1993 and Wharton's response of April 12 in the files at the Carter Library.

11. Steven A. Holmes, "Nicaragua to Get Blocked U.S. Aid: Administration Cites Progress on Issues of Concern in Releasing $50 million," *The New York Times*, April 3, 1993..

12. The Carter Center collaborated with the United Nations Development Program to assess the magnitude of and propose solutions for the property issue. See the following reports from the Carter Center: "Report on a Property Issues Conference," Montelimar, July 4–5, 1995, p. 2; "Nicaraguan Property Disputes," April 1995. The data on the number of claims, beneficiaries, and owners changed over time as new claims were made. The data cited in this chapter were current as of July 1995.

13. In addition to the reports above, a good summary of the conference can be found in "Jimmy Carter's Compromise in Nicaragua," *The Economist*, June 15, 1995, p. 29.

14. David Gonzalez, "Among Unpaid Wages of a Revolution: Competing Claims on Land in Nicaragua," *The New York Times*, September 10, 2000, p. 14.

15. For a good summary and analysis of the election, see Jennifer L. McCoy and Shelley A. McConnell, "Nicaragua: Beyond the Revolution," *Current History* (February 1997): 75–80; and the Carter Center, *The Observation of the 1996 Nicaraguan Elections: Special Report of the Council of Freely Elected Heads of Government* (Atlanta, Ga.: February 1997).

16. For a good but very critical analysis of the pact and politics in the Aleman years, see David Dye with Jack Spence and George Vickers, *Patchwork Democracy: Nicaraguan Politics Ten Years After the Fall* (Cambridge, Mass.: Hemispheric Initiatives, 2000).

17. David Gonzalez, "Nicaraguan Voters Reject Ortega's Bid for the Presidency," November 6, 2001.

Chapter 17

1. Interview with Alfonso Robelo, July 29–30, 1983, San José, Costa Rica.

2. Adolfo Calero, a conservative businessman, for example, left Nicaragua in December 1982 and subsequently became a leader of the contras.

3. See Robert A. Pastor, *Exiting the Whirlpool: U.S. Foreign Policy Toward Latin America* (Boulder, Colo.: Westview Press, 2001), ch. 8.

4. Quoted in Arthur M. Schlesinger Jr., *A Thousand Days: John F. Kennedy in the White House* (Boston: Houghton Mifflin, 1965), p. 769.

5. For a comparison, see Cole Blasier, *The Hovering Giant: U.S. Responses to Revolutionary Change in Latin America* (Pittsburgh: University of Pittsburgh Press, 1985); and Pastor, *Exiting the Whirlpool*, ch. 9.

6. Richard E. Welch Jr., *Response to Revolution: The United States and the Cuban Revolution, 1959–61* (Chapel Hill: University of North Carolina Press, 1985), p. 24.

7. Arthur M. Schlesinger Jr., "Foreign Policy and the American Character," *Foreign Affairs* (Fall 1983): 1.

8. Lucian W. Pye and Sidney Verba, eds., *Political Culture and Political Development* (Princeton: Princeton University Press, 1965); and Gabriel A. Almond and Sidney Verba, eds., *The Civic Culture Revisited* (Boston: Little, Brown, 1980).

9. This question was posed but never satisfactorily answered by Raymond Bonner, *Waltzing with a Dictator: The Marcoses and the Making of American Policy* (New York: Times Books, 1987), p. 447.

10. John E. Rielly, ed., *American Public Opinion and U.S. Foreign Policy 1975* (Chicago: Council on Foreign Relations, 1975), p. 22.

11. Cited in Thomas M. Leonard, "The United States and Central America, 1955–60," *Valley Forge Journal* (June 1986): 65.

12. Barry Sussman, "Poll Finds a Majority Fears Entanglement in Central America," *Washington Post,* May 25, 1983, pp. A1, 20.

13. In the cases of Trujillo and Duvalier, Presidents Eisenhower and Kennedy insisted on virtually impossible conditions before they would consider toppling the dictators. See U.S. Senate, Select Committee to Study Governmental Operations with Respect to Intelligence Activities, *Alleged Assassination Plots Involving Foreign Leaders,* November 20, 1975, pp. 191–205. On Haiti, see Edwin Martin, "Haiti: A Case Study in Futility," *SAIS Review* (Summer 1981); and on the Philippines, see Paul Laxalt, "My Conversations with Ferdinand Marcos, A Lesson in Personal Diplomacy," *Policy Review* (Summer 1986): 2–5.. Laxalt said that President Reagan refused to tell Marcos to resign. Unlike these presidents, Carter did not promote a rebellion against a leftist government.In the case of Vietnam, Stanley Karnow, in his book *Vietnam: A History* (New York: Penguin, 1986), commented on why that case might have inhibited future presidents: "America's responsibility for Diem's death haunted U.S. leaders during the years ahead, prompting them to assume a larger burden in Vietnam" (p. 278).

14. In a letter to the *Times of the Americas,* March 25, 1987, Carter denied that his administration had ever provided any funds or support for the contras, and in numerous interviews, he confirmed that he would never have done so if he had a second term. When the FSLN's support for the FMLN became known, his inclination was to support OAS action against Nicaragua.

15. Don Oberdorfer, "U.S. Pressing for Democratic Succession in Philippines," *Washington Post,* March 12, 1985, p. A11.

16. Cited in *Newsweek,* May 25, 1987, p. 19.

17. Stephen Kinzer, "Why Nicaragua Picked a Curious Time to Strike," *New York Times,* March 30, 1986, p. E2.

18. Neil A. Lewis, "Reagan Sees Fatal Flaws in Central American Pact," *New York Times,* September 13, 1987, p. A24. In a later address to Congress, Reagan said that if Congress did not approve the aid, "the Sandinista Communists [would] continue the consolidation of their dictatorial regime and the subversion of Central America." Excerpts printed in *New York Times,* February 3, 1988, p. A10.

19. For an in-depth discussion, see *Condemned to Repetition: The United States and Nicaragua* (Princeton University Press, 1987), ch. 15.

20. Robert A. Kagan, *A Twilight Struggle: American Power and Nicaragua, 1977–90* (New York: Free Press, 1996), pp. 722–723.

INDEX

340 ❖ Index